Book 1

Literature & Comprehension

Language Arts

Lesson Guide

Book Staff and Contributors

Kristen Kinney-Haines *Director, Primary Literacy*
Alane Gernon-Paulsen *Content Specialist*
Anna Day *Senior Instructional Designer*
Cheryl Howard, Lenna King *Instructional Designers*
Mary Beck Desmond *Senior Text Editor*
Karen Ingebretsen, Allyson Jacob *Text Editors*
Suzanne Montazer *Creative Director, Print and ePublishing*
Sasha Blanton *Art Director*
Carol Leigh *Print Visual Designer*
Stephanie Shaw Williams *Cover Designer*
Kandee Dyczko, Tisha Ruibal *Writers*
Amy Eward *Senior Manager, Writers*
Susan Raley *Senior Manager, Editors*
Deanna Lacek *Project Manager*
David Johnson *Director, Program Management Grades K–8*

Maria Szalay *Executive Vice President, Product Development*
John Holdren *Senior Vice President, Content and Curriculum*
David Pelizzari *Vice President, K12 Content*
Kim Barcas *Vice President, Creative*
Laura Seuschek *Vice President, Assessment and Research*
Aaron Hall *Vice President, Program Management*

Lisa Dimaio Iekel *Senior Production Manager*
Ray Traugott *Production Manager*

Credits

About K12 Inc.

K12 Inc., a technology-based education company, is the nation's leading provider of proprietary curriculum and online education programs to students in grades K–12. K^{12} provides its curriculum and academic services to online schools, traditional classrooms, blended school programs, and directly to families. K12 Inc. also operates the K^{12} International Academy, an accredited, diploma-granting online private school serving students worldwide. K^{12}'s mission is to provide any child the curriculum and tools to maximize success in life, regardless of geographic, financial, or demographic circumstances. K12 Inc. is accredited by CITA. More information can be found at www.K12.com.

978-1-60153-210-7
Printed by R.R. Donnelley, Kendallville, IN, USA, May 2016

Contents

Literature & Comprehension

K¹² Language Arts Green

General Overview

K¹² Language Arts Green lays a strong foundation for beginning readers and writers. A well-balanced Language Arts program provides instruction on getting words off the page (reading) as well putting words on the page (writing). According to the National Reading Panel, a comprehensive reading program includes fluency, text comprehension, spelling, vocabulary, and writing skills. Language Arts Green provides this instruction through six separate-yet-related programs.

You will spend about two hours a day working with Language Arts Green. The tables describe the programs, the time you can expect to spend on them, and the overarching Big Ideas that are covered.

Program	Daily Lesson Time (approximate)	Online/Offline
K¹² Language Arts PhonicsWorks Advanced	50 minutes in Days 1–90 30 minutes in Days 91–180	Each lesson: 15–30 minutes offline, 15–20 minutes online
Big Ideas		

- Readers must understand that print carries meaning and there is a connection between letters and sounds.
- Fluent readers blend sounds represented by letters into words.
- Breaking words into syllables helps us read and spell unfamiliar words.
- Good readers practice reading grade-level text with fluency.
- Reading sight words helps young readers read complete sentences and short stories.

Program	Daily Lesson Time (approximate)	Online/Offline
K¹² Language Arts Green Literature & Comprehension	45 minutes	All offline

Big Ideas

- *Read Aloud*   Students follow along as a proficient reader models fluent, expressive reading; what good readers think about as they read; and how good readers use strategies to understand text.
- *Shared Reading*   Students practice the reading behaviors of proficient readers with the support of a proficient reader.
- *Guided Reading*   A proficient reader helps students preview and prepare for reading, and then students use the skills and strategies of proficient readers to read texts.
- *Fluency*   The ability to decode text quickly, smoothly, and automatically allows readers to focus on comprehension.
- *Comprehension*   Comprehension requires readers to actively think, ask themselves questions, and synthesize information to make meaning from their reading.
- *Analysis*   Readers must pay careful attention to language and literary elements to appreciate the underlying meaning or message of an author's work.
- *Enjoyment*   To develop a lifelong love of reading, new readers should independently read for their own enjoyment.

Program	Daily Lesson Time (approximate)	Online/Offline
K¹² Language Arts Green Spelling	15 minutes (Days 91–180 only)	Each unit: 4 offline lessons, 1 online review

Big Ideas

- Spelling represents sounds, syllables, and meaningful parts of words.
- The spelling of all English words can be explained by rules or patterns related to word origins.
- Students benefit from spelling instruction that gradually builds on previously mastered concepts of letter–sound relationships.
- Engaging spelling activities help students develop spelling skills needed for both writing and reading.
- Spelling ability correlates to reading comprehension ability.

Program	Daily Lesson Time (approximate)	Online/Offline
K¹² Language Arts Green Vocabulary	15 minutes	All online

Big Ideas

- Vocabulary words are words we need to know to communicate and understand.
- A *speaking vocabulary* includes the words we know and can use when speaking.
- A *reading vocabulary* includes the words we know and can read with understanding.
- A *listening vocabulary* includes the words we know and understand when we hear them.
- A *writing vocabulary* includes the words we know and understand when we write.
- The more we read, the more our vocabulary grows.
- Early learners acquire vocabulary through active exposure (by talking and listening, being read to, and receiving explicit instruction).

Program	Daily Lesson Time (approximate)	Online/Offline
K¹² Language Arts Green Writing Skills	15 minutes (Days 91–180 only)	Each unit (approximately): 4 offline lessons, 1 online lesson

Big Ideas

Composition

- Developing writers should study models of good writing.
- Writing can be broken out into a series of steps, or a process, that will help developing writers become more proficient.
- All writers revise, and revision is best performed in discrete tasks.

Grammar, Usage, and Mechanics (GUM)

- Using different kinds of sentences helps writers and speakers express their ideas accurately.
- A noun is a basic part of speech. Understanding nouns gives students a basic vocabulary for building sentences and understanding how language works.
- Recognizing and using action verbs helps writers make their work specific and interesting to readers.
- The use of descriptive adjectives can turn an ordinary piece of writing into one that enables the audience to form clear mental pictures of a scene.

Program	Daily Lesson Time (approximate)	Online/Offline
K¹² Language Arts Green Handwriting	10 minutes	All offline

Big Ideas

- Instruction in posture, pencil grip, and letter formation improves students' handwriting skills.
- Proper modeling of letter formation is imperative for developing handwriting skills.
- Students who have formal instruction in handwriting are more engaged in composition writing.

Structure

PhonicsWorks, Literature & Comprehension, Spelling, Vocabulary, Writing Skills, and Handwriting are independent programs that work together to give students a complete, well-balanced education in Language Arts.

1. **PhonicsWorks Advanced**   Students review basic letter–sound correspondences before moving into more advanced patterns. Through careful reading, rereading, and writing of words, students develop fluency to later aid in comprehension.

2. **Literature & Comprehension**   Students learn and later apply a wide variety of reading and comprehension strategies as they participate in read-aloud, shared-reading, and guided-reading activities with texts that cover a wide variety of genres. Activities emphasize deeper comprehension and analysis of text while developing a love of literature. Students also study how language is used in reading selections, providing a foundation for Writing Skills instruction in the second half of the year.

3. **Spelling**   In the second half of the year, students learn to focus on spelling patterns that are necessary to be fluent, proficient readers, writers, and spellers.

4. **Vocabulary**   Students increase their vocabulary by learning the meanings of groups of related words. Vocabulary skills help students read and compose written material.

5. **Writing Skills**   Beginning in the second half of the year, students learn about grammar, usage, and mechanics and learn about and use writing strategies as they write a variety of compositions.

6. **Handwriting**   For the first half of the year, students practice handwriting at a pace that meets their needs. For the second part of the year, students may continue to practice handwriting skills as they complete written work in other programs.

First-grade students grow and change quite a bit over the course of a year. As students begin first grade, they learn by doing. By the end of the year, students are thinking more abstractly, and they are able to process information a little differently. Students also learn to read and write more fluently as they progress through first grade. K[12] Language Arts Green accommodates the changing needs of students by adapting the instruction in several programs.

▶ **Phonics instructional time decreases** as students become more knowledgeable about sounds and letters and have increased reading fluency.
▶ **Literature lessons progress** from an adult reading aloud to students to having students read more independently.
▶ **Spelling instruction increases** as students become ready to learn about and apply spelling patterns.
▶ **Writing instruction increases** after students master the basics of handwriting and are ready to learn about how to put words and thoughts together.

To accommodate these changing needs, K[12] Language Arts Green is a bit different from the first part of the year to the last.

Days 1–90	
PhonicsWorks Advanced	**50 minutes**
Literature & Comprehension	**45 minutes**
Vocabulary	**15 minutes**
Handwriting	**10 minutes**

Days 91–180		
PhonicsWorks Advanced	**30 minutes**	PhonicsWorks lesson time decreases.
Literature & Comprehension	**45 minutes**	
Spelling	**15 minutes**	Spelling instruction using *K[12] Spelling Handbook* begins.
Vocabulary	**15 minutes**	
Writing Skills	**15 minutes**	Writing Skills instruction addressing composition and grammar, usage, and mechanics begins.
Handwriting	**⊕ OPTIONAL 10 minutes**	Students practice handwriting on their own or as they complete assigned work in other programs.

You will be notified in Advance Preparation 10 days before the Spelling and Writing Skills programs begin. When you see the notification, you should

1. Unpack the materials for these programs and preview them before the lessons begin on Day 91.

2. Review the Spelling program overview at the front of the *K12 Spelling Handbook* and the Writing Skills program overview at the front of this Lesson Guide.

3. View the online program introductions in Unit 1, Lesson 1, of the Spelling and Writing Skills programs.

Flexible Lesson Planning

A key aspect of K12 is the flexibility we offer students. Doing things that work best for them is vital to students' mastery. The structure of K12 Language Arts Green, with the separate programs, allows you to work on one skill at a time, which gives you flexibility. You will be able to

▸ **Find content more easily.** The descriptive titles in the lesson lists online and in the Lesson Guide allow you to find lessons and activities quickly.

▸ **Manage progress more easily.** You can track progress, mastery, and attendance by program so you can see at a glance how a student is progressing in each. This tracking will allow you to better customize your schedule to meet students' needs.

▸ **Pace work appropriately for students.** The focused lessons enable you to identify skills that students need to spend more or less time on and make adjustments. You can decide the pace that works best for students in each program. For example, a student may work through two Vocabulary lessons at a time but need to spend some extra time on Phonics.

▸ **Control your own schedule.** You can arrange lessons to meet your needs.

TIP Get to know the different lesson types and then set up your lesson schedule in the best way for you and your students.

How to Work Through a Lesson

Preview and Prepare

1. **Prepare in advance.** Schedule time to plan at the beginning of each week and before each school day. You may want to look ahead at any assessments or writing assignments so you know what students are working toward in each unit.

2. **Check the Lesson Guide or the online lesson** to see the lesson plan and read any instructions for completing the lesson.

3. **Complete Advance Preparation** before you begin a lesson. Look for Advance Preparation in the Lesson Guide or the online lesson.

4. **Preview the Lesson Guide** so you are prepared to teach the offline activities. You may also want to preview the online lesson and the word lists for Vocabulary.

5. **Gather the materials** listed in the Lesson Guide or the online lesson before you begin. You should always have paper and pencil available in addition to any other materials that are listed.

6. **Set up the workspace** for offline activities or move students to the computer to complete online activities.

TIP You might want to check the materials and Advance Preparation for the week in addition to reviewing them before each lesson so you know of any materials or tasks that may require some extra time or planning. For example, you may need to plan a trip to the library to get a book or go to the craft store for special materials.

Where to Begin?

For programs with both offline and online components, there is more than one way to begin a lesson. Either way will get you where you need to go.

Beginning Online   If you begin from the online lesson, the lesson screens will walk you through what you need to do, including gathering materials and moving offline if necessary.

- ► If the lesson begins with online activities, students will need to come to the computer and complete them.
- ► If the lesson begins with offline activities, gather the materials listed and begin the activities described in the lesson plan with students when you're ready.

Beginning Offline   You may choose to begin a lesson by first checking the lesson plan for the day in the Lesson Guide. The table on the first page of the lesson plan will indicate whether the lesson begins with online or offline activities.

- ► If the lesson begins with online activities, students will need to move to the computer and complete them.
- ► If the lesson begins with offline activities, gather the materials listed and begin the activities described in the lesson plan with students when you're ready.

After you've completed a unit or two in a particular program, you'll be familiar with the pattern of the units and lessons, and you'll know exactly where and how to begin.

Complete Activities with Students

Offline Activities   During offline activities, you will work closely with students away from the computer. Follow the instructions in the Lesson Guide for completing these activities.

Online Activities   Online activities take place at the computer. At first, you may need to help students learn how to navigate and use the online activities. You may also need to provide support when activities cover new or challenging content. Eventually, students will complete online activities with minimal support from you.

Work with Students to Complete Assessments

Offline Assessments   Students will complete offline assessments in Phonics, Literature & Comprehension, Writing Skills, and Spelling. After students complete the assessments offline, you will need to enter assessment scores in the Online School.

Online Assessments   Students will complete online assessments, called Unit Checkpoints, in Vocabulary. Because these assessments are all online, the computer will score them for you. You do not need to enter these assessment scores in the Online School.

Track Progress in Portfolios

K[12] recommends keeping students' work samples in a portfolio as a record of their progress. A simple folder, large envelope, or three-ring binder would work. Place offline assessments, Activity Book pages, and handwriting samples in the portfolio. Look back through the portfolio monthly and at the end of the year with students. Celebrate their progress and achievements.

How to Use This Book

K¹² Language Arts Lesson Guide contains information that will be extremely helpful to you as you prepare to begin K¹² Language Arts Green and on a daily basis as you work through the programs. Here is what the Lesson Guide contains and how you should use it.

What Is in the Lesson Guide	What You Should Do with It
Overviews of each of the programs included in K¹² Language Arts Green, including instructional philosophies, materials, and unit and lesson structure for the programs	• **Read the overviews** of the programs as you prepare to begin K¹² Language Arts Green. • **Refer back to the overview** information if you have questions as you work through the programs.
Glossary of key terms used in Literature & Comprehension and Writing Skills	• **Use the glossary** any time you need to look up a keyword used in Literature & Comprehension or Writing Skills.
Lesson plans for teaching • Literature & Comprehension lessons • Writing Skills lessons	• **Scan the unit and lesson overviews** for the lessons you will be working on each day. • **Follow the instructions** in the lesson plans to complete the activities with students. • **Use the answer keys** to check students' work on Activity Book pages and offline assessments.

Following are examples of the unit overview, lesson overview, and activity instructions that you will see in the lesson plans for teaching a Literature & Comprehension or Writing Skills lesson.

Unit Overview

There is one unit overview page per unit.

Unit Title
Each unit has a unique title that reflects the purpose or content of the unit.

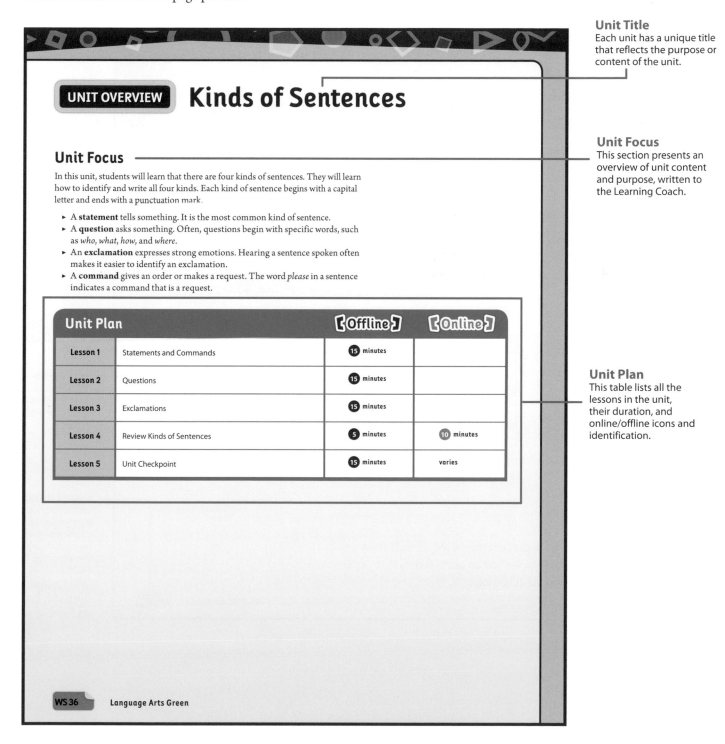

UNIT OVERVIEW Kinds of Sentences

Unit Focus

In this unit, students will learn that there are four kinds of sentences. They will learn how to identify and write all four kinds. Each kind of sentence begins with a capital letter and ends with a punctuation mark.

- ▸ A **statement** tells something. It is the most common kind of sentence.
- ▸ A **question** asks something. Often, questions begin with specific words, such as *who*, *what*, *how*, and *where*.
- ▸ An **exclamation** expresses strong emotions. Hearing a sentence spoken often makes it easier to identify an exclamation.
- ▸ A **command** gives an order or makes a request. The word *please* in a sentence indicates a command that is a request.

Unit Plan		**Offline**	**Online**
Lesson 1	Statements and Commands	**15** minutes	
Lesson 2	Questions	**15** minutes	
Lesson 3	Exclamations	**15** minutes	
Lesson 4	Review Kinds of Sentences	**5** minutes	**10** minutes
Lesson 5	Unit Checkpoint	**15** minutes	varies

Unit Focus
This section presents an overview of unit content and purpose, written to the Learning Coach.

Unit Plan
This table lists all the lessons in the unit, their duration, and online/offline icons and identification.

WS 36   Language Arts Green

Lesson Overview

Each Literature & Comprehension and Writing Skills lesson has a lesson overview page.

Lesson Title
The title indicates the lesson topic.

Lesson Overview Table
This table has an overview of the lesson's activities, their approximate times, and whether they take place offline or online.

This section of the lesson overview page includes Advance Preparation, Big Ideas, and Content Background, if any, that you need to know.

Advance Preparation
This information is what you need to prepare before beginning the lesson.

Big Ideas
Students will work toward these major organizing ideas in Language Arts.

Content Background
You might need this information to help you better understand the content you will be teaching.

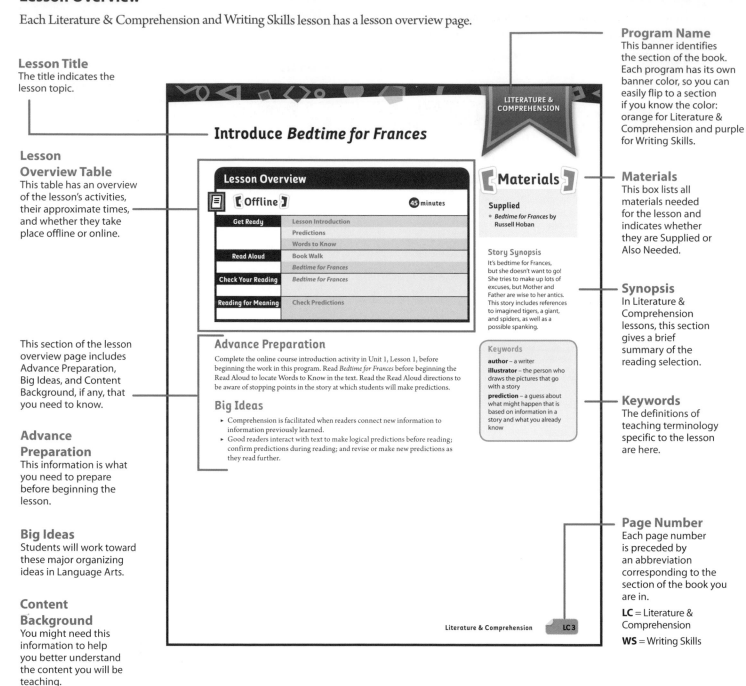

Introduce *Bedtime for Frances*

LITERATURE & COMPREHENSION

Lesson Overview		
⟨ Offline ⟩		**45** minutes
Get Ready	Lesson Introduction	
	Predictions	
	Words to Know	
Read Aloud	Book Walk	
	Bedtime for Frances	
Check Your Reading	*Bedtime for Frances*	
Reading for Meaning	Check Predictions	

Materials

Supplied
• *Bedtime for Frances* by Russell Hoban

Story Synopsis
It's bedtime for Frances, but she doesn't want to go! She tries to make up lots of excuses, but Mother and Father are wise to her antics. This story includes references to imagined tigers, a giant, and spiders, as well as a possible spanking.

Keywords
author – a writer
illustrator – the person who draws the pictures that go with a story
prediction – a guess about what might happen that is based on information in a story and what you already know

Advance Preparation
Complete the online course introduction activity in Unit 1, Lesson 1, before beginning the work in this program. Read *Bedtime for Frances* before beginning the Read Aloud to locate Words to Know in the text. Read the Read Aloud directions to be aware of stopping points in the story at which students will make predictions.

Big Ideas
▶ Comprehension is facilitated when readers connect new information to information previously learned.
▶ Good readers interact with text to make logical predictions before reading; confirm predictions during reading; and revise or make new predictions as they read further.

Literature & Comprehension — **LC 3**

Program Name
This banner identifies the section of the book. Each program has its own banner color, so you can easily flip to a section if you know the color: orange for Literature & Comprehension and purple for Writing Skills.

Materials
This box lists all materials needed for the lesson and indicates whether they are Supplied or Also Needed.

Synopsis
In Literature & Comprehension lessons, this section gives a brief summary of the reading selection.

Keywords
The definitions of teaching terminology specific to the lesson are here.

Page Number
Each page number is preceded by an abbreviation corresponding to the section of the book you are in.

LC = Literature & Comprehension

WS = Writing Skills

Activity Instructions

Lesson plans in the Literature & Comprehension and Writing Skills sections of the Lesson Guide include detailed instructions for each activity.

Program Name
This banner identifies the section of the book. Literature & Comprehension has an orange banner and Writing Skills has a purple banner.

Activity Type
These labels tell you what kind of activity you are working on.

Activity Description
This text describes what will happen in the activity. For offline activities, it provides step-by-step instructions. Answers are in magenta text.

Objectives
These learning goals indicate what students should be able to do as a result of the lesson.

Activity Book Page Answer Key
A miniature version of the Activity Book page is included in the Lesson Guide, with answers to help you check students' work.

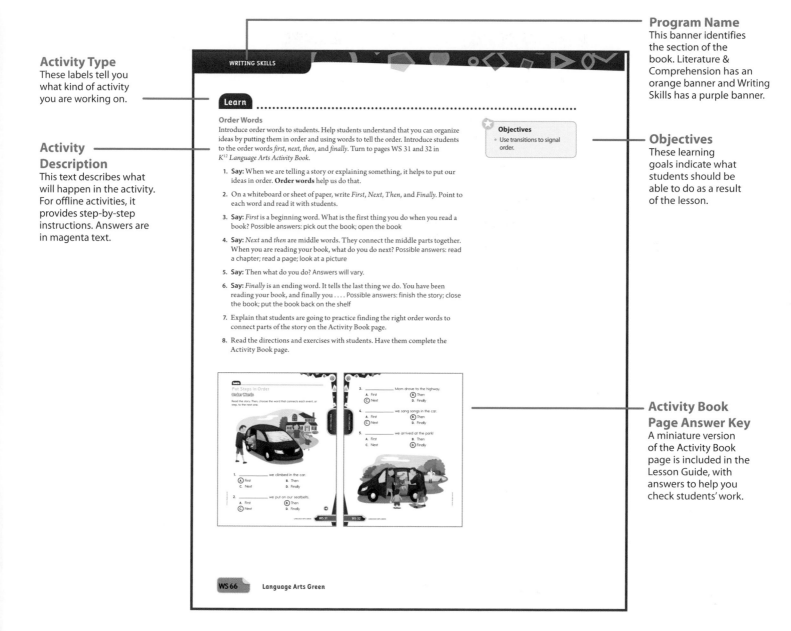

Look for Icons

The lesson plans contain icons to help you quickly see key elements as you work through the lesson. Look for these icons as you use the lesson plans.

Icon	Description
🖥 【Online】	Shows that an activity is online.
📄 【Offline】	Shows that an activity is offline.
TIP	Tips offer additional advice to help you explain the content.
 ✏️	This pencil appears next to activities that provide students with the opportunity to practice their handwriting.
 🎖	This blue ribbon indicates that you have reached a milestone that should be rewarded, usually by adding a sticker to the My Accomplishments chart.
➕ OPTIONAL:	Indicates that an activity is optional.
Reading Aid	Shows that you will use a Reading Aid from the Activity Book with this activity.

TIP Use a bookmark or a sticky note to mark the lesson that you are working on in Literature & Comprehension and in Writing Skills. These markers will help you quickly find the page you need each day.

My Accomplishments Chart

Research shows that rewarding students for quality work can increase their motivation. To help you reward students, you will receive a My Accomplishments chart and sticker sheet for use throughout K¹² Language Arts Green. This chart gives students a tangible record of their progress and accomplishments throughout Literature & Comprehension, Spelling, Vocabulary, and Writing Skills. There is also extra space that you can use to track progress for other accomplishments, like reading additional books, if you wish.

Help students proudly display and share their accomplishments with others by placing the chart somewhere visible, such as on the refrigerator or wall. Throughout the lessons, look for the reward icon 🎗, which indicates when and where students should place a sticker on the chart. Encourage students to set goals and watch their stickers accumulate. Praise students to help them understand the connection between their own growing skill set and the My Accomplishments chart. (For specific information about how to use the chart in each program, see the My Accomplishments Chart section in the following individual program overviews.)

K¹² My Journal

Research demonstrates that emerging writers are more motivated and become more confident when writing about self-selected topics. Journal writing allows young writers to explore and express themselves in a nonthreatening environment and make connections to their present knowledge. You will receive *K¹² My Journal* for use throughout K¹² Language Arts Green. Students will use the journal as they complete some lessons in Literature & Comprehension and Writing Skills, but they can also use the journal to write on their own. The journal has three sections that you will use as you work through lessons or on your own.

- ▶ **Thoughts and Experiences** has pages with space for drawing and writing and other pages for just writing. You will be directed to use these pages in some Literature & Comprehension lessons, but you can also encourage students to write in this section at any time.
- ▶ **Ideas** has some prompts to help students start writing. You can use the pages in this section at any time.
- ▶ **Writing Skills** has prompts that students will use to freewrite and make connections to the things that they learn as they complete the lessons in Writing Skills.

Noodleverse

Do your students have a favorite online activity? Do you wish you could find a favorite activity or practice a skill without hunting through lessons? If so, you and your students will love exploring Noodleverse—K¹²'s fun, engaging portal to many of the review and practice activities in the programs. The online Vocabulary, Spelling, and Phonics lessons contain links to Noodleverse, where students can create a "buddy" to help them explore, navigate to fun locations to browse activities, and mark activities as favorites for quick access later. You'll be able to pull up a site map listing every activity, organized by program and topic.

Here are some of the Language Arts items that can be found in Noodleverse:

▶ Phonics review and practice activities
▶ Vocabulary review and practice activities
▶ Spelling review and practice activities
▶ Writing Skills review and practice activities
▶ Handwriting practice activity
▶ Audio recordings of stories and poems from *K¹² Classics for Young Readers, Volume A*
▶ Book browser for choosing books in Literature & Comprehension and lesson materials for those books, including printable book report projects
▶ Printable Story Cards and graphic organizers

K¹² Language Arts PhonicsWorks Advanced Overview

The PhonicsWorks materials are separate from the K¹² Language Arts Green materials, so you will not find PhonicsWorks lesson plans in *K¹² Language Arts Lesson Guide* or activity pages in *K¹² Language Arts Activity Book*. Please refer to the PhonicsWorks Advanced Kit for all phonics materials.

K¹² Language Arts Green Literature & Comprehension Overview

Program	Daily Lesson Time (approximate)	Online/Offline
K¹² Language Arts Green Literature & Comprehension	45 minutes	All offline

Structure and Materials	
24 units that vary in length and structure, depending on the number and length of literary selections • 18 units of fiction, nonfiction, and poetry • 2 Reader's Choice units • 4 Checkpoints (2 Mid-Semester Checkpoints and 2 Semester Checkpoints)	**Materials** • *K¹² Language Arts Lesson Guide* • *K¹² Language Arts Activity Book* • *K¹² Language Arts Assessment Book* • *K¹² Classics for Young Readers, Volume A* • *K¹² My Journal* • Literature & Comprehension Support Materials • 10 Story Cards • 4 *K¹² World* nonfiction magazines: *Earth and Sky, People and Places of the Past, The Science of Inventing, Critter and Creature Stories* • 18 trade books

Philosophy

K¹² Language Arts Literature & Comprehension includes four effective instructional approaches to reading: read aloud, shared reading, guided reading, and independent reading. Each approach contributes to students' skill level and ability to apply specific reading strategies.

Read Aloud

What Is It?   The **Learning Coach reads aloud to students** from carefully selected texts of various genres. The texts have features that lend themselves to modeling what good readers do. While reading aloud, the **Learning Coach will model** the following behaviors for students: fluent, expressive reading; what good readers think about as they read; and how good readers use strategies to understand text.

Why We Do It   Reading aloud engages students in an enjoyable experience that promotes a love of reading. It is an opportunity to share quality literature that is too challenging for students to read independently. Listening to stories helps students build vocabulary knowledge and develop a sense of story structure.

What Does It Look Like?   The Learning Coach and students sit together so that everyone can see the text and pictures or illustrations. While reading aloud, the Learning Coach tracks with his or her finger so students can follow along. While reading, the Learning Coach models the behaviors of a good reader by doing some or all of the following:

- ▶ Emphasize Words to Know in the text.
- ▶ Use the pictures or illustrations to help determine word meanings (if appropriate).
- ▶ Stop to ask questions or have students make predictions.

Shared Reading

What Is It?   Shared reading is an interactive reading experience that happens when **students join in the reading of a text** while guided by a proficient reader (in this case, the Learning Coach). Students must be able to clearly see the text and follow along as the Learning Coach points to the words. Students gradually assume more responsibility for the reading as their skill level and confidence increases.

Why We Do It   Shared reading gives students a chance to practice the reading behaviors of proficient readers with the support of a proficient reader. Through shared reading, students develop an awareness of the relationship between the spoken and printed word. They learn print concepts and conventions, and they are exposed to early reading strategies such as word-by-word matching. They learn where to focus their attention as they read. They also acquire a sense of story structure and the ability to predict while being exposed to the process of reading extended texts. Shared reading also familiarizes students with a collection of texts that they can use for independent reading and as resources for word study and writing.

What Does It Look Like?   As in read-aloud activities, the Learning Coach and students sit together so everyone can see the text and the pictures or illustrations. The Learning Coach reads aloud, tracking with his or her finger so students can follow along. Students chime in to read parts of the story that they are familiar with. While reading, the Learning Coach will

- ▶ Model the behaviors of a good reader, as in read-aloud activities.
- ▶ Stop to discuss questions with students during the reading.
- ▶ Reread texts to examine features (for example, the use of quotation marks for dialogue or the author's use of descriptive language in the text).
- ▶ Give students specific tasks to allow them to participate in the reading (for example, reading a character's quotations or reading a section expressively).

Guided Reading

What Is It?   In guided reading, students read books specifically selected to challenge them and give them problem-solving opportunities. The Learning Coach introduces the new book to students and provides instruction that will support and enable **students to read the text themselves**. In guided reading, the Learning Coach's focused instruction helps students develop the decoding and comprehension strategies necessary to move on to texts at the next level of difficulty.

Why We Do It   Guided reading gives students the chance to apply strategies they already know to read a new text. During these Learning Coach-supported lessons, students also acquire and practice new reading strategies as they problem solve and read for meaning. While the Learning Coach provides assistance, the ultimate goal is for students to read independently. Through shared reading, students have learned how print works and how to monitor their understanding of text. Guided reading is the natural next step during which students learn to apply problem-solving strategies when they encounter difficulties decoding and understanding text.

What Does It Look Like?   The **Learning Coach guides students through a preview** of a text to prepare **students to read it on their own**. As in read-aloud activities, the Learning Coach and student sit together so that everyone can see the text and the pictures or illustrations. To prepare for reading, the Learning Coach will preview with students by doing some or all of the following:

- ▶ Look at pictures or illustrations and discuss what they show about the text.
- ▶ Examine words and phrases in the text and discuss what they mean (for example, find the words *Frog* and *Toad* and talk about why they have capital letters).
- ▶ Scan the pages to find information (for example, what the character says he likes).
- ▶ Practice reading certain words or phrases.
- ▶ Make predictions based on the information in the text.
- ▶ Model strategies for reading (for example, using pictures to determine word meaning).

After previewing with the Learning Coach, **students will read the text aloud.** If necessary, the **Learning Coach may offer support** by doing one of the following:

- ▶ Read aloud to students.
- ▶ Read aloud as students chime in.
- ▶ Take turns reading aloud (alternate pages or sections with students).

Independent Reading

What Is It?   When students do independent reading, they often choose their own books from a wide range of reading materials and read on their own for an extended block of time. During independent reading, students need to read books at a level just right for them, called their *independent level*. Independent reading is introduced in K¹² Language Arts Orange.

Approaches to Reading in K¹² Language Arts Green

In K¹² Language Arts Green Literature & Comprehension, students move from read aloud to shared reading to guided reading over the course of the year.

When in Program	Reading Approach	Learning Coach Responsibilities
First Third (Units 1–8)	**Read Aloud**	• Read to students. • Model reading strategies. • Discuss readings with students.
Second Third (Units 9–16)	**Shared Reading**	• Read with students; have students chime in and read parts of the selections. • Model reading strategies. • Discuss readings with students
Last Third (Units 17–24)	**Guided Reading**	• Model reading strategies. • Preview selections to prepare students to read. • Support students as they read. • Discuss readings with students.

TIP Look in the first lesson of the first unit of this program in the Online School for more information about the different approaches to reading in K¹² Language Arts Green.

Overview of Literature & Comprehension Lessons

Materials

The following materials are supplied for Literature & Comprehension:

K¹² Language Arts Lesson Guide

K¹² Language Arts Activity Book

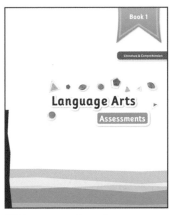

K¹² Language Arts Assessments

K¹² Classics for Young Readers, Volume A

K¹² World: Earth and Sky

K¹² World: People and Places of the Past

K¹² World: The Science of Inventing

K¹² World: Critter and Creature Stories

K¹² My Journal

Literature & Comprehension Support Materials

Story Cards

The following trade books are also supplied:

- *A Picture for Harold's Room* by Crockett Johnson
- *Amelia Bedelia* by Peggy Parish
- *And I Mean It, Stanley* by Crosby Bonsall
- *Bedtime for Frances* by Russell Hoban
- *Danny and the Dinosaur* by Syd Hoff
- *Frog and Toad Are Friends* by Arnold Lobel
- *Harry and the Lady Next Door* by Gene Zion
- *Listen, My Children: Poems for First Graders*
- *Little Bear* by Else Holmelund Minarik
- *No Fighting, No Biting!* by Else Holmelund Minarik
- *Owl at Home* by Arnold Lobel
- *Ready . . . Set . . . Read!: The Beginning Reader's Treasury*
- *Sylvester and the Magic Pebble* by William Steig
- *Tales of Amanda Pig* by Jean Van Leeuwen
- *The First Thanksgiving* by Linda Hayward
- *The Legend of the Bluebonnet* by Tomie dePaola
- *Weather: Poems for All Seasons*
- *Who Will Be My Friends?* by Syd Hoff

You should always have paper and pencils available. You will also need the following general materials to complete Activity Book pages:

- crayons or colored pencils
- glue
- scissors (Safety note: When students are working with scissors, please supervise them to make sure they use their scissors safely and stay seated.)

Additional materials, ranging from index cards to library books, may be needed for certain lessons.

Using the Activity Book

Keep in mind that students will write in and tear out pages from the Activity Book; you may want to store loose Activity Book pages in a three-ring binder. Remember to build students' portfolios with completed Activity Book pages.

You will find some special pages in the Activity Book for use with lessons that include shared-reading or guided-reading activities. When one of these pages is to be used, you will see the Reading Aid icon **Reading Aid** in the Lesson Guide. The Reading Aid is designed so that the Learning Coach can easily follow instructions for reading activities while simultaneously using one of the texts for reading.

TIP Look for instructions in Advance Preparation and tips within activities for saving and gathering materials that get used in more than one lesson.

Using the Journal

As students complete Literature & Comprehension lessons, they will occasionally use *K¹² My Journal* to record thoughts and ideas related to their work. You will be directed to turn to Thoughts and Experiences in the journal and then follow the instructions in the Lesson Guide for completing the journal activity. Thoughts and Experiences has pages with room for drawing and writing and pages for just writing.

Students may also write in their journal on their own. They may use pages in Thoughts and Experiences or in Ideas for writing on their own. The Ideas section has prompts to help students start writing. The Writing Skills section will be used in the Writing Skills lessons.

(TIP) Any time you are directed to use the journal in a lesson, you can print additional journal pages from the online lesson.

Using Support Materials

Literature & Comprehension Support Materials include posters (both wall-size and 8 ½ x 11 inches), bookmarks, and materials for completing book report projects.

The posters are included as a visual reminder for both you and students of different strategies readers use to improve their reading and comprehension. You may choose to hang the wall-size posters where you and students can easily refer to them during lessons. Take-along versions of the posters are provided in 8 ½ x 11-inch size. Additionally, two of the four bookmarks contain the reading and comprehension strategies.

A third bookmark has an inspirational quote on it, and the fourth provides room for students to write the names of books they have read. You may choose to give students the bookmarks one at a time as a motivational tool or reward, or you can give all of them to students at once. These are simply resources for to assist students in their journey to becoming independent readers.

Finally, Literature & Comprehension Support Materials include instructions, templates, and scoring aids for completing book report projects. Students will complete two book report projects as part of the Reader's Choice units in Literature & Comprehension. Encourage students to complete additional projects as they read books on their own.

(TIP) Links to additional book report project materials can be found in Noodleverse.

Lesson Structure

Literature & Comprehension consists of daily 45-minute lessons that build in a sequence designed to meet new readers' needs and that are developmentally appropriate for an early reader's growing comprehension abilities. The number of lessons in a unit will vary, and the lessons themselves will have different combinations of activities, but the activities will include prereading, reading, and postreading instruction.

The following chart is an overview of how activities might be sequenced in lessons. As you can see, you work with students to prepare for the reading and then uses one of the reading strategies to read with students. After reading, you will check students' comprehension before beginning a deeper analysis of the reading selection.

Day 1 Lesson Overview

Get Ready
- Lesson Introduction
- Main Ideas
- Words to Know

Read (Aloud, Shared, or Guided)
- Book Walk
- "Women in Space"

Check Your Reading "Women in Space"

Reading for Meaning Main Ideas in "Women in Space"

Day 2 Lesson Overview

Get Ready
- Lesson Introduction
- Finding Facts
- Words to Know

Read (Aloud, Shared, or Guided)
- Book Walk
- "Women in Space"

Reading for Meaning Facts in "Women in Space"

Looking at Language Exclamation Marks and Periods

Making Connections My Favorite Astronaut

+ OPTIONAL: Beyond the Lesson Learn More About Outer Space

The activities shown are an example of what you might see in the lessons for this program. Not every lesson will contain all these activities. In some lessons, you may read a selection more than once.

Lesson Activities

Lesson plans in the Literature & Comprehension section of this Lesson Guide include detailed instructions for each activity. Literature & Comprehension activity types include the following:

- **Get Ready (Offline)**   The Get Ready activities prepare students for that day's reading selection and lesson. They include instructions to help students build background knowledge and strategies needed for comprehension, and Words to Know, which are words from the selection that students should become familiar with.

- **Read Aloud, Shared Reading, Guided Reading (Offline)**   The Learning Coach and students complete prereading activities (Book Walk) and then read the selection using read-aloud, shared-reading, or guided-reading strategies. These activities might have a Reading Aid, which is a special kind of Activity Book page designed to help the Learning Coach.

- **Check Your Reading (Offline)**   The Learning Coach asks students questions to show general comprehension of the reading selection. Students will answer the questions orally. In most cases, these questions require students to know what happened in the selection.

- **Reading for Meaning (Offline)**   The Learning Coach works with students to help them develop a deeper understanding of the reading selection through application of comprehension strategies and analysis of the selection. These activities often have an Activity Book page to complete.

- **Looking at Language (Offline)**   The Learning Coach models thought processes by talking to students as they interact with the written text. These activities might have a Reading Aid, which is a special kind of Activity Book page designed to help the Learning Coach.

- **Making Connections (Offline)**   Students will apply information and strategies learned from lessons to the reading selection. These activities often involve students making a connection between and among texts or between the text and themselves or the larger world. These activities may or may not have an Activity Book page.

- **OPTIONAL Beyond the Lesson (Offline)**   These activities are for students who have extra time and interest in exploring the reading selection further. These activities are not required and can be skipped.

- **Peer Interaction (Offline)**   The Learning Coach will lead a discussion with students about a reading selection. Ideally, students should discuss their reading with their peers.

- **Semester Review (Offline)**   Students will review skills from the semester to prepare for the Semester Checkpoint.

- **Mid-Semester and Semester Checkpoints (Offline)**   Students will apply the skills learned in the program as they read fiction, nonfiction, and poetry selections.

- **More Practice (Online)**   After each Checkpoint, suggestions are provided for activities to help review and practice areas in which students may need extra work.

Noodleverse

In the Literature & Comprehension area of Noodleverse, you will find audio recordings of the literary selections in *K¹² Classics for Young Readers, Volume A*. You can also access extra copies of the book report project materials and Reader's Choice lesson materials. In addition, you can access printable graphic organizers and story cards for use in any of lessons.

My Accomplishments Chart

Rewards in Literature & Comprehension are tied to completing units. When students complete a unit, have them add a sticker for that unit to the My Accomplishments chart.

Reader's Choice Units

Throughout K¹² Language Arts Green Literature & Comprehension, Planning and Progress in the Online School will alert you to an approaching Reader's Choice unit (Units 4 and 16). These units are designed to give students an opportunity to choose books to read while fine-tuning their comprehension skills. Research indicates that providing opportunities for choice enhances performance and motivates early readers.

In each of the two Reader's Choice units, you and your students will have a bank of six texts to choose from. K¹² suggests that you discuss the possible texts with students to guarantee that they will engage with texts that interest them. Reader's Choice units are 11 lessons each. There are two important differences from other units in the program.

1. **You will need to acquire these texts on your own, through a library or bookstore.** To help you choose a text for a Reader's Choice unit, K¹² includes a brief synopsis of the story and information about grade and interest level.

2. Once you have selected the text, you will be prompted to *print* the accompanying lesson guide and activity pages. **These pages are not provided in this Lesson Guide or the Activity Book.**

To keep students engaged, deepen comprehension, and develop public speaking capabilities, they are required to complete a book report project as part of each Reader's Choice unit. Literature & Comprehension Support Materials include detailed instructions for creating, grading, and presenting a book report project.

K¹² Language Arts Green Spelling Overview

Program	Daily Lesson Time (approximate)	Online/Offline
K¹² Language Arts Green Spelling	15 minutes (Days 91–180 only)	Each unit: 4 offline lessons, 1 online review
Structure and Materials		
18 units with 5 lessons each	Materials • *K¹² Spelling Handbook*	

The Spelling materials are separate from the K¹² Language Arts Green materials, so you will not find Spelling lesson plans in *K¹² Language Arts Lesson Guide* or activity pages in *K¹² Language Arts Activity Book*. Please refer to *K¹² Spelling Handbook* for all materials related to the program.

K¹² Language Arts Green Vocabulary Overview

Program	Daily Lesson Time (approximate)	Online/Offline
K¹² Language Arts Green Vocabulary	15 minutes	All online
Structure and Materials		
18 units with 10 lessons each	Materials • *K¹² Language Arts Vocabulary Word Lists* Online Book	

Vocabulary is entirely online. Students will work through the online lessons with your supervision. You can access the word lists for all the units from the online lessons.

K¹² Language Arts Green Writing Skills Overview

Program	Daily Lesson Time (approximate)	Online/Offline
K¹² Language Arts Green Writing Skills	15 minutes (Days 91–180 only)	Each unit (approximately): 4 offline lessons, 1 online lesson

Structure and Materials	
18 units with 5 lessons each • 9 GUM units • 8 Composition units • 1 optional Composition unit	**Materials** • *K¹² Language Arts Lesson Guide* • *K¹² Language Arts Activity Book* • *K¹² Language Arts Assessments* • *K¹² My Journal* • 10 Story Cards

Philosophy

Learning to express one's ideas in writing is a fundamental requirement of an educated person. K¹² Language Arts Green Writing Skills takes a two-pronged approach to fulfilling this need. Grammar, Usage, and Mechanics (GUM) lessons teach students the nuts and bolts of communicating in standard written English. Composition lessons teach students how to think about, plan, organize, and write organized communications in a variety of forms. Writing Skills includes alternating units of GUM and Composition.

Grammar, Usage, and Mechanics (GUM)

What Is It?   The grammar, usage, and mechanics lessons give students practice in learning about sentences and the parts of speech that make up sentences; in using subjects, verbs, and pronouns correctly; and in discovering how capitalization and punctuation marks aid in conveying the message of sentences.

Why We Do It   While it is true that knowing grammar does not make someone a good writer, understanding how grammar works makes writing easier. When students know things like what a complete sentence is, what kind of punctuation is used within a sentence and at the end of a sentence, and which words need capital letters, they can spend their time focusing on ideas. When the focus is on ideas, not on mechanics, writing becomes more fluent and expressive.

Composition

What Is It?   In composition lessons, students practice to become more fluent and expressive writers. In these lessons, students learn to write in a variety of forms. They start by using a journal to encourage fluid and creative thought. They use freewriting techniques and build upon their ideas to learn more structured forms. They learn to write sentences and to connect those sentences to form a group of related ideas into a paragraph. They will write short narrative and informative compositions as well as create basic explanatory texts. They will write a response to literature and practice basic presentation skills.

Why We Do It   Research shows that daily writing practice is essential for the developing writer. The lessons are based on a process-writing model of instruction. Research demonstrates that engaging in a variety of prewriting techniques (such as freewriting) and planning activities helps novice writers learn to transform their ideas into organized writing. Throughout each unit, students will practice skills in discrete steps, and they will ultimately write a polished piece of writing, ready to be "published" or shared. Students will learn that the writing process is not a straight line forward and that writing always means rewriting for improvement. As you help students through these lessons, encourage them to express their thoughts and ideas. Student writing is not adult writing. Expect errors in basic sentence structure, but encourage students to express their thoughts in written form.

Overview of Writing Skills Lessons

Materials

The following materials are supplied for Writing Skills:

K¹² Language Arts Lesson Guide

K¹² Language Arts Activity Book

K¹² Language Arts Assessments

K¹² My Journal

Story Cards

You should always have paper and pencils available for students. You might sometimes also need the following general materials to complete the Activity Book pages:

- 3½ x 5-inch index cards
- crayons or colored pencils
- glue
- scissors (Safety note: When students are working with scissors, please supervise students to make sure they use their scissors safely and stay seated.)

Keeping a Writing Portfolio

Students will write in and tear out pages of the Activity Book, so periodically place some of the Activity Book pages in a student writing portfolio. In addition, save students' graphic organizers, drafts, and published compositions in the portfolio to keep track of their growth as writers. Consult the portfolio regularly and keep it as a record to share with teachers. Share the work with students so that they can see the progress they have made and celebrate it. Remember that student writing is not adult writing. Do not expect perfection, but rather look for progress over time and clarity of thought and intent.

The Activity Book contains pages with examples of different types of writing or other kinds of materials that students will refer to over the course of a unit. Look for tips in the Lesson Guide alerting you to store these materials for further use. Be sure to keep these pages in a safe place so you can easily find them and refer to them.

Using the Journal

As students complete Writing Skills lessons, they will freewrite about topics and ideas in Writing Skills of *K¹² My Journal.* You will find specific instructions in the Lesson Guide to help students get started and to encourage their writing. Students may use Thoughts and Experiences and Ideas of the journal to write on their own.

TIP You can print additional copies of the journal pages used in the Writing Skills lessons from the online lessons.

Lesson Structure

Writing Skills consists of 18 units. The units alternate: Odd-numbered units are about grammar, usage, and mechanics (GUM), and even-numbered units are about composition.

All units are five lessons long, with each lesson taking about 15 minutes to complete. Although the GUM and Composition units look similar, there are several key differences:

- Composition units begin with a freewriting activity, using the journal on Day 1.
- GUM units include an online review lesson on Day 4. Composition units are entirely offline.
- GUM units end with a Unit Checkpoint on Day 5. Composition units end with a Write Now activity, which is a writing assignment.

Day 1 Lesson Overview

GUM	Composition
[Offline] **15** minutes	**[Offline]** **15** minutes
Get Ready Learn Try It	Get Ready Try It: Freewrite (Journal)

Days 2–3 Lesson Overview

GUM	Composition
[Offline] **15** minutes	**[Offline]** **15** minutes
Get Ready Learn Try It	Get Ready Learn Try It

Day 4 Lesson Overview

GUM	Composition
[Online] **10** minutes	**[Offline]** **15** minutes
Review	Get Ready Learn Try It **✚ OPTIONAL:** Peer Interaction
[Offline] **5** minutes	
Try It: Journal	

Day 5 Lesson Overview

GUM	Composition
[Offline] **15** minutes	**[Offline]** **15** minutes
Unit Checkpoint	Get Ready Learn Write Now
[Online] varies	**[Online]** varies
More Practice	More Practice

Lesson Activities

Lesson plans in the Writing Skills section of this Lesson Guide include detailed descriptions or instructions for each activity. Writing Skills lessons include the following types of activities:

- **Get Ready (Offline)** The Get Ready is a short activity to prepare students for the new skills that they will learn in the lesson. Often the Get Ready draws on students' previous knowledge or builds background knowledge in preparation for the new skill. Sometimes students will preview examples of different types of writing or work with other kinds of examples as part of the Get Ready.

- **Learn (Offline)** Students learn a new skill. The examples and tips in the Lesson Guide provide the Learning Coach with the information needed to explain the new skill. Often the Learn is accompanied by an Activity Book page that contains an explanation of the new skill and an example that students can refer to as they progress through the program.

- **Try It (Offline)** Students practice using the new skill that they have learned by completing a page in the Activity Book. Sometimes students will freewrite in their journal or continue to work on a piece of writing that they started earlier.

- **Review (Online)** Each odd-numbered unit includes an online activity to provide students with an opportunity to review and practice the grammar, usage, and mechanics (GUM) skills they have learned in that unit. Students will also have several days to review the GUM skills learned throughout the semester before completing the Semester Checkpoint.

- **Unit and Semester Checkpoints (Offline)** Each GUM unit ends with an offline Unit Checkpoint, which tests the skills that students have learned in the unit. An offline Semester Checkpoint covers the GUM skills learned in the entire semester.

- **Write Now (Offline)** Each Composition unit ends with a writing assignment. Students complete the assignment that they have been planning, drafting, and revising throughout the unit. The Learning Coach evaluates that writing on a three-point scale for purpose and content, structure and organization, and grammar and mechanics. Sample papers (available online) help the Learning Coach evaluate the strength of the writing and areas in which students can improve.

- **More Practice (Online)** After each Checkpoint or Write Now, suggestions are provided for activities to help review and practice areas in which students may need extra work, along with links to access these materials.

- **Peer Interaction (Offline)** Some composition assignments include Peer Interaction, in which students share their writing with a peer or anyone else willing to give feedback. If time allows, students can benefit from this interaction by using the feedback to revise their work.

Noodleverse

In the Writing Skills area of Noodleverse, students can access all the online review activities from the program. You can also access printable graphic organizers and story cards for use in any of your lessons.

My Accomplishments Chart

Rewards in GUM units of Writing Skills are tied to completing Unit Checkpoints. Each time students score 80 percent or higher on a Unit Checkpoint, have them add a sticker for that unit to the My Accomplishments chart. If students score lower than 80 percent, review each Checkpoint exercise with them and work with them to correct any exercises they missed.

Rewards in the Composition units of Writing Skills are tied to completing the Write Now assignments in each unit. When students' writing achieves "meets objectives" in all three categories on the grading rubric, have them add a sticker for that unit to the My Accomplishments chart. If students' work scores "does not meet objectives" in any category, help them review and revise their work to achieve "meets objectives."

K¹² Language Arts Green Handwriting Overview

Program	Daily Lesson Time (approximate)	Online/Offline
K¹² Language Arts Green Handwriting	10 minutes	All offline
Structure and Materials		
36 units with 5 lessons each	**Materials** • *My Printing Book* • *1st Grade Printing Teacher's Guide* • Lined paper	

Philosophy

K¹² supplies the proven Handwriting Without Tears® program for students in kindergarten through grade 3. This gentle, multisensory approach focuses on careful practice at a pace that suits students' fine motor skills development.

Overview of Handwriting Lessons

Materials

The following books and materials are supplied for Handwriting:

- *My Printing Book*
- *1st Grade Printing Teacher's Guide*
- One package of specially lined writing paper for Handwriting Without Tears
  If you need more of this paper, the following options are available:
  - Online lesson openers provide a handwriting sheet that you can print and photocopy.
  - You can order more wide double-lined notebook paper directly from Handwriting Without Tears at http://www.hwtears.com/.

These materials are separate from *K¹² Language Arts Lesson Guide* and *K¹² Language Arts Activity Book*.

Lesson Structure

K¹² Handwriting is entirely offline and uses the supplied Handwriting Without Tears materials. Before beginning the program, become familiar with *1st Grade Printing Teacher's Guide*. The guide includes a Teaching Guidelines chart to help you plan students' handwriting lessons.

In each lesson, you will work with students for 10 minutes. (You may want to set a timer for 10 minutes; most students enjoy the Handwriting program, so it's easy to lose track of time and do too much in one day.)

Students should complete as many workbook pages as they can, picking up where they left off during the previous Handwriting lesson and continuing from there. They are not expected to complete a set number of pages during the 10-minute lessons. Be sure to monitor students' writing time so you can help them develop good letter formation habits.

Depending on students' pace, the workbook should take 8 to 12 weeks of instruction. Move as quickly or as slowly as students need. When students have completed the workbooks, have them use the packaged lined writing paper from Handwriting Without Tears to practice their handwriting. Also look for the Handwriting icon throughout the Lesson Guide. This icon indicates that the associated activity provides a perfect opportunity to practice proper handwriting, and if students pay careful attention to their handwriting, this time can also count as Handwriting time.

K¹² Language Arts Green Keywords

Literature and Comprehension

alliteration – the use of words with the same or close to the same beginning sounds

author – a writer

author's purpose – the reason the author wrote a text: to entertain, to inform, to express an opinion, or to persuade

autobiography – the story of a person's life written by that person

biography – the story of someone's life written by another person

brainstorming – an early step in writing that helps a writer come up with as many ideas about a topic as possible

caption – writing under a picture that describes the picture

cause – the reason something happens

character – a person or animal in a story

compare – to explain how two or more things are alike

comprehension – understanding

connection – a link readers make between themselves, information in text, and the world around them

context – the parts of a sentence or passage surrounding a word

context clue – a word or phrase in a text that helps you figure out the meaning of an unknown word

contrast – to explain how two or more things are different

decode – to sound out a word

detail – a piece of information in a text

dialogue – the words that characters say in a written work

draft – an early effort at a piece of writing, not the finished work

drama – another word for *play*

effect – the result of a cause

fable – a story that teaches a lesson and may contain animal characters

fact – something that can be proven true

fairy tale – a folktale with magical elements

fantasy – a story with characters, settings, or other elements that could not really exist

fiction – make-believe stories

first-person point of view – the telling of a story by a character in that story, using pronouns such as *I*, *me*, and *we*

folktale – a story passed down through a culture for many years that may have human, animal, or magical characters

genre – a category for classifying literary works

glossary – a list of important terms and their meanings that is usually found in the back of a book

graphic organizer – a visual tool used to show relationships between key concepts; formats include webs, diagrams, and charts

illustration – a drawing

illustrator – the person who draws the pictures that go with a story

imagery – language that helps readers imagine how something looks, sounds, smells, feels, or tastes

infer – to use clues and what you already know to make a guess

inference – a guess you make using the clues in a text and what you already know

informational text – text written to explain and give information on a topic

legend – a story that is passed down for many years to teach the values of a culture; a legend may or may not contain some true events or people

line – a row of words in a poem

literal level – a reference to text information that is directly stated

literal recall – the ability to describe information stated directly in a text

literature – made-up stories, true stories, poems, and plays

main character – an important person, animal, or other being who is central to the plot

main idea – the most important idea in a paragraph or text

moral – the lesson of a story, particularly a fable

narrative – text genre that tells a story; a narrative text usually includes characters, setting, and plot

narrator – the teller of a story

news – information about, or report of, recent events

nonfiction – writings about true things

opinion – something that a person thinks or believes, but which cannot be proven to be true

personification – giving human qualities to something that is not human
Example: The thunder shouted from the clouds.

plot – what happens in a story

point of view – the perspective a story is told from

predictable text – text written with rhyme, rhythm, and repetition

prediction – a guess about what might happen that is based on information in a story and what you already know

print features – formatting that draws attention to words in text, such as bold type, underlining, and capital letters

prior knowledge – things you already know from past experience

problem – an issue a character must solve in a story

realistic fiction – a made-up story that has no magical elements

retelling – using your own words to tell a story that you have listened to or read

rhyme – when two or more words have the same ending sounds
Example: cat and *hat* rhyme

rhythm – a pattern of accented and unaccented syllables; a distinctive beat

scriptal information – things you already know from past experience

self-correct – to correct an error without prompting while reading text aloud

self-monitor – to notice if you do or do not understand what you are reading

self-question – to ask questions of yourself as you read to check your understanding

sensory language – language that appeals to the five senses

sequence – order

setting – when and where a story takes place

simile – a comparison between two things using the words *like* or *as*
Example: He was as quiet as a mouse.

solution – how a character solves a problem in a story

stanza – a group of lines in a poem

story events – the things that happen in a story; the plot

story structure elements – components of a story; they include character, setting, plot, problem, and solution

summarize – to tell in order the most important ideas or events of a text

Literature and Comprehension *continued*

summary – a short retelling that includes only the most important ideas or events of a text

supporting detail – a detail that gives more information about a main idea

table of contents – a list at the start of a book that gives the titles of the book's stories, poems, articles, chapters, or nonfiction pieces and the pages where they can be found

text feature – part of a text that helps a reader locate information and determine what is most important; some examples are the title, table of contents, headings, pictures, and glossary

text structure – the organizational pattern of a text, such as cause and effect, compare and contrast, and chronological order

text support – a graphic feature that helps a reader better understand text, such as a picture, chart, or map

theme – the author's message or big idea

time line – a line showing dates and events in the order that they happened

tone – the author's feelings toward the subject and/or characters of a text

topic – the subject of a text

visual text support – a graphic feature that helps a reader better understand text, such as a picture, chart, or map

visualize – to picture things in your mind as you read

Writing Skills (Composition)

audience – a writer's readers

body (of a friendly letter) – the main text of a friendly letter

book report – a piece of writing that gives information, a summary, and an opinion about a book

book review – a piece of writing that gives an opinion about a book and tells about it

brainstorming – before writing, a way for the writer to come up with ideas

chronological order – a way to organize that puts details in time order

closing (of a friendly letter) – the part of the friendly letter that follows the body
Example: Your friend or Love

coherence – of writing, the smooth connection of ideas in a paragraph or essay

command – a kind of sentence that gives an order or makes a request

comparison – a look at how two things are alike

complete sentence – a group of words that tells a complete thought

concluding sentence – the last sentence of a paragraph; often summarizes the paragraph

conclusion – the final paragraph of a written work

conjunction – a word used to join parts of a sentence, such as *and*, *but*, and *or*

content – the information or ideas in a piece of writing

contrast – a look at how two things are different

declarative sentence – a group of words that makes a statement

definition – a statement that tells what a word means

description – writing that uses words that show how something looks, sounds, feels, tastes, or smells
Example: The sky is a soft, powdery blue, and the golden sun feels warm on my face.

detail – a fact or description that tells more about a topic

dialogue – the words spoken between people

dictionary – a reference work made up of words with their definitions, in alphabetical order

drafting – of writing, the stage or step in which the writer first writes the piece

encyclopedia – a reference work made up of articles on many topics, usually in alphabetical order

example – a specific instance of something, used to illustrate an idea

exclamation – a kind of sentence that shows strong feeling

exclamatory sentence – a group of words that shows strong feeling

experience story – a story about something that happened to the writer

fact – a statement that can be proven true

feedback – information given to help improve a piece of writing

fiction – a story created from the imagination; fiction is not documentation of fact

focus – the direction or emphasis of a piece of writing; writing with a focus sticks to the main idea and does not include lots of ideas that are unrelated

freewriting – a way for a writer to pick a topic and write as much as possible about it within a set time limit

friendly letter – a kind of letter used to share thoughts, feeling, and news

graphic – a picture, photograph, map, diagram, or other image

graphic organizer – a visual device, such as a diagram or chart, that helps a writer plan a piece of writing

greeting – the part of a letter that begins with the word *Dear* followed by a person's name; also called the salutation

heading – the first part of a letter that has the writer's address and the date

how-to paper – a paragraph or essay that explains how to do or make something

imperative sentence – a group of words that gives a command or makes a request

interrogative sentence – a group of words that asks a question

introductory sentence – the first sentence in a piece of writing

journal – a notebook where a writer regularly records experiences and ideas

logical order – a way to organize that groups details in a way that makes sense

main idea – the most important point of the paragraph

narrative – a kind of writing that tells a story

news – information about, or report of, recent events

nonfiction – writing that presents facts and information to explain, describe, or persuade; for example, newspaper articles and biographies are nonfiction

Writing Skills (Composition) *continued*

opinion – a statement of belief that cannot be proven true; the opposite of a fact

order of importance – a way to organize that presents details from least to most important, or from most to least important

order words – words that connect ideas or a series of steps, or create a sequence, such as *first, next, later, finally*

organization – of a piece of writing, the way the ideas are arranged

outline – an organized list of topics in an essay

paragraph – a group of sentences about one topic

paraphrase – to restate information in one's own words

personal narrative – an essay about a personal experience of the writer

plagiarism – using another person's words without giving that person credit as a source

plot – what happens in a story; the sequence of events

point of view – the perspective from which a story is told

presentation – an oral report, usually with visuals

prewriting – the stage or step of writing in which a writer chooses a topic, gathers ideas, and plans what to write

proofreading – the stage or step of the writing process in which the writer checks for errors in grammar, punctuation, capitalization, and spelling

publishing – the stage or step of the writing process in which the writer makes a clean copy of the piece and shares it

purpose – the reason for writing

question – a kind of sentence that asks something

quotation – a report of the exact words spoken or written by a person; usually placed within quotation marks

reason – a statement that explains why something is or why it should be

reference – a work that contains useful information for a writer, such as an encyclopedia, a dictionary, or a website

research – to find information through study rather than through personal experience

revising – the stage or step of the writing process in which the writer rereads and edits the draft, correcting errors and making changes in content or organization that improve the piece

rubric – the criteria used to evaluate a piece of writing

sentence – a group of words that tells a complete thought

sentence combining – to join two sentences that have similar parts into one sentence

sequence – the order in which things happen

setting – where and when a literary work takes place

showing language – words used to create pictures in the reader's mind, rather than words that merely tell what happened
Example: The sun blazed on the street, and my bare feet sizzled like a frying egg each time I took a step.
[as opposed to] The sun was hot, and my bare feet burned each time I took a step.

signature – the end of a letter where the writer writes his or her name

source – a provider of information; a book, a historical document, online materials, and an interviewee are all sources

speaker tag – the part of a dialogue that identifies who is speaking

statement – a kind of sentence that tells something

story map – a kind of a graphic organizer that helps a writer plan a story

structure – the way a piece of writing is organized

style – the words the writer chooses and the way the writer arranges the words into sentences

summarize – to restate briefly the main points of a text

supporting details – the sentences that give information about the main idea or topic sentence

time order – the arrangement of ideas according to when they happened

topic – the subject of a piece of writing

topic sentence – the sentence that expresses the main idea of the paragraph

transition – a word or phrase that connects ideas

visual – a graphic, picture, or photograph

visual aid – a graphic, picture, photograph, or prop used in a presentation

website – a place on the Internet devoted to a specific organization, group, or individual

writing process – a series of five steps (which can be repeated) to follow during writing: prewriting, drafting, revising, proofreading, and publishing

Writing Skills (GUM)

action verb – a word that shows action

adjective – a word that describes a noun or a pronoun

article – the adjective *a, an,* or *the*

command – a kind of sentence that gives an order or makes a request

common noun – a word that names any person, place, or thing

contraction – a shortened word or words where an apostrophe replaces missing letters

demonstrative adjective – one of four describing words—*this, that, these, those*—that point out an object or objects

exclamation – a kind of sentence that shows strong feeling

future tense – a form of a verb that names an action that will happen later

indefinite pronoun – the form of a pronoun that refers to an unnamed person or group

irregular verb – a verb that does not add *–d* or *–ed* to the present form to make the past and the past participle

noun – a word that names a person, place, or thing

past tense – the form of the verb that tells what already has happened

personal pronoun – a word that takes the place of a noun

plural – more than one of something

possessive noun – the form of a noun that shows ownership

possessive pronoun – the form of a pronoun that shows ownership

predicate – the verb or verb phrase in a sentence

present tense – the verb form that tells what is happening now

pronoun – a word that takes the place of one or more nouns

proper noun – a word that names a specific person, place, or thing

question – a kind of sentence that asks something

sentence – a group of words that tells a complete thought

singular – one of something

statement – a kind of sentence that tells something

subject – a word or words that tell whom or what the sentence is about

verb – a word that shows action

words in a series – a list of words in a sentence that are separated by commas

Literature & Comprehension

How Are You Feeling?

Unit Focus

In this unit, students will explore feelings—a child's feelings about bedtime and the feelings invoked by descriptive poems. This unit follows the read-aloud instructional approach. The read-aloud and other instructional approaches to reading are explained in detail in the online course introduction activity in Unit 1, Lesson 1. Before you begin the work in this program, complete the online course introduction activity. In this unit, students will

- ► Listen to stories and poems.
- ► Observe fluent, expressive reading.
- ► Learn about the strategy of predicting and why it is important.
- ► Explore the structure and elements of poems.
- ► Explore the ways that poets create rhyme and rhythm.
- ► Learn about descriptive language and how it is used in poetry to create detailed pictures in a reader's mind.

Unit Plan

[Offline]

Lesson 1	Introduce *Bedtime for Frances*	45 minutes a day
Lesson 2	Explore *Bedtime for Frances*	
Lesson 3	Explore Poems About Games	
Lesson 4	Explore "Sing a Song of People"	
Lesson 5	Explore Poems About Animals (A)	
Lesson 6	Explore "Table Manners"	
Lesson 7	Your Choice	

Introduce *Bedtime for Frances*

Lesson Overview

[Offline]   **45** minutes

Get Ready	Lesson Introduction
	Predictions
	Words to Know
Read Aloud	Book Walk
	Bedtime for Frances
Check Your Reading	*Bedtime for Frances*
Reading for Meaning	Check Predictions

Materials

Supplied

- *Bedtime for Frances* by Russell Hoban

Story Synopsis

It's bedtime for Frances, but she doesn't want to go! She tries to make up lots of excuses, but Mother and Father are wise to her antics. This story includes references to imagined tigers, a giant, and spiders, as well as a possible spanking.

Keywords

author – a writer

illustrator – the person who draws the pictures that go with a story

prediction – a guess about what might happen that is based on information in a story and what you already know

Advance Preparation

Complete the online course introduction activity in Unit 1, Lesson 1, before beginning the work in this program. Read *Bedtime for Frances* before beginning the Read Aloud to locate Words to Know in the text. Read the Read Aloud directions to be aware of stopping points in the story at which students will make predictions.

Big Ideas

- ▸ Comprehension is facilitated when readers connect new information to information previously learned.
- ▸ Good readers interact with text to make logical predictions before reading; confirm predictions during reading; and revise or make new predictions as they read further.

 **Offline** **45** minutes

Work **together** with students to complete Get Ready, Read Aloud, Check Your Reading, and Reading for Meaning activities.

Get Ready ••

Lesson Introduction
Prepare students for listening to and discussing *Bedtime for Frances* by Russell Hoban.

1. Tell students that you are going to read *Bedtime for Frances*, which is a book about a character who has a hard time going to sleep.

2. Explain that before you read the book, you will get ready by discussing

   ▸ What the author and illustrator of a story do
   ▸ How we make predictions while reading a story and why it's important to make predictions

> **Objectives**
> - Make predictions before and during reading.
> - Build vocabulary through listening, reading, and discussion.
> - Use new vocabulary in written and spoken sentences.

Predictions
Explore how to make a prediction.

1. Tell students that **good readers make predictions**, or guesses, about what will happen in a story. We use clues in the story and what we know from our own experiences to predict what will happen next.

2. Explain that making predictions helps us be active readers. It makes us want to keep reading a story to see if what we predict happens or not.

3. Have students practice making a prediction.
   Say: Alicia went into the garage to find her old fishing pole. She put it in the van next to a picnic basket. Then Alicia and her dad got in the van.

   ▸ What do you think will happen next? Possible answers: Alicia and her dad will go fishing; they will drive to a lake; they will go on a picnic.
   ▸ What clues in the story made you think this? Possible answers: the fishing pole; the picnic basket; Alicia and her dad getting into the van.

TIP Predictions are neither right nor wrong. We make the best prediction we can, based on the available information. Do not describe a prediction as "wrong" because this may discourage students from making predictions.

Words to Know

Before reading *Bedtime for Frances*, go over Words to Know with students.

1. Read aloud each word or phrase and have students repeat it.

2. Ask students if they know what each word or phrase means.

   ▸ If students know a word's or phrase's meaning, have them define it and use it in a sentence.
   ▸ If students don't know a word's or phrase's meaning, read them the definition and discuss the word or phrase with them.

all of a sudden – at once; happening quickly and without warning
bathrobe – a loose piece of clothing worn before or after taking a bath or over pajamas
ceiling – the part of a room that is above your head
curtain – a piece of cloth that covers a window to keep out the light
thump – a loud, dull sound of one thing hitting another

Read Aloud

Book Walk

Prepare students for reading by taking them on a Book Walk of *Bedtime for Frances*. Scan the beginning of the book together and ask students to make predictions about the story. Answers to questions may vary.

1. Have students look at the picture on the cover. Point to and read aloud the **book title**.

   ▸ What do you think the book is about?

2. Read aloud the **name of the author**. Tell students that an author is the person who writes a story or book.

3. Read aloud the **name of the illustrator**. Tell students that an illustrator is the person that makes the pictures for a story or book.

4. Have students look at the **pictures up to page 11**. Then discuss the following questions to prepare for reading.

   ▸ Where do you think the story takes place?
   ▸ What do you think might happen in the story?
   ▸ Did you ever want to stay up past your bedtime? If so, what did you do to try to stay awake? Did it work?

Objectives

- Make predictions based on text, illustrations, and/or prior knowledge.
- Make predictions before and during reading.
- Activate prior knowledge by previewing text and/or discussing topic.
- Read and listen to a variety of texts for information and pleasure independently or as part of a group.

Bedtime for Frances

It's time to read aloud the story and ask students to make predictions.

1. Have students sit next to you so that they can see the pictures and words while you read aloud.

2. **Begin to read aloud. Pause at the following points in the story** to ask students what they predict will happen next. Jot down their predictions for later reference.

   ▸ Page 11: after Frances thinks she sees a tiger in her room
   ▸ Page 15: after Frances thinks there's a giant in her room
   ▸ Page 19: after Frances thinks about things that might come out of the crack in the ceiling
   ▸ Page 23: after Frances sees the curtains blowing and goes to tell her parents
   ▸ Page 29: after Frances sees a moth bumping against the window

3. **Continue to read aloud the story.**

   ▸ Track with your finger so students can follow along.
   ▸ Emphasize Words to Know as you come to them. If appropriate, use the pictures to help show what each word means.
   ▸ Remember to stop at the listed points listed and have students make predictions.

Check Your Reading

Bedtime for Frances

Check students' comprehension of *Bedtime for Frances*.

1. Have students retell *Bedtime for Frances* in their own words to develop grammar, vocabulary, comprehension, and fluency skills.

2. Ask students the following questions.

   ▸ What does an author do? write stories or books
   ▸ What does an illustrator do? draw pictures to go with a story or book
   ▸ Does Frances want to go to bed? No   How do you know Frances doesn't want to go to bed? Possible answers: She asks for a glass of milk; she can't fall asleep; she keeps getting out of bed; she's not tired.
   ▸ What does Frances do while she is trying to fall asleep? She sings a song she makes up.   Does it help her fall asleep? No   Why not? It makes her think about tigers.
   ▸ What are some of the things that Frances worries about while she tries to fall asleep? Possible answers: tigers; a giant; spiders; something behind the curtains

 TIP If students have trouble responding to a question, help them locate the answer in the text or pictures.

Objectives
• Retell or dramatize a story.
• Describe the role of author and/or illustrator.
• Answer questions requiring literal recall of details.

Reading for Meaning

Check Predictions

Revisit the predictions students made while reading the text.

Objectives
- Evaluate predictions.

1. Remind students that good readers make predictions when they read a story.

2. **Ask them the following questions** to review and discuss the predictions they made while reading *Bedtime for Frances*. **Refer to the predictions you jotted down, as necessary.** Answers to questions may vary.

   ▸ What did you predict would happen after Frances thinks she see a tiger in her room?

   ▸ Were you surprised at how Mother and Father act when Frances tells them about the giant in her room?

   ▸ What did you predict would happen when Frances thinks a spider might come out of the crack in the ceiling? What really happens? She goes to get her father.

   ▸ What did you predict would happen after Frances sees the curtains moving? What clues from the story or your own experiences did you use to make your prediction?

   ▸ What did you predict would happen after Frances sees a moth bumping against the window? What really happens? She falls asleep.

3. Conclude by explaining that it's okay if our predictions don't happen. Tell students to keep the following things in mind:

   ▸ **Good readers make predictions that make sense** based on the story up to that point.

   ▸ **Good readers change their predictions** as they read further and get more information.

   ▸ Even if our predictions don't happen, **making predictions is important because it helps us be active readers**.

Explore *Bedtime for Frances*

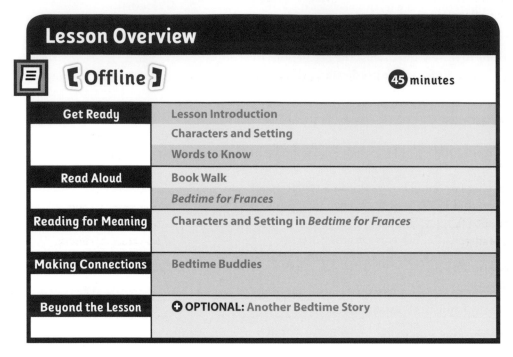

Lesson Overview

Offline

45 minutes

Get Ready	Lesson Introduction
	Characters and Setting
	Words to Know
Read Aloud	Book Walk
	Bedtime for Frances
Reading for Meaning	Characters and Setting in *Bedtime for Frances*
Making Connections	Bedtime Buddies
Beyond the Lesson	⊕ OPTIONAL: Another Bedtime Story

Materials

Supplied
- *Bedtime for Frances* by Russell Hoban
- *K¹² Language Arts Activity Book*, p. LC 1

Also Needed
- crayons

Keywords
character – a person or animal in a story
setting – when and where a story takes place

Advance Preparation

Review the Reading for Meaning and Making Connections to familiarize yourself with the questions and answers.

Big Ideas

► Comprehension requires an understanding of story structure.
► An awareness of story structure elements (setting, characters, plot) provides readers a foundation for constructing meaning when reading new stories and writing their own stories.

 **45** minutes

Work **together** with students to complete offline Get Ready, Read Aloud, Reading for Meaning, Making Connections, and Beyond the Lesson activities.

Get Ready

Lesson Introduction
Prepare students for listening to and discussing *Bedtime for Frances* by Russell Hoban.

1. Explain that when you're learning to read, it's important to reread stories because with every reading, you

   ▸ Are able to read more and more of the words on your own.
   ▸ Are able to remember more of what happens in the story.
   ▸ Discover something new about a familiar story.
   ▸ Build your confidence as a reader.

2. Tell students that you will reread *Bedtime for Frances* to focus on the story elements of characters and settings.

> **Objectives**
> - Identify character(s).
> - Identify the main character(s).
> - Identify setting.
> - Increase concept and content vocabulary.
> - Build vocabulary through listening, reading, and discussion.
> - Use new vocabulary in written and spoken sentences.

Characters and Setting
Explore the story elements of characters and setting.

1. Tell students that **the people in a story are called characters**. In some stories and books, animals are characters.

2. Explain that there's usually one character who is more important than the other characters in a story. The most important character is the one who does and talks the most. The most important character is called the **main character**.

3. Tell students that **where and when a story takes place is called the setting**.

4. Have students practice identifying characters, the main character, and the setting. **Read aloud** the following short story.

   Julia, Pablo, and their mother went to the park in the afternoon. Julia went to play on the slide, while Mother sat on a bench to read a magazine. Pablo played with his toys on the grass.

   Julia ran up the slide's ladder and shouted, "Watch me!" to her mother.

   Then Julia ran over to the sandbox, where she built a sandcastle. "Look what I did!" Julia hollered to her mother.

   Next, Julia ran over to the swings. When she was high in the air, Julia yelled to her mother, "Look how high I can swing!"

   Julia finished swinging and ran over to the blanket to ask Pablo to play with her. Just then, Mother said it was time to go. Julia skipped all the way home while she sang, "Skip, skip, watch me skip!"

5. Ask students the following questions.

   ▸ Who are the characters in the story? Julia; Pablo; Mother
   ▸ Who is the main, or most important, character in the story? Julia
     How do you know Julia is the main character? Julia does most of the
     things in the story; she talks the most.
   ▸ Where does the story take place? at the park
   ▸ When does the story happen? in the afternoon

6. Explain that when good readers hear or read a story, they pay attention to who
   the characters are, who the most important character is, and where and when
   the story takes place. Knowing these things helps make the story easier to
   understand and fun to read.

Words to Know

Before reading *Bedtime for Frances*, go over Words to Know with students.

1. Read aloud each word or phrase and have students repeat it.

2. Ask students if they know what each word or phrase means.

   ▸ If students know a word's or phrase's meaning, have them define it and use
     it in a sentence.
   ▸ If students don't know a word's or phrase's meaning, read them the
     definition and discuss the word or phrase with them.

all of a sudden – at once; happening quickly and without warning
bathrobe – a loose piece of clothing worn before or after taking a bath or
over pajamas
ceiling – the part of a room that is above your head
curtain – a piece of cloth that covers a window to keep out the light
thump – a loud, dull sound of one thing hitting another

Read Aloud

Book Walk

Prepare students by taking them on a Book Walk of *Bedtime for Frances*. Scan the
book together to revisit the characters and events.

1. Point to and read aloud the **book title**.

2. Point to and read aloud the **name of the author**.

3. Point to and read aloud the **name of the illustrator**.

4. Look through the book. Have students describe what they see in the **pictures**.
   Answers to questions may vary.

   ▸ What time is your bedtime?
   ▸ What do you do just before you go to bed?
   ▸ Do you always fall asleep right away, or do you sometimes have trouble?
     What do you do if you have trouble falling asleep?

Objectives

• Activate prior knowledge
  by previewing text and/or
  discussing topic.

• Read and listen to a variety
  of texts for information and
  pleasure independently or
  as part of a group.

Bedtime for Frances
It's time to reread the story.

1. Have students sit next to you so that they can see the pictures and words while you read aloud the story.

2. Explain to students that you are going to reread the story aloud. Ask them to listen carefully for

   ► Who the characters are
   ► Who the most important character is
   ► Where and when the story takes place

3. **Read aloud the entire story.** Track with your finger so students can follow along.

Reading for Meaning ....

Characters and Setting in *Bedtime for Frances*
Check students' comprehension of *Bedtime for Frances*.

1. Have students retell *Bedtime for Frances* in their own words to develop grammar, vocabulary, comprehension, and fluency skills.

2. Ask students the following questions.

   ► Who are the characters in *Bedtime for Frances*? Frances; Father; Mother
   ► Who is the main, or most important, character in the story? Frances
   ► How do you know Frances is the main character? What clues are in the story? Frances does most of the things in the story; she talks the most.
   ► Where does the story take place? in Frances's home; in Frances's bedroom
   ► When does the story happen? at 7:00 at night; at night; at bedtime

Objectives
- Retell or dramatize a story.
- Identify character(s).
- Identify the main character(s).
- Identify setting.

Making Connections ....

Bedtime Buddies
Help students make a personal connection to *Bedtime for Frances* by drawing a picture of themselves in bed with something that helps them fall asleep. Turn to page LC 1 in *K¹² Language Arts Activity Book*.

1. Ask students what Frances took to bed to help her fall asleep. a teddy bear and a doll

   ► If students have trouble recalling what Frances had in bed with her, refer to the words and pictures on pages 8–10 in *Bedtime for Frances*.

2. On the Activity Book page, have students draw a picture of themselves in bed with an item that helps them fall asleep, such as a favorite doll, stuffed animal, or blanket.

   ► If students don't take anything to bed with them, have them draw something that they imagine they might like to use.
   ► If students enjoy drawing, encourage them to include other parts of their bedroom, such as the dresser, window, rug, or door.

Objectives
- Make connections with text: text-to-text, text-to-self, text-to-world.
- Demonstrate understanding through drawing, discussion, drama, and/or writing.

3. Have students explain their drawing and how their bedtime item helps them fall asleep.

4. Read aloud the sentence starter at the bottom and ask students how they would complete it.

5. Write the words students dictate on the line.

   ► If students are ready to write on their own, allow them to do so.

6. Have students read aloud the completed sentence **with** you as you track the words with your finger.

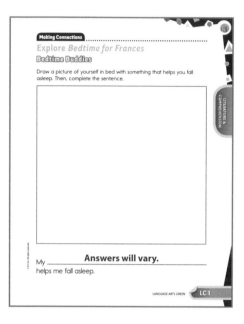

Beyond the Lesson

⊕ OPTIONAL: Another Bedtime Story

This activity is OPTIONAL. It is intended for students who have extra time and would benefit from reading an additional book with a topic that's similar to *Bedtime for Frances*. Feel free to skip this activity.

1. Go to a library and look for a copy of *Can't You Sleep, Little Bear?* by Martin Waddell or *Bedtime for Bear* by Bonny Becker.

2. Lead a Book Walk and then read aloud the story.

3. Have students tell how the book that they chose is similar to and different from *Bedtime for Frances*. Be sure they describe how the characters and settings are alike and different.

4. Ask students to tell which book is their favorite and why.

Objectives

- Make connections with text: text-to-text, text-to-self, text-to-world.
- Compare and contrast story structure elements across texts.

Explore Poems About Games

Lesson Overview

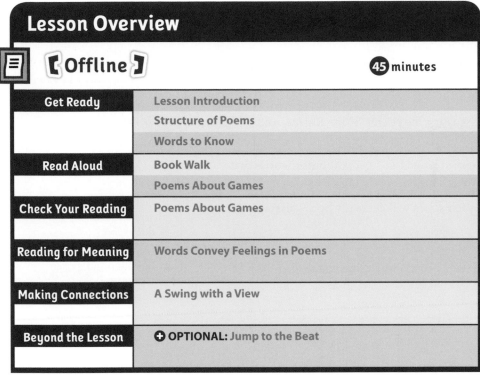

[Offline]   **45** minutes

Get Ready	Lesson Introduction
	Structure of Poems
	Words to Know
Read Aloud	Book Walk
	Poems About Games
Check Your Reading	Poems About Games
Reading for Meaning	Words Convey Feelings in Poems
Making Connections	A Swing with a View
Beyond the Lesson	⊕ OPTIONAL: Jump to the Beat

Advance Preparation

Read "Rope Rhyme" and "The Swing" before beginning the Read Aloud to locate Words to Know in the text.

Big Ideas

▸ Poems are different from prose in structure and content. They are generally organized in lines and often contain rhymes.

▸ Readers must focus on the specific language of a text to aid in interpretation.

[Materials]

Supplied
- *Listen, My Children: Poems for First Graders*, pp. 8, 11
- *K¹² Language Arts Activity Book*, p. LC 2

Also Needed
- crayons
- household objects – jump rope (optional)

Poetry Synopses

Eloise Greenfield describes the rhythmic sounds of jumping rope, while Robert Louis Stevenson expresses the thrill of soaring on a swing.

Keywords

rhyme – when two or more words have the same ending sounds; for example, *cat* and *hat* rhyme

rhythm – a pattern of accented and unaccented syllables; a distinctive beat

stanza – a group of lines in a poem

tone – the author's feelings toward the subject and/or characters of a text

 **Offline** **45** minutes

Work **together** with students to complete offline Get Ready, Read Aloud, Check Your Reading, Reading for Meaning, Making Connections, and Beyond the Lesson activities.

Get Ready

Lesson Introduction

Prepare students for listening to and discussing the poems "Rope Rhyme" and "The Swing."

1. Tell students that you are going to read aloud two poems about activities that they may have done before—jumping rope and swinging on a swing.

2. Explain that before you read the poems, you will get ready by discussing how

   ▸ Poems are made up of stanzas.
   ▸ Poems often have words that rhyme.
   ▸ Poets use words to make you feel a certain way when you read or hear a poem.

 Objectives

- Identify structure of poems and poetic elements: rhyme, rhythm, repetition, and/or alliteration.
- Build vocabulary through listening, reading, and discussion.
- Use new vocabulary in written and spoken sentences.

Structure of Poems

Introduce the structure of poems and the poetic element of rhyme.

1. Tell students that **poetry** is a special kind of writing that is different from fiction and nonfiction.

2. The person who writes a poem is called a **poet**. Poets share feelings or experiences with others by carefully choosing the words that make up their poems.

3. Explain that a poem is usually written in short lines that are grouped together. A group of these lines is called a **stanza**.

4. Tell students that the words at the ends of the lines in a stanza can sometimes rhyme.

5. Read aloud the following poem.

   I found a bug
   Under the rug.

   Say: The words *bug* and *rug* both end with the *ug* sound, so they **rhyme**.

6. Tell students to listen for more rhyming words. Then read aloud the following poem.

   I have a cat.
   Her name is Pat.

   ▸ Which word rhymes with *cat*? *Pat*
   ▸ Can you think of another word that rhymes with *cat* and *Pat*? Possible answers: *hat; sat; fat; mat*

Words to Know

Before reading "Rope Rhyme" and "The Swing," go over Words to Know with students.

1. Read aloud each word or phrase and have students repeat them.

2. Ask students if they know what each word or phrase means.

   ▸ If students know a word's or phrase's meaning, have them define it and use it in a sentence.
   ▸ If students don't know a word's or phrase's meaning, read them the definition and discuss the word or phrase with them.

cattle – cows
clappedy-slappedy – the sound that a jump rope makes when it hits the ground
countryside – the land outside a city
pleasantest – nicest

Read Aloud

Book Walk

Prepare students by taking them on a Book Walk of "Rope Rhyme" and "The Swing." Scan the poems together and ask students to make predictions about the poems. Answers to questions may vary.

1. Turn to the **table of contents** in *Listen, My Children*. Help students find "Rope Rhyme" and turn to that page.

2. Point to and read aloud the **title of the poem** and the **name of the poet**.

   ▸ What do you think the poem is about?
   ▸ Do you ever jump rope?
   ▸ If so, do you sing songs when you jump rope? What songs?

3. Return to the **table of contents** and help students find "The Swing." Turn to that page.

4. Point to and read aloud the **title of the poem** and the **name of the poet**.

   ▸ What do you think the poem is about?
   ▸ Do you like to swing?
   ▸ How does it feel to be on a swing?

Objectives
- Activate prior knowledge by previewing text and/or discussing topic.
- Make predictions based on text, illustrations, and/or prior knowledge.
- Listen to and discuss poetry.

Poems About Games
It's time to read aloud the poems.

1. Have students sit next to you so that they can see the pictures and words while you read aloud.

2. Explain to students that as you read aloud, they should listen for words that rhyme, or have the same ending sounds.

3. Tell students to think about how the poems make them feel as they listen to the words.

4. **Read aloud both poems.** Track with your finger so students can follow along. Emphasize Words to Know as you come to them. If appropriate, use the pictures to help show what each word means.

Check Your Reading ....

Poems About Games
Check general comprehension of the poems and understanding of words that rhyme.

1. Ask the following questions about "Rope Rhyme."
   ▸ What is the poet describing in the poem? jumping rope; the sounds you hear when you jump rope
   ▸ What are some things the poet says you can do while you're jumping rope? Possible answers: bounce; kick; giggle; spin; count to a hundred; count by ten

2. Reread the lines from "Rope Rhyme" that end with the words *ground* and *sound* and then ask the following questions.
   ▸ What word in the poem rhymes with *ground*? *sound*
   ▸ Do the words *clappedy-slappedy* rhyme? Yes

3. Ask the following question about "The Swing."
   ▸ What does the poet see when he "swings up in the air" and looks "over the wall"? river; trees; cattle

4. Reread the lines from "The Swing" that end with the words *swing* and *thing* and then ask the following question.
   ▸ Which word rhymes with, or has the same ending sound as, *swing*? *thing*

5. Reread the lines from "The Swing" that end with the words *blue* and *do* and then ask the following question.
   ▸ Which word rhymes with *blue*? *do*

Objectives
- Answer questions requiring literal recall of details.
- Identify structure of poems and poetic elements: rhyme, rhythm, repetition, and/or alliteration.

Reading for Meaning

Words Convey Feelings in Poems

Explore how the words of a poem can convey a feeling.

1. Remind students that poets share their feelings or experiences with others by carefully choosing the words that make up their poems. The words of a poem can make the reader feel things, such as happy or sad. **Read aloud the following poem, with enthusiasm.**

   The sun is shining so bright today
   Let's grab a ball, go out and play!
   A game of tag—that sounds fun, too
   Let's run around, just me and you!

   ▸ How does this poem make you feel? Help students recognize that the poem might make them feel happy, energetic, or excited about playing outside.
   ▸ What word or words in the poem make you feel this way? If students have trouble answering, suggest that the words *play, fun, tag,* and *run* help the reader think of enjoyable things and feel happy.

2. **Reread "Rope Rhyme" aloud,** and then ask the following question.

   ▸ How do you think the poet feels about jumping rope? She enjoys it; she thinks it's fun.

3. **Read aloud the following stanza from "Rope Rhyme"** by Eloise Greenfield.

   Get set, ready now, jump right in
   Bounce and kick and giggle and spin

   ▸ What words are clues that the poet thinks jumping rope is fun? *bounce and kick; giggle and spin*

4. Point to the last three words of "Rope Rhyme."

   ▸ Why do you think the poet wrote the last three words of the poem this way? to make it look like the words are jumping out like a child would jump out while jumping rope

5. **Reread "The Swing" aloud,** and then ask the following questions.

   ▸ What is the poem "The Swing" about? what it feels like to swing; what the poet can see while he's swinging
   ▸ Why do you think the poet says that going up on a swing is "the pleasantest thing"? He thinks it's fun.
   ▸ What words do you hear repeated many times in the poem? *up* and *down*
   ▸ Why do you think the poet uses the words *up* and *down* so many times? because a swing goes up and down; to help the reader think about being on a swing
   ▸ How do you think the poet wants to make you feel when you listen to the poem? happy; like you're on a swing

Objectives
- Identify words and phrases that reveal the tone of a text.
- Listen to and discuss poetry.

Making Connections

A Swing with a View

Have students draw a picture inspired by the poem "The Swing." Turn to page LC 2 in *K¹² Language Arts Activity Book.*

1. **Say:** How are the poems "The Swing" and "Rope Rhyme" alike? They both tell about something that's fun to do.

2. Remind students that in "The Swing," the poet describes what he can see when he's on a swing.

3. Have students think about their favorite place to play on a swing.

4. On the Activity Book page, have students draw a picture of what they see (or what they would like to see) when they swing high in the air.

5. Ask students to describe their drawing when done.

6. Read aloud the sentence starter at the bottom and ask students how they would complete it.

7. Write the words students dictate on the line.

   ▸ If students are ready to write on their own, allow them to do so.

8. Have students read aloud the completed sentence **with** you as you track the words with your finger.

Objectives

- Make connections with text: text-to-text, text-to-self, text-to-world.
- Demonstrate understanding through drawing, discussion, drama, and/or writing.

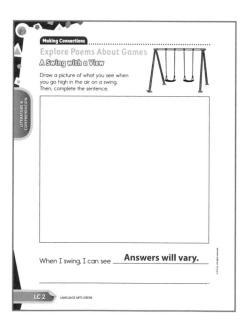

Beyond the Lesson

⊕ OPTIONAL: Jump to the Beat

This activity is OPTIONAL. It is intended for students who have extra time and would benefit from learning the rhythm of a poem. Feel free to skip this activity.

1. Tell students that it's fun to clap, jump up and down, or jump a rope to the beat of poems like "Rope Rhyme." You can hear the beat by listening for the words in the poem that are emphasized.

2. Read aloud "Rope Rhyme" by Eloise Greenfield, and clap whenever you say a boldface word. Have students clap along with you.

> **Get** set, **ready** now, **jump** right **in**
> **Bounce** and **kick** and **giggle** and **spin**
> **Listen** to the **rope** when it **hits** the **ground**
> **Listen** to that **clap**pedy-**slap**pedy **sound**
> **Jump** right **up** when it **tells** you **to**
> **Come** back **down**, what**ever** you **do**
> **Count** to a **hun**dred, **count** by **ten**
> **Start** to **count** all **over** a**gain**
> **That's** what **jumping** is **all** a**bout**
> **Get** set, **ready** now, **jump** right **out**!

3. Repeat Step 2 to help students become more familiar with the beat of the poem.

   ▶ Why do you think the poet wrote the poem with such a strong beat?
   to make you think about how you jump up and down when you jump rope

4. Read aloud "Rope Rhyme" while students jump up and down in place. Explain how they should jump up on the beat when you clap.

5. If students know how to jump rope, have them jump rope to the beat. If not, skip this step.

6. If time allows, look for additional poems with beats that students can clap or jump to by searching for "jump rope rhymes" on the Internet.

TIP Tell students that learning how to clap or jump to the beat of a poem might take a lot of practice, and that they shouldn't get discouraged.

Objectives
- Respond to poetic devices of rhyme, rhythm, and/or alliteration.
- Locate information using features of text and electronic media.

Explore "Sing a Song of People"

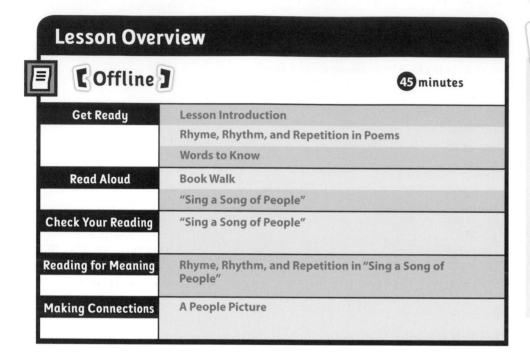

Lesson Overview

[Offline]   **45** minutes

Get Ready	Lesson Introduction
	Rhyme, Rhythm, and Repetition in Poems
	Words to Know
Read Aloud	Book Walk
	"Sing a Song of People"
Check Your Reading	"Sing a Song of People"
Reading for Meaning	Rhyme, Rhythm, and Repetition in "Sing a Song of People"
Making Connections	A People Picture

Materials

Supplied

- *Listen, My Children: Poems for First Graders*, pp. 6–7
- *K¹² Language Arts Activity Book*, p. LC 3

Also Needed

- crayons
- scissors, round-end safety (optional)
- glue stick (optional)
- household objects – magazines (optional)

Poetry Synopsis

All sorts of people bustle around a big city—quiet, loud, walking, riding, fast, and slow.

Keywords

imagery – language that helps readers imagine how something looks, sounds, smells, feels, or tastes

rhyme – when two or more words have the same ending sounds; for example, *cat* and *hat* rhyme

rhythm – a pattern of accented and unaccented syllables; a distinctive beat

stanza – a group of lines in a poem

Advance Preparation

Read "Sing a Song of People" before beginning the Read Aloud to locate Words to Know in the text.

Big Ideas

▶ Poems are different from prose in structure and content. They are generally organized in lines and often contain rhymes.

▶ Readers must focus on the specific language of a text to aid in interpretation.

▶ The use of imagery and sensory language creates detailed pictures in the reader's mind, so the reader can understand and appreciate the ideas and feelings the writer conveys.

 **45** minutes

Work **together** with students to complete Get Ready, Read Aloud, Check Your Reading, Reading for Meaning, and Making Connections activities.

Get Ready

Lesson Introduction
Prepare students for listening to and discussing "Sing a Song of People."

1. Tell students that you are going to read a poem about a place where you can see people and watch what they do.

2. Explain that before you read the poem, you will get ready by discussing how

   ▸ Poems often rhyme.
   ▸ Poems often have rhythm, or a beat.
   ▸ Poets repeat and rhyme words to create rhythm.

Rhyme, Rhythm, and Repetition in Poems
Introduce the poetic elements of rhyme, rhythm, and repetition.

1. Tell students that a poem is usually written in short lines that are grouped together.

2. Explain that the words in a poem can sometimes rhyme. Then **read aloud the following poem.**

   I like to eat my toast.
   I like to chew my gum.
   I like to sing my song.
   I like to bang my drum.

   Say: The words *gum* and *drum* both end with *–um*, so they **rhyme**.

3. Tell students that poets sometimes use the same words over and over in a poem. When you use the same words more than once, you *repeat* them.

4. Reread the poem.

   ▸ What words are repeated in the poem? *I like to* and *my*

5. Explain that poets repeat words in their poems to help create **rhythm**. The rhythm of a poem is like the beat of a song. You hear the rhythm by listening for particular words in the poem that are stressed, or said with more emphasis than others. Clapping to the rhythm of a poem helps you hear the beat.
   Say: Listen as I read the poem and clap on the beat. (Clap on the words in boldface.)

   I **like** to **eat** my **toast**.
   I **like** to **chew** my **gum**.
   I **like** to **sing** my **song**.
   I **like** to **bang** my **drum**.

Objectives
- Listen to and discuss poetry.
- Identify structure of poems and poetic elements: rhyme, rhythm, repetition, and/or alliteration.
- Build vocabulary through listening, reading, and discussion.
- Use new vocabulary in written and spoken sentences.

▶ What can we hear when we clap along with the poem? the beat of the poem; the rhythm of the poem

6. Reread the poem, having students clap along with you so they can practice hearing the beat.

7. Tell students that poets often use descriptive words that help readers see or imagine pictures and hear sounds in their head. Poets do this to make a poem come to life, or seem real, to readers.

8. Have students close their eyes as you reread the poem. Answers to questions may vary.

▶ What do you see, or imagine, in your head when you listen to the poem? What sounds do you imagine that you hear?

▶ What words in the poem helped you see those pictures and hear those sounds?

Words to Know
Before reading "Sing a Song of People," go over Words to Know with students.

1. Read aloud each word and have students repeat it.

2. Ask students if they know what each word means.

▶ If students know a word's meaning, have them define it and use it in a sentence.

▶ If students don't know a word's meaning, read them the definition and discuss the word with them.

elevator – a small room that carries people or things from one floor of a building to another
singly – alone; one at a time
subway – a train in the city that carries passengers underground
taxi – a car that carries people who pay for a ride; a cab

Read Aloud

Book Walk
Prepare students by taking them on a Book Walk of "Sing a Song of People." Scan the poem together and ask students to make predictions about it.

1. Turn to the **table of contents** in *Listen, My Children*. Help students find "Sing a Song of People" and turn to that page.

2. Point to and read aloud the **title of the poem** and the **name of the poet**.

▶ What do you think the poem is about? Answers will vary.

▶ Have you ever been to a big city? What was it like? Did you see lots of people? Answers will vary.

▶ Can you think of another place where you would see a lot of people? Possible answers: at a sports game; at the zoo; at the movies

Objectives
- Make predictions based on text, illustrations, and/or prior knowledge.
- Activate prior knowledge by previewing text and/or discussing topic.
- Listen to and discuss poetry.

3. Point to the first group of lines in the poem and tell students that a group of lines in a poem is called a **stanza**.

4. Point to and read aloud the words *slow* and *go* in the first stanza. Remind students that words in a poem can sometimes rhyme. Tell students that rhyming words often appear at the ends of lines.

"Sing a Song of People"

It's time to read aloud the poem.

1. Have students sit next to you so that they can see the pictures and words while you read aloud.

2. Explain to students that as you read aloud, they should do the following:

   ▸ Listen for repeated words, or words that are said over and over.
   ▸ Think about the words that help them see pictures in their head.
   ▸ Listen for the rhythm, or beat, of the poem.

3. **Read aloud the entire poem.** Track with your finger so students can follow along. Emphasize Words to Know as you come to them. If appropriate, use the pictures to help show what each word means.

TIP Read the poem at a quick pace to accentuate the idea of people rushing around the city.

Check Your Reading

"Sing a Song of People"

Check students' comprehension of "Sing a Song of People."

1. Have students tell what "Sing a Song of People" is about in their own words to develop grammar, vocabulary, comprehension, and fluency skills.

2. Ask students the following questions.

   ▸ What are some ways that people walk in the poem? Possible answers: fast; slow; by themselves; in crowds
   ▸ What are some things people do while they rush around the city? Possible answers: talk; laugh; smile
   ▸ How do people go up and down in tall buildings? They ride elevators.

3. Remind students that poets often use descriptive words to help readers see pictures in their head.

4. Have students close their eyes and listen as you reread the second stanza of "Sing a Song of People."

   ▸ What do you see in your head when you hear these words? Possible answers: People walking or rushing around; people sitting on the bus, in a taxi, or on the subway.

Objectives
- Listen to and discuss poetry.
- Answer questions requiring literal recall of details.
- Identify author's use of imagery and descriptive language.
- Use visualizing to aid understanding of text.

5. Have students close their eyes and listen as you reread the third stanza of the poem.

   ▶ What do you see in your head when you hear these words? Possible answers: people wearing hats; people going in and out of doors; rain; people with umbrellas; tall buildings

TIP If students have trouble responding to a question, reread the appropriate lines and help them locate the answer in the poem.

Reading for Meaning

Rhyme, Rhythm, and Repetition in "Sing a Song of People"
Explore poetic elements with students.

1. Remind students that poets often rhyme and repeat words to help create rhythm, or a beat.

2. Reread the first four lines of the second stanza of "Sing a Song of People."

   ▶ What word does the poet use over and over in these lines? *people*
   ▶ What word rhymes with *bus*? *us*

3. Reread the fourth stanza of "Sing a Song of People."

   ▶ What word does the poet repeat in the stanza? *people*
   ▶ Why do you think the poet uses the word *people* over and over? Guide students to recognize that the poet wants readers to imagine crowds of people.
   ▶ What word rhymes with *crowd*? *loud*
   ▶ What do you hear in your head when you listen to the words of this stanza? Possible answers: people talking; people laughing; the sound of footsteps
   ▶ What words do you think help you imagine these things? Possible answers: *walking; talking; laughing*

4. Reread the last stanza of "Sing a Song of People."

   ▶ What words, or phrase, does the poet repeat in the stanza? *sing a song of people*
   ▶ What word rhymes with *go*? *know*

5. Reread the entire poem. **Have students clap on the beat** to practice recognizing rhythm.

   ▶ How does the rhythm, or beat, of the poem make you feel? What does it make you think of? Guide students to recognize that the rhythm might make them feel excited or rushed. It might make them think of the sounds of people who are always on the move.

Objectives
- Listen to and discuss poetry.
- Identify structure of poems and poetic elements: rhyme, rhythm, repetition, and/or alliteration.
- Identify the effects of rhyme and rhythm.

Making Connections ....

A People Picture

Students will demonstrate understanding by drawing a picture inspired by the poem "Sing a Song of People." Turn to page LC 3 in *K¹² Language Arts Activity Book*.

1. Remind students that "Sing a Song of People" describes different ways people move around a city.

2. Have students think about what they imagined in their head while they listened to the poem.

3. On the Activity Book page, have students draw a picture of one of the ways the poet describes people moving in "Sing a Song of People."

4. Ask students to describe their drawing when done.

   ▸ Do the words in "Sing a Song of People" make you think of a place that you have visited? What was it like? Was it fun to be around so many people? **Answers will vary.**

5. Read aloud the sentence starter at the bottom and ask students how they would complete it.

6. Write the words students dictate on the blank line.

   ▸ If students are ready to write on their own, allow them to do so.

7. Have students read aloud the completed sentence **with** you as you track the words with your finger.

TIP If students struggle with drawing, suggest that they cut out and glue down pictures from magazines to create their picture instead.

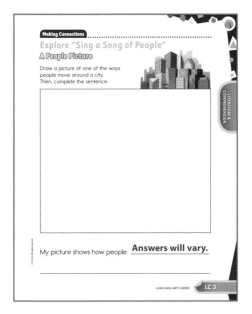

Objectives
- Demonstrate visualizing through drawing, discussion, and/or writing.
- Make connections with text: text-to-text, text-to-self, text-to-world.

Explore Poems About Animals (A)

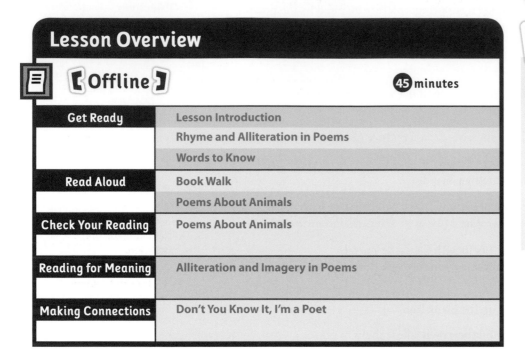

Lesson Overview

Offline
45 minutes

Get Ready	Lesson Introduction
	Rhyme and Alliteration in Poems
	Words to Know
Read Aloud	Book Walk
	Poems About Animals
Check Your Reading	Poems About Animals
Reading for Meaning	Alliteration and Imagery in Poems
Making Connections	Don't You Know It, I'm a Poet

Materials

Supplied
- *Listen, My Children: Poems for First Graders*, pp. 9, 13
- *K¹² Language Arts Activity Book*, p. LC 4

Also Needed
- whiteboard (optional)
- crayons

Poetry Synopses

One poet ponders a cow of an unusual color, while another mismatches an assortment of animals and the sounds that they produce.

Keywords

alliteration – the use of words with the same or close to the same beginning sounds

imagery – language that helps readers imagine how something looks, sounds, smells, feels, or tastes

rhyme – when two or more words have the same ending sounds; for example, *cat* and *hat* rhyme

stanza – a group of lines in a poem

Advance Preparation

Write the poem in the Get Ready on a whiteboard or sheet of paper. Read "The Purple Cow" and "I Know All the Sounds that the Animals Make" before beginning the Read Aloud to locate Words to Know in the text.

Big Ideas

▶ Poems are different from prose in structure and content. They are generally organized in lines and often contain rhymes.

▶ Readers must focus on the specific language of a text to aid in interpretation.

▶ The use of imagery and sensory language creates detailed pictures in the reader's mind, so the reader can understand and appreciate the ideas and feelings the writer conveys.

 **45 minutes**

Work **together** with students to complete Get Ready, Read Aloud, Check Your Reading, Reading for Meaning, and Making Connections activities.

Get Ready

Lesson Introduction

Prepare students for listening to and discussing "The Purple Cow" and "I Know All the Sounds that the Animals Make."

1. Tell students that you are going to read two poems: one about a purple cow, and another about the sounds that animals make.

2. Explain that before you read the poems, you'll get ready by discussing how

   ▸ Poems often rhyme.
   ▸ Poems often have words that begin with the same sound.
   ▸ Poets use words that make you imagine pictures or sounds in your head.

> **Objectives**
> - Listen to and discuss poetry.
> - Identify structure of poems and poetic elements: rhyme, rhythm, repetition, and/or alliteration.
> - Build vocabulary through listening, reading, and discussion.
> - Use new vocabulary in written and spoken sentences.

Rhyme and Alliteration in Poems

Introduce the poetic elements of rhyme and alliteration.

1. Remind students that a poem is usually written in short lines that are grouped together. A group of these lines is called a **stanza**.

2. Explain that the words at the ends of the lines in a stanza can sometimes rhyme.

3. **Read aloud the poem** that you wrote on a whiteboard or sheet of paper.

   I saw a single star
   That sparkled from afar.

4. Point to the words at the end of each line.
   Say: The words *star* and *afar* are at the ends of the lines. Both end with *–ar*, which means they **rhyme**.

5. Tell students that poets sometimes use several words that begin with the same sound to make those words stand out and to make a poem fun to listen to and pleasing to the ear.

6. Reread the poem.

   ▸ What words in the poem begin with the same sound? *saw; single; star; sparkled*

7. Remind students that poets also use descriptive words that help readers imagine pictures in their head.

   ▸ What do you imagine in your head when you hear the poem?
   Answers will vary.

TIP There is no need to teach students the term *alliteration* at this time.

Words to Know

Before reading "The Purple Cow" and "I Know All the Sounds that the Animals Make," go over Words to Know with students.

1. Read aloud each word and have students repeat it.

2. Ask students if they know what each word means.

   ▸ If students know a word's meaning, have them define it and use it in a sentence.
   ▸ If students don't know a word's meaning, read them the definition and discuss the word with them.

marvel – to be filled with surprise
moment – a particular point in time
wake – to stop sleeping

Read Aloud

Book Walk

Prepare students by taking them on a Book Walk of "The Purple Cow" and "I Know All the Sounds that the Animals Make." Scan the poems together and ask students to make predictions about them. Answers to questions may vary.

1. Turn to the **table of contents** in *Listen, My Children*. Help students find "The Purple Cow" and turn to that page.

2. Point to and read aloud the **title of the poem** and the **name of the poet**.

   ▸ What do you think the poem is about?
   ▸ Do you think a cow can really be purple? Why or why not?

3. Return to the **table of contents** and help students find "I Know All the Sounds that the Animals Make." Turn to that page.

4. Point to and read aloud the **title of the poem** and the **name of the poet**.

   ▸ What do you think the poem is about?
   ▸ What animal sounds do you already know?
   ▸ What is your favorite animal sound to imitate?

Objectives
- Make predictions based on text, illustrations, and/or prior knowledge.
- Activate prior knowledge by previewing text and/or discussing topic.
- Listen to and discuss poetry.

Poems About Animals

It's time to read aloud the poems.

1. Have students sit next to you so that they can see the pictures and words while you read aloud.

2. Explain to students that as you read aloud, they should do the following:

   ▸ Listen for words that rhyme, or end with the same sound.
   ▸ Listen for words that begin with the same sound.
   ▸ Think about what they see and hear in their head.

3. **Read aloud both poems.** Track with your finger so students can follow along. Emphasize Words to Know as you come to them.

Check Your Reading

Poems About Animals

Check students' comprehension of "The Purple Cow" and "I Know All the Sounds that the Animals Make."

1. Have students tell what each poem is about in their own words to develop grammar, vocabulary, comprehension, and fluency skills.

2. Ask students the following questions about "The Purple Cow."

   ► What does the poet describe in the poem? a purple cow
   ► Does the poet want to be a purple cow? No   How do you know? He says, "I'd rather see than be one."

3. Reread the entire poem, telling students to listen for words that rhyme.

   ► What word rhymes with *cow*? *anyhow*
   ► What two words in the last line rhyme? *see* and *be*

4. Ask the following question about "I Know All the Sounds that the Animals Make."

   ► What is the poem about? how the poet likes to make animal sounds

5. Reread the first two lines of the second stanza.

   ► What sound does the poet say a cat makes? a squeak
   ► What animal does the poet say "oinks"? a bear

 TIP If students have trouble responding to a question, reread the appropriate lines and help them locate the answer in the poem.

Reading for Meaning

Alliteration and Imagery in Poems

Explore the poetic element of alliteration and the poet's use of imagery.

1. Remind students that poets sometimes use words to help readers imagine pictures in their heads.

2. Reread "The Purple Cow."

   ► Describe what the words in the poem make you imagine. What word or words do you think made you imagine that? Answers will vary.

3. Remind students that poets sometimes use words that begin with the same sound to make the words stand out and make the poem fun to listen to.

4. Reread the second line in the second stanza of "I Know All the Sounds that the Animals Make."

   ► What two words in this line from the poem begin with the same sound? *honk* and *hog*

5. Reread the third line in the second stanza of "I Know All the Sounds that the Animals Make."

   ► What words in this line from the poem begin with the same sounds? *croak* and *cow*; *bark* and *bee*

6. Reread all of "I Know All the Sounds that the Animals Make."

   ▸ What do the words of the poem help you imagine? Guide students to recognize that they might see animals making the wrong sounds, such as a bee barking like a dog.

   ▸ Which part of the poem do you like best? Answers will vary.   What did that part of the poem make you imagine in your head? Be sure students describe how the animal is making the wrong sound.   What words helped you imagine that? Answers will vary.

Making Connections

 Don't You Know It, I'm a Poet

Have students demonstrate fluent speaking by reciting the poem "The Purple Cow." Then have them show their understanding of rhyming by creating a new poem with the same rhyming pattern as "The Purple Cow." Turn to page LC 4 in *K¹² Language Arts Activity Book*.

Objectives
- Recite short poems or rhymes.
- Respond to text through art, writing, and/or drama.
- Create mental imagery using sensory and descriptive language.
- Identify and replicate the pattern of a poem.

1. Turn to page 9 in *Listen, My Children*. Tell students that you are going to reread "The Purple Cow" line by line, and that they are going to repeat the words after you so they can learn to say the poem by heart.

   ▸ Read aloud the first line in the poem and then pause so students can recite the words.
   ▸ Continue reading a line and pausing until students have memorized it.
   ▸ Repeat these two actions until students have learned the entire poem.

2. Have students recite the entire poem on their own.

3. Point out that the last word in line 1 rhymes with the last word in line 3, and that the last word in line 2 rhymes with the last word in line 4. This is called a **rhyming pattern**.

4. Tell students that you are going to read another poem with the same rhyming pattern as "The Purple Cow," and then they will make a poem of their own.

5. Read aloud the poem on the Activity Book page, emphasizing the last word in each line to ensure students hear the rhyming pattern.

6. Have students use a crayon to circle the rhyming words at the ends of lines 1 and 3. Have them use a different-color crayon to circle the rhyming words at the ends of lines 2 and 4.

7. Point to the blank lines in the poem at the bottom of the page. Tell students they will choose words that rhyme to create their own poem, based on the poem they have just heard.

8. Read aloud the poem, pausing at each blank line so students can choose a word.

9. Help students write the missing words in the blanks.

   ▸ Be sure students pick pairs of words that rhyme.
   ▸ Remind students that one pair of rhyming words should appear at the ends of lines 1 and 3, and another pair should appear at the ends of lines 2 and 4.

10. Help students write their name on the blank line next to the title. Have them read aloud the completed poem **with** you as you track the words with your finger.

11. Ask students to describe what the words of their new poem help them imagine in their head.

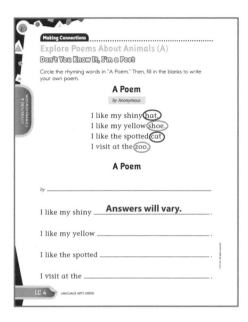

Explore "Table Manners"

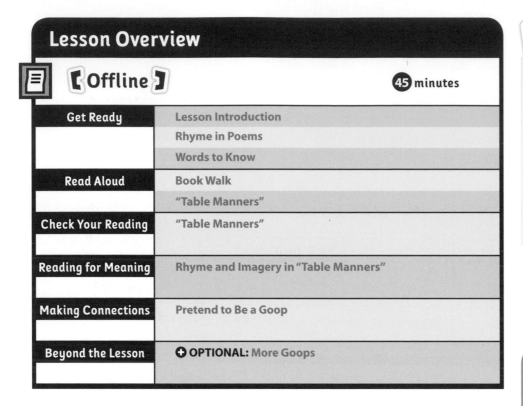

Lesson Overview

[Offline]   45 minutes

Get Ready	Lesson Introduction
	Rhyme in Poems
	Words to Know
Read Aloud	Book Walk
	"Table Manners"
Check Your Reading	"Table Manners"
Reading for Meaning	Rhyme and Imagery in "Table Manners"
Making Connections	Pretend to Be a Goop
Beyond the Lesson	⊕ OPTIONAL: More Goops

[Materials]

Supplied
- *Listen, My Children: Poems for First Graders*, p. 12
- *K¹² My Journal*, pp. 2–53

Also Needed
- household objects – plates, bowls, cups, forks, spoons, napkins

Poetry Synopsis

The Goops have many habits, but using good table manners isn't one of them!

Keywords

rhyme – when two or more words have the same ending sounds; for example, *cat* and *hat* rhyme

Advance Preparation

Read "Table Manners" before beginning the Read Aloud to locate Words to Know in the text.

Big Ideas

▸ Poems are different from prose in structure and content. They are generally organized in lines and often contain rhymes.

▸ Readers must focus on the specific language of a text to aid in interpretation.

▸ The use of imagery and sensory language creates detailed pictures in the reader's mind, so the reader can understand and appreciate the ideas and feelings the writer conveys.

 **45 minutes**

Work **together** with students to complete Get Ready, Read Aloud, Check Your Reading, Reading for Meaning, Making Connections, and Beyond the Lesson activities.

Get Ready

Lesson Introduction

Prepare students for listening to and discussing "Table Manners."

1. Tell students that you are going to read a poem about a family that has bad table manners.

2. Explain that before you read the poem, you'll get ready by discussing how

   ▸ Poems often rhyme.
   ▸ Poets use words to help readers see pictures and hear sounds in their head.

Objectives
- Listen to and discuss poetry.
- Identify structure of poems and poetic elements: rhyme, rhythm, repetition, and/or alliteration.
- Build vocabulary through listening, reading, and discussion.
- Use new vocabulary in written and spoken sentences.

Rhyme in Poems

Reinforce the poetic element of rhyme.

1. Remind students that the words at the ends of the lines in a stanza of a poem often rhyme.

2. Tell them that sometimes two words in the same line rhyme. **Read aloud the following poem.**

   My name is Mike;
   I like to ride my bike.

   ▸ What words in the poem rhyme? *Mike, like, bike*
   ▸ What do we call it when words end with the same sound? a rhyme

Words to Know

Before reading "Table Manners," go over Words to Know with students.

1. Read aloud each word and have students repeat it.

2. Ask students if they know what each word means.

   ▸ If students know a word's meaning, have them define it and use it in a sentence.
   ▸ If students don't know a word's meaning, read them the definition and discuss the word with them.

disgusting – awful; sickening
lead – to live

Read Aloud

Book Walk

Prepare students by taking them on a Book Walk of "Table Manners." Scan the poem together and ask students to make predictions about it.

1. Turn to the **table of contents** in *Listen, My Children*. Help students find "Table Manners" and turn to that page.

2. Point to and read aloud the **title of the poem** and the **name of the poet**.

   ► What do you think the poem is about? Answers will vary.
   ► What are some good table manners? Possible answers: chewing food with your mouth closed; using a napkin to wipe your mouth
   ► What are some bad table manners? Possible answers: talking with your mouth full; wiping your mouth with your bare hand
   ► Do you use good or bad table manners, or both? Answers will vary.

"Table Manners"

It's time to read aloud the poem.

1. Have students sit next to you so that they can see the pictures and words while you read aloud.

2. Explain to students that as you read aloud, they should do the following:

   ► Listen for words that rhyme.
   ► Think about the words that help them see pictures in their head.

3. **Read aloud the entire poem.** Track with your finger so students can follow along. Emphasize Words to Know as you come to them.

Check Your Reading

"Table Manners"

Check students' comprehension of "Table Manners."

1. Have students tell what "Table Manners" is about in their own words to develop grammar, vocabulary, comprehension, and fluency skills.

2. Ask students the following questions.

   ► Who are the Goops? a family with bad table manners
   ► What do the Goops do with their knives? lick them
   ► How do the Goops chew their food? loud; fast
   ► Does the poet want to be a Goop? No

TIP If students have trouble responding to a question, reread the appropriate lines and help them locate the answer in the poem.

Objectives
- Listen to and discuss poetry.
- Answer questions requiring literal recall of details.

Reading for Meaning

Rhyme and Imagery in "Table Manners"
Check students' ability to recognize rhyme and imagery.

1. Remind students that poets use words to make rhymes and help readers see and hear things in their head.

2. Reread the first four lines of "Table Manners," telling students to listen for words that rhyme.

   ▸ What word rhymes with *knives*? *lives*
   ▸ What word rhymes with *broth*? *tablecloth*

3. Reread the last four lines of the poem, telling students to listen for words that rhyme.

   ▸ What word rhymes with *chew*? *you*
   ▸ What word rhymes with *why*? *I*

4. Reread the first four lines of the poem.

   ▸ What do you see in your head when you hear these lines? Possible answers: people licking their fingers and knives; people spilling things; people making a mess at the dinner table
   ▸ What words do you think helped you imagine these things? Answers will vary.

5. Reread the fifth and sixth lines of the poem.

   ▸ What do you hear in your head when you listen to these lines? Possible answers: people talking; people chewing their food loudly
   ▸ What words do you think helped you imagine these things? Answers will vary.

Objectives
- Listen to and discuss poetry.
- Identify structure of poems and poetic elements: rhyme, rhythm, repetition, and/or alliteration.
- Identify author's use of imagery and descriptive language.
- Use visualizing to aid understanding of text.

Making Connections

Pretend to Be a Goop
Students will demonstrate understanding of "Table Manners" by acting out a meal with the Goops. Gather *K¹² My Journal* and have students turn to the next available page for **writing** in Thoughts and Experiences. Also gather the plates, bowls, cups, forks, spoons, and napkins.

1. Remind students that in "Table Manners" the poet describes how the Goops eat their food. Answers to questions may vary.

   ▸ Do the Goops remind you of anybody you know?
   ▸ Do you ever eat like the Goops?

2. Have students act out a meal with the Goops.

   ▸ Encourage students to make loud noises and use all the bad table manners that they can think of.

3. Have students describe what it might be like to be a Goop.

4. Have students explain why they think it would be fun to be a Goop and then have them tell why they think it would be disgusting.

Objectives
- Respond to text through art, writing, and/or drama.
- Make connections with text: text-to-text, text-to-self, text-to-world.

5. Have them say a few sentences that express their thoughts.

   ▶ Use a sentence starter such as, "I would like to be a Goop because . . . ."
   ▶ Be sure students give an example of why they would or would not like to be a Goop.

6. In the journal, write the words students dictate.

   ▶ If students are ready to write on their own, allow them to do so.

7. Have students read aloud the completed sentence(s) **with** you as you track the words with your finger.

 Reward: Add a sticker for this unit on the My Accomplishments chart to mark successful completion of the unit.

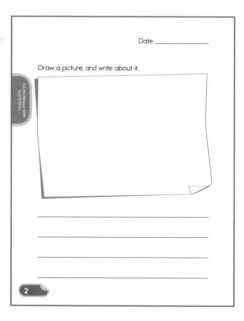

Beyond the Lesson

 OPTIONAL: More Goops

This activity is OPTIONAL. It is intended for students who have extra time and would benefit from listening to additional poems about the Goops. Feel free to skip this activity.

1. Go to a library and look for a copy of *More Goops and How Not to Be Them* by Gelett Burgess. Or get a free copy online at www.gutenberg.org (search by book title).

2. Lead a Book Walk and then read aloud one or more of the poems.

3. Have students tell how the Goops show more bad manners. Answers to questions may vary.

   ▶ Which bad behavior do you think is the worst? Why?
   ▶ How are the poems in *More Goops and How Not to Be Them* like the poem "Table Manners"?

> **Objectives**
> - Make connections with text: text-to-text, text-to-self, text-to-world.
> - Listen to and discuss poetry.

Let's Share
Through Stories

Unit Focus

In this unit, students will explore legends and storytelling traditions of different cultures. This unit follows the read-aloud instructional approach (see the instructional approaches to reading in the introductory lesson for this program). In this unit, students will

▶ Listen to legends and a nonfiction article.
▶ Practice the strategy of making predictions.
▶ Learn about the strategy of setting a purpose for reading and why it's important.
▶ Learn about characteristics of legends.
▶ Explore main characters and their actions.
▶ Learn about facts and text features found in nonfiction articles.
▶ Explore using text and picture clues to define unknown words.

Unit Plan

Offline

Lesson 1	Introduce *The Legend of the Bluebonnet*	**45** minutes a day
Lesson 2	Explore *The Legend of the Bluebonnet*	
Lesson 3	Introduce "The Legend of the Dipper"	
Lesson 4	Explore "The Legend of the Dipper"	
Lesson 5	Introduce "Telling Stories Around the World"	
Lesson 6	Explore "Telling Stories Around the World"	
Lesson 7	Introduce "Medio Pollito: The Little Half-Chick"	
Lesson 8	Explore "Medio Polito: The Little Half-Chick"	
Lesson 9	Your Choice	

Introduce *The Legend of the Bluebonnet*

Lesson Overview

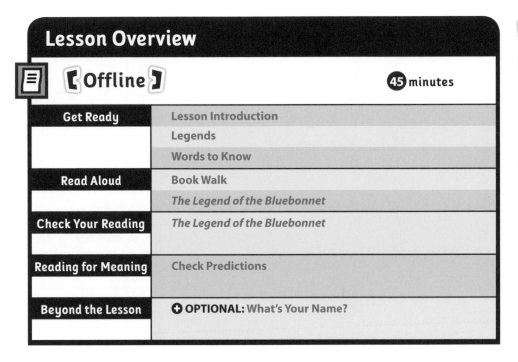

Offline		45 minutes
Get Ready	Lesson Introduction	
	Legends	
	Words to Know	
Read Aloud	Book Walk	
	The Legend of the Bluebonnet	
Check Your Reading	*The Legend of the Bluebonnet*	
Reading for Meaning	Check Predictions	
Beyond the Lesson	⊕ OPTIONAL: What's Your Name?	

Advance Preparation

Read *The Legend of the Bluebonnet* before beginning the Read Aloud to locate Words to Know in the text. Read the Read Aloud directions to be aware of stopping points in the story at which students will make predictions. Since this book has no page numbers, you should bookmark pages with stopping points.

Big Ideas

► Good readers interact with text to make logical predictions before reading; confirm predictions during reading; and revise or make new predictions as they read further.
► Exposing readers to a wide variety of genres provides them with a wide range of background knowledge and increases their vocabulary.

Materials

Supplied
- *The Legend of the Bluebonnet* by Tomie dePaola

Also Needed
- whiteboard (optional)

Story Synopsis

The Great Spirits have spoken: Someone must make a great sacrifice to save the People from a severe drought. Who will give up their most valued possession? What will it be? This book includes brief references to drought, famine, and death, as well as the Comanche belief in a shaman and Great Spirits.

Keywords

genre – a category for classifying literary works

legend – a story that is passed down for many years to teach the values of a culture; a legend may or may not contain some true events or people

prediction – a guess about what might happen that is based on information in a story and what you already know

[Offline] **45** minutes

Work **together** with students to complete Get Ready, Read Aloud, Check Your Reading, Reading for Meaning, and Beyond the Lesson activities.

Get Ready ....

Lesson Introduction

Prepare students for listening to and discussing *The Legend of the Bluebonnet*.

1. Tell students that you are going to read a book called *The Legend of the Bluebonnet*, a story about a courageous Native American girl and what she does for her people.

2. Explain that before you read the book, you will get ready by discussing what makes a story a legend.

3. Tell students that they will make predictions about what will happen at certain points in the story.

> ### Objectives
> - Identify genre.
> - Identify characteristics of different genres.
> - Build vocabulary through listening, reading, and discussion.
> - Use new vocabulary in written and spoken sentences.

Legends

Introduce the kind of story known as a legend.

1. Explain that a **legend** is a story that is very old and has been told by a group of people for many years. A legend can be about a person who may have been real, but it can't be proven. That person is sometimes described as a hero, such as in the legend of Robin Hood. In that story, Robin Hood is a hero who steals from the rich and gives to the poor.

2. Tell students that a legend can also explain why something happens in nature, such as why the sky is blue. It may include events that could have really happened and other events that could not happen in real life.

3. Read aloud the following legend.

   Long ago, there were very few apple trees in America. A man who loved apples felt this was a shame. He thought everyone should have apples. So the man started to collect apple seeds in a big sack. Once the sack was full of seeds, he set out on a journey walking across America. Every so often, the man would stop and plant a few of the seeds on a hill or in an empty field. Before long, apple trees were growing where they had never been seen before. And it was all because of the man who we now know as Johnny Appleseed.

   ▶ What does the story explain? why there are lots of apple trees in America
   ▶ What do we call a story that tries to explain something? a legend
   ▶ What part of the legend is true? that there are apple trees in America

TIP Although an objective for this lesson is to identify genre, there is no need to introduce the term to students at this time.

Words to Know

Before reading *The Legend of the Bluebonnet*, go over Words to Know with students.

1. Read aloud each word and have students repeat it.

2. Ask students if they know what each word means.

   ▸ If students know a word's meaning, have them define it and use it in a sentence.

   ▸ If students don't know a word's meaning, read them the definition and discuss the word with them.

cease – to stop something

drought – when it doesn't rain for a long, long time

famine – when many people have little or no food to eat

offering – something special that's given up to help others

possession – something you own

sacrifice – to give up something special to help others

shaman – a person that some people in Native American groups believe has special powers to heal the sick and speak with spirits

valued – a description of something that is very important and people are grateful for

Read Aloud ....

Book Walk

Prepare students for reading by taking them on a Book Walk of *The Legend of the Bluebonnet*. Scan the **beginning of the book together** and ask students to make predictions about the story. Answers to questions may vary.

1. Have students look at the picture on the cover. Point to and read aloud the **book title**.

   ▸ What do you think the book is about?

2. Have students point to the **name of the author and illustrator**. Read the name of the author and illustrator.

3. Have students look at the **pictures, up to the picture of the people gathered in a circle** around the man dressed in red and holding feathers.

   ▸ Where do you think the story takes place?
   ▸ What do you think might happen in the story?
   ▸ Did you ever give away something of yours to make someone else happy? What was it? Was it hard to give it up?
   ▸ Do you know any stories that have been passed down through your family? What is the story?

 Do not show all the pictures in the story. This will allow students to make predictions based on what they hear, not what they've seen.

> **Objectives**
> - Activate prior knowledge by previewing text and/or discussing topic.
> - Listen and respond to texts representing a variety of cultures, time periods, and traditions.
> - Make predictions based on text, illustrations, and/or prior knowledge.
> - Make predictions before and during reading.

The Legend of the Bluebonnet

It's time to read aloud the story and ask students to make predictions.

1. Have students sit next to you so that they can see the pictures and words while you read aloud.

2. **Begin to read aloud.** Pause at the following points in the story to ask students what they predict will happen next. Jot down their predictions for later reference.

   ► After the shaman tells the People what they must do to end the drought
   ► After She-Who-Is-Alone creeps out of her tipi after everyone is asleep
   ► After She-Who-Is-Alone asks the Great Spirits to accept her doll, her most valued possession
   ► After She-Who-Is-Alone wakes up in the morning
   ► After the People come out of their tipis and see all the flowers

3. **Continue to read aloud the story.**

   ► Track with your finger so students can follow along.
   ► Emphasize Words to Know as you come to them. If appropriate, use the pictures to help show what each word means.
   ► Remember to stop at the listed points and have students make predictions.

Check Your Reading

The Legend of the Bluebonnet

Check students' comprehension of *The Legend of the Bluebonnet*.

1. Have students retell *The Legend of the Bluebonnet* in their own words to develop grammar, vocabulary, comprehension, and fluency skills.

2. Ask students the following questions.

   ► What does the shaman say the People need to do to end the drought? They need to sacrifice their most valued possession.
   ► Why doesn't the warrior sacrifice his new bow? He says he's sure it's not what the Great Spirits want.
   ► Why doesn't the woman sacrifice her special blanket? She doesn't think it's what the Great Spirits want.
   ► What does She-Who-Is-Alone say is her most valued possession? her warrior doll
   ► What kind of story is *The Legend of the Bluebonnet*? a legend
   ► What does the legend explain? why bluebonnets bloom in Texas every year
   ► Can you prove bluebonnets bloom because She-Who-Is-Alone sacrifices her doll? No
   ► Do you think the legend is true? Why or why not? Answers will vary.

 TIP If students have trouble responding to a question, help them locate the answer in the text or pictures.

> **Objectives**
> - Retell or dramatize a story.
> - Answer questions requiring literal recall of details.
> - Identify genre.
> - Identify characteristics of different genres.

Reading for Meaning

Check Predictions

Revisit the predictions students made while listening to *The Legend of the Bluebonnet*.

1. Remind students that good readers make predictions when they read a story.

2. Ask students the following questions to review and discuss the predictions they made while reading *The Legend of the Bluebonnet*. **Refer to the predictions you jotted down, as necessary.** Answers to questions may vary.

   ▶ What did you predict would happen after the shaman tells the People what they must do to end the drought?
   ▶ Were you surprised that some of the People did not want to give up their possessions? Why or why not?
   ▶ What did you predict would happen after She-Who-Is-Alone creeps out of her tipi after everyone is asleep? What really happens? She-Who-Is-Alone asks the Great Spirits to accept her warrior doll.
   ▶ Were you surprised that She-Who-Is-Alone throws her doll into the fire? What clues from the story or your own experiences did you use to make your prediction?
   ▶ What did you predict would happen after She-Who-Is-Alone wakes up in the morning? What really happens? She-Who-Is-Alone sees the ground is covered with blue flowers.
   ▶ Were you surprised by what happens after the People come out of their tipis and see all the flowers? Why or why not?

3. Conclude by telling students that it's okay if our predictions don't happen. Even if our predictions don't happen, **making predictions is important because it helps us be active readers**.

Objectives
- Evaluate predictions.

Beyond the Lesson

⊕ OPTIONAL: What's Your Name?

This activity is OPTIONAL. It is intended for students who have extra time and would benefit from connecting to the story by coming up with their own descriptive name. Feel free to skip this activity.

1. Remind students She-Who-Is-Alone becomes known as One-Who-Dearly-Loved-Her-People after she sacrifices her warrior doll to help the People.

2. Have students think of descriptive names for themselves.

Objectives
- Make connections with text: text-to-text, text-to-self, text-to-world.

3. Discuss the following questions to help students brainstorm ideas for their own descriptive names.

   ▸ What is your favorite thing to do? Example name: He-Who-Loves-To-Swim
   ▸ What are you really good at? Example name: She-Who-Is-Good-At-Math
   ▸ What are some ways you help your family? Example name: He-Who-Feeds-The-Cat
   ▸ What kind of stories do you like? Example name: He-Who-Loves-Mysteries
   ▸ What is something you really like? Example name: She-Who-Loves-Rainbows
   ▸ What is something special that people say about you? Example names: He-Who-Has-A-Great-Smile, She-Who-Always-Helps-Her-Brother

4. Have students dictate the name they decide on.

5. Write the name students dictate on a whiteboard or sheet of paper.

6. Have students read aloud the completed name **with** you as you track the words with your finger.

7. Have students explain why they chose their name and why it's an appropriate name for them.

Explore *The Legend of the Bluebonnet*

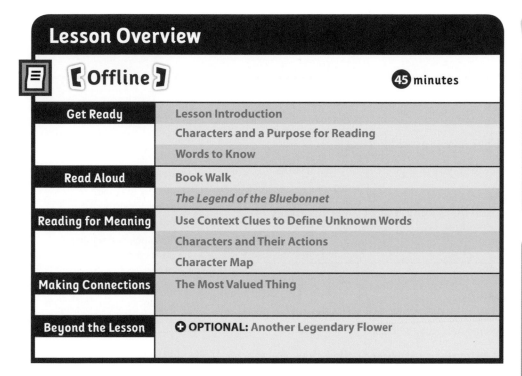

Lesson Overview

[Offline]　　　　　　　　**45** minutes

Get Ready	Lesson Introduction
	Characters and a Purpose for Reading
	Words to Know
Read Aloud	Book Walk
	The Legend of the Bluebonnet
Reading for Meaning	Use Context Clues to Define Unknown Words
	Characters and Their Actions
	Character Map
Making Connections	The Most Valued Thing
Beyond the Lesson	⊕ OPTIONAL: Another Legendary Flower

Advance Preparation

Review Reading for Meaning and Making Connections to familiarize yourself with the questions and answers.

Big Ideas

▸ Comprehension entails having and knowing a purpose for reading.
▸ An awareness of story structure elements (setting, characters, plot) provides readers a foundation for constructing meaning when reading new stories and writing their own stories.
▸ To understand and interpret a story, readers need to understand and describe characters and what they do.

[Materials]

Supplied
- *The Legend of the Bluebonnet* by Tomie dePaola
- *K¹² Language Arts Activity Book*, p. LC 5
- *K¹² My Journal*, pp. 2–53

Keywords

character – a person or animal in a story
main character – an important person, animal, or other being who is central to the plot
story structure elements – components of a story; they include character, setting, plot, problem, and solution

 **Offline** **45** minutes

Work **together** with students to complete Get Ready, Read Aloud, Reading for Meaning, Making Connections, and Beyond the Lesson activities.

Get Ready

Lesson Introduction
Prepare students for listening to and discussing *The Legend of the Bluebonnet*.

1. Tell students that you will reread *The Legend of the Bluebonnet*.

2. Explain that before you reread the story, you will get ready by discussing

   ▶ How we can learn about characters by what they say and do.
   ▶ How to set a purpose, or a reason for reading, and why it is important to do so.

 Objectives
- Set a purpose for reading.
- Identify character(s).
- Describe character(s).
- Identify the main character(s).
- Build vocabulary through listening, reading, and discussion.
- Use new vocabulary in written and spoken sentences.

Characters and a Purpose for Reading
Explore the story elements of characters and their actions, and setting a purpose for reading. Turn to page LC 5 in *K¹² Language Arts Activity Book*.

1. Tell students that the **people and animals in a story are called characters**.

2. We can learn many things about a story's characters. We can learn what they look like. We can learn what they are like by what they say and do.

3. Read aloud the following story.

   Grace, Maddy, and Estelle are sisters who share a bedroom. They all have brown hair and green eyes. One morning, Grace told her sisters that it was time to clean up their room. But Maddy and Estelle said they'd rather go outside and play. Grace went back to their bedroom and picked up all the clothes that were on the floor. Then she dusted the dresser and cleaned the mirror. The last thing Grace did was vacuum the rug. When Maddy and Estelle came inside from playing, they were surprised at how wonderful their room looked, and they thanked Grace for cleaning it.

   ▶ Who are the characters in the story? Grace; Maddy; Estelle
   ▶ What do Grace, Maddy, and Estelle look like? brown hair; green eyes
   ▶ Does Grace like having a messy room? No   How can you tell? She says that it's time to clean their room.

4. Explain that one character is usually more important than the other characters in a story. The most important character is the one who does and talks the most. The most important character is called the **main character**.

   ▸ Who is the main, or most important, character in the story? Grace
   ▸ How do you know Grace is the main character? She does most of the things in the story.

5. Explain to students that after they listen to *The Legend of the Bluebonnet*, they will complete a chart called a **character map** about She-Who-Is-Alone. On the Activity Book page, they will add information about another character later.

6. Point to and read aloud the statements and questions in the left column and then ask the following question.

   ▸ What do you think you should listen for as I read the story aloud? answers to the questions on the chart; information about She-Who-Is-Alone

7. Tell students that good readers usually have a purpose, or reason for reading a story. Having a reason for reading helps readers focus on what's important and remember what they read.

8. Explain to students that listening for information about She-Who-Is-Alone is their purpose, or reason for listening to *The Legend of the Bluebonnet*. If they listen for information about She-Who-Is-Alone, it will be easier for them to remember the story and complete the character map.

9. Keep the map nearby for use during the Reading for Meaning.

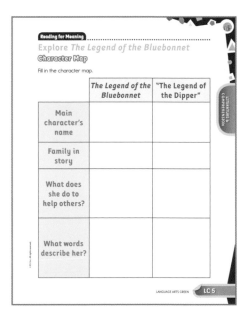

Words to Know

Before reading *The Legend of the Bluebonnet*, go over Words to Know with students.

1. Read aloud each word and have students repeat it.

2. Ask students if they know what each word means.

   ▸ If students know a word's meaning, have them define it and use it in a sentence.
   ▸ If students don't know a word's meaning, read them the definition and discuss the word with them.

cease – to stop something
drought – when it doesn't rain for a long, long time
famine – when many people have little or no food to eat
offering – something special that's given up to help others
possession – something you own
sacrifice – to give up something special to help others
shaman – a person that some people in Native American groups believe has special powers to heal the sick and speak with spirits
valued – a description of something that is very important and people are grateful for

Read Aloud

Book Walk

Prepare students by taking them on a Book Walk of *The Legend of the Bluebonnet*. Scan the book together to revisit the characters and events.

1. Read aloud the **book title**.

2. Read aloud the name of the **author** and **illustrator**.

3. Look through the book. Have students review the **pictures**. Answers to questions may vary.

   ▸ What do you own that you care about the most?
   ▸ Why is it so important to you?
   ▸ Do you think you would give it up if it would help others?

Objectives

- Activate prior knowledge by previewing text and/or discussing topic.
- Listen and respond to texts representing a variety of cultures, time periods, and traditions.

The Legend of the Bluebonnet

It's time to reread the story.

1. Have students sit next to you so that they can see the pictures and words while you read aloud.

2. Tell students to listen carefully for information about the characters, especially She-Who-Is-Alone.

3. **Read aloud the entire story.** Track with your finger so students can follow along. Emphasize Words to Know as you come to them. If appropriate, use the pictures to help show what each word means.

Reading for Meaning

Use Context Clues to Define Unknown Words

Check students' ability to use text and picture clues to determine a word's meaning.

1. Have students retell *The Legend of the Bluebonnet* in their own words to develop grammar, vocabulary, comprehension, and fluency skills.

2. Turn to the page with the picture of She-Who-Is-Alone standing near the dying council fire and holding her doll after everyone has returned to their tipis. Read aloud the text on the right-hand page.

   ▸ What do you think the word *tipi* means? a kind of home   What clues in the text and the picture help you figure this out? The text says the girl slept in a tipi, and the picture shows a kind of home that people could live in.

3. Turn to the page with the picture of She-Who-Is-Alone putting her warrior doll into the fire and read aloud the text below the picture.

   ▸ What does the word *thrust* mean? to push   How does the picture help you figure this out? It shows She-Who-Is-Alone shoving her warrior doll into the fire.

4. Turn to the picture of She-Who-Is-Alone scattering ashes on the hilltop and read aloud the text on the page.

   ▸ What does the word *scatter* mean? to toss in every direction   What clues in the text and the picture help you figure this out? The text says She-Who-Is-Alone scatters the ashes to the winds, and the picture shows her tossing the ashes in the air, where they blow away.

Objectives

- Retell or dramatize a story.
- Use illustrations to aid understanding of text.
- Use context and sentence structure to determine meaning of words, phrases, and/or sentences.
- Identify the main character(s).
- Describe character(s).
- Identify details that explain characters' actions and feelings.
- Demonstrate understanding through graphic organizers.

Characters and Their Actions

Explore the story elements of characters and their actions with students.

1. Remind students that thinking about **what the characters are like and what they do** can help a reader better understand the characters and the story.

2. Ask the following questions.

   ▸ Who is the main character in the story? She-Who-Is-Alone   How do you know she is the main character? She does most of the things in the story.
   ▸ What does She-Who-Is-Alone love more than all other things? her warrior doll

▸ Why does She-Who-Is-Alone love her warrior doll so much? because it's all she has left of her family; because it reminds her of her parents

▸ Why doesn't the warrior sacrifice his new bow after the shaman says the People must sacrifice the most valued possession among them? He says that he's sure the Great Spirits don't want his bow.   What does this tell you about the warrior? He doesn't want to give up his bow.

▸ Why does She-Who-Is-Alone put her warrior doll in the fire? It's the thing she values the most; she knows that if she sacrifices it, it will end the drought and help the People.

▸ Why do the People dance and sing as the rain begins to fall at the end of the story? to thank the Great Spirits for ending the drought

▸ What is She-Who-Is-Alone's new name at the end of the story? One-Who-Dearly-Loved-Her-People   Why do you think she is given this new name? because she gave up the thing that was most important to her to help the People

▸ Do you think *One-Who-Dearly-Loved-Her-People* is a good name for the girl? Why or why not? Answers will vary.

Character Map

Check students' ability to describe the main character of *The Legend of the Bluebonnet*. Turn to page LC 5 in *K¹² Language Arts Activity Book*.

1. Point to and read aloud the first statement on the character map.

2. Write what students dictate in the first box under the heading *The Legend of the Bluebonnet*.

3. Repeat Steps 2 and 3 until all the boxes are filled in.

TIP Keep the Activity Book page in a safe place for use after reading "The Legend of the Dipper."

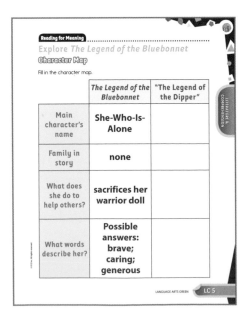

Making Connections

The Most Valued Thing

Have students draw a picture of their most valued possession. Gather *K¹² My Journal* and have students turn to the next available page for **drawing and writing** in Thoughts and Experiences.

1. Remind students that She-Who-Is-Alone gives the thing she loves the most to help the People.

2. Have students think about their most valued possession. If students have trouble thinking of something they value, suggest items that you know they care about. Examples might be a special stuffed animal or toy, or a special gift they have received from a family member.

3. In the journal, have students draw a picture of their most valued possession.

4. Ask students to explain why they care so much about the item in their picture.

5. Have students dictate a sentence about their most valued possession.

   ▸ A possible sentence starter might be, "My most valued possession is . . . ."
   ▸ Another possible sentence starter might be, "This is my most valued possession because . . . ."

6. Write the words students dictate below the picture.

   ▸ If students are ready to write on their own, allow them to do so.

7. Have students read aloud the completed sentence **with** you as you track the words with your finger.

TIP The amount of time students need to complete this activity will vary. Students need only work for the remaining time of the lesson.

Objectives

- Respond to text through art, writing, and/or drama.
- Make connections with text: text-to-text, text-to-self, text-to-world.

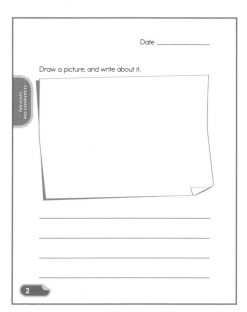

Beyond the Lesson

⊕ OPTIONAL: Another Legendary Flower

This activity is OPTIONAL. It is intended for students who have extra time and would benefit from reading an additional book written by the same author about the legend of another flower. Feel free to skip this activity.

1. Go to a library and look for a copy of *The Legend of the Indian Paintbrush* by Tomie dePaola.

2. Lead a Book Walk and then read aloud the story.

3. Have students tell how the books are alike and different.

   ▸ Be sure students tell how the main characters are alike and different.

4. Ask them to explain why the story is a legend.

5. Have students tell which story is their favorite and why.

Objectives

- Compare and contrast two texts on the same topic.
- Compare and contrast story structure elements across texts.
- Identify characteristics of different genres.

Introduce "The Legend of the Dipper"

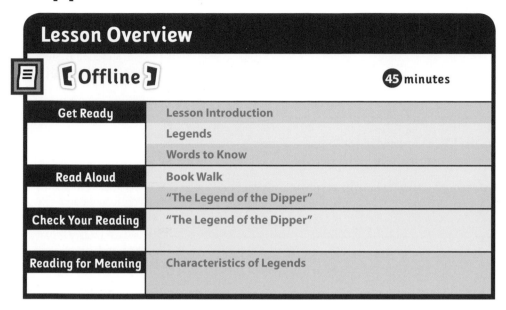

Lesson Overview

[Offline]   **45** minutes

Get Ready	Lesson Introduction
	Legends
	Words to Know
Read Aloud	Book Walk
	"The Legend of the Dipper"
Check Your Reading	"The Legend of the Dipper"
Reading for Meaning	Characteristics of Legends

Advance Preparation

Read "The Legend of the Dipper" before beginning the Read Aloud to locate Words to Know in the text.

Big Ideas

Exposing readers to a wide variety of genres provides them with a wide range of background knowledge and increases their vocabulary.

[Materials]

Supplied

- *"The Legend of the Dipper," K¹² Classics for Young Readers, Volume A,* pp. 2–9

Story Synopsis

In the midst of a drought, a little girl needs to find some water to help her ailing mother. On her way back from a distant mountain spring, the selfless little girl stops to let others take a sip from her tin dipper.

Keywords

genre – a category for classifying literary works

legend – a story that is passed down for many years to teach the values of a culture; a legend may or may not contain some true events or people

 **45** minutes

Work **together** with students to complete Get Ready, Read Aloud, Check Your Reading, and Reading for Meaning activities.

Get Ready ···

Lesson Introduction
Prepare students for listening to and discussing "The Legend of the Dipper."

1. Tell students that you are going to read "The Legend of the Dipper," a story about a girl who is willing to help others before she helps herself.

2. Explain that before you read the story, you will get ready by reviewing what makes a story a legend.

> **Objectives**
> - Identify genre.
> - Identify characteristics of different genres.
> - Build vocabulary through listening, reading, and discussion.
> - Use new vocabulary in written and spoken sentences.

Legends
Review the kind of story known as a legend.

1. Ask students if they remember what a legend is. Have them tell you what a legend is.

2. If students cannot tell you what a legend is, remind them of the following **characteristics of a legend**.

   ▶ It is a story that is very old and has been told for many years.
   ▶ It might be about a person who may have been real, but it can't be proven.
   ▶ It often has a character who is a hero.

3. Tell students that a legend can also explain why something happens in nature, such as why there are rainbows. Legends may include events that could have really happened and other events that could not happen in real life.

4. Read aloud the following story.

   Long, long ago, there was a beautiful goddess who lived on an island. But the goddess had a very bad temper. She would stomp her feet so hard it would make the ground shake. She would dig her magic stick into the sides of the mountains to make fire pour out of them, turning them into volcanoes.

   One day, the goddess and her sister got into a terrible fight. The ground shook for days, and the fire and smoke from the volcanoes filled the sky. When it was all over, many new fiery mountains had popped up. We call them the Hawaiian Islands.

   ▶ Is the story a legend? Yes
   ▶ How do you know? What parts of the story tell you it's a legend? Guide students to recognize that: The story took place "long, long ago"; it explains something that happened in nature, the creation of the Hawaiian Islands; it has events that could not happen in real life.

Words to Know

Before reading "The Legend of the Dipper," go over Words to Know with students.

1. Read aloud each word or phrase and have students repeat it.

2. Ask students if they know what each word or phrase means.

   ▸ If students know a word's or phrase's meaning, have them define it and use it in a sentence.
   ▸ If students don't know a word's or phrase's meaning, read them the definition and discuss the word or phrase with them.

by and by – before long; after a while
dipper – a large, deep spoon with a long handle; a ladle
flow – to pour out of
parched – dried up; in need of water
servant – a helper; someone who works in another person's home
spring – a place where water rises up from under the ground
unselfish – generous; giving

Read Aloud

Book Walk

Prepare students for reading by taking them on a Book Walk of "The Legend of the Dipper." Scan the story together and ask students to make predictions about the story. Answers to questions may vary.

1. Point to the **table of contents**. Help students find the selection and turn to that page.

2. Point to and read aloud the **title of the story**.

   ▸ What do you think the story is about?

3. Have students look at the **pictures**.

   ▸ Where do you think the story takes place?
   ▸ What do you think might happen in the story?
   ▸ Can you think of a legend? What is it about?

Objectives

- Activate prior knowledge by previewing text and/or discussing topic.
- Make predictions based on text, illustrations, and/or prior knowledge.
- Listen and respond to texts representing a variety of cultures, time periods, and traditions.

"The Legend of the Dipper"

It's time to read aloud the story.

1. Have students sit next to you so that they can see the pictures and words while you read aloud.

2. Tell students to listen for clues that tell them the story is a legend.

3. **Read aloud the entire story.** Track with your finger so students can follow along. Emphasize Words to Know as you come to them. If appropriate, use the pictures to help show what each word means.

Check Your Reading

"The Legend of the Dipper"
Check students' comprehension of "The Legend of the Dipper."

1. Have students retell "The Legend of the Dipper" in their own words to develop grammar, vocabulary, comprehension, and fluency skills.

2. Ask students the following questions.

   ▶ Why are the flowers drooping and the creeks and rivers dried up at the beginning of the story? It hasn't rained for a long time.

   ▶ Why does the little girl want to find water? She thinks it will make her sick mother feel better.

   ▶ Where does she find water? in the mountains; at a spring

   ▶ What does the little girl do when she passes a thirsty dog on the road? She puts some water in her hand so the dog can lap it up.

   ▶ What happens to the little girl's tin dipper after she gives the dog some water? It turns into silver.

   ▶ What happens to the dipper after the little girl gives the servant some water? It turns into gold.

   ▶ What happens when the stranger spills water on the ground? A fountain of water bubbles up.

TIP If students have trouble responding to a question, help them locate the answer in the text or pictures.

Reading for Meaning

Characteristics of Legends
Check students' understanding of the characteristics of legends.

▶ What kind of story is "The Legend of the Dipper"? a legend

▶ Is it possible that it doesn't rain for so long that flowers droop and rivers dry up? Yes

▶ Is it possible that a little girl could bring back water in a dipper for her mother to drink? Yes

▶ Could a dipper really change from tin to silver or gold? No

▶ Is it possible that a spring would bubble up where someone spilled water on the ground? No

▶ Is it likely that the dipper in the sky is made out of diamonds? No

▶ What does "The Legend of the Dipper" explain? why the dipper is in the night sky

▶ Which parts of the legend do you think could have really happened? Which parts do you think are make-believe? Be sure students' responses match the answers to the previous questions in this activity.

Explore "The Legend of the Dipper"

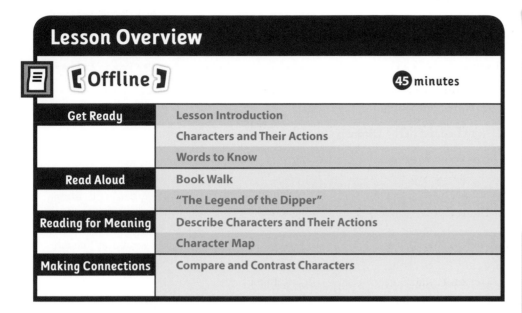

Lesson Overview

【Offline 】 45 minutes

Get Ready	Lesson Introduction
	Characters and Their Actions
	Words to Know
Read Aloud	Book Walk
	"The Legend of the Dipper"
Reading for Meaning	Describe Characters and Their Actions
	Character Map
Making Connections	Compare and Contrast Characters

Advance Preparation

Gather the partially completed page LC 5 (Character Map) in *K¹² Language Arts Activity Book*. Review Reading for Meaning and Making Connections to familiarize yourself with the questions and answers.

Big Ideas

▸ Comprehension entails having and knowing a purpose for reading.
▸ An awareness of story structure elements (setting, characters, plot) provides readers a foundation for constructing meaning when reading new stories and writing their own stories.
▸ To understand and interpret a story, readers need to understand and describe characters and what they do.

【 Materials 】

Supplied

- "The Legend of the Dipper," *K¹² Classics for Young Readers, Volume A*, pp. 2–9
- *K¹² Language Arts Activity Book*, p. LC 5

Keywords

character – a person or animal in a story
compare – to explain how two or more things are alike
contrast – to explain how two or more things are different
main character – an important person, animal, or other being who is central to the plot
story structure elements – components of a story; they include character, setting, plot, problem, and solution

[Offline] 45 minutes

Work **together** with students to complete Get Ready, Read Aloud, Reading for Meaning, and Making Connections activities.

Get Ready

Lesson Introduction

Prepare students for listening to and discussing "The Legend of the Dipper."

1. Tell students that you will reread "The Legend of the Dipper."

2. Explain that before you read the story, you will get ready by reviewing

   ▶ How we can learn about characters from what they say and do
   ▶ What it means to have a purpose for reading and why it's important

Objectives
- Set a purpose for reading.
- Identify character(s).
- Identify the main character(s).
- Identify details that explain characters' actions and feelings.
- Build vocabulary through listening, reading, and discussion.
- Use new vocabulary in written and spoken sentences.

Characters and Their Actions

Explore the story element of character and learn about setting a purpose for reading. Gather the partially completed character map on page LC 5 in *K¹² Language Arts Activity Book*.

1. Have students explain what a character is and what makes a character the main character. If students have trouble explaining, remind them of the following.

   ▶ The people and animals in a story are called **characters**.
   ▶ The character who does and talks the most is the **main character**.

2. Remind students that we can learn a lot about a story's characters from what they say and do.

3. Read aloud the following story.

   Jason, Mario, and Paco are friends who are on the same soccer team. "I just know we're going to win today," said Paco as they put on their gear. "I can just feel it!" During the game, someone passed Paco the ball. He ran down the field and scored a goal at the last minute. His team won the game, just like he thought they would! On their way home, Paco asked his friends to come to his house and celebrate. "Ice cream for everyone!" he shouted.

   ▶ Who are the characters in the story? Jason; Mario; Paco
   ▶ Who is the main, or most important, character in the story? Paco
   ▶ How do you know Paco is the main character? He says and does the most in the story.
   ▶ How do you think Paco feels at the end of the game? excited; happy   Why do you think he feels that way? His team won; he scored the winning goal.
   ▶ Why does Paco ask his friends to come over to his house after the game? because he wants to celebrate winning the game and have ice cream

4. Remind students that good readers have a purpose, or reason for reading a story. A purpose helps them focus on the important information in a story and remember what they read.

5. Explain to students that after they listen to "The Legend of the Dipper," they will complete another part of the **character map** on the Activity Book page. This part of the character map will be about the little girl in "The Legend of the Dipper."

6. Point to and read aloud the statements and questions in the left column and then ask the following question.

   ▸ What do you think is your purpose, or reason for listening to "The Legend of the Dipper?" to get information about the little girl

7. Keep the character map nearby for use during the Reading for Meaning.

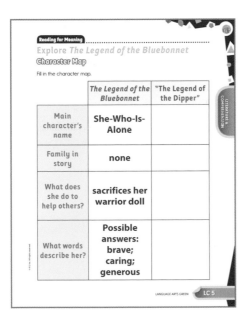

Words to Know

Before reading "The Legend of the Dipper," go over Words to Know with students.

1. Read aloud each word or phrase and have students repeat it.

2. Ask students if they know what each word or phrase means.

   ▸ If students know a word's or phrase's meaning, have them define it and use it in a sentence.
   ▸ If students don't know a word's or phrase's meaning, read them the definition and discuss the word or phrase with them.

by and by – before long; after a while
dipper – a large, deep spoon with a long handle; a ladle
flow – to pour out of
parched – dried up; in need of water
servant – a helper; someone who works in another person's home
spring – a place where water rises up from under the ground
unselfish – generous; giving

Read Aloud

Book Walk

Prepare students by taking them on a Book Walk of "The Legend of the Dipper." Scan the story together to revisit the characters and events.

1. Point to the **table of contents**. Help students find the selection and turn to that page.

2. Read aloud the **story title**.

3. Have students review the **pictures in the story**.

4. Point to the picture of the girl and the thirsty dog on page 5.

   ► Who are these characters? the little girl; the thirsty dog
   ► Why is the dog so thirsty? It hasn't rained in a long time.
   ► Do you think you would share your water with a thirsty dog if you were thirsty, too? Answers will vary.

Objectives
- Activate prior knowledge by previewing text and/or discussing topic.
- Listen and respond to texts representing a variety of cultures, time periods, and traditions.

"The Legend of the Dipper"

It's time to reread "The Legend of the Dipper."

1. Have students sit next to you so that they can see the pictures and words while you read the story aloud.

2. Tell students to listen carefully for information about the characters, especially the little girl.

3. **Read aloud the entire story.** Track with your finger so students can follow along. Emphasize Words to Know as you come to them. If appropriate, use the pictures to help show what each word means.

Reading for Meaning

Describe Characters and Their Actions

Explore the story structure elements of characters and their actions.

1. Have students retell "The Legend of the Dipper" in their own words to develop grammar, vocabulary, comprehension, and fluency skills.

2. Remind students that thinking about **what the characters are like and what they do** can help a reader better understand the characters and the story.

3. Ask the following questions.

   ► Who are some of the characters in the story? the little girl; the mother; the dog; the old servant; the stranger
   ► Who is the main character? the little girl   How do you know she is the main character? She says and does most of the things in the story.

Objectives
- Retell or dramatize a story.
- Identify character(s).
- Identify the main character(s).
- Describe character(s).
- Identify details that explain characters' actions and feelings.
- Demonstrate understanding through graphic organizers.

- ▸ Why does the little girl go looking for water? Her mother is sick, and the little girl thinks water will help her feel better.
- ▸ Why does the little girl share the dipper of water with the dog? She could tell he was thirsty.
- ▸ Why does the mother tell the girl to give some water to the old servant? because the servant had worked hard all day
- ▸ Why does the stranger pour water on the ground? to make a spring bubble up; so all the people and animals will have water
- ▸ Why does the stranger put the dipper in the sky? to remind everyone of the little girl who shared her water with everybody
- ▸ What words could you use to describe the little girl? Possible answers: kind; caring; unselfish; giving

TIP If students have trouble responding to a question, help them locate the answer in the text or pictures.

Character Map

Check students' ability to describe the main character of "The Legend of the Dipper." Gather the partially completed character map on page LC 5 in *K¹² Language Arts Activity Book*.

1. Remind students that they are going to fill out a character map.

2. Point to and read aloud the first statement on the character map.

3. Write what students dictate in the first box under the heading "The Legend of the Dipper."

4. Repeat Steps 2 and 3 until all the boxes are filled in.

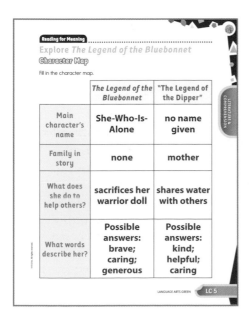

Making Connections

Compare and Contrast Characters

Have students compare and contrast characters from *The Legend of the Bluebonnet* and "The Legend of the Dipper."

1. Tell students that discussing how characters are alike and different helps readers better understand what kind of people the characters are and why they act the way they do.

2. Explain that they will refer to the character map to discuss the characters from two legends. Doing so will help them understand the type of character they might find in a legend.

3. Ask the following questions.

   ▸ How are the two characters alike? Possible answers: They are both main characters; they are both living in a place that is having a drought; both girls do something to help others; the things the girls do cause something special to happen.

   ▸ How are the two characters different? Possible answers: One girl is Native American, and the other one isn't; one character has a name, and the other doesn't; She-Who-Is-Alone doesn't have a family, and the little girl has a mother; She-Who-Is-Alone burns her doll, and the little girl shares water with others.

   ▸ Do you think these two characters are heroes? Why do you think that? Be sure students provide examples from the story to support their answers.

   ▸ What words could you use to describe both characters? Possible answers: helpful; caring; unselfish; kind

TIP Keep page LC 5 in *K¹² Language Arts Activity Book* in a safe place for reference when students read "Medio Pollito: The Little Half-Chick."

Objectives

- Describe character(s).
- Compare and contrast story structure elements across texts.
- Make connections with text: text-to-text, text-to-self, text-to-world.

Introduce "Telling Stories Around the World"

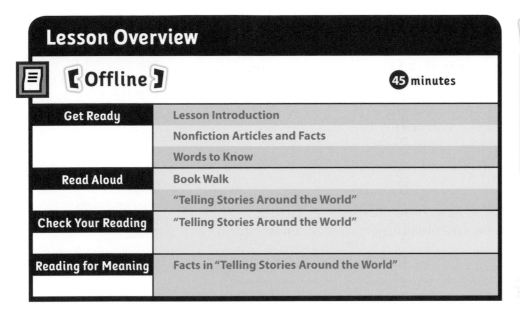

Lesson Overview

[Offline] **45** minutes

Get Ready	Lesson Introduction
	Nonfiction Articles and Facts
	Words to Know
Read Aloud	Book Walk
	"Telling Stories Around the World"
Check Your Reading	"Telling Stories Around the World"
Reading for Meaning	Facts in "Telling Stories Around the World"

Advance Preparation

Read "Telling Stories Around the World" before beginning the Read Aloud to locate Words to Know in the text.

Big Ideas

▶ Exposing readers to a wide variety of genres provides them with a wide range of background knowledge and increases their vocabulary.
▶ Nonfiction texts differ from fiction texts in that they describe real or true things in life, rather than things made up by the author.

[Materials]

Supplied

● "Telling Stories Around the World," *K¹² World: Critter and Creature Stories*, pp. 2–15

Article Synopsis

People have been telling stories since the dawn of time. Storytelling serves many purposes, such as passing on cultural history and beliefs, explaining the world around us, and entertaining friends and family.

Keywords

fact – something that can be proven true
genre – a category for classifying literary works
informational text – text written to explain and give information on a topic
nonfiction – writings about true things

 **45** minutes

Work **together** with students to complete Get Ready, Read Aloud, Check Your Reading, and Reading for Meaning activities.

Get Ready

Lesson Introduction

Prepare students for listening to and discussing "Telling Stories Around the World."

1. Tell students that you are going to read "Telling Stories Around the World," a nonfiction magazine article that explains why and how different groups of people tell stories.

2. Explain that before you read the article, you will get ready by

   ▸ Learning about a kind of writing called nonfiction
   ▸ Talking about what makes a fact

 Objectives
- Identify facts.
- Build vocabulary through listening, reading, and discussion.
- Use new vocabulary in written and spoken sentences.
- Increase concept and content vocabulary.

Nonfiction Articles and Facts

Introduce the genre of nonfiction and what makes a fact.

1. Explain that magazine articles are often about real things. This kind of writing is called **nonfiction**. It is also called **informational text**.

2. If something is true and real, it is called a **fact**. Nonfiction articles are about real things, so they are filled with facts.

3. If you can't prove something is true, it can't be called a fact. It's important to recognize facts so that we can know if information is true or not.

4. Discuss the following questions about facts with students.

   ▸ What is your name? Your name is a fact. You can prove what your name is.
   ▸ Can apples can be red, yellow, or green? Yes. You can prove that apples can be red, yellow, or green, so it is a fact.
   ▸ Can a cow jump over the moon? No. You can't prove that a cow can jump over the moon, so it is not a fact.

TIP Although an objective for this lesson is to identify genre, there is no need to introduce the term to students at this time.

Words to Know

Before reading "Telling Stories Around the World," go over Words to Know with students.

1. Read aloud each word and have students repeat it.

2. Ask students if they know what each word means.

   ► If students know a word's meaning, have them define it and use it in a sentence.

   ► If students don't know a word's meaning, read them the definition and discuss the word with them.

actor – a person whose job is to act

belief – an idea or feeling that is accepted as true

griot – a professional storyteller in West Africa who retells the history and traditions of a group of people

leprechaun – in Irish stories, a small man who has magical powers

ordinary – normal or regular

response – an answer or reply

tradition – the beliefs and ways of doing things that are passed from parents to children within a community over many years

train – to teach a person or animal how to do something

Read Aloud

Book Walk

Prepare students by taking them on a Book Walk of "Telling Stories Around the World." Scan the magazine article together and ask students to make predictions about the text. Answers to questions may vary.

1. Tell students that the list of titles at the beginning of a magazine or book is called the **table of contents**. The table of contents in a magazine tells which articles are in the magazine and the page number where each article begins.

2. Have students locate the table of contents in *Critter and Creature Stories*. Help them find the selection and turn to that page.

3. Point to and read aloud the **title of the article**.

4. Have students look at the **pictures in the article**.

   ► What do you think the article is about?
   ► Do you like to listen to stories? What is your favorite story?

5. Point to and read aloud any headers, captions, or other features that stand out.

   ► What do you think the article might tell us about stories and the people who tell them?

Objectives

- Identify the function of and locate information with a table of contents.
- Activate prior knowledge by previewing text and/or discussing topic.
- Make predictions based on text, illustrations, and/or prior knowledge.
- Read and listen to a variety of texts for information and pleasure independently or as part of a group.

"Telling Stories Around the World"

It's time to read aloud the article.

1. Have students sit next to you so that they can see the pictures and words while you read aloud.

2. Tell students to listen for facts, or things that are true.

3. **Read aloud the entire article.** Track with your finger so students can follow along. Emphasize Words to Know as you come to them. If appropriate, use the pictures to help show what each word means.

Check Your Reading

"Telling Stories Around the World"

Check students' comprehension of "Telling Stories Around the World."

1. Have students retell "Telling Stories Around the World" in their own words to develop grammar, vocabulary, comprehension, and fluency skills.

2. Ask students the following questions.

   ▸ What is a table of contents? a list of titles at the beginning of a magazine or a book   Why would we use a table of contents in a magazine? to find the page that an article starts on

   ▸ According to the article, what is something people in the past did for fun, since they didn't have television or computers? tell stories

   ▸ Why do people tell "how" and "why" stories, such as why the giraffe has a long neck? to explain things; to make sense of the world

   ▸ Many African stories are about a character called Anansi. What kind of animal is Anansi? a spider

   ▸ Some Native American stories tell about a character who is very smart and tricky. What is the name of this animal character? Coyote

   ▸ What group of people told stories about leprechauns? the Irish

TIP If students have trouble responding to a question, help them locate the answer in the article's text or pictures.

Objectives

- Retell or dramatize a story.
- Identify the function of and locate information with a table of contents.
- Answer questions requiring literal recall of details.

Reading for Meaning

Facts in "Telling Stories Around the World"

Explore facts in nonfiction articles.

Objectives

- Identify genre.
- Identify facts.
- Identify facts in informational text.

1. Remind students that many magazine articles are about real things and include facts.

2. Ask students the following questions.

   ▶ The article "Telling Stories Around the World" tells about real things. What do we call this kind of writing? nonfiction

   ▶ What do we call something that we can prove is true? a fact

   ▶ Long ago in Ireland, there were trained storytellers who worked for the chiefs and princes. Is this a fact? Yes   How do you know it's a fact? You can prove it; it's true.

   ▶ What kind of stories did the people in Ireland like to hear? stories about magical creatures   Is this a fact? Yes

   ▶ Native Americans tell stories about the animals that live around them. Is this a fact? Yes

   ▶ Telling stories is part of African tradition. Is this a fact? Yes   How do you know it's a fact? You can prove it; it's true.

   ▶ Where can you hear storytellers today? Possible answers: at home; at the library; on TV; on the radio; at school

Explore "Telling Stories Around the World"

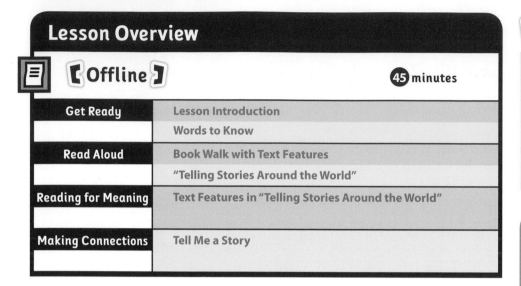

Lesson Overview

[Offline]   45 minutes

Get Ready	Lesson Introduction
	Words to Know
Read Aloud	Book Walk with Text Features
	"Telling Stories Around the World"
Reading for Meaning	Text Features in "Telling Stories Around the World"
Making Connections	Tell Me a Story

Advance Preparation

Review Reading for Meaning and Making Connections to familiarize yourself with the questions and answers.

Big Ideas

Comprehension is facilitated by an understanding of physical presentation (for example, headings, subheads, graphics, and other features).

[Materials]

Supplied

- "Telling Stories Around the World," *K¹² World: Critter and Creature Stories*, pp. 2–15
- *K¹² My Journal*, pp. 2–53

Keywords

informational text – text written to explain and give information on a topic

text feature – part of a text that helps a reader locate information and determine what is most important; some examples are the title, table of contents, headings, pictures, and glossary

 **Offline** ⓽ minutes

Work **together** with students to complete Get Ready, Read Aloud, Reading for Meaning, and Making Connections activities.

Get Ready ·

Lesson Introduction

Prepare students for listening to and discussing "Telling Stories Around the World."

1. Tell students that you are going to reread an article about storytelling traditions of different groups of people.

2. Explain that before you read the article, you will get ready by

   ► Learning about the features of nonfiction articles
   ► Talking about the information each type of text feature provides

> **Objectives**
> * Build vocabulary through listening, reading, and discussion.
> * Use new vocabulary in written and spoken sentences.
> * Increase concept and content vocabulary.

Words to Know

Before reading "Telling Stories Around the World," go over Words to Know with students.

1. Read aloud each word and have students repeat it.

2. Ask students if they know what each word means.

   ► If students know a word's meaning, have them define it and use it in a sentence.
   ► If students don't know a word's meaning, read them the definition and discuss the word with them.

actor – a person whose job is to act

belief – an idea or feeling that is accepted as true

griot – a professional storyteller in West Africa who retells the history and traditions of a group of people

leprechaun – in Irish stories, a small man who has magical powers

ordinary – normal or regular

response – an answer or reply

tradition – the beliefs and ways of doing things that are passed from parents to children within a community over many years

train – to teach a person or animal how to do something

Read Aloud •

Book Walk with Text Features

Prepare students by taking them on a Book Walk of "Telling Stories Around the World." Scan the magazine article together to revisit the text and point out text features.

1. Turn to the article.

2. Tell students that magazine articles have features that help readers better understand the information in the article.

3. Turn to page 2 and point to the title of the article. Explain that the title usually tells us what the article is about.

4. Point to the picture on page 7. Explain that pictures help show ideas that are in the article.
   Say: This picture shows someone telling a story. It helps the reader better understand what storytelling is and what the article is about.

5. Point to the text near the picture on page 6. Tell students that the text near the picture is called a *caption*. It gives information about the picture. Read aloud the caption.

6. Point to the word *tradition* on page 7. Explain that some words in the article are darker, or bold, so that we will notice them. This word is bold because it's an important word in the article. We can find out what this word means in the back of the magazine on page 44.

7. Turn to page 7 and point to the heading. Explain that articles can be broken up into sections, and a heading tells what a section is about. An article's headings can help us figure out where to find certain information.
   Say: This heading tells readers that this section of the article is about African stories. If I want to find information about African stories, this is the section I would look in.

8. Turn to page 10 and point to and read aloud the heading.

   ▶ What do you think this part of the article is about? Native American stories

9. Point to the picture at the top of page 11 and read aloud the caption.

   ▶ What is the text near the picture called? a caption   What does this caption tell us? that Coyote is a character in Native American stories

---

"Telling Stories Around the World"

It's time to reread the article.

1. Have students sit next to you so that they can see the pictures and words while you read the aloud.

2. Tell students to think about how the features of an article help readers better understand the information in the article.

3. **Read aloud the entire article.** Track with your finger so students can follow along. Emphasize Words to Know as you come to them. If appropriate, use the pictures to help show what each word means.

Objectives

- Activate prior knowledge by previewing text and/or discussing topic.
- Identify features of informational text.
- Identify purpose of and information provided by informational text features.
- Read and listen to a variety of texts for information and pleasure independently or as part of a group.

Reading for Meaning

Text Features in "Telling Stories Around the World"
Explore text features in magazine articles.

1. Remind students that good readers use text features, such as headings, pictures, and captions, to better understand the information in a magazine article.

2. Point to the picture on page 4 of the magazine and read aloud the caption next to it.

   ▸ What information does this picture and caption give us? They tell us that a story might explain why blue flowers cover the hills of Texas.

3. Point to and read aloud the heading on page 10.

   ▸ What is this called? a heading
   ▸ What does this heading tell us? that this part of the article is about Native American stories

4. Point to the picture on page 11 and read aloud the caption above it.

   ▸ What information does this picture and caption give us? what goes on at a powwow and that storytelling is part of powwows

5. Where should I look if I want to read about Irish stories? pages 12 and 13

6. Point to the word *leprechauns* on page 13.

   ▸ Why is this word darker than the other words? It's an important word in the article. Where can we find out what this word means? in the back of the magazine

7. Point to the pictures on page 14 and read aloud the caption near them.

   ▸ Why do you think these pictures are part of the article? Guide students to understand that they show how we still like to listen to stories today, and how much fun stories are.

Objectives
- Identify features of informational text.
- Identify purpose of and information provided by informational text features.
- Locate information using features of text and electronic media.

Making Connections

Tell Me a Story
Have students describe a favorite story. Gather *K¹² My Journal* and have students turn to the next available page for **writing** in Thoughts and Experiences.

1. Tell students that family members like to tell stories, especially at family gatherings, such as Thanksgiving Day.

2. Explain that family stories might be about ancestors, family members, and funny things that have happened over the years. They are good memories that are shared over and over again.

Objectives
- Respond to text through art, writing, and/or drama.
- Make connections with text: text-to-text, text-to-self, text-to-world.

3. Ask students if there is a story that someone in their family likes to tell whenever their family gets together. Example story topics could be "how your parents met," "the day you were born," or "the day of the big blizzard."
Say: Do you have a favorite family story that you like to listen to? If somebody is going to tell you a story, what story do you ask to hear?

4. Have students tell the story. If students are having trouble getting started, you might share one of your favorite family stories.

5. Have them say a few sentences about their favorite story.

   ▸ A possible sentence starter could be, "My favorite story is about . . . ."

6. Write the words students dictate.

   ▸ If students are ready to write on their own, allow them to do so.

7. Have students read aloud the completed sentence(s) **with** you as you track the words with your finger.

TIP The amount of time students need to complete this activity will vary. Students need only work for the remainder of the lesson time.

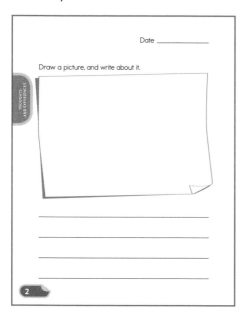

Introduce "Medio Pollito: The Little Half-Chick"

Lesson Overview

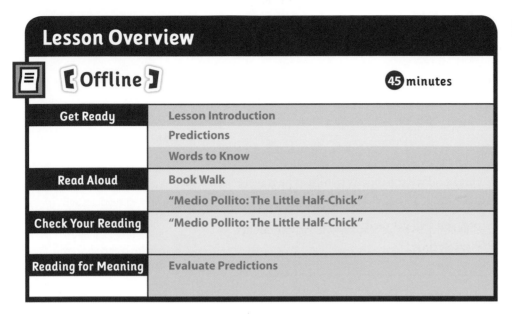

Offline			**45** minutes
Get Ready	Lesson Introduction		
	Predictions		
	Words to Know		
Read Aloud	Book Walk		
	"Medio Pollito: The Little Half-Chick"		
Check Your Reading	"Medio Pollito: The Little Half-Chick"		
Reading for Meaning	Evaluate Predictions		

Advance Preparation

Read "Medio Pollito: The Little Half-Chick" before beginning the Read Aloud to locate Words to Know in the text.

Big Ideas

Good readers interact with text to make logical predictions before reading; confirm predictions during reading; and revise or make new predictions as they read further.

Materials

Supplied

- "Medio Pollito: The Little Half-Chick," *K¹² Classics for Young Readers, Volume A*, pp. 10–25

Story Synopsis

Medio Pollito might be only half a chick, but he has twice the attitude! One day, he decides he's had enough of dull country life and heads to the big city to meet the king. The little half-chick soon learns the consequences of being unwilling to help others in need as he hops along the road to Madrid.

Keywords

prediction – a guess about what might happen that is based on information in a story and what you already know

 **45** minutes

Work **together** with students to complete Get Ready, Read Aloud, Check Your Reading, and Reading for Meaning activities.

Get Ready

Lesson Introduction

Prepare students for listening to and discussing "Medio Pollito: The Little Half-Chick."

1. Tell students that you are going to read "Medio Pollito: The Little Half-Chick," a story about an odd little chick and what happens to him as he travels to Madrid.

2. Explain that before you read the story, you will get ready by discussing how and why we make predictions when we read.

Objectives
- Make predictions based on text, illustrations, and/or prior knowledge.
- Build vocabulary through listening, reading, and discussion.
- Use new vocabulary in written and spoken sentences.

Predictions

Explore how and why readers make predictions when they read.

1. Have students explain what predictions are and how we make them when we read. If students have trouble responding, remind them of the following.

   ▸ **Predictions** are guesses about what will happen in a story.
   ▸ We use clues in the story and what we know from our personal experience to make predictions.

2. Have students explain why we make predictions.

   ▸ If students have trouble responding, remind them that making predictions makes us want to keep reading a story to see if what we predict happens or not.

3. Read aloud the following story.

   Marla was hungry, so she went in the kitchen to make a sandwich. Just as she was about to take a bite out of it, the doorbell rang.

   ▸ What do you think will happen next? Possible answers: Marla will put down the sandwich and go answer the door; Marla will go ahead and eat the sandwich.
   ▸ What clues in the story or your own experience made you predict this? The doorbell rang so somebody needs to answer the door; I know when I'm hungry, I want to eat right away.

TIP Predictions are neither right nor wrong. We make the best prediction we can, based on the available information. Do not describe a prediction as "wrong" because this may discourage students from making predictions.

Words to Know

Before reading "Medio Pollito: The Little Half-Chick," go over Words to Know with students.

1. Read aloud each word and have students repeat it.

2. Ask students if they know what each word means.

   ▶ If students know a word's meaning, have them define it and use it in a sentence.
   ▶ If students don't know a word's meaning, read them the definition and discuss the word with them.

advice – a suggestion about what to do in a particular situation
odd – strange; not ordinary
peculiar – unusual; different
perch – to sit in a high place
pity – to feel sorry for someone or something
rude – not polite; unkind
steeple – the pointed top of a tower

Read Aloud

Book Walk

Prepare students for reading by taking them on a Book Walk of "Medio Pollito: The Little Half-Chick." Scan the **beginning of the story together** and ask students to make predictions. Answers to questions may vary.

1. Point to the **table of contents**. Help students find the selection and turn to that page.

2. Point to and read aloud the **title of the story**.

   ▶ What do you think the story is about?

3. Have students look at the **picture on the first page of the story**.

   ▶ Where do you think the story takes place?
   ▶ What do you think might happen in the story?
   ▶ Do you think it's important to help others?
   ▶ Did you ever need help but no one would stop to help you?

Objectives

- Activate prior knowledge by previewing text and/or discussing topic.
- Make predictions based on text, illustrations, and/or prior knowledge.
- Make predictions before and during reading.
- Listen and respond to texts representing a variety of cultures, time periods, and traditions.

"Medio Pollito: The Little Half-Chick"

It's time to read aloud the story.

1. Have students sit next to you so that they can see the pictures and words while you read aloud.

2. **Begin to read aloud.** Pause at the following points in the story to ask students what they predict will happen next. Jot down their predictions for later reference.

   ▶ Page 10: after Medio Pollito is born
   ▶ Page 17: after the fire asks Medio Pollito for help
   ▶ Page 18: after the wind asks Medio Pollito for help
   ▶ Page 21: after Medio Pollito asks the fire not to burn him
   ▶ Page 22: when Medio Pollito asks the wind to let him rest

3. **Continue to read aloud the story.**

   ▶ Track with your finger so students can follow along.
   ▶ Emphasize Words to Know as you come to them. If appropriate, use the pictures to help show what each word means.
   ▶ Remember to stop at the points listed above and have students make predictions.

 Medio Pollito is pronounced MAY-dee-oh poh-YEE-toh.

Check Your Reading

"Medio Pollito: The Little Half-Chick"

Check students' comprehension of "Medio Pollito: The Little Half-Chick."

1. Have students retell "Medio Pollito: The Little Half-Chick" in their own words to develop grammar, vocabulary, comprehension, and fluency skills.

2. Ask students the following questions.

   ▶ What does Medio Pollito look like? like half a chick, with only one leg, one wing, and one eye
   ▶ How does Medio Pollito get around? He hops on his one leg.
   ▶ Why does Medio Pollito want to go to Madrid? He thinks the farm is dull; he wants to see the king.
   ▶ Why does the fire by the road need help? It's about to go out.
   ▶ Why does the wind ask Medio Pollito for help? It is caught in the branches of a tree.
   ▶ What does the king's cook do with Medio Pollito? He puts Medio Pollito in the soup pot.
   ▶ What does the wind do with Medio Pollito at the end of the story? It blows him through town and puts him on top of a church steeple.

 Objectives
- Retell or dramatize a story.
- Answer questions requiring literal recall of details.

 If students have trouble responding to a question, help them locate the answer in the text or pictures.

Reading for Meaning

Evaluate Predictions

Revisit the predictions students made while listening to "Medio Pollito: The Little Half-Chick."

1. Remind students that good readers make predictions when they read.

2. Ask them the following questions to review and discuss the predictions students made while listening to the story. **Refer to the predictions you jotted down, as necessary.** Answers to questions may vary.

   ▸ What did you predict would happen after Medio Pollito is born? What information did you use to predict that?

   ▸ What did you predict would happen after the fire asks Medio Pollito for help? Were you surprised by what really happens?

   ▸ What did you predict would happen after the wind asks Medio Pollito for help? What clues from the story and your personal experience helped you make this prediction?

   ▸ What did you predict would happen after Medio Pollito asks the fire to stop burning him? Why did you predict that?

   ▸ What did you predict would happen after Medio Pollito asks the wind to let him rest? Were you surprised by what the wind does to Medio Pollito?

Explore "Medio Pollito: The Little Half-Chick"

Lesson Overview

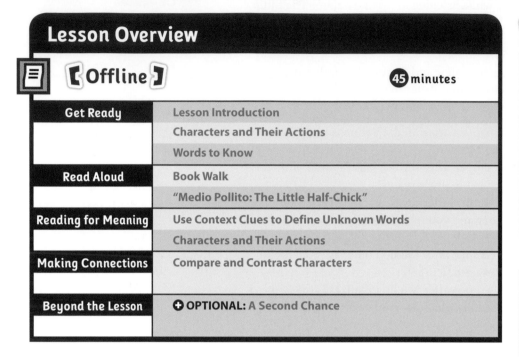

Offline		**45** minutes
Get Ready	Lesson Introduction	
	Characters and Their Actions	
	Words to Know	
Read Aloud	Book Walk	
	"Medio Pollito: The Little Half-Chick"	
Reading for Meaning	Use Context Clues to Define Unknown Words	
	Characters and Their Actions	
Making Connections	Compare and Contrast Characters	
Beyond the Lesson	⊕ OPTIONAL: A Second Chance	

Materials

Supplied
- "Medio Pollito: The Little Half-Chick," *K¹² Classics for Young Readers, Volume A,* pp. 10–25
- *K¹² Language Arts Activity Book,* pp. LC 5–6
- *K¹² My Journal,* pp. 2–53 (optional)

Keywords

character – a person or animal in a story

compare – to explain how two or more things are alike

context – the parts of a sentence or passage surrounding a word

contrast – to explain how two or more things are different

story structure elements – components of a story; they include character, setting, plot, problem, and solution

Advance Preparation

Gather completed page LC 5 (Character Map) in *K¹² Language Arts Activity Book.* Review Reading for Meaning and Making Connections to familiarize yourself with the questions and answers.

Big Ideas

▸ To understand and interpret a story, readers need to understand and describe characters and what they do.

▸ Early learners acquire vocabulary through active exposure (by talking and listening, being read to, and receiving explicit instruction).

 **45 minutes**

Work **together** with students to complete Get Ready, Read Aloud, Reading for Meaning, Making Connections, and Beyond the Lesson activities.

Get Ready

Lesson Introduction

Prepare students for listening to and discussing "Medio Pollito: The Little Half-Chick."

1. Tell students that you are going to reread "Medio Pollito: The Little Half-Chick."

2. Explain that before you reread the story, you will get ready by reviewing characters and what we can learn about characters from what they say and do.

Characters and Their Actions

Review the story structure element of characters and their actions.

1. Have students explain what a character is and what makes a character the main character. If students have trouble answering, remind them of the following.

   ▸ The people and animals in a story are called **characters**.
   ▸ The character who does and talks the most is the **main character**.

2. Remind students that we can learn a lot about a story's characters from what they say and do.

3. Read aloud the following story.

   Sasha and her friend, Tran, sat down at a table in the library to study. When Sasha put her backpack under the table, she saw a set of car keys on the floor. "Look what I found!" Sasha said to Tran as she held up the keys. "I think I should give these keys to the librarian so he can put them in the lost and found." Sasha went to the counter and explained to the librarian where she found the keys. "I sure hope the person who lost those keys figures out where they are!" she said to Tran when she sat back down at the table.

   ▸ Who are the characters in the story? Sasha; Tran; the librarian
   ▸ Who is the main, or most important, character in the story? Sasha
   ▸ What does Sasha do after she finds the keys? She shows them to Tran; she gives them to the librarian.
   ▸ Why does Sasha give the keys to the librarian? so he can put them in the lost and found
   ▸ How do you think Sasha feels about the person who lost keys? worried

Objectives
- Identify character(s).
- Identify the main character(s).
- Describe character(s).
- Identify details that explain characters' actions and feelings.
- Build vocabulary through listening, reading, and discussion.
- Use new vocabulary in written and spoken sentences.

Words to Know

Before reading "Medio Pollito: The Little Half-Chick," go over Words to Know with students.

1. Read aloud each word and have students repeat it.

2. Ask students if they know what each word means.

   ▸ If students know a word's meaning, have them define it and use it in a sentence.
   ▸ If students don't know a word's meaning, read them the definition and discuss the word with them.

advice – a suggestion about what to do in a particular situation
odd – strange; not ordinary
peculiar – unusual; different
perch – to sit in a high place
pity – to feel sorry for someone or something
rude – impolite; unkind
steeple – the pointed top of a tower

Read Aloud

Book Walk

Prepare students by taking them on a Book Walk of "Medio Pollito: The Little Half-Chick." Scan the book together to revisit the characters and events.

1. Point to the **table of contents**. Help students find the selection and turn to that page.

2. Read aloud the **story title**.

3. Have students review the **pictures**.

4. Point to the **picture on the first page of the story**.

   ▸ Who are these characters? Medio Pollito; his mother; the other chicks
   ▸ What do you remember about Medio Pollito? Possible answers: He wants to go to Madrid; he doesn't help others; he's rude; he gets thrown in a soup pot.
   ▸ Do you think it would be fun to go somewhere by yourself? Where would you like to go? Answers will vary.

Objectives

• Activate prior knowledge by previewing text and/or discussing topic.
• Listen and respond to texts representing a variety of cultures, time periods, and traditions.

"Medio Pollito: The Little Half-Chick"

It's time to reread the story.

1. Have students sit next to you so that they can see the pictures and words while you read the story aloud.

2. Tell students to listen for who the characters are and what they do.

3. **Read aloud the entire story.** Track with your finger so students can follow along. Emphasize Words to Know as you come to them. If appropriate, use the pictures to help show what each word means.

Use Context Clues to Define Unknown Words

Check students' ability to use text and picture clues to determine a word's meaning.

1. Have students retell "Medio Pollito: The Little Half-Chick" in their own words to develop grammar, vocabulary, comprehension, and fluency skills.

2. Remind students that good readers can sometimes figure out the meaning of unknown words by listening to nearby words and looking at the pictures.

3. Read aloud the following sentences from the story.

    "His brothers and sisters were all good, obedient chickens. When their mother clucked at them, those 12 chicks chirped and ran to her side."

    ▶ What does the word *obedient* mean? does what one is told   What clue is in the text? The text says that the brothers and sisters were good chicks, and they ran to their mother when she clucked at them.

4. Turn to page 16 and have students look at the picture at the top of the page. Read aloud the following sentence from the story.

    "The stream was choked and overgrown with weeds, so its waters could not flow freely."

    ▶ What does the phrase *choked and overgrown* mean? plugged up; blocked   How do the text and picture help you figure this out? The story says the "waters could not flow freely," and the picture shows lots of weeds growing in the stream.

5. Turn to page 18 and have students look at the picture at the top of the page. Read aloud the following sentences from the story.

    "There, the wind was caught and entangled in the tree's branches. 'Oh! Medio Pollito,' called the wind. 'Please climb up here and help me get free of these branches. I cannot get away, and it is so uncomfortable.'"

    ▶ What does the word *entangled* mean? twisted up; tangled   What clues are in the text and the picture? The wind says it can't get away, and the picture shows the wind twisted around and tangled in the tree branches.

6. Turn to page 24 and have the students look at the picture on the page. Read aloud the following sentence from the story.

    "There, the wind left the half-chick fastened to the top of the steeple."

    ▶ What does the word *fastened* mean? stuck to   How do the text and picture help you figure this out? The story says the wind fastened the half-chick to the top of the steeple, and the picture shows Medio Pollito stuck on top of it.

Objectives

- Retell or dramatize a story.
- Use context and sentence structure to determine meaning of words, phrases, and/or sentences.
- Use illustrations to aid understanding of text.
- Identify character(s).
- Identify the main character(s).
- Describe character(s).
- Identify details that explain characters' actions and feelings.

Characters and Their Actions

Explore characters and their actions.

1. Remind students that thinking about **what the characters are like and what they do** can help a reader better understand the characters and the story.

2. Ask the following questions.

   ▸ Who are some of the characters in the story? Medio Pollito; his mother; the other chicks; the stream (or the water); the fire; the wind; the cook

   ▸ Who is the main character? How do you know? Medio Pollito, because he does and talks the most in the story

   ▸ What does Medio Pollito look like when he's born? a black and yellow chick that's cut in half

   ▸ Why does the water ask Medio Pollito to help clear away the weeds? because the water is choking   What does Medio Pollito do? He tells the water that he doesn't want to waste his time helping him.

   ▸ Why does the fire ask Medio Pollito to put some sticks and dry leaves on him? because the fire is about to go out   What does Medio Pollito do? He tells the fire he has better things to do.

   ▸ Why does the cook put Medio Pollito in a soup pot? to make chicken broth   What do the fire and the water do when Medio Pollito is in the soup pot and he asks them to stop hurting him? They tell Medio Pollito that he's being punished for not helping them, and they don't help him.

   ▸ Why does the wind blow Medio Pollito up to the top of a steeple? to punish Medio Pollito for not helping him when he was caught in the tree

   ▸ Why are the water, the fire, and the wind so angry with Medio Pollito? He didn't help them when they needed help.

TIP If students have trouble responding to a question, help them locate the answer in the text or pictures.

Making Connections

Compare and Contrast Characters

Help students compare Medio Pollito to the little girl in "The Legend of the Dipper." They will explore how characters in the two stories are alike and different. Gather the completed character map on page LC 5 and turn to page LC 6 in *K¹² Language Arts Activity Book*.

1. Refer to the completed character map and have students review what they said about the little girl in "The Legend of the Dipper."

2. In the Compare and Contrast Characters chart, point to and read aloud the first column heading, "Words that describe."

3. Write what students dictate in the first row of boxes for the appropriate characters' names.

4. Repeat Steps 3 and 4 until the chart is completed.

Objectives

- Compare and contrast story structure elements across texts.
- Describe character(s).
- Identify details that explain characters' actions and feelings.
- Demonstrate understanding through graphic organizers.
- Demonstrate understanding through drawing, discussion, drama, and/or writing.

5. Ask the following questions to encourage discussion and comparisons of the two characters.

 ▸ How are the two characters alike? They both meet other characters on the road.

 ▸ How are the two characters different? Possible answers: Medio Pollito is selfish and doesn't help others; the little girl is nice and helps other people; something bad happens to Medio Pollito; something good happens to the little girl.

 ▸ Why do you think something bad happens to Medio Pollito at the end of the story? because he is mean and doesn't help others

 ▸ Why do you think good things happen to the little girl at the end of "The Legend of the Dipper"? because she is nice and helps others

 ▸ If you could be friends with one of these characters, which would you choose? Why? Be sure to have students give examples from the stories to support their answer.

Reward: Add a sticker for this unit on the My Accomplishments chart to mark successful completion of the unit.

Reading for Meaning

Explore *The Legend of the Bluebonnet*
Character Map

Fill in the character map.

	The Legend of the Bluebonnet	"The Legend of the Dipper"
Main character's name	She-Who-Is-Alone	no name given
Family in story	none	mother
What does she do to help others?	sacrifices her warrior doll	shares water with others
What words describe her?	Possible answers: brave; caring; generous	Possible answers: kind; helpful; caring

LANGUAGE ARTS GREEN   LC 5

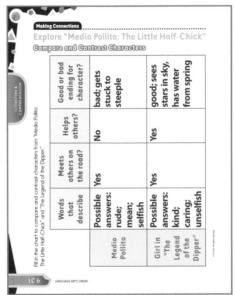

Making Connections

Explore "Medio Pollito: The Little Half-Chick"
Compare and Contrast Characters

Fill in the chart to compare and contrast characters from "Medio Pollito: The Little Half-Chick" and "The Legend of the Dipper."

	Words that describe	Meets others on the road?	Helps others?	Good or bad ending for character?
Medio Pollito	Possible answers: rude; mean; selfish	Yes	No	bad; gets stuck to steeple
Girl in "The Legend of the Dipper"	Possible answers: kind; caring; unselfish	Yes	Yes	good; sees stars in sky, has water from spring

LC 6   LANGUAGE ARTS GREEN

Beyond the Lesson

✛ OPTIONAL: A Second Chance

This activity is OPTIONAL. It is intended for students who have extra time and would benefit from predicting what would happen next in "Medio Pollito: The Little Half-Chick" if the story were to continue. Feel free to skip this activity. Gather *K¹² My Journal* and have students turn to the next available page for **writing** in Thoughts and Experiences.

Objectives

- Demonstrate understanding through drawing, discussion, drama, and/or writing.
- Make predictions based on text, illustrations, and/or prior knowledge.

1. Tell students the weather vane breaks during a bad storm, and Medio Pollito is free again!

2. Ask students to predict what will happen next. Have them think about the following questions.

   ▸ Will Medio Pollito feel bad for the way he treated others and apologize to the water, the fire, and the wind?
   ▸ Will Medio Pollito hop back to the palace to try and see the king again?
   ▸ Will Medio Pollito be just as rude as he was before, or will he use his second chance to be kind?
   ▸ Will Medio Pollito decide he's had enough of the city and hop back home to his mother?

3. Write down what students dictate.

4. Have students read aloud their prediction **with** you as you track the words with your finger.

There's Magic in the Air

Unit Focus

In this unit, students will explore poems and stories with magical elements. This unit follows the read-aloud instructional approach (see the instructional approaches to reading in the introductory lesson for this program). In this unit, students will

- ► Listen to poems and stories.
- ► Explore the genre of poetry and the characteristics of poems.
- ► Explore the strategy of visualizing.
- ► Explore the strategy of making predictions.
- ► Learn about cause and effect.
- ► Practice identifying setting.
- ► Use picture clues to identify setting and define unknown words.
- ► Learn about the order of events in a story.

Unit Plan   [Offline]

Lesson 1	Explore "Wynken, Blynken, and Nod"	**45** minutes a day
Lesson 2	Introduce *Sylvester and the Magic Pebble*	
Lesson 3	Explore *Sylvester and the Magic Pebble*	
Lesson 4	Explore "The Owl and the Pussycat"	
Lesson 5	Introduce "King Midas"	
Lesson 6	Explore "King Midas"	
Lesson 7	Your Choice	

Explore "Wynken, Blynken, and Nod"

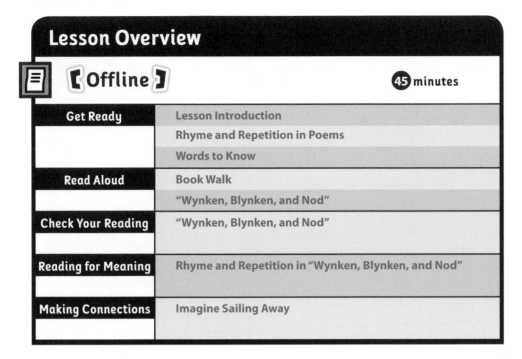

Lesson Overview

[Offline]   45 minutes

Get Ready	Lesson Introduction
	Rhyme and Repetition in Poems
	Words to Know
Read Aloud	Book Walk
	"Wynken, Blynken, and Nod"
Check Your Reading	"Wynken, Blynken, and Nod"
Reading for Meaning	Rhyme and Repetition in "Wynken, Blynken, and Nod"
Making Connections	Imagine Sailing Away

Materials

Supplied

- *Listen, My Children: Poems for First Graders*, pp. 16–18
- *K¹² Language Arts Activity Book*, p. LC 7

Also Needed

- whiteboard (optional)
- crayons

Poetry Synopsis

This well-loved poem describes three youngsters and their nocturnal fishing expedition in the night sky.

Keywords

genre – a category for classifying literary works

repetition – the use of a word or phrase more than once

rhyme – when two or more words have the same ending sounds; for example, *cat* and *hat* rhyme

stanza – a group of lines in a poem

visualize – to picture things in your mind as you read

Advance Preparation

Write the poem in the Get Ready on a whiteboard or sheet of paper. Read "Wynken, Blynken, and Nod" before beginning the Read Aloud to locate Words to Know in the text.

Big Ideas

- ▸ Exposing readers to a wide variety of genres provides them with a wide range of background knowledge and increases their vocabulary.
- ▸ Poems are different from prose in structure and content. They are generally organized in lines and often contain rhymes.
- ▸ Readers who visualize, or form mental pictures, while they read have better recall of text than those who do not.

[Offline] 45 minutes

Work **together** with students to complete Get Ready, Read Aloud, Check Your Reading, Reading for Meaning, and Making Connections activities.

Get Ready ....

Lesson Introduction

Prepare students for listening to and discussing "Wynken, Blynken, and Nod."

1. Tell students that you are going to read a poem about three characters that go on a nighttime fishing expedition.

2. Explain that before you read the poem, you'll get ready by discussing

   ▸ A type of writing called poetry
   ▸ How poems often have words that rhyme and words that are very descriptive
   ▸ How poems sometimes have words or lines that are repeated over and over

> **Objectives**
> - Identify structure of poems and poetic elements: rhyme, rhythm, repetition, and/or alliteration.
> - Identify genre.
> - Build vocabulary through listening, reading, and discussion.
> - Use new vocabulary in written and spoken sentences.

Rhyme and Repetition in Poems

Explore the genre of poetry and the poetic elements of rhyme and repetition.

1. Tell students that there are many kinds of writing. One kind is called **poetry**. Poems make up this kind of writing.

2. Explain that there are certain things about poems that help us recognize that they are poems.

   ▸ Poems are often written in short lines grouped together.
   ▸ Poems also often have descriptive words that help readers imagine things in their minds.
   ▸ Poems often have words that **rhyme**.

3. Explain that another thing we might find in many poems is **repetition**, or words that are said over and over. Poets repeat words to make them stand out so that the reader knows what's important. Repeated words also make the poem fun to listen to.

4. **Read aloud the following poem** from a whiteboard or sheet of paper. Tell students to listen for words that are said over and over, and for words that rhyme. **Point to the words that rhyme at the ends of lines as you come to them**.

"I don't want to feed the cat."
So says stubborn Stan.
"I don't like to wear a hat."
So says stubborn Stan.
"I don't want to sweep the mat."
So says stubborn Stan.

> ► What words rhyme with *cat*? *hat* and *mat*
> ► What words are said over and over in the poem? *I don't want to* and *So says stubborn Stan*
> ► What do we call the kind of writing that is written in short lines grouped together, has rhyming words at the ends of lines, and has words that are said over and over? poetry; a poem

5. Read aloud the poem again, encouraging students to chime in when you come to repeated words.

Words to Know

Before reading "Wynken, Blynken, and Nod," go over Words to Know with students.

1. Read aloud each word and have students repeat it.

2. Ask students if they know what each word means.

> ► If students know a word's meaning, have them define it and use it in a sentence.
> ► If students don't know a word's meaning, read them the definition and discuss the word with them.

afeared – frightened; scared
cast – to throw
dew – tiny drops of water that form on the ground and other things such as grass and flowers during the night
ruffle – to move
'twas – a short way of saying "it was"
wee – little; very small

Read Aloud

Book Walk

Prepare students by taking them on a Book Walk of "Wynken, Blynken, and Nod." Scan the poem together and ask students to make predictions about the poem.

1. Turn to the **table of contents** in *Listen, My Children*. Help students find "Wynken, Blynken, and Nod" and turn to that page.

2. Point to and read aloud the **title of the poem** and the **name of the poet**. Answers to questions may vary.

   ▶ What do you think the poem is about?

   ▶ Have you ever had an interesting dream? What was it about?

3. Point to the first stanza in the poem. Remind students that the lines of a poem that are grouped together are called **stanzas**. A stanza in a poem is like a paragraph in a story.

4. Point to and read aloud the words *night* and *light* at the ends of the lines in the first stanza. Remind students that the words at the ends of the lines in a stanza can sometimes rhyme.

"Wynken, Blynken, and Nod"

It's time to read aloud the poem.

1. Have students sit next to you so that they can see the pictures and words while you read aloud.

2. Explain to students that as you read the poem, they should

   ▶ Listen for words that rhyme at the ends of lines.

   ▶ Listen for words that are said over and over.

   ▶ Try to imagine pictures in their heads as they listen to the poem's words.

3. **Read aloud the entire poem.** Track with your finger so students can follow along. Emphasize Words to Know as you come to them. If appropriate, use the picture to help show what each word means.

Objectives

- Make predictions based on text, illustrations, and/or prior knowledge.
- Activate prior knowledge by previewing text and/or discussing topic.
- Listen to and discuss poetry.

Check Your Reading

"Wynken, Blynken, and Nod"
Check students' comprehension of "Wynken, Blynken, and Nod."

1. Have students tell what "Wynken, Blynken, and Nod" is about in their own words to develop grammar, vocabulary, comprehension, and fluency skills.

2. Ask students the following questions.

   ▸ What do Wynken, Blynken, and Nod use for a boat? a wooden shoe
   ▸ Who asks Wynken, Blynken, and Nod where they are going? the moon
   ▸ What kind of fish do Wynken, Blynken, and Nod want to catch? herring
   ▸ What are the herring fish? stars
   ▸ What are Wynken and Blynken? two little eyes   What is Nod? a little head   What is the wooden shoe? a bed

TIP If students have trouble responding to a question, help them locate the answer in the poem.

Objectives
- Listen to and discuss poetry.
- Answer questions requiring literal recall of details.

Reading for Meaning

Rhyme and Repetition in "Wynken, Blynken, and Nod"
Explore the poetic elements of rhyme and repetition.

1. Remind students that poets often rhyme and repeat words to make a poem fun to read and so the repeated words will stand out.

   ▸ What kind of writing is "Wynken, Blynken, and Nod"? a poem; poetry

2. Point to one of the stanzas of the poem.

   ▸ What is a group of lines in a poem called? a stanza

3. Reread the first four lines of the poem, telling students to listen for words that rhyme.

   ▸ What word rhymes with *night*? *light*
   ▸ What word rhymes with *shoe*? *dew*

4. Reread the first four lines of the third stanza of the poem, telling students to listen for words that rhyme.

   ▸ What word rhymes with *threw*? *shoe*
   ▸ What word rhymes with *foam*? *home*

5. Reread the first four lines of the fourth stanza of the poem, telling students to listen for words that rhyme.

   ▸ What word rhymes with *eyes*? *skies*
   ▸ What word rhymes with *head*? *bed*

6. Reread the last line of all fours stanzas of the poem, telling students to listen for words that are said over and over.

   ▸ What words do you hear over and over again? *fishermen three* and *Wynken, Blynken, and Nod*

Objectives
- Listen to and discuss poetry.
- Identify genre.
- Identify structure of poems and poetic elements: rhyme, rhythm, repetition, and/or alliteration.

Making Connections

• •

Imagine Sailing Away

Guide students to practice visualizing by listening to "Wynken, Blynken, and Nod."
Have them draw a picture showing what they imagine as they listen to the poem.
Turn to page LC 7 in *K¹² Language Arts Activity Book*.

1. Tell students that good readers **visualize** while reading or listening to a poem—meaning that they imagine pictures in their mind based on the words they read or hear.

2. Explain that visualizing is an important strategy because seeing pictures in your mind as you read makes it easier to remember a story.

3. Remind students that poets often use descriptive words, which make it easier to visualize, or imagine pictures as we listen to the words.

4. Have students close their eyes and listen as you read aloud the following words from the poem.

   Sailed on a river of crystal light / Into a sea of dew.

   ▸ What do you imagine when you hear those words? Answers will vary.

5. Tell students that some people might imagine a boat on a shining, white river or a sparkling ocean when they hear those lines from the poem.

6. Explain that visualizing is a strategy that can help readers enjoy and better understand what they read. For example, visualizing what a character or a place in a story looks like can help you better understand those parts of a story.

7. Point out that in "Wynken, Blynken, and Nod," the poet uses many descriptive words that help readers visualize, or imagine pictures in their head.

8. Tell students to close their eyes and think about what they see in their mind as they listen to you **reread the poem**.

Objectives

• Use visualizing to aid understanding of text.

• Demonstrate visualizing through drawing, discussion, and/or writing.

9. On the Activity Book page, have students draw a picture of something they imagined as they listened to the poem.

10. Ask students to describe their drawing.

11. Read aloud the sentence starter located at the bottom of the page and ask students how they would complete it.

12. Write the words students dictate on the blank line.

   ▸ If students are ready to write on their own, allow them to do so.

13. Have students read aloud the completed sentence **with** you as you track the words with your finger.

TIP The amount of time students need to complete this activity will vary. Students need only work for the remaining time of the lesson.

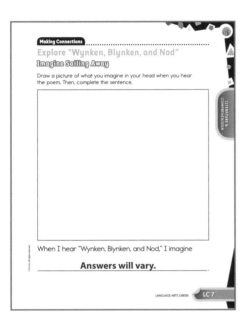

Making Connections

Explore "Wynken, Blynken, and Nod"

Imagine Sailing Away

Draw a picture of what you imagine in your head when you hear the poem. Then, complete the sentence.

When I hear "Wynken, Blynken, and Nod," I imagine

Answers will vary.

LANGUAGE ARTS GREEN   LC 7

Introduce *Sylvester and the Magic Pebble*

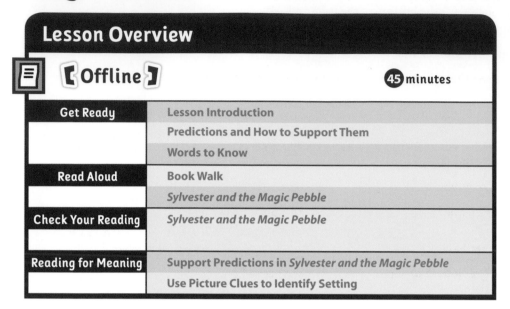

Lesson Overview

[Offline]   45 minutes

Get Ready	Lesson Introduction
	Predictions and How to Support Them
	Words to Know
Read Aloud	Book Walk
	Sylvester and the Magic Pebble
Check Your Reading	*Sylvester and the Magic Pebble*
Reading for Meaning	Support Predictions in *Sylvester and the Magic Pebble*
	Use Picture Clues to Identify Setting

Materials

Supplied

- *Sylvester and the Magic Pebble* by William Steig

Story Synopsis

While on vacation, Sylvester finds a magic red pebble. He thinks he is the luckiest donkey in the world, because now all of his dreams will come true. Unfortunately, one hasty choice causes Sylvester to learn the hard way that you should be careful what you wish for.

Keywords

author – a writer

prediction – a guess about what might happen that is based on information in a story and what you already know

setting – when and where a story takes place

Advance Preparation

Read *Sylvester and the Magic Pebble* before beginning the Read Aloud to locate Words to Know in the text. Read the Read Aloud directions to be aware of stopping points in the story at which students will make predictions. Since this book has no page numbers, you should bookmark pages with stopping points.

Big Ideas

- ▶ Good readers interact with text to make logical predictions before reading; confirm predictions during reading; and revise or make new predictions as they read further.
- ▶ An awareness of story structure elements (setting, characters, plot) provides readers a foundation for constructing meaning when reading new stories and writing their own stories.

 **45 minutes**

Work **together** with students to complete Get Ready, Read Aloud, Check Your Reading, and Reading for Meaning activities.

Get Ready

Lesson Introduction

Prepare students for listening to and discussing *Sylvester and the Magic Pebble*.

1. Tell students that you are going to read a book called *Sylvester and the Magic Pebble*, a story about a donkey who finds a pebble that has very special powers.

2. Explain that before you read the story, you will get ready by discussing

   ▶ How readers make predictions while they read using clues in the story and from their own experiences
   ▶ Why it's important to make predictions

3. Tell students that they will make predictions about what will happen at certain points in the story.

Predictions and How to Support Them

Explore how to make and support a prediction.

1. Tell students that **good readers make predictions**, or guesses, about what will happen in a story. We use clues in the story and what we know from our own experiences to predict what will happen next.

2. Explain that making predictions helps us be active readers. It makes us want to keep reading a story to see if what we predict happens or not.

3. Have students practice making and supporting a prediction. **Read aloud** the following scenario.

   It was very, very cold outside when Maleek woke up Saturday morning. "I just heard Foster's Pond froze solid last night," his father said as they sat down at the kitchen table.

   "At last!" Maleek exclaimed. "Now I can finally try out my new ice skates." He gobbled up his breakfast, and then he ran to his room to get his skates out of the closet.

> **Objectives**
> - Make predictions based on text, illustrations, and/or prior knowledge.
> - Make predictions before and during reading.
> - Support predictions with evidence from text and/or prior knowledge.
> - Build vocabulary through listening, reading, and discussion.
> - Use new vocabulary in written and spoken sentences.

- ▶ What do you think will happen next? Maleek will go ice skating.
- ▶ What clues in the story make you think this? Maleek says that he will try out his new ice skates, and he runs to his room to get them.
- ▶ What do you know from your own experiences that helped you make this prediction? Possible answers: A pond has to be frozen before you can skate on it; they may say that if they get something new, they want to try it out as soon as possible; they may say that if they get something out of the closet, they are going to use it.

TIP Predictions are neither right nor wrong. We make the best prediction we can, based on the available information. Do not describe a prediction as "wrong" because this may discourage students from making predictions.

Words to Know

Before reading *Sylvester and the Magic Pebble*, go over Words to Know with students.

1. Read aloud each word or phrase and have students repeat it.

2. Ask students if they know what each word or phrase means.

   - ▶ If students know a word's or phrase's meaning, have them define it and use it in a sentence.
   - ▶ If students don't know a word's or phrase's meaning, read them the definition and discuss the word or phrase with them.

amaze – to surprise; to shock
conclude – to figure out
extraordinary – unusual; extra special
gratify – to make happen; to grant
less than an instant – to happen very quickly
pace – to walk back and forth
safe – a locked metal box that holds special things

Read Aloud

Book Walk

Prepare students for reading by taking them on a Book Walk of *Sylvester and the Magic Pebble*. Scan the beginning of the book together and ask students to make predictions. Answers to questions may vary.

1. Have students look at the picture on the cover. Point to and read aloud the **book title**.

   ▶ What do you think the book is about?

2. Have students point to the **name of the author**. Read aloud the name of the author and then have students repeat the name after you.

3. Have students look at the **pictures up to the page with Sylvester sitting on the grass during a thunderstorm**.

   ▶ Where do you think the story takes place?
   ▶ What do you think might happen in the story?
   ▶ Do you collect anything special? What is it?

> **Objectives**
> - Identify author.
> - Activate prior knowledge by previewing text and/or discussing topic.
> - Read and listen to a variety of texts for information and pleasure independently or as part of a group.
> - Make predictions based on text, illustrations, and/or prior knowledge.
> - Make predictions before and during reading.

Sylvester and the Magic Pebble

It's time to read aloud the story and ask students to make predictions.

1. Have students sit next to you so that they can see the pictures and words while you read aloud.

2. Tell students to listen for clues in the story about what might happen next.

3. **Begin to read aloud.** Pause at the following points in the story to ask students what they predict will happen next. Jot down their predictions for later reference.

   ▶ After Sylvester starts to walk home to show his father and mother the magic pebble
   ▶ After Sylvester realizes that there's almost no chance of turning back into a donkey
   ▶ After all the dogs in Oatsdale look for Sylvester
   ▶ After Mrs. Duncan sits on the rock that is Sylvester
   ▶ After Mr. Duncan puts the magic pebble on the rock that is Sylvester

4. **Continue to read aloud the story.**

   ▶ Track with your finger so students can follow along.
   ▶ Emphasize Words to Know as you come to them. If appropriate, use the pictures to help show what each word means.
   ▶ Remember to stop at the points listed above and have students make predictions.

Check Your Reading

Sylvester and the Magic Pebble

Check students' comprehension of *Sylvester and the Magic Pebble*.

1. Have students retell *Sylvester and the Magic Pebble* in their own words to develop grammar, vocabulary, comprehension, and fluency skills.

2. Ask students the following questions.

   ▶ Who wrote *Sylvester and the Magic Pebble*? William Steig
   ▶ Where does Sylvester live? What is the name of his town? Oatsdale
   ▶ What is the weather like at the beginning of the story? It's raining.
   ▶ What is the weather like after Sylvester holds the pebble and wishes it would stop raining? It's sunny.   What does Sylvester believe made it stop raining? the red pebble
   ▶ Where is Sylvester when he runs into the lion? on Strawberry Hill
   ▶ When Sylvester doesn't come home, what are some of the things his parents do to try and find him? Possible answers: They ask the neighbors if they've seen him; they go to the police station; they have all the dogs look for him.
   ▶ What does Mr. Duncan find while on a picnic at Strawberry Hill? the red pebble

TIP If students have trouble responding to a question, help them locate the answer in the text or pictures.

Objectives
- Retell or dramatize a story.
- Identify author.
- Answer questions requiring literal recall of details.
- Identify setting.

Reading for Meaning

Support Predictions in *Sylvester and the Magic Pebble*

Revisit the predictions students made while reading the text.

1. Remind students that good readers make predictions by using clues in the words and pictures when they read a story. Good readers can explain what clues they used to make a prediction.

2. Ask students the following questions. **Have students explain how they made a particular prediction by citing clues from the story and personal experience.** Refer to the predictions you jotted down, as necessary. Answers to questions may vary.

   ▶ What did you predict would happen after Sylvester starts to walk home to show his father and mother the magic pebble? What clues did you use to make this prediction?
   ▶ What did you predict would happen after Sylvester realizes that there's almost no chance of turning back into a donkey? What clues did you use to make this prediction?
   ▶ What did you predict would happen after all the dogs in Oatsdale look for Sylvester? What clues did you use to make this prediction?
   ▶ What did you predict would happen after Mrs. Duncan sits on the rock that is Sylvester? What clues did you use to make this prediction?
   ▶ What did you predict would happen after Mr. Duncan puts the magic pebble on the rock that is Sylvester? What clues did you use to make this prediction?

Objectives
- Support predictions with evidence from text and/or prior knowledge.
- Use illustrations to aid understanding of text.
- Identify setting.

Use Picture Clues to Identify Setting

Explore clues in pictures.

1. Remind students that where and when a story happens is called the **setting**. When a story happens can be the time of day or a season of the year.

2. Tell students that while the words of a story can tell us the setting, pictures often give more clues to help readers figure out where and when a story is taking place and what the setting is like.

3. Explain that the setting can change during the story. For example, the characters may go from one place to another. Also, as time passes in the story, the seasons may change. We can often see these changes in the pictures.

4. Turn to the first picture in the story.

   ▸ Where is the story taking place here? in Sylvester's house   What clues are in the picture? Sylvester is sitting at a table and his father is sitting in a chair. These are things that are inside of a house.

5. Turn to the picture of Sylvester as a rock under the night sky.

   ▸ What time of day is it? nighttime   What clues are in the picture? It's dark and the stars are out.

6. Turn to the picture of Mr. and Mrs. Duncan speaking to the policemen. Read aloud the text at the top of the page.

   ▸ Where are Mr. and Mrs. Duncan? at the police station   How do you know? The story says that they went to the police; there's a policeman behind a desk, so they must be inside a building.

7. Turn to the picture of Sylvester as a rock in a fall landscape.

   ▸ What time of year is it? fall   What clues are in the picture? The leaves on the trees are orange and brown, and they are falling off the branches, which happens in the fall.

8. Turn to the picture of Sylvester as a rock in a snowy landscape.

   ▸ Has the time of year changed? Yes   What time of year is it now? winter   What clues are in the picture? There are no leaves on the trees; it's snowing, which happens in the winter.

9. Turn to the last picture in the story.

   ▸ Where are Mr. and Mrs. Duncan and Sylvester? at home   What clues are in the picture? Everyone is sitting on a couch, and a couch would be inside a house.

Explore *Sylvester and the Magic Pebble*

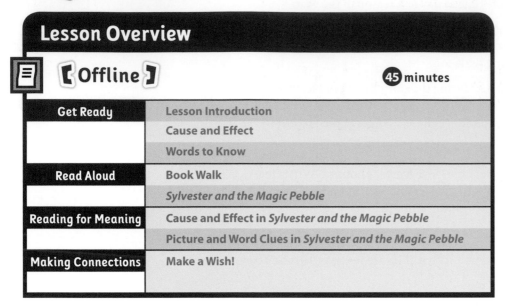

Lesson Overview

[Offline]   **45** minutes

Get Ready	Lesson Introduction
	Cause and Effect
	Words to Know
Read Aloud	Book Walk
	Sylvester and the Magic Pebble
Reading for Meaning	Cause and Effect in *Sylvester and the Magic Pebble*
	Picture and Word Clues in *Sylvester and the Magic Pebble*
Making Connections	Make a Wish!

Materials

Supplied

- *Sylvester and the Magic Pebble* by William Steig
- *K¹² My Journal*, pp. 2–53

Also Needed

- household objects – pebbles, red paint, paintbrushes

Keywords

cause – the reason something happens

context – the parts of a sentence or passage surrounding a word

context clue – a word or phrase in a text that helps you figure out the meaning of an unknown word

effect – the result of a cause

Advance Preparation

Review Reading for Meaning and Making Connections to familiarize yourself with the questions and answers.

Big Ideas

▶ Comprehension entails an understanding of the organizational patterns of text.

▶ Early learners acquire vocabulary through active exposure (by talking and listening, being read to, and receiving explicit instruction).

▶ Verbalizing your thoughts while modeling a reading strategy allows students to see what goes on inside the head of an effective reader; it makes visible the normally hidden process of comprehending text.

 **Offline** **45** minutes

Work **together** with students to complete Get Ready, Read Aloud, Reading for Meaning, and Making Connections activities.

Get Ready

Lesson Introduction

Prepare students for listening to and discussing *Sylvester and the Magic Pebble.*

1. Tell students that you are going to read *Sylvester and the Magic Pebble* again.

2. Explain that before you read the story, you will get ready by discussing

   ▸ How one thing can cause another thing to happen
   ▸ How an event can cause a character to do something

3. Tell students that they will also practice using word and picture clues to figure out the meaning of unknown words.

Objectives
- Identify examples of cause and effect.
- Build vocabulary through listening, reading, and discussion.
- Use new vocabulary in written and spoken sentences.

Cause and Effect

Explore cause and effect, and have students practice identifying examples.

1. Tell students that doing one thing can make another thing happen. The thing that you do is called the **cause**, and the thing that happens is called the **effect**.

2. Explain that sometimes the cause and effect are things you can see and touch. Other times, they are things you say or do. Examples of cause and effect are all around us.

   Cause: You knock over a glass of milk.
   Effect: Milk spills all over the table.

   Cause: A boy's balloon pops.
   Effect: The boy starts to cry.

   Cause: You see a coin on the sidewalk.
   Effect: You pick up the coin.

3. Have students practice figuring out cause-and-effect relationships.

   ▸ Everything outside is wet. What might have caused this? It rained.
   ▸ You drop a glass on the floor. What might happen, or what is the effect? The glass might break.

Words to Know

Before reading *Sylvester and the Magic Pebble*, go over Words to Know with students.

1. Read aloud each word or phrase and have students repeat it.

2. Ask students if they know what each word or phrase means.

   ▸ If students know a word's or phrase's meaning, have them define it and use it in a sentence.

   ▸ If students don't know a word's or phrase's meaning, read them the definition and discuss the word or phrase with them.

amaze – to surprise; to shock
conclude – to figure out
extraordinary – unusual; extra special
gratify – to make happen; to grant
less than an instant – to happen very quickly
pace – to walk back and forth
safe – a locked metal box that holds special things

Read Aloud ....

Book Walk

Prepare students by taking them on a Book Walk of *Sylvester and the Magic Pebble*. Scan the book together to revisit the characters and events.

1. Read aloud the **book title**.

2. Read aloud the **name of the author**.

   ▸ What does an author do? write books; write stories

3. Look through the book. Have students review the **pictures**.

   ▸ Who are some of the characters in the story? Possible answers: Sylvester; his parents; the lion; the policemen

   ▸ What are some things that happen in the story because of the red pebble? Possible answers: It stops and starts raining; Sylvester turns into a rock; Sylvester changes back into a donkey.

Objectives

- Describe role of author and/or illustrator.
- Activate prior knowledge by previewing text and/or discussing topic.
- Read and listen to a variety of texts for information and pleasure independently or as part of a group.

Sylvester and the Magic Pebble

It's time to reread the story.

1. Have students sit next to you so that they can see the pictures and words while you read aloud the story.

2. Tell students to listen for things that cause other things to happen and what makes characters do things.

3. Remind them to look at pictures to better understand the story.

4. **Read aloud the entire story.** Track with your finger so students can follow along. Emphasize Words to Know as you come to them. If appropriate, use the pictures to help show what each word means.

Reading for Meaning

Cause and Effect in *Sylvester and the Magic Pebble*
Explore cause-and-effect relationships.

1. Have students retell *Sylvester and the Magic Pebble* in their own words to develop grammar, vocabulary, comprehension, and fluency skills.

2. Remind students that doing one thing can make another thing happen, and an event can cause a character to do something.

3. Ask the following questions.

   ▸ Why does Sylvester pick up the red pebble? He collects pebbles.
   ▸ What happens when Sylvester holds the red pebble and wishes it would stop raining? It stops raining immediately.
   ▸ What happens when Sylvester sees the lion? He's scared and he wishes he were a rock.
   ▸ One day, a wolf sits on the rock and howls. What causes the wolf to do this? The wolf is hungry.
   ▸ What happens, or what is the effect, when the rock gets warm from Mrs. Duncan sitting on it? Sylvester wakes up.
   ▸ Why does Mr. Duncan pick up the red pebble? because he knows Sylvester would have liked to add it to his pebble collection
   ▸ What causes Sylvester to change from a rock back into a donkey? The magic pebble is on his back and he wishes he were himself.

Picture and Word Clues in *Sylvester and the Magic Pebble*
Explore using picture and word clues to define unknown words.

1. Explain to students that looking at a story's pictures while listening to the story can help them figure out what a word means.

2. Tell students that you will show them how to do this while sharing your thoughts aloud. This is so students can know what goes on in the mind of a good reader as you figure out what a word means.

3. Turn to the two pages with pictures of Sylvester sitting in the rain on the left page and Sylvester sitting in the sun on the right page. Read aloud the text at the bottom of the page on the right.
   Say: I'm not sure what the word *ceased* means. When I look at the pictures, I see that first Sylvester is sitting in the rain and then he's sitting in the sun. The story says that the rained stopped, and it says that the sun was shining as if the rain never existed. I think that *ceased* means "stopped right away."

Objectives
- Retell or dramatize a story.
- Identify details that explain characters' actions and feelings.
- Describe cause-and-effect relationships in text.
- Use illustrations to aid understanding of text.
- Use context and sentence structure to determine meaning of words, phrases, and/or sentences.

4. Turn to the picture of Mrs. Duncan talking to the pig at a fence. Read aloud the sentence at the bottom of the page.

  ▸ What does *inquiring* mean? asking   What is happening in the story that helped you figure this out? Sylvester's parents are trying to figure out where he is.   What clues in the picture helped you figure this out? Mr. and Mrs. Duncan look like they're talking to the animals, so they're probably asking if anybody has seen Sylvester.

5. Turn to picture of Sylvester and his mother hugging each other and Mr. Duncan jumping for joy. Read aloud the sentence at the bottom of the page.

  ▸ What does *embraces* mean? hugs   What is happening in the story that helped you figure this out? Sylvester just turned back into a donkey, and everybody is happy.   What clues in the picture helped you figure this out? Mrs. Duncan and Sylvester have their arms wrapped around each other, like when you give someone a hug.

Making Connections

Make a Wish!

Guide students to make a connection to *Sylvester and the Magic Pebble* by using their own magic pebble to make a wish. Gather *K¹² My Journal* and have students turn to the next available page for **drawing and writing** in Thoughts and Experiences. Also gather the pebbles, paint, and paintbrushes. (If you don't have any paint, you can use a red permanent marker.)

1. Have students paint the pebbles red and then set the pebbles aside to dry.

2. Remind students that the magic pebble Sylvester found was red. If you have a group of students, have them discuss the following questions with each other. If not, have the student discuss the questions with you.

  ▸ What are some of the things Sylvester wished for? to make it stop raining; to make it start raining; to turn into a rock; to be himself again

  ▸ Do you think they were very good wishes? Why or why not? Answers will vary.

3. Tell students to hold a pebble in their hand and make a wish.

4. Have students draw a picture of what they wished for in their journal.

5. Ask students to describe their drawing in one or two sentences.

Objectives

- Demonstrate understanding through drawing, discussion, drama, and/or writing.
- Make connections with text: text-to-text, text-to-self, text-to-world.
- Continue a conversation through multiple exchanges.
- Speak audibly and clearly to express thoughts, feelings, and ideas.
- Share work with an audience.

6. Write the sentence(s) students dictate below their picture.

7. Have students read aloud the completed sentence(s) **with** you as you track the words with your finger.

8. If you have a group of students, have them share their pictures, and discuss what they wished for and why. If you do not have a group, discuss the picture with the student, and share something that you would wish for and why.

TIP Supervise students to make sure they do not choke on small objects. The amount of time students need to complete this activity will vary. Students need only work for the remaining time of the lesson.

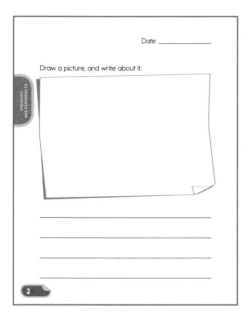

Explore "The Owl and the Pussycat"

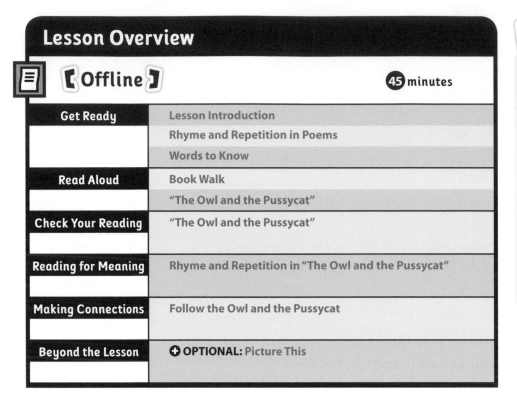

Lesson Overview

Offline   45 minutes

Get Ready	Lesson Introduction
	Rhyme and Repetition in Poems
	Words to Know
Read Aloud	Book Walk
	"The Owl and the Pussycat"
Check Your Reading	"The Owl and the Pussycat"
Reading for Meaning	Rhyme and Repetition in "The Owl and the Pussycat"
Making Connections	Follow the Owl and the Pussycat
Beyond the Lesson	⊕ OPTIONAL: Picture This

Materials

Supplied

- *Listen, My Children: Poems for First Graders*, pp. 14–15
- *K¹² Language Arts Activity Book*, pp. LC 9–11
- *K¹² My Journal*, pp. 2–53

Also Needed

- whiteboard (optional)
- scissors, round-end safety
- glue
- crayons (optional)

Poetry Synopsis

The Owl and the Pussycat sail away, fall in love, get married, and dance by the light of the moon, the moon, the moon, dance by the light of the moon.

Keywords

genre – a category for classifying literary works

rhyme – when two or more words have the same ending sounds; for example, *cat* and *hat* rhyme

sequence – order

visualize – to picture things in your mind as you read

Advance Preparation

Write the poem in the Get Ready on a whiteboard or a sheet of paper. Read "The Owl and the Pussycat" before beginning the Read Aloud to locate Words to Know in the text.

Big Ideas

▸ Exposing readers to a wide variety of genres provides them with a wide range of background knowledge and increases their vocabulary.

▸ Poems are different from prose in structure and content. They are generally organized in lines and often contain rhymes.

▸ Readers who visualize, or form mental pictures, while they read have better recall of text than those who do not.

▸ Comprehension entails an understanding of the organizational patterns of text.

 **45** minutes

Work **together** with students to complete Get Ready, Read Aloud, Check Your Reading, Reading for Meaning, Making Connections, and Beyond the Lesson activities.

Get Ready

Lesson Introduction

Prepare students for listening to and discussing "The Owl and the Pussycat."

1. Tell students that you are going to read a poem about the adventures of an owl and a pussycat who sail away in a boat.

2. Tell them that before you read the poem, you'll get ready by reviewing

   ► A type of writing called poetry
   ► How poems are written in stanzas and have words that are very descriptive
   ► How poems have rhyming words and sometimes have words or lines that are repeated over and over

---

Rhyme and Repetition in Poems

Review the genre of poetry and the poetic elements of rhyme and repetition.

1. Ask students to tell you what they remember about the kind of writing called **poetry**.

2. If students have trouble recalling characteristics of poetry, remind them of the following.

   ► Poems make up this group of writing.
   ► Poems are often written in short lines called stanzas.
   ► Poems often have descriptive words that help readers imagine things in their minds.
   ► Poems often have words that rhyme and may sometimes have repeated words.

3. **Read aloud the poem** on the whiteboard or sheet of paper. Tell students to listen for words that are said over and over, and for words that rhyme. **Point to the words that rhyme at the end of lines as you come to them.**

   I like to play in the sun, the sun
   I like to play in the sun.
   In the sun I have fun, I have fun
   In the sun I have fun, fun, fun.

⭐ **Objectives**

- Listen to and discuss poetry.
- Identify structure of poems and poetic elements: rhyme, rhythm, repetition, and/or alliteration.
- Activate prior knowledge by previewing text and/or discussing topic.
- Build vocabulary through listening, reading, and discussion.
- Use new vocabulary in written and spoken sentences.

4. Ask students the following questions.

> ▸ Which word rhymes with *sun*? *fun*
> ▸ Which words are said over and over in the poem? Accept any of the repeated words or phrases in the poem.

5. Read aloud the poem again, encouraging students to chime in when you come to repeated words.

Words to Know

Before reading "The Owl and the Pussycat," go over Words to Know with students.

1. Read aloud each word and have students repeat it.

2. Ask students if they know what each word means.

> ▸ If students know a word's meaning, have them define it and use it in a sentence.
> ▸ If students don't know a word's meaning, read them the definition and discuss the word with them.

fowl – a bird
tarry – to put off starting something; to delay

Read Aloud

Book Walk

Prepare students by taking them on a Book Walk of "The Owl and the Pussycat." Scan the poem together and ask students to make predictions about the poem.

1. Turn to the **table of contents** in *Listen, My Children*. Help students find "The Owl and the Pussycat" and turn to that page.

2. Point to and read aloud the **title of the poem** and the **name of the poet**. Answers to questions may vary.

> ▸ What do you think the poem is about?
> ▸ Have you ever been on a boat? Did you sail on a river, a lake, or an ocean? Where did you go? Did you have fun?
> ▸ Where would you go if you could sail away?

Objectives
- Make predictions based on text, illustrations, and/or prior knowledge.
- Activate prior knowledge by previewing text and/or discussing topic.
- Listen to and discuss poetry.

"The Owl and the Pussycat"

It's time to read aloud the poem.

1. Have students sit next to you so that they can see the pictures and words while you read aloud.

2. Explain to students that as you read the poem, they should

   ► Listen for words that rhyme.
   ► Listen for words that are said over and over.
   ► Think about the order in which things happen.

3. **Read aloud the entire poem.** Track with your finger so students can follow along. Emphasize Words to Know as you come to them. If appropriate, use the pictures to help show what each word means.

Check Your Reading

"The Owl and the Pussycat"

Check students' comprehension of "The Owl and the Pussycat."

Objectives

● Retell or dramatize a story.
● Answer questions requiring literal recall of details.

1. Have students tell what "The Owl and the Pussycat" is about in their own words to develop grammar, vocabulary, comprehension, and fluency skills.

2. Ask students the following questions.

   ► What is something that the Owl and the Pussycat take with them on the boat? honey; money
   ► What instrument does the Owl play while he sings? a guitar
   ► How long do the Owl and the Pussycat sail? a year and a day
   ► Where do the Owl and the Pussycat find a ring? in Piggy's nose
   ► Who marries the Owl and the Pussycat? the Turkey
   ► Where do the Owl and the Pussycat dance? on the edge of the sand

TIP If students have trouble responding to a question, help them locate the answer in the text or picture.

Reading for Meaning

Rhyme and Repetition in "The Owl and the Pussycat"
Explore the poetic elements of rhyme and repetition.

1. Remind students that poems often have words that rhyme and repeated words or phrases.

    ▶ What kind of writing is "The Owl and the Pussycat"? *poetry; a poem*

2. Reread the first four lines of the first stanza, telling students to listen for words that rhyme.

    ▶ What word rhymes with *boat*? *note*

3. Reread the first four lines of the second stanza, telling students to listen for words that rhyme.

    ▶ What word rhymes with *owl*? *fowl*
    ▶ What word rhymes with *sing*? *ring*

4. Reread the last five lines of the second stanza, telling students to listen for words that are repeated.

    ▶ Which words are repeated in these lines of the poem? *His nose; With a ring at the end of his nose*

5. Reread the last five lines of the last stanza, telling students to listen for words that are repeated.

    ▶ Which words are repeated in these lines of the poem? *The moon; They danced by the light of the moon*

Objectives
- Listen to and discuss poetry.
- Identify genre.
- Identify structure of poems and poetic elements: rhyme, rhythm, repetition, and/or alliteration.

Making Connections

Follow the Owl and the Pussycat
Have students demonstrate their ability to recall a sequence of events and read simple directions. Turn to pages LC 9–11 in *K¹² Language Arts Activity Book*.

1. Tell students that the order in which things happen in a story is called the **sequence**. One way that readers can check if they understand what they read is by telling the sequence of events.

2. Explain that students will use pictures to show the order, or sequence, of the things that happen in "The Owl and the Pussycat." They will also practice reading and following simple directions.

3. Have students read the directions on the Activity Book page. Help them, if necessary.

Objectives
- Follow written directions.
- Identify story sequence.
- Sequence pictures illustrating story events.
- Retell a story using various media.

4. Have students cut out pictures from "The Owl and the Pussycat," put them in order, and glue them down.

5. Have them retell the sequence of events in the poem using the pictures as a guide.

TIP Refer back to "The Owl and the Pussycat" if students have trouble recalling the order of events in the poem.

Beyond the Lesson

⊕ OPTIONAL: Picture This

This activity is OPTIONAL. It is intended for students who have extra time and would benefit from practicing visualizing as they listen to "The Owl and the Pussycat." Feel free to skip this activity. Gather *K¹² My Journal* and have students turn to the next available page for **drawing and writing** in Thoughts and Experiences.

1. Remind students that good readers visualize, or see pictures in their mind, as they read or listen to stories.

2. Tell students to close their eyes and think about what they see in their mind as they listen to you read "The Owl and the Pussycat."

Objectives
- Demonstrate visualizing through drawing, discussion, and/or writing.

3. Have students draw a picture of something they imagined while listening to the poem.

4. Have students explain the picture in their journal and then ask them to tell you a sentence that describes what they imagined.

   ▶ Use a sentence starter such as, "When I listened to the poem, I saw . . . ."

5. In their journal, write the sentence students dictate below their picture.

6. Have students read aloud the completed sentence **with** you as you track the words with your finger.

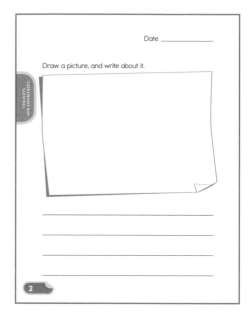

Introduce "King Midas"

Lesson Overview

[Offline]   **45** minutes

Get Ready	Lesson Introduction
	Personal Experience and Predictions
	Words to Know
Read Aloud	Book Walk
	"King Midas"
Check Your Reading	"King Midas"
Reading for Meaning	Support Predictions in "King Midas"
	Use Text and Pictures to Identify Setting

Advance Preparation

Read "King Midas" before beginning the Read Aloud to locate Words to Know in the text.

Big Ideas

▸ Good readers interact with text to make logical predictions before reading; confirm predictions during reading; and revise or make new predictions as they read further.

▸ Comprehension is facilitated when readers connect new information to information previously learned.

▸ An awareness of story structure elements (setting, characters, plot) provides readers a foundation for constructing meaning when reading new stories and writing their own stories.

Materials

Supplied

- "King Midas," *K¹² Classics for Young Readers, Volume A*, pp. 26–33

Story Synopsis

A stranger offers King Midas the Golden Touch, and the king gladly accepts this marvelous gift. What could possibly be worth more than gold?

Keywords

prediction – a guess about what might happen that is based on information in a story and what you already know

setting – when and where a story takes place

[Offline] **45** minutes

Work **together** with students to complete Get Ready, Read Aloud, Check Your
Reading, and Reading for Meaning activities.

Get Ready

Lesson Introduction
Prepare students for listening to and discussing "King Midas."

1. Tell students that you are going to read "King Midas," a story about a man who
   says he loves gold more than anything.

2. Explain that before you read the story, you will get ready by discussing how
   readers use personal knowledge and experience to make predictions.

3. Tell students that they will make predictions about what will happen at certain
   points in the story.

Personal Experience and Predictions
Explore how we use personal knowledge and experience to make predictions.

1. Explain to students that we make predictions all the time. For example,

   ▸ If you step outside and the clouds are dark and the wind is blowing, you
     might predict, or guess, that it's going to rain—so you go back inside and
     get an umbrella.
   ▸ If you plan to spend a few hours playing at the park, you might predict that
     you'll get hungry—so you pack a snack to take with you.

2. Tell students that these predictions are based on personal knowledge and
   experience. We look at what is around us and compare it to what's happened in
   the past. Making predictions helps us be prepared for what might happen next.

3. Explain that sometimes the personal knowledge we use to make a prediction
   about a story comes from having heard a similar story or a different version of
   the same story.

> **Objectives**
> - Make predictions based on text, illustrations, and/or prior knowledge.
> - Make predictions before and during reading.
> - Support predictions with evidence from text and/or prior knowledge.
> - Identify setting.
> - Build vocabulary through listening, reading, and discussion.
> - Use new vocabulary in written and spoken sentences.

4. Have students practice making and supporting a prediction.

Say: I'm going to tell you the beginning of a story that may sound familiar. Once upon a time there were three little ducks. One day their mother told them that it was time for them to leave home and make their way in the world. So off they went. The first little duck found some leaves by a little pond. He thought the pond would make a fine home, so he built a house out of the leaves. The second little duck found some twigs by a large lake.

  ▸ What does this story remind you of? "The Three Little Pigs"
  ▸ What do you think will happen next? The second little duck will build a house out of twigs.
  ▸ What do you know from your own experiences that helped you make your prediction? Students may say that in the "Three Little Pigs," the pigs each build a house.

TIP Predictions are neither right nor wrong. We make the best prediction we can, based on the available information. Do not describe a prediction as "wrong" because this may discourage students from making predictions.

Words to Know

Before reading "King Midas," go over Words to Know with students.

1. Read aloud each word and have students repeat it.

2. Ask students if they know what each word means.

  ▸ If students know a word's meaning, have them define it and use it in a sentence.
  ▸ If students don't know a word's meaning, read them the definition and discuss the word with them.

pitcher – a container, usually with a handle and a spout, that holds liquids
treasure – wealth and riches, such as gold, jewels, and money

Read Aloud

Book Walk

Prepare students for reading by taking them on a Book Walk of "King Midas." Scan the beginning of the story together and ask students to make predictions about the story. Answers to questions may vary.

1. Turn to the **table of contents** in *K¹² Classics for Young Readers, Volume A.* Help students find the selection and turn to that page.

2. Point to and read aloud the **title of the story**.

   ▸ What do you think the story might be about?

3. Have students **look at the pictures on the first two pages of the story**.

   ▸ Where do you think the story takes place?
   ▸ What do you think might happen in the story?
   ▸ Have you ever made a wish that came true? How did it make you feel?

"King Midas"

It's time to read aloud the story and ask students to make predictions.

1. Have students sit next to you so that they can see the pictures and words while you read aloud.

2. Tell students to listen for clues in the story about what might happen next.

3. **Begin to read aloud.** Pause at the following points in the story to ask students what they predict will happen next. Jot down their predictions for later reference.

   ▸ Page 27: After the stranger asks King Midas what wish would make him happy
   ▸ Page 28: After King Midas wakes up with the Golden Touch
   ▸ Page 30: After King Midas kisses Marygold
   ▸ Page 31: After King Midas says he would give up all his money to get back his little girl

4. **Continue to read aloud the story.**

   ▸ Track with your finger so students can follow along.
   ▸ Emphasize Words to Know as you come to them. If appropriate, use the pictures to help show what each word means.
   ▸ Remember to stop at the points listed above and have students make predictions.

Objectives

- Activate prior knowledge by previewing text and/or discussing topic.
- Listen and respond to texts representing a variety of cultures, time periods, and traditions.
- Make predictions based on text, illustrations, and/or prior knowledge.
- Make predictions before and during reading.

Check Your Reading

· ·

"King Midas"
Check students' comprehension of "King Midas."

1. Have students retell "King Midas" in their own words to develop grammar, vocabulary, comprehension, and fluency skills.

2. Ask students the following questions.

   ▶ What is the name of King Midas's daughter? Marygold
   ▶ Who does King Midas find in his treasure room? a stranger
   ▶ What does King Midas do when he wakes up with the Golden Touch? He touches the things around him and changes them to gold.
   ▶ Why does King Midas go into the garden? to touch all the leaves and flowers; to make the most beautiful garden in the world
   ▶ What happens when King Midas drinks some water? It turns into gold.

(TIP) If students have trouble responding to a question, help them locate the answer in the text or pictures.

Objectives
- Retell or dramatize a story.
- Answer questions requiring literal recall of details.

Reading for Meaning

· ·

Support Predictions in "King Midas"
Revisit the predictions students made while reading the text.

1. Remind students that good readers make predictions by using clues in the words and pictures of a story, along with knowledge from personal experiences. Good readers can explain what clues they used to make a prediction.

2. Explain to students that sometimes the personal knowledge we use to help us make predictions comes from having heard a similar story or a different version of the same story.

3. Ask students the following questions. Refer to the predictions you jotted down, as necessary. **Have students explain how they made a particular prediction by citing clues from the story and personal experience.** Answers to questions may vary.

   ▶ Have you ever heard another version of King Midas before this one?
   ▶ What did you predict would happen after the stranger asks King Midas what he wishes for? What clues did you use to make this prediction?
   ▶ What did you predict would happen after King Midas wakes up with the Golden Touch? What clues did you use to make this prediction?
   ▶ What did you predict would happen after King Midas kisses Marygold? What clues did you use to make this prediction?
   ▶ What did you predict would happen after King Midas says he would give up all his money to get back his little girl? What clues did you use to make this prediction?

Objectives
- Support predictions with evidence from text and/or prior knowledge.
- Use illustrations to aid understanding of text.
- Identify setting.

Use Text and Pictures to Identify Setting

Explore how to figure out a story's setting.

1. Remind students that the **setting** of a story is where and when the story takes place. A story can have more than one setting.

2. Tell students that along with the words, the pictures in a story often give clues to help readers better understand the story and its setting.

3. Turn to page 27 and point to the picture.

   ▸ Where is King Midas? in his treasure room   How do you know? The story says so, and there is treasure all around Midas.

   ▸ What is it like in the treasure room? There is so much gold and so many jewels that Midas has to stand on top of them.   What does that tell you about King Midas? He's very rich.

4. Turn to pages 28 and 29 and point to the picture.

   ▸ What is the setting here? the garden   How do you know? The story says that Midas went into the garden; there are plants, grass, and flowers in the picture.

5. Turn to pages 30 and 31. Read the first sentence and point to the picture.

   ▸ What time of day is it? Possible answers: morning; daytime   How do you know? The story says that Midas went to eat breakfast; the picture shows the sun is in the sky.

Explore "King Midas"

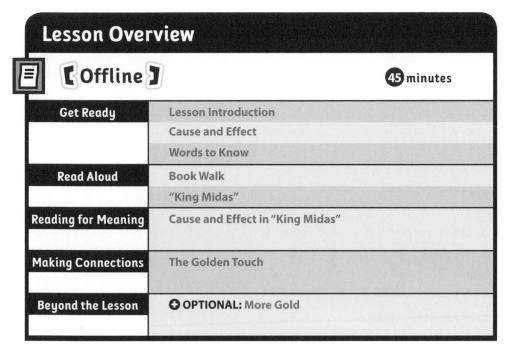

Lesson Overview

[Offline]   45 minutes

Get Ready	Lesson Introduction
	Cause and Effect
	Words to Know
Read Aloud	Book Walk
	"King Midas"
Reading for Meaning	Cause and Effect in "King Midas"
Making Connections	The Golden Touch
Beyond the Lesson	⊕ OPTIONAL: More Gold

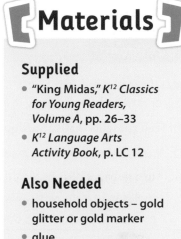

[Materials]

Supplied
- "King Midas," *K¹² Classics for Young Readers, Volume A*, pp. 26–33
- *K¹² Language Arts Activity Book*, p. LC 12

Also Needed
- household objects – gold glitter or gold marker
- glue

Keywords
cause – the reason something happens
effect – the result of a cause

Big Ideas

Comprehension entails an understanding of the organizational patterns of text.

 **Offline** **45** minutes

Work **together** with students to complete Get Ready, Read Aloud, Reading for Meaning, Making Connections, and Beyond the Lesson activities.

Get Ready

Lesson Introduction

Prepare students for listening to and discussing "King Midas."

1. Tell students that you are going to read "King Midas" again.

2. Explain that before you read the story, you will get ready by reviewing
   ▶ How one thing can cause another thing to happen
   ▶ How an event can cause a character to do something

 Objectives
- Identify examples of cause and effect.
- Build vocabulary through listening, reading, and discussion.
- Use new vocabulary in written and spoken sentences.

Cause and Effect

Review cause and effect, and have students practice identifying examples.

1. Have students give an example of a cause and its effect.
   ▶ If students have trouble recalling the concept, remind them that doing one thing can make another thing happen. The thing that you do is called the **cause**, and the thing that happens is called the **effect**.

2. Remind them that sometimes the cause and effect are things you can see and touch. Other times, they are things you say or do.

   Cause: You are thirsty.
   Effect: You drink a glass of water.

   Cause: You give your mother a flower.
   Effect: Your mother gives you a hug.

3. Give students a cause and have them identify the effect.
   ▶ You kick a ball. What happens, or what is the effect? The ball moves.

4. Give students an effect and have them identify the cause.
   ▶ The dirty dishes in the sink are gone. What might have caused this? Someone washed them and put them away.

Words to Know

Before reading "King Midas," review Words to Know with students.

1. Read aloud each word and have students repeat it.

2. Ask students if they know what each word means.

   ▸ If students know a word's meaning, have them define it and use it in a sentence.
   ▸ If students don't know a word's meaning, read them the definition and discuss the word with them.

pitcher – a container, usually with a handle and a spout, that holds liquids
treasure – wealth and riches, such as gold, jewels, and money

Read Aloud

Book Walk

Prepare students by taking them on a Book Walk of "King Midas." Scan the story together to revisit the characters and events.

1. Turn to the selection in *K¹² Classics for Young Readers, Volume A.* Point to and read aloud the **title of the story**.

2. Have students review the **pictures**.

3. Point to the picture of the girl on page 26.

   ▸ Who is this character? Marygold; King Midas's daughter

4. Point to the pictures on pages 30 and 31.

   ▸ What caused these things to turn to gold? King Midas touched them.
   ▸ How did King Midas get the Golden Touch? He wished for it, and the stranger gave him his wish.

Objectives
- Activate prior knowledge by previewing text and/or discussing topic.
- Listen and respond to texts representing a variety of cultures, time periods, and traditions.

"King Midas"

It's time to reread the story.

1. Have students sit next to you so that they can see the pictures and words while you read aloud.

2. Tell students to listen for things that cause other things to happen, and what makes characters do things.

3. **Read aloud the entire story.** Track with your finger so students can follow along.

Reading for Meaning

Cause and Effect in "King Midas"
Explore cause-and-effect relationships.

1. Have students retell "King Midas" in their own words to develop grammar, vocabulary, comprehension, and fluency skills.

2. Remind students that doing one thing can make another thing happen, and an event can cause a character to do something.

3. Ask the following questions.

   ▸ Why does King Midas say he would pick buttercups and dandelions if they were as golden as they look? because he loves gold
   ▸ Why does the stranger give King Midas the Golden Touch? because the king says it would make him happy
   ▸ What causes the bed and table to turn to gold? King Midas touches them.
   ▸ What happens, or what is the effect, when King Midas touches the fish on his plate? It turns to gold.
   ▸ Why does King Midas start to cry? because he accidently turns his daughter into gold
   ▸ What lesson does King Midas learn at the end of the story? that his daughter is more important than gold; that gold is not everything
   What causes King Midas to learn this? Possible answers: not being able to eat or drink because everything turns to gold; turning his daughter into gold
   ▸ What lesson can we learn from the story? Possible answers: Gold is nice to look at, but you can't eat it; the people we love are more precious than gold.

Objectives

- Retell or dramatize a story.
- Describe cause-and-effect relationships in text.
- Identify details that explain characters' actions and feelings.
- Identify the moral or lesson of a text.

Making Connections

The Golden Touch
Guide students to make a connection to "King Midas" when they turn something they love into gold. Turn to page LC 12 in *K¹² Language Arts Activity Book*, and gather the glue and gold glitter.

1. Have students think about something they own that they love.

2. Give students the following verbal directions to have them practice following three-step directions. (If glitter is not available, use a gold marker or crayon.)

   ▸ Use a pencil to draw a picture of something you own that you love.
   ▸ Spread a thin layer of glue on the item you drew.
   ▸ Glue gold glitter on your picture.

3. Ask students to describe their drawing.

4. Read aloud the sentence starter at the bottom of the page and ask students how they would complete the sentence.

Objectives

- Demonstrate understanding through drawing, discussion, drama, and/or writing.
- Make connections with text: text-to-text, text-to-self, text-to-world.
- Follow two- or three-step oral directions.
- Share work with an audience.
- Continue a conversation through multiple exchanges.
- Speak audibly and clearly to express thoughts, feelings, and ideas.

5. Write the words students dictate on the blank lines.

   ▸ If students are ready to write on their own, allow them to do so.

6. Have students read aloud the completed sentence **with** you as you track the words with your finger.

7. If you have a group of students, have them share and discuss their pictures with each other. If you do not have a group, have the student share and discuss the picture with you. Ask the following questions to encourage discussion. Answers to questions may vary.

   ▸ What did you turn to gold and why?
   ▸ Do you think you would enjoy this item more if it were gold, or just as it normally is?
   ▸ Do you think you would ever want the Golden Touch? Why or why not?

 The amount of time students need to complete this activity will vary. Students need only work for the remaining time of the lesson.

Reward: Add a sticker for this unit on the My Accomplishments chart to mark successful completion of the unit.

Beyond the Lesson

● OPTIONAL: More Gold

This activity is OPTIONAL. It is intended for students who have extra time and would enjoy listening to another version of the King Midas story. Feel free to skip this activity.

1. Go to a library and look for a copy of *King Midas: A Golden Tale* by John Warren Stewig.

2. Lead a Book Walk and then begin to read aloud the story.

3. Stop at some points in the story and ask students to make a prediction about what will happen next. Remind them that knowledge from the story "King Midas" that you read during the lesson can help them make predictions.

4. Have students tell how the stories are alike and different. Be sure students describe how the characters and settings are alike and different.

5. Ask them to tell which story is their favorite and why.

Objectives

- Make predictions based on text, illustrations, and/or prior knowledge.
- Make predictions before and during reading.
- Compare and contrast story structure elements across texts.
- Compare and contrasts two texts on the same topic.

How's the Weather?

Unit Focus

In this unit, students will explore different types of writing related to wind, weather, and rainbows. This unit follows the read-aloud instructional approach (see the instructional approaches to reading in the introductory lesson for this program). In this unit, students will

- ▶ Listen to poems, a legend, and a nonfiction article.
- ▶ Explore the genre of poetry and the characteristics of poems, including rhyme, repetition, alliteration, and personification.
- ▶ Learn how to draw and support conclusions, and practice making inferences.
- ▶ Learn how to self-monitor their understanding of text through the strategies of retelling and asking questions.
- ▶ Learn about setting a purpose for reading.
- ▶ Practice identifying the speaker of a poem.
- ▶ Explore the facts and features of nonfiction text.

Unit Plan   [Offline]

Lesson 1	Explore Poems About the Weather (A)	**45** minutes a day
Lesson 2	Introduce "Strong Wind's Bride"	
Lesson 3	Explore "Strong Wind's Bride"	
Lesson 4	Explore Poems About the Weather (B)	
Lesson 5	Introduce "Shedding Light on Rainbows"	
Lesson 6	Explore "Shedding Light on Rainbows"	
Lesson 7	Explore Poems About the Weather (C)	
Lesson 8	Your Choice	

Explore Poems About the Weather (A)

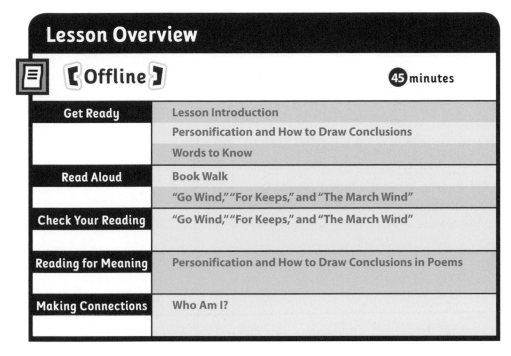

Lesson Overview

Offline
45 minutes

Get Ready	Lesson Introduction
	Personification and How to Draw Conclusions
	Words to Know
Read Aloud	Book Walk
	"Go Wind," "For Keeps," and "The March Wind"
Check Your Reading	"Go Wind," "For Keeps," and "The March Wind"
Reading for Meaning	Personification and How to Draw Conclusions in Poems
Making Connections	Who Am I?

Advance Preparation

Read "Go Wind," "For Keeps," and "The March Wind" before beginning the Read Aloud to locate Words to Know in the text.

Big Ideas

▸ Poems are different from prose in structure and content. They are generally organized in lines and often contain rhymes.
▸ Good readers use prior knowledge and text clues to infer, or draw conclusions about what is implied but not directly stated in text.
▸ Readers must focus on the specific language of a text to aid in interpretation.

Materials

Supplied

• *Weather: Poems for All Seasons*, pp. 20–21, 24–27
• *K¹² Language Arts Activity Book*, p. LC 13

Poetry Synopses

The wind comes alive in three breezy poems.

Keywords

conclusion – a reasoned decision made about something not stated directly in a text through the consideration of information provided and what is already known

italic – text that slants toward the right

personification – giving human qualities to something that is not human; for example: "The thunder shouted from the clouds."

rhyme – when two or more words have the same ending sounds; for example, *cat* and *hat* rhyme

[Offline] 45 minutes

Work **together** with students to complete Get Ready, Read Aloud, Check Your Reading, Reading for Meaning, and Making Connections activities.

Get Ready

Lesson Introduction

Prepare students for listening to and discussing poems about the wind.

1. Tell students that you are going to read "Go Wind," "For Keeps," and "The March Wind." All three poems are about the wind.

2. Tell students that you will read the poems more than one time. Explain that when you're learning to read poetry, it's important to reread the poems because with every reading, you

   ▸ Become more familiar with the poems, so you are able to read more and more of the words on your own.
   ▸ Learn something new about the poems that you didn't think about during the first reading.
   ▸ Build your confidence as a reader.

3. Explain to students that before you read the poems, you will get ready by discussing how

   ▸ Poets sometimes make things that aren't human sound like they are.
   ▸ You can figure out things about the poems that the poets don't directly say.
   ▸ You can draw conclusions based on information in a poem and on pictures, prior knowledge, and personal experience.

Objectives

- Listen to and discuss poetry.
- Identify literary devices: personification and/or simile.
- Draw conclusions using text, illustrations, and/or prior knowledge.
- Support conclusions with evidence from text and/or prior knowledge.
- Activate prior knowledge by previewing text and/or discussing topic.
- Build vocabulary through listening, reading, and discussion.
- Use new vocabulary in written and spoken sentences.

Personification and How to Draw Conclusions

Introduce the literary device of personification and discuss how to draw a conclusion.

1. Tell students that poets sometimes make animals or objects sound like they're human. For example, a poet might say, "the star winked at the moon." We know that a star isn't human and can't really wink. But poets do this to help us imagine an interesting picture and think about certain feelings, such as joy or sadness.

2. Tell students to listen for ways that a poet makes an object sound as though it were human. **Read aloud the following poem.**

   The thirsty flower thanked the rain
   For the sip of water that eased her pain.

   ▸ How does the poet make the flower sound human? by saying she's thirsty and that she thanks the rain
   ▸ Can a flower feel thirst or pain? No   Why not? It isn't human.
   ▸ Can a flower thank the rain? No   Why not? It isn't human, and neither is the rain.
   ▸ Why does the poet describe the flower as though it were human? to help us imagine an interesting picture of the flower; to help us think about feelings

3. Tell students that sometimes a poet doesn't tell us everything in the words of a poem. Good readers look for clues in the words and pictures to help them figure out things, such as how a character feels.

4. Explain that along with the words and pictures, good readers think about what they know from personal experience to help them figure out things that the poet doesn't say directly. When readers do this, they **draw a conclusion**. A conclusion is based on what you read and pictures you see, together with your knowledge learned from personal experience.

   ▸ How is the flower feeling in the poem? What feelings does the poet want you to think about? Possible answers: feeling thirsty; feeling grateful; feeling thankful
   ▸ What do you think the weather was like before it rained? dry; hot; no rain   How did you figure that out, or draw that conclusion? The flower was thirsty and in pain because she didn't have water.   What do you know from your own experience that helped you draw this conclusion? Possible answers: Plants get dry when there's no rain; plants get dry in hot weather.

5. Tell students that as they listen to poetry, they should listen for the words that the poet uses to describe things. They should also use the pictures and their own experience to draw conclusions.

(TIP) Although an objective for this lesson is to identify personification, there is no need to introduce the term to students at this time.

Words to Know

Before reading "Go Wind," "For Keeps," and "The March Wind," go over Words to Know with students.

1. Read aloud each word or phrase and have students repeat it.

2. Ask students if they know what each word or phrase means.

   ▸ If students know a word's or phrase's meaning, have them define it and use it in a sentence.
   ▸ If students don't know a word's or phrase's meaning, read them the definition and discuss the word or phrase with them.

fling – to throw
flock – a group of birds
huff and puff – to blow air out hard and fast
strew – to spread here and there; to scatter
to and fro – back and forth
tug of war – a contest in which people pull a rope from both ends in opposite directions

Read Aloud

Book Walk

Prepare students by taking them on a Book Walk of "Go Wind," "For Keeps," and "The March Wind." Scan the poems together and ask students to make predictions about the poems.

1. Turn to the first poem, "Go Wind," on pages 20 and 21 in *Weather: Poems for All Seasons*.

2. Point to and read aloud the **title of the poem** and the **name of the poet**. Have students repeat the poet's name.

3. Have students study the **pictures**. Answers to questions may vary.

   ▸ What do you think the poem is about?
   ▸ What are some things that you've seen the wind blow around your neighborhood?

4. Point to the words *wheee* and *me*. Explain that these two words are written with slanting letters called italic. Using italic shows that the words should be read differently, with more emphasis.

5. Turn to the second poem, "For Keeps," on pages 24 and 25.

Objectives
- Make predictions based on text, illustrations, and/or prior knowledge.
- Activate prior knowledge by previewing text and/or discussing topic.
- Listen to and discuss poetry.
- Identify author.

6. Point to and read aloud the **title of the poem** and the **name of the poet**. Have students repeat the poet's name.

7. Have students study the **picture**. Answers to questions may vary.

   ▶ What do you think the poem is about?
   ▶ What do you like to do on a windy day?

8. Turn to the third poem, "The March Wind," on pages 26 and 27.

9. Point to and read aloud the **title of the poem** and the **name of the poet**. Have students repeat the poet's name. Explain that *anonymous* means that no one knows who wrote the poem.

10. Have students study the **picture**.

   ▶ What do you think the poem is about? Answers will vary.
   ▶ Why is the girl holding on to the post in the picture? Possible answers: She's trying not to blow away; she's trying to stand up straight.
     Why is the boy's cap above his head? The wind blew it off.

"Go Wind," "For Keeps," and "The March Wind"
It's time to read aloud the poems.

1. Have students sit next to you so that they can see the pictures and words while you read aloud.

2. Tell students to listen carefully to words that rhyme, as well as ways that poets make things sound as though they were human.

3. Tell students to listen for hints to help them figure out things that the poets don't say directly.

4. **Read aloud all three poems.** Track with your finger so students can follow along. Emphasize Words to Know as you come to them. If appropriate, use the pictures to help show what each word means.

5. Remember to point to and emphasize the words *wheee* and *me* in "Go Wind."

Check Your Reading

"Go Wind," "For Keeps," and "The March Wind"

Check students' comprehension of the poems.

1. Reread "Go Wind" aloud, encouraging students to chime in and read with you. Then have students say in their own words what the poem is about.

   ▶ What is blowing things around in the poem? the wind
   ▶ Reread the last six lines of "Go Wind." Which words rhyme with *go*? *blow* and *no*
   ▶ Point to the words *wheee* and *me*. Why are the letters in these words slanting? to show they need to be said with more emphasis; to show they should be said differently

2. Reread "For Keeps" aloud, encouraging students to chime in and read with you. Then have students say in their own words what the poem is about.

   ▶ What color is the kite? red
   ▶ Who tries to steal the kite? Old March Wind; the wind
   ▶ Who helps the poet fly her kite? Daddy
   ▶ Reread the last four lines of "For Keeps." What word rhymes with *tight*? *kite*

3. Reread "The March Wind" aloud, encouraging students to chime in and read with you. Then have students say in their own words what the poem is about.

   ▶ Point to the name of the author. Who wrote this poem? Anonymous What does *anonymous* mean? No one knows who wrote the poem.
   ▶ Reread the first stanza of "The March Wind." What word rhymes with *play*? *day*
   ▶ Reread the second stanza of "The March Wind." What word rhymes with *down*? *brown*   What word rhymes with *fro*? *low*

TIP If students have trouble responding to a question, help them locate the answer in the text.

Objectives

- Listen to and discuss poetry.
- Answer questions requiring literal recall of details.
- Identify structure of poems and poetic elements: rhyme, rhythm, repetition, and/or alliteration.
- Identify and describe the use of print features: boldface, underlining, highlighting, italic, capital letters.
- Identify author.

Reading for Meaning

Personification and How to Draw Conclusions in Poems
Explore personification and drawing conclusions.

1. Remind students that poets make poems interesting by making things sound like they're human. We can also figure out things, or draw a conclusion, about a poem by listening for things the poet hints at but doesn't actually say.

2. Check students' ability to recognize and comprehend personification.

   ▸ In "For Keeps," what kinds of things does the poet say about Old March Wind that makes it sound like it's a person? Possible answers: He had a tug of war; he tried to steal the kite; he gave up. Can the wind really steal a kite? No Why not? It isn't a person.
   ▸ In "The March Wind," how does the poet make the wind sound human? What things does the wind say it does? Possible answers: go to work; play; whistle; toss and shake branches; wake up flowers

3. Check students' ability to draw a conclusion.

   ▸ Read aloud the last six lines of "Go Wind." What does the poet mean when she says, "No wind, no/Not me—/not *me*"? She doesn't want the wind to blow her away.
   ▸ In "For Keeps," what does the poet mean when she says Old March Wind "tried to steal my new red kite"? The wind blew so hard it almost pulled the kite string out of her hands. Does the poet say directly that the wind blew really hard and almost pulled the kite out of her hands? No How did you draw that conclusion? What clues from the poem and personal experience helped you figure that out? Possible answers: When you have a tug of war, you pull really hard; when the wind is blowing really hard, it can feel like it's pulling things.
   ▸ Who is speaking in the poem "The March Wind"? the wind How can you tell? the word *I*

Objectives
- Identify literary devices: personification and/or simile.
- Draw conclusions using text, illustrations, and/or prior knowledge.
- Support conclusions with evidence from text and/or prior knowledge.
- Identify the narrator of a text.
- Identify first-person point of view.

Making Connections

Who Am I?

Check students' ability to draw conclusions to solve riddles. Turn to page LC 13 in *K¹² Language Arts Activity Book*.

1. Remind students that they can figure out things that a poet doesn't say directly. Tell them that a riddle is a good example of a text that gives readers clues to help them figure out something.

2. Read aloud the first riddle on the Activity Book page as you track the words with your finger.

3. Have students figure out the answer. the sky

   ▸ If students have trouble answering, give them a hint, such as, "If you were outside, you could look up and see it."

4. Help students write the answer on the blank line.

5. Repeat Steps 2–4 for the second riddle. a carrot

   ▸ If students have trouble answering, give them a hint, such as, "It's something you can eat as a snack" or "It's a vegetable."

6. Ask students about how they solved the riddles.

   ▸ What hints in the riddle and clues from your own experience helped you figure out that the answer to Riddle 1 is the sky? What do you know from your own experience that helped you figure it out? Students may say that they know the sky is blue during the daytime but it's black at night when the sun is gone.

   ▸ What hints in the riddle and clues from your own experience helped you figure out that the answer to Riddle 2 is a carrot? Students may say that they know carrots are orange, grow underground, and crunch when they chew them.

Objectives

- Draw conclusions using text, illustrations, and/or prior knowledge.
- Support conclusions with evidence from text and/or prior knowledge.

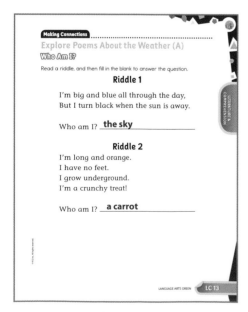

Introduce "Strong Wind's Bride"

Lesson Overview

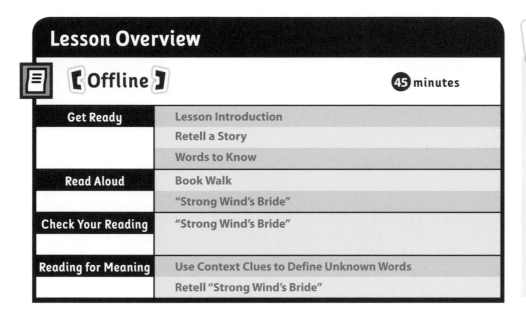

Offline — 45 minutes

Get Ready	Lesson Introduction
	Retell a Story
	Words to Know
Read Aloud	Book Walk
	"Strong Wind's Bride"
Check Your Reading	"Strong Wind's Bride"
Reading for Meaning	Use Context Clues to Define Unknown Words
	Retell "Strong Wind's Bride"

Advance Preparation

Read "Strong Wind's Bride" before beginning the Read Aloud to locate Words to Know in the text.

Big Ideas

► Comprehension entails an understanding of story structure.
► Comprehension requires the reader to self-monitor understanding.
► Early learners acquire vocabulary through active exposure (by talking and listening, being read to, and receiving explicit instruction).
► Verbalizing your thoughts while modeling a reading strategy allows students to see what goes on inside the head of an effective reader; it makes visible the normally hidden process of comprehending text.

Materials

Supplied
- "Strong Wind's Bride," *K¹² Classics for Young Readers, Volume A*, pp. 34–45
- Story Card B
- *K¹² Language Arts Activity Book*, pp. LC 15–17

Also Needed
- scissors, round-end safety
- glue stick

Story Synopsis

In this Native American version of "Cinderella," the young women of a village are asked to describe the invisible Strong Wind to become his bride. Many pretend to see the mighty warrior, but only the girl with an honest and true heart can actually see him.

Keywords

context clue – a word or phrase in a text that helps you figure out the meaning of an unknown word
illustration – a drawing
retelling – using your own words to tell a story that you have listened to or read

[Offline] 45 minutes

Work **together** with students to complete Get Ready, Read Aloud, Check Your Reading, and Reading for Meaning activities.

Get Ready

Lesson Introduction

Prepare students for listening to and discussing "Strong Wind's Bride."

1. Tell students that you are going to read "Strong Wind's Bride," a Native American story that is similar to the fairy tale "Cinderella."

2. Explain that before you read the story, you will get ready by discussing how to retell the stories we listen to or read.

Retell a Story

Introduce how to retell a story.

1. Tell students that one way we can check that we understand a story is by telling the story in our own words. We call this **retelling**.

2. Explain to students that when good readers retell a story, they **tell the most important things that happen in the beginning, middle, and end of the story**. They mention where the story takes place, the characters, and the things that the characters do.

3. Gather Story Card B. Have students look at the picture of the family riding bikes and having a picnic in the park.
   Say: Last Saturday, the Franklin family packed up lots of food and games, and then got on their bikes and rode to the park. Dad grilled burgers for lunch, while the kids rode their bikes and flew their new kites. Later, the whole family joined in a game of volleyball. When it got cold, the family packed up their gear and rode their bikes home. Everyone went to bed early that night because they were so tired from riding their bikes and playing at the park all day.

   ‣ In what part of the story does the Franklin family pack up lots of food? the beginning   Retell that part of the story. The Franklin family packed up food and games, and rode their bikes to the park.
   ‣ In what part of the story does Dad grill burgers? the middle   Retell that part of the story. Dad grilled burgers; the kids rode their bikes and flew kites; everyone played volleyball.
   ‣ In what part of the story does the family go home? the end   Retell that part of the story. The family rode their bikes home; they all went to bed early because they were so tired.

Objectives

- Identify the beginning, middle, and end of a story.
- Retell the beginning, middle, and end of a story.
- Self-monitor comprehension of text.
- Activate prior knowledge by previewing text and/or discussing topic.
- Build vocabulary through listening, reading, and discussion.
- Use new vocabulary in written and spoken sentences.

4. Have students retell the entire story. The retelling should include the same information students gave when they retold the beginning, middle, and end of the story.

5. Guide students think about their retellings. Answers to questions may vary.

> ▸ Did your retelling include the important characters?
> ▸ Did it include most of the important things that happened?
> ▸ Do you think you understand the story?

 TIP If students forgot to mention characters or important events in their retelling, have them retell the story again as you ask questions such as, "Who is in the story? What did they do?" If students don't think they understand the story, reread it aloud, pausing to let students ask questions as you read.

Words to Know

Before reading "Strong Wind's Bride," go over Words to Know with students.

1. Read aloud each word and have students repeat it.

2. Ask students if they know what each word means.

> ▸ If students know a word's meaning, have them define it and use it in a sentence.
> ▸ If students don't know a word's meaning, read them the definition and discuss the word with them.

appearance – the way somebody or something looks
cord – a strong, thick string
hide – animal skin
jealous – feeling angry or bitter because you want what someone else has
strut – to walk in a way that shows you are proud and think that you are important

Read Aloud

Book Walk

Prepare students for reading by taking them on a Book Walk of "Strong Wind's Bride." Scan the story together and ask students to make predictions about the story. Answers to questions may vary.

1. Turn to the **table of contents** in *K¹² Classics for Young Readers, Volume A*. Help students find the selection and turn to that page.

2. Point to and read aloud the **title of the story**.

> ▸ What do you think the story is about?

3. Have students look at the **pictures of the story**.

> ▸ Where do you think the story takes place?
> ▸ What do you think might happen in the story?
> ▸ What do you know about "Cinderella"? What are some things that happen in that story?

 TIP *Algonquian* is pronounced al-GAHN-kwee-uhn.

> **Objectives**
> - Make predictions based on text, illustrations, and/or prior knowledge.
> - Activate prior knowledge by previewing text and/or discussing topic.
> - Listen and respond to texts representing a variety of cultures, time periods, and traditions.

"Strong Wind's Bride"

It's time to read aloud the story.

1. Have students sit next to you so that they can see the pictures and words while you read aloud.

2. Remind them to listen carefully so they can retell who the characters are and what happens in the beginning, middle, and end of the story.

3. Encourage students to look at the pictures to help them better understand the story and unknown words.

4. **Read aloud the entire story.** Track with your finger so students can follow along. Emphasize Words to Know as you come to them. If appropriate, use the pictures to help show what each word means.

Check Your Reading

"Strong Wind's Bride"

Check students' comprehension of "Strong Wind's Bride."

▶ What does Strong Wind's sister do with her brother's moccasins every night? hangs them on the wall

▶ In the story, there is a poor man who has three daughters. Why does the youngest daughter have a burnt face? Her older sisters make her work over a fire; sparks from the fire have burned her face.

▶ Why do many village girls walk to Strong Wind's wigwam? because he is looking for a bride

▶ What must a village girl do before she can marry Strong Wind? She must to be able to prove that she can see him; she must answer the question Strong Wind's sister asks.

▶ What does Strong Wind use to pull his sled? a rainbow

▶ What happens when Strong Wind's sister gives the burnt-faced girl a bath? Possible answers: Her burns and scars disappear; her skin becomes smooth; her hair grows back.

 If students have trouble responding to a question, help them locate the answer in the text or pictures.

Objectives
- Answer questions requiring literal recall of details.

Reading for Meaning

Use Context Clues to Define Unknown Words

Check students' ability to use context clues and pictures to determine the meaning of words.

1. Remind students that sometimes the words and pictures in a story can help a reader figure out what an unknown word means.

2. Tell students that you will show them how to figure out the meaning of a word while explaining to them what you are thinking as you do it. This will help them know what goes on in a good reader's mind as the reader figures out the meaning of a word.

3. Turn to page 35 of "Strong Wind's Bride." Read aloud the first paragraph on the page.
   Say: I'm not sure what *shore* means in the sentence "One spring day, Strong Wind's sister walked along the shore of the lake to the nearby village." The sentence mentions *the lake*, and I see in the picture that people are walking on the land next to the lake. I think *shore* means the land next to the lake.

   ► Does *the land next to the lake* make sense in the sentence? "One spring day, Strong Wind's sister walked along the land next to the lake to the nearby village." Yes

4. Point to the picture on page 34 of "Strong Wind's Bride" and have students study it. Read aloud the last two sentences on page 34. Tell students that when they answer the following question, they should think aloud like you did.

   ► What do you think *moccasins* means? a kind of shoe; As students think aloud, they should mention that the story says Strong Wind's sister hangs up his moccasins when he comes home, and that the picture shows a pair of shoes hanging from a wall.

5. Have students study the picture on page 35. Read aloud the first sentence in the second paragraph on page 35. Tell students to think aloud when they answer the following question.

   ► What do you think *wigwam* means? a kind of house; As students think aloud, they should mention that the story says Strong Wind's sister waits by the wigwam, and the picture shows her standing in front of a kind of house with a doorway.

Objectives

- Demonstrate understanding by thinking aloud.
- Use context and sentence structure to determine meaning of words, phrases, and/or sentences.
- Use illustrations to aid understanding of text.
- Follow written directions.
- Sequence pictures illustrating story events.
- Retell a story using various media.
- Retell the beginning, middle, and end of a story.
- Self-monitor comprehension of text.

6. Turn to page 36 of "Strong Wind's Bride." Have students study the picture on the page. Read aloud the text on the page.

▸ What do you think *untruthful* means? not telling the truth; lying; not honest   What clues in the story and picture help you figure this out? The story says that Strong Wind's sister knows that the girls are lying because they give the wrong answer to her question, and the picture shows a girl who looks like she's ashamed for doing something wrong.

Retell "Strong Wind's Bride"

Check students' ability to retell "Strong Wind's Bride" and their understanding of the story's sequence. Turn to pages LC 15–17 in *K[12] Language Arts Activity Book*.

1. Have students read aloud the directions at the top of the page.

2. Have students cut out the pictures on page LC 15 and glue them to page LC 17 in the order in which the events took place in the story.

▸ If necessary, have students refer back to the story to determine the order of the pictures.

3. Have students retell "Strong Wind's Bride" by referring to the pictures and answering the following questions.

▸ What happens in the beginning of the story? Possible answer: Strong Wind's sister tells the people that her brother will marry the girl who can see him. Many girls from the village go see Strong Wind's sister. The girls can't see Strong Wind, but many of them lie and say they can.

▸ What happens in the middle of the story? Possible answer: A man in the village has three daughters. The two older daughters are mean to the youngest one and make her do all the work. The two older daughters go to see Strong Wind's sister. They lie and say they can see Strong Wind, but all they see are his moccasins. They go home in shame. When the youngest sister says that she might see Strong Wind, the older sisters laugh at her.

▸ What happens at the end of the story? Possible answer: The youngest sister goes to see Strong Wind's sister. She is truthful, and she can see Strong Wind. Strong Wind and the girl get married.

4. Have students retell the entire story in sequence. Their retelling should include the same information given when they did retellings of the beginning, middle, and end of the story.

5. Guide students to think about their retelling. Answers to questions may vary.

   ▶ Did your retelling include the important characters?
   ▶ Did it include most of the important things that happened, in the correct order?
   ▶ Do you think you understand the story?

TIP If students forgot to mention characters or important events in their retelling, have them retell the story again as you ask questions such as, "Who is in the story? What did they do?" If students don't think they understand the story, reread the story aloud, pausing to let students ask questions as you read.

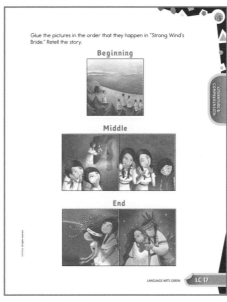

Explore "Strong Wind's Bride"

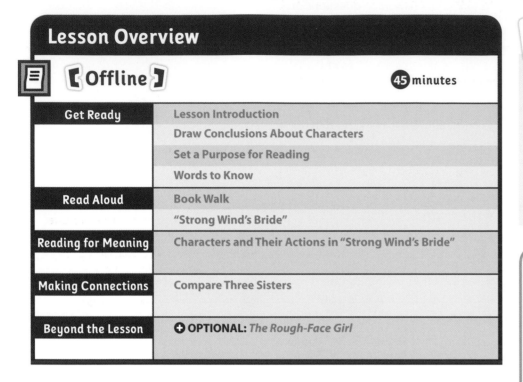

Lesson Overview

Offline — 45 minutes

Get Ready	Lesson Introduction
	Draw Conclusions About Characters
	Set a Purpose for Reading
	Words to Know
Read Aloud	Book Walk
	"Strong Wind's Bride"
Reading for Meaning	Characters and Their Actions in "Strong Wind's Bride"
Making Connections	Compare Three Sisters
Beyond the Lesson	⊕ OPTIONAL: *The Rough-Face Girl*

Materials

Supplied

- "Strong Wind's Bride," *K¹² Classics for Young Readers, Volume A,* pp. 34–45
- *K¹² Language Arts Activity Book,* p. LC 18
- *K¹² My Journal,* pp. 2–53

Keywords

character – a person or animal in a story

compare – to explain how two or more things are alike

conclusion – a reasoned decision made about something not stated directly in a text through the consideration of information provided and what is already known

contrast – to explain how two or more things are different

Big Ideas

- ▸ Good readers use prior knowledge and text clues to infer, or draw conclusions about, what is implied but not directly stated in text.
- ▸ An awareness of story structure elements (setting, characters, plot) provides readers a foundation for constructing meaning when reading new stories and writing their own stories.
- ▸ To understand and interpret a story, readers need to understand and describe characters and what they do.
- ▸ Comprehension entails having and knowing a purpose for reading.
- ▸ Comprehension entails asking and answering questions about text.

 **Offline** **45** minutes

Work **together** with students to complete Get Ready, Read Aloud, Reading for Meaning, Making Connections, and Beyond the Lesson activities.

Get Ready

Lesson Introduction
Prepare students for listening to and discussing "Strong Wind's Bride."

1. Tell students that you will reread "Strong Wind's Bride."

2. Explain that before you reread the story, you will get ready by discussing

   ▸ What a character's words and actions tell us about the character
   ▸ What it means to have a purpose for reading
   ▸ Why it's important to have a purpose for reading

 Objectives
- Draw conclusions using text, illustrations, and/or prior knowledge.
- Set a purpose for reading.
- Generate questions and seek information to answer questions.
- Build vocabulary through listening, reading, and discussion.
- Use new vocabulary in written and spoken sentences.

Draw Conclusions About Characters
Explore characters and the conclusions we can draw about them.

1. Remind students that characters' words and actions help us to figure out, or draw conclusions about, what characters are like.

2. Explain to students that we can draw conclusions about the characters in "Strong Wind's Bride" based on their words and actions. For example, many of the girls from the village say that they can see Strong Wind when they really can't see him. We can draw the conclusion that the girls want Strong Wind to choose them for his wife.

   ▸ What other conclusions can we draw about the girls from the village? Possible answers: They are not honest; they are not truthful; they want to get married; they think Strong Wind would be a good husband.

Set a Purpose for Reading
Explore how to set a purpose for reading. Gather *K¹² My Journal* and have students turn to the next available page for **writing** in Thoughts and Experiences.

1. Remind students that good readers have a purpose, or reason, for reading a story. A reader's purpose could be to read for fun or to find out certain information. Having a purpose for reading helps readers focus on the important information in a story and remember what they read.

2. Tell students they will be completing an activity in which they will compare the three sisters in the story.

   ▸ What do you think is your purpose, or reason, for listening to "Strong Wind's Bride?" to get information about the sisters

3. Explain that one way readers can prepare to gather information from a story is to think of questions they would like to find answers for.

4. Have students dictate at least three questions about the sisters that they would like to find answers for. Write what students say in the journal.

  ▸ If students have trouble thinking of questions, give them an example question that you'd like to find an answer for.

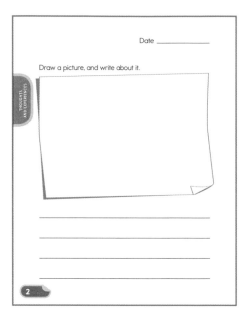

Words to Know

Before reading "Strong Wind's Bride," go over Words to Know with students.

1. Read aloud each word and have students repeat it.

2. Ask students if they know what each word means.

  ▸ If students know a word's meaning, have them define it and use it in a sentence.
  ▸ If students don't know a word's meaning, read them the definition and discuss the word with them.

appearance – the way somebody or something looks
cord – a strong, thick string
hide – animal skin
jealous – feeling angry or bitter because you want what someone else has
strut – to walk in a way that shows you are proud and think that you are important

Read Aloud

Book Walk

Prepare students by taking them on a Book Walk of "Strong Wind's Bride." Scan the story together to revisit the characters and events.

1. Turn to the selection in *K¹² Classics for Young Readers, Volume A*. Read aloud the **title of the story**.

2. Have students review the **pictures of the story**.

3. Point to the picture of the three girls on page 40.

   ▸ Who are these characters? the three sisters
   ▸ Why do two of the sisters have long braids and nice clothes, while the third one does not? The two older sisters cut off the younger sister's braids and make her wear rags.

Objectives

- Activate prior knowledge by previewing text and/or discussing topic.
- Listen and respond to texts representing a variety of cultures, time periods, and traditions.

"Strong Wind's Bride"

It's time to reread the story.

1. Have students sit next to you so that they can see the pictures and words while you read aloud the story.

2. Tell students to listen carefully for information about the sisters and for answers to their questions about them.

3. **Read aloud the entire story.** Track with your finger so students can follow along. Emphasize Words to Know as you come to them. If appropriate, use the pictures to help show what each word means.

Reading for Meaning

Characters and Their Actions in "Strong Wind's Bride"

Check students' ability to describe and draw conclusions about characters. Gather *K¹² My Journal* and have students turn to the page with their questions about the story.

1. Have students retell "Strong Wind's Bride" in their own words to develop grammar, vocabulary, comprehension, and fluency skills.

2. Read aloud the first question in the journal while tracking with your finger.

3. Have students answer the question verbally.

   ▸ If students have trouble responding to a question, help them locate the answer in the text or pictures.
   ▸ If the answer cannot be found in the story, explain that sometimes our questions are not answered directly in the story. But we can often guess what the answer may be, based on the story's events and characters' actions.

Objectives

- Retell or dramatize a story.
- Generate questions and seek information to answer questions.
- Describe character(s).
- Identify details that explain characters' actions and feelings.
- Draw conclusions using text, illustrations, and/or prior knowledge.

4. Ask students the following questions. Skip any questions that were already answered in the journaling activity.

▶ Why do the older sisters cut of the youngest sister's braids and give her rags to wear? They are jealous of her.

▶ The older sisters say to their sister, "Now who will want to marry you, you ugly burnt-faced girl!" What can you figure out, or what conclusions can you draw, about the older sisters? Possible answers: They're mean; they're bullies; they don't like their sister.

▶ Why do you think the older sisters wear jewelry and their finest clothes when they go to meet Strong Wind's sister? Guide students to recognize that the sisters think Strong Wind will want to marry them if they look pretty.

▶ Why do the older sisters say that they can see Strong Wind when they really can't? They want to marry him; he will only marry somebody that can see him.   What does this tell us about the older sisters? Possible answers: They are liars; they are not honest; they think they can trick Strong Wind's sister.

▶ What do the older sisters say when their younger sister says that maybe she will see Strong Wind? They say that Strong Wind would never marry her with her scarred face and chopped-off braids.   What does this tell us about the older sisters? Possible answers: They think that looks are very important; they think that Strong Wind will only marry somebody who is pretty.

▶ Why do Strong Wind's sister's eyes light up when the burnt-face girl says Strong Wind pulls his sled with a rainbow? because she knows that the girl can really see Strong Wind

Making Connections

 Compare Three Sisters

Help students use a graphic organizer to compare characters in "Strong Wind's Bride." Turn to page LC 18 in *K¹² Language Arts Activity Book*.

1. In the Compare Three Sisters chart, point to the characters' names at the top of the columns and read them aloud. Point to and read aloud the first row heading, "How they look."

2. Help students write their answers in the first row of boxes for the appropriate characters.

3. Repeat Steps 1 and 2 until the chart is complete.

4. Ask the following questions to encourage discussion and comparison of the characters.

   ▸ How are the older sisters and the youngest sister alike? They all go to see Strong Wind's sister.

   ▸ How are the older sisters and the youngest sister different? Possible answers: The older sisters are cruel and jealous, and the youngest sister is kind and gentle; the older sisters are sent away because they lie, and the youngest sister marries Strong Wind because she is honest.

   ▸ If you had to choose a sister to be friends with, which would you choose and why? Be sure to have students give examples from the story to support their answer.

   ▸ Why do you think the youngest sister can see Strong Wind but her sisters can't? Answers will vary.

Objectives

- Compare and contrast story structure elements within a text.
- Demonstrate understanding through graphic organizers.
- Draw conclusions using text, illustrations, and/or prior knowledge.

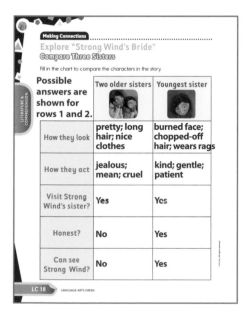

Beyond the Lesson

⊕ OPTIONAL: *The Rough-Face Girl*

This activity is OPTIONAL. It is intended for students who have extra time and would enjoy reading another version of "Strong Wind's Bride." Feel free to skip this activity.

1. Go to a library for a copy of *The Rough-Face Girl* by Rafe Martin.

2. Lead a Book Walk and then read aloud the story.

3. Have students tell how "Strong Wind's Bride" and *The Rough-Face Girl* are alike and different. Be sure students describe how the beginning, middle, and end of the stories are alike and different.

4. Discuss how the characters are alike and different in the two stories.

5. Ask students to tell which version of the story is their favorite and why.

Objectives

- Compare and contrast two texts on the same topic.
- Compare and contrast story structure elements across texts.

Explore Poems About the Weather (B)

Lesson Overview

Offline — **45** minutes

Get Ready	Lesson Introduction
	Poetic Elements and Narration
	Words to Know
Read Aloud	Book Walk
	"To Walk in Warm Rain," "Rain," and "Thunder"
Check Your Reading	"To Walk in Warm Rain," "Rain," and "Thunder"
Reading for Meaning	Poetic Elements and Narration
Making Connections	Write a Rain Poem

Advance Preparation

Read "To Walk in Warm Rain," "Rain," and "Thunder" before beginning the Read Aloud to locate Words to Know in the text.

Big Ideas

▶ Poems are different from prose in structure and content. They are generally organized in lines and often contain rhymes.

▶ Readers must focus on the specific language of a text to aid in interpretation.

Materials

Supplied

● *Weather: Poems for All Seasons*, pp. 31, 35, 36–37

● *K¹² Language Arts Activity Book*, p. LC 19

Also Needed

● crayons

Poetry Synopses

Different aspects of the rain are described in three poems.

Keywords

alliteration – the use of words with the same or close to the same beginning sounds

first-person point of view – the telling of a story by a character in that story, using pronouns such as *I*, *me*, and *we*

italic – text that slants toward the right

narrator – the teller of a story

rhyme – when two or more words have the same ending sounds; for example, *cat* and *hat* rhyme

 **Offline** **45** minutes

Work **together** with students to complete Get Ready, Read Aloud, Check Your Reading, Reading for Meaning, and Making Connections activities.

Get Ready

Lesson Introduction

Prepare students for listening to and discussing poems about rain.

1. Tell students that you are going to read "To Walk in Warm Rain," "Rain," and "Thunder." All three poems are about the rain in some way.

2. Explain to students that before you read the poems, you will get ready by discussing how a poet

   ▸ Can be the person speaking in a poem.
   ▸ Sometimes starts many words in a poem with the same sound.

Poetic Elements and Narration

Introduce the concept of a narrator and review alliteration.

1. Explain to students that the person speaking in a poem is called the **narrator**. Sometimes we can tell that the narrator is the person who wrote the poem. We can tell that the poet is the narrator when we hear words such as *I*, *my*, and *me* in the poem.

2. Remind students that poets sometimes start many words in a poem with the same sound.

3. Tell students to listen carefully to hear who is speaking in a poem and to listen for repeated sounds. **Read aloud the poem.**

   The Snow
   by Art Friday
   I like to see the snow drift down
   A cold, white blanket that covers my town.

   ▸ Who is speaking in the poem? the poet; Art Friday   How can you tell? the words *I* and *my*
   ▸ Reread the first line of the poem. What two words begin with the sound /s/? *see* and *snow*
   ▸ Reread the second line of the poem. What two words begin with the sound /k/? *cold* and *covers*

4. Tell students that when they listen to poetry, they should listen for clues about who is speaking and notice how the sounds of the poem are pleasing to the ear.

TIP Although an objective for this lesson is to identify first-person point of view, there is no need to introduce the term to students.

 Objectives

- Listen to and discuss poetry.
- Identify first-person point of view.
- Identify the narrator of a text.
- Identify structure of poems and poetic elements: rhyme, rhythm, repetition, and/or alliteration.
- Build vocabulary through listening, reading, and discussion.
- Use new vocabulary in written and spoken sentences.

Words to Know

Before reading "To Walk in Warm Rain," "Rain," and "Thunder," go over Words to Know with students.

1. Read aloud each word and have students repeat it.

2. Ask students if they know what each word means.

   ▶ If students know a word's meaning, have them define it and use it in a sentence.

   ▶ If students don't know a word's meaning, read them the definition and discuss the word with them.

drain – a pipe that carries water away from a sink or bathtub
rumbling – a low, heavy sound
whip – to move quickly

Read Aloud

Book Walk

Prepare students by taking them on a Book Walk of "To Walk in Warm Rain," "Rain," and "Thunder." Scan the poems together and ask students to make predictions about the poems. Answers to questions may vary.

1. Turn to "To Walk in Warm Rain" on page 31 in *Weather: Poems for All Seasons.*

2. Point to and read aloud the **title of the poem** and the **name of the poet**. Have students repeat the poet's name.

3. Have students study the **picture**.

   ▶ What do you think the poem is about?
   ▶ Have you ever played in the rain?

4. Turn to "Rain" on page 35.

5. Point to and read aloud the **title of the poem** and the **name of the poet**. Have students repeat the poet's name.

6. Have students study the **pictures**.

   ▶ What do you think the poem is about?
   ▶ Why do you think the girl is outside in shorts in one picture and inside wearing a sweater in the other picture? because it's warm outside in the first picture and it's cold outside in the second one

7. Turn to "Thunder" on pages 36 and 37.

8. Point to and read aloud the **title of the poem** and the **name of the poet**. Have students repeat the poet's name.

Objectives
- Make predictions based on text, illustrations, and/or prior knowledge.
- Activate prior knowledge by previewing text and/or discussing topic.
- Listen to and discuss poetry.

9. Have students study the **pictures**.

   ▸ What do you think the poem is about?
   ▸ Why do you think the boy is covering his ears in the picture? Thunder makes a loud noise.
   ▸ Have you ever heard thunder? Did it scare you?

10. Point to the word *must*. Explain that the letters are slanting to show that the word should be read differently, or with more emphasis.

11. Point to the word *LOUD*. Explain that it is written with capital letters so the reader knows to say it with a loud voice.

"To Walk in Warm Rain," "Rain," and "Thunder"

It's time to read aloud the poems.

1. Have students sit next to you so that they can see the pictures and words while you read aloud.

2. Tell students to listen carefully to hear who the narrator is, or who is speaking in the poems.

3. Remind students to listen for sounds that repeat at the beginning of words, as well as words that rhyme.

4. **Read aloud all three poems.** Track with your finger so students can follow along. Emphasize Words to Know as you come to them. If appropriate, use the pictures to help show what each word means.

5. Remember to emphasize the words *must* and *LOUD* in the poem "Thunder."

Check Your Reading

"To Walk in Warm Rain," "Rain," and "Thunder"

Check students' comprehension of the poems.

1. Reread "To Walk in Warm Rain" aloud, encouraging students to chime in and read with you. Then have students say in their own words what the poem is about.

   ▸ Point to the name of the poet. Who wrote this poem? David McCord
   ▸ What happens when you walk in warm rain? You get wetter and wetter.
   ▸ Reread the two lines that end with *rain* and *drain*. What word rhymes with *rain*? *drain*

2. Reread "Rain" aloud, encouraging students to chime in and read with you. Then have students say in their own words what the poem is about.

   ▸ What words does the poet use to describe summer rain? *soft* and *cool*
   ▸ What word does the poet use to describe winter rain? *cold*
   ▸ Reread the first stanza of the poem. What word rhymes with *cool*? *pool*

Objectives

- Identify author.
- Listen to and discuss poetry.
- Answer questions requiring literal recall of details.
- Identify structure of poems and poetic elements: rhyme, rhythm, repetition, and/or alliteration.
- Identify and describe the use of print features: boldface, underlining, highlighting, italic, capital letters.

3. Reread "Thunder" aloud, encouraging students to chime in and read with you. Then have students say in their own words what the poem is about.

▸ What words does the poet use to describe the sound of thunder? Possible answers: *crashing; cracking; racing; roaring; rumbling*

▸ Point to the word *must*. Why are the letters in this word slanting? to show that you should read this word differently than the rest of the words in the poem; to show that you should emphasize this word

▸ Point to the word *LOUD*. Why is this word written in all capital letters? to show that you should read it in a loud voice

TIP If students have trouble responding to a question, help them locate the answer in the text or pictures.

Reading for Meaning

Poetic Elements and Narration
Check students' ability to recognize alliteration and first-person point of view in poems.

1. Remind students that poets make poems interesting by starting words with the same sound and repeating words.

2. Reread the first two lines of "To Walk in Warm Rain."

▸ What sound do you hear at the beginning of many of the words? /w/ Which words begin with sound /w/? *walk, warm,* and *wetter*

3. Reread the entire poem "To Walk in Warm Rain."

▸ What phrases are repeated in the poem? *To walk in warm rain* and *and get wetter and wetter*

4. Reread "Rain."

▸ Who is speaking in this poem? the poet; the author   How do you know? the word *I*

5. Reread the text on page 36 of "Thunder."

▸ What words begin with the sound /k/? *crashing* and *cracking*

▸ The word *racing* begins with the sound /r/. What other word begins with the sound /r/? *roaring*

Objectives

- Identify structure of poems and poetic elements: rhyme, rhythm, repetition, and/or alliteration.
- Identify the narrator of a text.
- Identify first-person point of view.
- Support conclusions with evidence from text and/or prior knowledge.

Making Connections

Write a Rain Poem

Check students' understanding of rhyme as they write their own rain poem. Turn to page LC 19 in *K¹² Language Arts Activity Book*.

1. Remind students that poems often have words that rhyme at the ends of lines.

2. Tell them they will choose pairs of rhyming words to write their own poem about the rain.

3. Read aloud the poem, pausing at each blank line so students can choose a word.

   ▸ Tell students that one pair of rhyming words should appear at the ends of lines 1 and 3, and another pair should appear at the ends of lines 2 and 4.
   ▸ Read aloud the first row of words in the word bank and have students choose a word to fill in the blank at the end of line 1.
   ▸ Read aloud the second row and have students choose a word to fill in the blank at the end of line 2.
   ▸ Reread the words in the first row of the word bank and have students choose a word to fill in the blank at the end of line 3.
   ▸ Reread the words in the second row and have students choose a word to fill in the blank at the end of line 4.
   ▸ If students wish to use rhyming words that are not in the word bank, allow them to do so.

4. Help students write the words they chose in the blanks.

   ▸ If students are ready to write on their own, allow them to do so.

5. Have students write their name on the blank line under the title.

Objectives
- Identify structure of poems and poetic elements: rhyme, rhythm, repetition, and/or alliteration.
- Demonstrate visualizing through drawing, discussion, and/or writing.

6. Have students read aloud the completed poem **with** you as you track the words with your finger. Answers to questions may vary.

  ▸ What word is said over and over in the poem? *rain*
  ▸ Which rhyming words did you choose for the ends of lines 1 and 3?
  ▸ Which words did you choose for lines 2 and 4?
  ▸ What do you imagine in your head when you hear the poem?

7. If time allows, have students draw a picture that shows what they imagine in their head when they hear their poem.

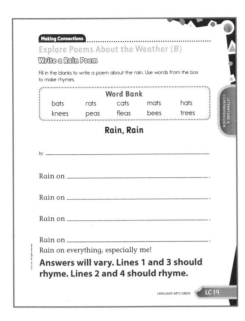

Introduce "Shedding Light on Rainbows"

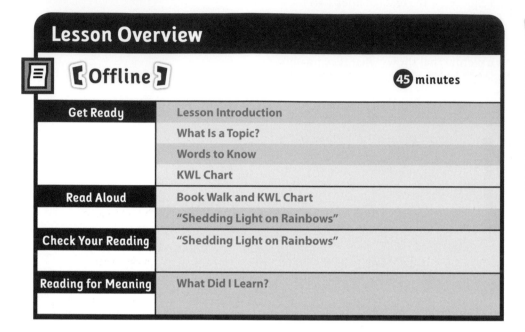

Lesson Overview

[Offline] 45 minutes

Get Ready	Lesson Introduction
	What Is a Topic?
	Words to Know
	KWL Chart
Read Aloud	Book Walk and KWL Chart
	"Shedding Light on Rainbows"
Check Your Reading	"Shedding Light on Rainbows"
Reading for Meaning	What Did I Learn?

Advance Preparation

Read "Shedding Light on Rainbows" before beginning the Read Aloud to locate Words to Know in the text.

Big Ideas

▸ Comprehension entails having and knowing a purpose for reading.
▸ Activating prior knowledge provides a framework for a reader to organize and connect new information to information previously learned; readers that activate prior knowledge before reading are more likely to understand and recall what they read.
▸ Comprehension entails asking and answering questions about the text.

[Materials]

Supplied
- "Shedding Light on Rainbows," *K¹² World: Earth and Sky*, pp. 2–11
- *K¹² Language Arts Activity Book*, p. LC 20

Article Synopsis

Rainbows have fascinated people throughout the ages. Just what is the science behind these magical displays of color?

Keywords

prior knowledge – things you already know from past experience
topic – the subject of a text

 **45** minutes

Work **together** with students to complete Get Ready, Read Aloud, Check Your Reading, and Reading for Meaning activities.

Get Ready ....

Lesson Introduction
Prepare students for listening to and discussing "Shedding Light on Rainbows."

1. Tell students that you are going to read "Shedding Light on Rainbows," a nonfiction magazine article that explains what causes rainbows.

2. Explain that before you read the article, you will get ready by discussing
   ▸ How to identify the topic of an article
   ▸ Having a purpose, or reason, for reading a text

 Objectives
- Identify the topic.
- Build vocabulary through listening, reading, and discussion.
- Use new vocabulary in written and spoken sentences.
- Increase concept and content vocabulary.
- Set a purpose for reading.
- Generate questions and seek information to answer questions.
- Demonstrate understanding through graphic organizers.
- Activate prior knowledge by previewing text and/or discussing topic.

What Is a Topic?
Introduce students to the idea of a topic.

1. Tell students that every magazine article has a **topic**. The topic is what the article is about. Good readers can figure out the topic by thinking about the title of an article and asking, "What is this article mostly about?"

2. Have students practice naming the topic of an article.
   Say: Listen carefully as I read the title of an article and what it's about. In the article "Beautiful Blue Whales," the author tells interesting facts about the largest animal on earth.
   ▸ What do you think is the topic of the article "Beautiful Blue Whales"? blue whales

3. Tell students that when they read articles, they should try to figure out what the topic is.

Words to Know

Before reading "Shedding Light on Rainbows," go over Words to Know with students.

1. Read aloud each word and have students repeat it.

2. Ask students if they know what each word means.

   ▸ If students know a word's meaning, have them define it and use it in a sentence.
   ▸ If students don't know a word's meaning, read them the definition and discuss the word with them.

arch – to make a curved line
band – stripe
prism – a block of clear glass that separates light passing through it into the colors of the rainbow

 Prism is pronounced PRIH-zuhm.

KWL Chart

Introduce students to prereading activities and reading for a specific purpose. Turn to page LC 20 in *K¹² Language Arts Activity Book*.

1. **Say:** This is called a KWL (Know/Want to know/Learn chart). It will help us get ready to read. It will also help us organize our thoughts on what we want to know.

2. **Point** to the K column.
   Say: The K stands for **know**. A good reader asks, "What do I already know about this subject?" before he or she reads an article.

   ▸ Thinking about what we already know helps get our brain ready to learn more about the subject.

3. **Point** to the W column.
   Say: The W stands for **want**. A good reader asks, "What do I want to know, or wonder, about this subject?" before he or she reads an article.

   ▸ Good readers ask questions about what they want to know and then look for the answers while they read. Looking for the answers to our questions is the **purpose** for reading this article.
   ▸ Asking questions helps readers better understand what they read because they focus on the important information to answer their questions. They're also motivated to read to find answers to their questions.

4. **Point** to the L column.

   Say: The L stands for **learn**. Good readers think about what they've learned after they read an article.

5. Tell students that they will work on the K and W columns of the chart before they begin reading. They will complete the L column after they read.

TIP Students will not complete the chart in this activity. Keep the Activity Book page in a safe place so students can complete it later.

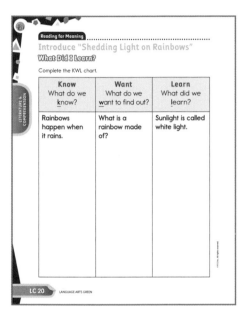

Read Aloud

Book Walk and KWL Chart

Prepare students by taking them on a Book Walk of "Shedding Light on Rainbows." Scan the magazine article together and ask students to make predictions about the text. Gather the KWL chart on page LC 20 in *K¹² Language Arts Activity Book*. Answers to questions may vary.

1. Turn to the **table of contents** in *K¹² World: Earth and Sky*. Help students find the selection and turn to that page.

2. Point to and read aloud the **title of the article**.

   ▸ What do you think the article will be about?

3. Have students look at the **pictures of the article**. Explain that as they look through the article, you will help them begin filling out the KWL chart.

4. Explain to students that the KWL chart has an example in each column to help them understand the kind of statements or questions that will go in each column.

Objectives

- Make predictions based on text, illustrations, and/or prior knowledge.
- Activate prior knowledge by previewing text and/or discussing topic.
- Generate questions and seek information to answer questions.
- Read and listen to a variety of texts for information and pleasure independently or as part of a group.

5. Ask the following questions and discuss the examples in each column to help students complete the K and W columns.

   ▶ What do you already know about rainbows? (Write each fact students dictate in the K column of the KWL chart.)

   ▶ What are three things about rainbows that you want to learn, or wonder about? (Write students' questions in the W column of the chart.)

   If students have difficulty thinking of things they'd like to learn, suggest one or more of the following questions: What are rainbows made of? Where do we usually see rainbows? What are the colors of the rainbow?

6. Point to and read aloud any headings, captions, or other features that stand out in the article.

   ▶ What do you think the article might tell us about rainbows?

7. Keep the KWL chart in a safe place so students can complete it later.

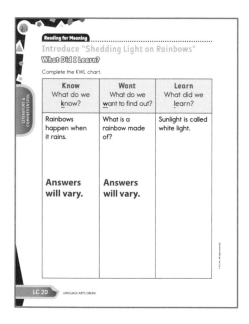

"Shedding Light on Rainbows"

It's time to read aloud the article.

1. Have students sit next to you so that they can see the pictures and words while you read aloud.

2. Tell students to listen carefully to figure out the topic of the article and to hear if the article answers any of their questions.

3. **Read aloud the entire article.** Track with your finger so students can follow along. Emphasize Words to Know as you come to them. If appropriate, use the pictures to help show what each word means.

Check Your Reading

"Shedding Light on Rainbows"
Check students' comprehension of "Shedding Light on Rainbows."

1. Have students retell "Shedding Light on Rainbows" in their own words to develop grammar, vocabulary, comprehension, and fluency skills.

2. Ask students the following questions.

   ▶ What is the topic of the article? rainbows
   ▶ What question did you ask yourself to figure out the topic? What is this article mostly about?
   ▶ Why did people of the past make up stories about rainbows? to explain what causes rainbows
   ▶ What happens when white light goes through a prism? It turns into a rainbow; it shows all the colors of the rainbow.
   ▶ What are the colors of the rainbow? red, orange, yellow, green, blue, indigo, and violet
   ▶ Where does the sun need to be for you to see a rainbow when it rains? behind you and low in the sky

 TIP If students have trouble responding to a question, help them locate the answer in the text or pictures.

 Objectives
- Retell or dramatize a story.
- Identify the topic.
- Answer questions requiring literal recall of details.

Reading for Meaning

What Did I Learn?
Have students use the KWL chart to record answers to the questions they previously generated and what they learn from the article. Gather the partially completed KWL chart on page LC 20 in *K¹² Language Arts Activity Book.*

1. Read aloud the first question written in the W column of the KWL chart.

   ▶ Ask students if they heard the answer in the article. If students know the answer, write it in the L column of the chart across from the question.
   ▶ If the answer is in the article but students cannot remember it, return to the article and help students locate the answer. Then write it in the L column across from the question.
   ▶ If the answer is not in the article, leave the area across from the question blank. Explain to students that we don't always find the answers to our questions in the articles we read. But asking the questions still helps us become better readers because it helps us read or listen carefully to a text.

 Objectives
- Demonstrate understanding through graphic organizers.
- Generate questions and seek information to answer questions.
- Identify important details in informational text.

2. Repeat Step 1 for each of the remaining questions in the W column.

3. After the last question is answered, have students tell any additional facts that they learned about rainbows, and write them at the end of the L column.

4. Keep the KWL chart in a safe place so students can use it to do more research later.

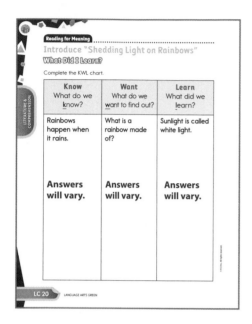

Reading for Meaning

Introduce "Shedding Light on Rainbows"

What Did I Learn?

Complete the KWL chart.

Know What do we know?	Want What do we want to find out?	Learn What did we learn?
Rainbows happen when it rains.	What is a rainbow made of?	Sunlight is called white light.
Answers will vary.	**Answers will vary.**	**Answers will vary.**

Explore "Shedding Light on Rainbows"

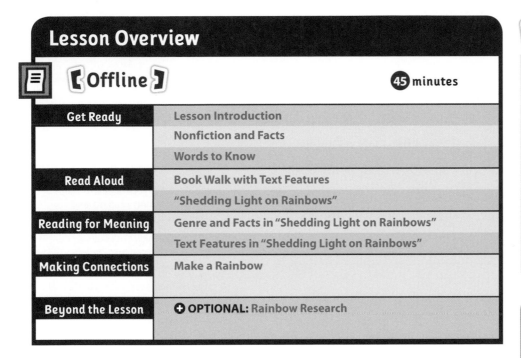

Lesson Overview

Offline · 45 minutes

Get Ready	Lesson Introduction
	Nonfiction and Facts
	Words to Know
Read Aloud	Book Walk with Text Features
	"Shedding Light on Rainbows"
Reading for Meaning	Genre and Facts in "Shedding Light on Rainbows"
	Text Features in "Shedding Light on Rainbows"
Making Connections	Make a Rainbow
Beyond the Lesson	✚ OPTIONAL: Rainbow Research

Materials

Supplied

- "Shedding Light on Rainbows," *K¹² World: Earth and Sky*, pp. 2–11
- *K¹² Language Arts Activity Book*, p. LC 20 (optional)

Also Needed

- household objects – garden hose

Keywords

fact – something that can be proven true

genre – a category for classifying literary works

informational text – text written to explain and give information on a topic

nonfiction – writings about true things

text feature – part of a text that helps a reader locate information and determine what is most important; some examples are the title, table of contents, headings, pictures, and glossary

Advance Preparation

For Making Connections, if a garden hose is unavailable, gather a spray bottle and fill it with water.

Big Ideas

- ▶ Nonfiction texts differ from fiction texts in that they describe real or true things in life, rather than things made up by the author.
- ▶ Exposing readers to a wide variety of genres provides them with a wide range of background knowledge and increases their vocabulary.
- ▶ Comprehension is facilitated by an understanding of physical presentation (for example, headings, subheads, graphics, and other features).

 **45 minutes**

Work **together** with students to complete Get Ready, Read Aloud, Reading for Meaning, Making Connections, and Beyond the Lesson activities.

Get Ready

Lesson Introduction

Prepare students for the listening to and discussing "Shedding Light on Rainbows."

1. Tell students that you are going to reread "Shedding Light on Rainbows."

2. Explain that before you read the article, you will get ready by discussing

   ▸ A kind of writing called nonfiction text
   ▸ The features found in nonfiction text, such as magazine articles
   ▸ How to recognize facts

 Objectives

- Identify genre.
- Identify facts in informational text.
- Build vocabulary through listening, reading, and discussion.
- Use new vocabulary in written and spoken sentences.
- Increase concept and content vocabulary.

Nonfiction and Facts

Explore the genre of nonfiction and how to recognize a fact.

1. Tell students that some kinds of writing are about true things. This kind of writing is called **nonfiction**. Nonfiction text can also be called **informational text** because it gives information.

2. Nonfiction articles are filled with **facts**. A fact is something that you can prove is true. If you can't prove something is true, it can't be called a fact. It's important to recognize facts so that we can know if information is true or not.

3. Ask students the following questions about facts.

   ▸ What city do you live in? Where you live is a fact. You can prove where you live.
   ▸ Do fish live in water? Yes, this is a fact. You can prove that fish live in water.
   ▸ Is there a moon in the sky? Yes, this is a fact. You can prove that there is a moon in the sky.

4. Tell students that good readers look for facts when they read nonfiction texts.

Words to Know

Before reading "Shedding Light on Rainbows," go over Words to Know with students.

1. Read aloud each word and have students repeat it.

2. Ask students if they know what each word means.

    ▸ If students know a word's meaning, have them define it and use it in a sentence.

    ▸ If students don't know a word's meaning, read them the definition and discuss the word with them.

arch – to make a curved line
band – stripe
prism – a block of clear glass that separates light passing through it into the colors of the rainbow

Read Aloud

Book Walk with Text Features

Prepare students by taking them on a Book Walk of "Shedding Light on Rainbows." Scan the magazine article together to revisit the text and point out text features.

1. Turn to the article.

2. Tell students that magazine articles have features that help readers better understand the information in the article.

3. Turn to pages 2 and 3 and point to the **title** of the article. Explain that the title usually tells us what the article is about.

4. On page 5, point to the **picture**. Explain that pictures help show ideas that are in the article.
    Say: This picture helps the reader better understand the story of Iris and how people imagined that her colorful clothes created a rainbow when she moved between heaven and earth.

5. On page 4, point to the **heading** "Colorful Tales." Explain that articles can be broken up into sections, and a heading tells what a section is about. An article's headings can help us figure out where to find certain information.
    Say: This heading tells readers that this part of the article is on stories about rainbows. If I want to find information on stories about rainbows, this is the section I would look in.

6. On page 6, point to the small text near the picture of the full-circle rainbow. Tell students that the text near the picture is called a **caption**. It gives information about the picture. Read the caption aloud.

Objectives

*   Activate prior knowledge by previewing text and/or discussing topic.
*   Identify features of informational text.
*   Identify purpose of and information provided by informational text features.
*   Read and listen to a variety of texts for information and pleasure independently or as part of a group.

7. On page 6, point to the word *prism*. Explain that some words in the article are darker, or bold, so that we will notice them. This word is bold because it's an important word in the article. We can find out what this word means in the glossary at the back of the magazine on page 51.

8. On page 6, point to the picture of the prism.

   ▸ What is this? a picture   Why do think this picture is in this section of the article? to show how light that goes through a prism turns into a rainbow

9. On page 8, point to the heading and read it aloud.

   ▸ What do you think this part of the article is about? prisms

---

"Shedding Light on Rainbows"

It's time to reread the article.

1. Have students sit next to you so that they can see the pictures and words while you read aloud the article.

2. Tell students to listen for facts in the article.

3. **Read aloud the entire article.** Track with your finger so that students can follow along.

Reading for Meaning

Genre and Facts in "Shedding Light on Rainbows"
Check students' understanding of facts and characteristics of nonfiction.

   ▸ Are rainbows real? Yes
   ▸ What does it mean if something is real? It means it's true and not made up; it's a fact.
   ▸ This article is about true things. What kind of writing is this? nonfiction; informational text
   ▸ Is it true that sunlight is filled with color? Yes   What do we call something that is true? a fact
   ▸ What happens when sunlight goes through a prism? It comes out as a rainbow; it shows all the colors of the rainbow.

Objectives
- Identify facts in informational text.
- Identify genre.
- Identify features of informational text.
- Identify purpose of and information provided by informational text features.
- Locate information using features of text and electronic media.

Text Features in "Shedding Light on Rainbows"
Check students' understanding of text features in magazine articles.

1. Remind students that text features, such as headings, pictures, and captions, can help us better understand the information in a magazine article.

2. On pages 2 and 3, point to the title of the article.

   ▸ What is this called? the title   What does the title tell the reader? What the topic is; what the article is about.

3. On page 4, point to the picture and read aloud the caption.

   ▸ How does this picture and caption help the reader understand information in the article? It shows how a rainbow can look like a ladder to heaven to the people in Polynesia.

4. On page 9, point to the heading and read it aloud.

   ▸ What is this called? a heading
   ▸ What does this heading tell us? that this part of the article explains what a prism is

5. On page 8, point to the word *bands*.

   ▸ Why is this word darker than the other words? It's an important word in the article.   Where can we find out what this word means? in the back of the magazine

6. Read aloud the heading for each part of the article.

   ▸ Where should I look if I want to find out how I can make a rainbow? the section called "How to Make a Rainbow"; the section that starts on page 10

Making Connections

Make a Rainbow

Check students' ability to follow verbal directions and connect to the topic of rainbows.

1. Remind students that a rainbow can appear at times other than when it rains.

2. Have students review the pictures on pages 10 and 11 of "Shedding Light on Rainbows," giving particular attention to the boy washing the car with a garden hose.

   ▸ Have you seen a rainbow recently? Was it raining when you saw it, or did something else make the rainbow? Answers will vary.

3. Take students outside in the early morning or late afternoon on a sunny day and have them pick up a garden hose with a spray nozzle.

4. Ask them if they recall where they need to stand to see a rainbow. with the sun behind them

5. Give students the following directions.
   Say: Stand with your back to the sun. Spray the water in front of you. Look for a rainbow.
   If students are using a spray bottle, have them spritz water in the air in front of them and look for a rainbow in the mist.

   ▸ Why does a rainbow appear in the spray? The water drops act like tiny prisms.
   ▸ What happens when light goes through a prism? It comes out as a rainbow.

Objectives
- Make connections with text: text-to-text, text-to-self, text-to-world.
- Follow two- or three-step oral directions.

Beyond the Lesson

⊕ OPTIONAL: Rainbow Research

This activity is OPTIONAL. It is intended for students who have extra time and would enjoy doing further research on rainbows. Feel free to skip this activity. Gather the completed KWL chart on page LC 20 in *K¹² Language Arts Activity Book*.

1. Help students look for answers to their unanswered questions about rainbows on their KWL chart. Use one or more of the following sources:

   ▸ encyclopedias
   ▸ science magazines, such as *National Geographic Kids*
   ▸ nonfiction library books about rainbows
   ▸ the Internet, using the search words "rainbow facts"

2. If students find an answer, write it in the L column across from the question in the W column.

3. If students find additional information about rainbows that they find interesting, write these facts at the end of the L column.

Objectives

- Demonstrate understanding through graphic organizers.
- Identify important details in informational text.
- Generate questions and seek information to answer questions.
- Locate information using features of text and electronic media.

Explore Poems About
the Weather (C)

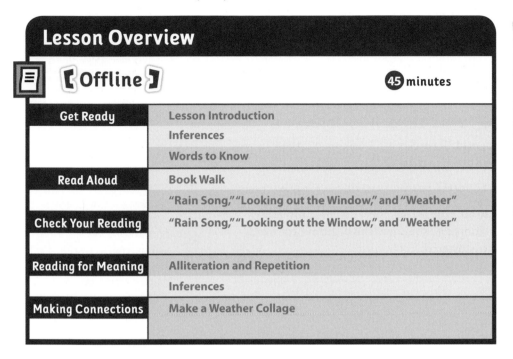

Lesson Overview

Offline   **45** minutes

Get Ready	Lesson Introduction
	Inferences
	Words to Know
Read Aloud	Book Walk
	"Rain Song," "Looking out the Window," and "Weather"
Check Your Reading	"Rain Song," "Looking out the Window," and "Weather"
Reading for Meaning	Alliteration and Repetition
	Inferences
Making Connections	Make a Weather Collage

Advance Preparation

Read "Rain Song," "Looking out the Window," and "Weather" before beginning the Read Aloud to locate Words to Know in the text. Gather magazines with pictures of outdoor scenes for Making Connections.

Big Ideas

- ▶ Readers must focus on the specific language of a text to aid in interpretation.
- ▶ Good readers use prior knowledge and text clues to infer or draw conclusions about what is implied but not directly stated in text.

Materials

Supplied

- *Weather: Poems for All Seasons,* pp. 54, 56, 59

Also Needed

- glue stick
- paper, construction
- scissors, round-end safety
- household objects – magazines

Poetry Synopses

Poets look at the different kinds of weather we experience throughout the year.

Keywords

alliteration – the use of words with the same or close to the same beginning sounds

inference – a guess you make using the clues in a text and what you already know

rhyme – when two or more words have the same ending sounds; for example, *cat* and *hat* rhyme

Offline · 45 minutes

Work **together** with students to complete Get Ready, Read Aloud, Check Your Reading, Reading for Meaning, and Making Connections activities.

Get Ready

Lesson Introduction

Prepare students for listening to and discussing poems about the weather.

1. Tell students that you are going to read "Rain Song," "Looking out the Window," and "Weather." All three poems are about the weather.

2. Explain to students that before reading the poems, you will get ready by

   ▸ Discussing how you can figure out things that poets don't say directly
   ▸ Reviewing how poets repeat words and sounds at the beginning of words to make their poems more interesting

Inferences

Explore making inferences.

1. Tell students that good readers are able to infer, or figure out, things in a poem that the poet does not say directly. Good readers think about **clues in the poem** and their own **prior knowledge**, or knowledge from past experience, to make inferences.

2. Have students practice making inferences. **Read aloud the poem.**

   Springtime
   by Art Friday
   Chirp! Chirp! Chirp!
   I hear all day
   Outside my window
   Spring's on its way!

   Chirp! Chirp! Chirp!
   Up in a tree
   A big, brown nest
   Eggs—one, two, three!

   ▸ What is making the chirping noise? birds   What clues helped you infer that? Possible answers: *chirp, tree, nest, eggs*   What do you know from personal experience that makes you say this? Students may say that they know that birds chirp, they live in trees, they make nests, and they lay eggs.

Objectives

- Listen to and discuss poetry.
- Make inferences based on text and/or prior knowledge.
- Support inferences with evidence from text and/or prior knowledge.
- Identify structure of poems and poetic elements: rhyme, rhythm, repetition, and/or alliteration.
- Activate prior knowledge by previewing text and/or discussing topic.
- Build vocabulary through listening, reading, and discussion.
- Use new vocabulary in written and spoken sentences.

3. Remind students that poets repeat words and sounds to make their poems more interesting.

   ▸ What word is repeated, or said over and over, in the poem? *chirp*

   ▸ Reread the second stanza of the poem. What two words begin with the /b/ sound? *big* and *brown*

Words to Know

Before reading "Rain Song," "Looking out the Window," and "Weather," go over Words to Know with students.

1. Read aloud each word and have students repeat it.

2. Ask students if they know what each word means.

   ▸ If students know a word's meaning, have them define it and use it in a sentence.

   ▸ If students don't know a word's meaning, read them the definition and discuss the word with them.

fair – pretty
oak – a kind of tree with strong, hard wood
petal – one of the colored parts around the center of a flower
pine – a tall evergreen tree with long, very thin, pointy leaves
tinkle – a soft sound
windowpane – a piece of glass inside the frame of a window

Read Aloud •

Book Walk

Prepare students by taking them on a Book Walk of "Rain Song," "Looking out the Window," and "Weather." Scan the poems together and ask students to make predictions about the poems.

1. Turn to "Rain Song" on page 54 in *Weather: Poems for All Seasons*.

2. Point to the **title of the poem** and the **name of the poet**, and read them aloud. Have students repeat the poet's name.

3. Have students study the **pictures**. Answers to questions may vary.

   ▸ Based on the pictures, what do you think the poem is about?

   ▸ Which season do you like the best? Why?

4. Turn to "Looking out the Window" on page 56.

5. Point to the **title of the poem** and the **name of the poet**, and read them aloud. Have students repeat the poet's name.

6. Have students study the **picture**. Answers to questions may vary.

   ▸ What do you think the poem is about?

   ▸ Do you ever look out a window to watch the weather? What kind of weather do you like to watch the best?

Objectives

• Make predictions based on text, illustrations, and/or prior knowledge.

• Activate prior knowledge by previewing text and/or discussing topic.

• Listen to and discuss poetry.

7. Turn to "Weather" on page 59.

8. Point to the **title of the poem** and the **name of the poet**, and read them aloud. Have students repeat the poet's name. Explain that *Anonymous* means no one knows who wrote the poem.

9. Have students study the **pictures**.

   ▸ What do you think the poem is about? Answers will vary.
   ▸ Why are the children dressed in different kinds of clothes in the pictures? to show we wear different kinds of clothes during different seasons   What do you know from personal experience that makes you say this? Possible answers: I know that if it's raining I need to wear a raincoat; I know that if I go ice skating I need to wear a sweater and mittens; I know it's hot in the summer, so I can wear shorts and a T-shirt.

"Rain Song," "Looking out the Window," and "Weather"

It's time to read aloud the poems.

1. Have students sit next to you so that they can see the pictures and words while you read aloud.

2. Tell students to look at the picture for each poem to see how it relates to the text.

3. **Read aloud all three poems.** Track with your finger so that students can follow along. Emphasize Words to Know as you come to them. If appropriate, use the pictures to help show what each word means.

Check Your Reading

"Rain Song," "Looking out the Window," and "Weather"

Check students' comprehension of the poems.

1. Reread "Rain Song" aloud, encouraging students to chime in and read with you. Then have students tell what the poem is about in their own words.

   ▸ Who wrote this poem? Leland B. Jacobs
   ▸ What color does the poet say the rain is in the spring? pink
   ▸ What color does the poet say the rain is in the fall? brown

2. Reread "Looking out the Window" aloud, encouraging students to chime in and read with you. Then have students tell what the poem is about in their own words.

   ▸ Who wrote this poem? Aileen Fisher
   ▸ What color does the poet say the wind is when it snows? white
   ▸ Reread the first stanza of the poem. What word rhymes with *shines*? *pines*
   ▸ Reread the second stanza of the poem. What word rhymes with *snows*? *blows*

Objectives

- Listen to and discuss poetry.
- Answer questions requiring literal recall of details.
- Identify structure of poems and poetic elements: rhyme, rhythm, repetition, and/or alliteration.
- Identify author.

3. Reread "Weather" aloud, encouraging students to chime in and read with you. Then have students tell what the poem is about in their own words.

  ▸ Point to the name of the author. Who wrote this poem? **Anonymous** What does *anonymous* mean? **No one knows who wrote the poem.**

  ▸ Reread the first four lines of the poem. What word rhymes with *not*? **hot**

(TIP) If students have trouble responding to a question, help them locate the answer in the text or pictures.

Reading for Meaning

Alliteration and Repetition

Check students' ability to recognize alliteration and repetition.

1. Remind students that poets make poems interesting by repeating sounds and words.

2. Reread the first two lines of "Rain Song."

  ▸ What words begin with the /p/ sound? *pink* and *petals*

3. Reread the first stanza of "Rain Song."

  ▸ What word is said over and over in the stanza? *rain*

4. Reread "Looking out the Window."

  ▸ What words are said over and over? *I like it when it*

5. Reread "Weather."

  ▸ What words are said over and over? *Whether the weather*

  ▸ What sound do you hear at the beginning of many of the words in the poem? /w/

6. Reread the last three lines of "Weather."

  ▸ The word *weather* begins with the /w/ sound. What other words begin with the /w/ sound? *we'll* and *whatever*

Objectives

- Identify structure of poems and poetic elements: rhyme, rhythm, repetition, and/or alliteration.
- Make inferences based on text and/or prior knowledge.
- Support inferences with evidence from text and/or prior knowledge.

Inferences

Check students' ability to make and support inferences.

1. Remind students that we can figure out things poets don't say directly by listening carefully to the words of poems, looking at pictures, and thinking about our own experiences.

2. Reread the second stanza of "Rain Song."

    ▶ What color does the poet say the rain is in the fall? brown   Why does the poet say the rain of fall is a brown rain? What is the poet talking about? The brown rain is leaves falling off trees.   What do you know from personal experience that makes you say this? Students may say that leaves turn brown in the fall, and then they fall off the trees.

3. Point to the pictures for "Rain Song."

    ▶ What do these four pictures show? the four seasons; spring, summer, fall, and winter   Why do you think these pictures are next to the poem? to show the seasons that are described in the poem

4. Point to the picture for "Looking out the Window."

    ▶ The people and the cat are looking out the windows in the picture. What do you notice about what's outside the windows? The weather is different outside each window.   Why do you think the picture looks like this? Possible answers: to show the different kinds of weather that are described in the poem; to show the sun, snow, and rain that are described in the poem; to show the weather in different seasons

5. Reread the first stanza of "Looking out the Window."

    ▶ What is shining on the oaks and pines? the sun   How did you figure this out? Possible answers: The sun is shining on the tree in the picture; the word *shines* must be about the sun.

6. Reread the second stanza of "Looking out the Window."

    ▶ What season do you think the poet is talking about? winter   What do you know from personal experience that makes you think this? Students may say that it snows in the winter.

Making Connections

Make a Weather Collage

Have students respond to poems about weather by creating a collage of the four seasons. Gather the magazines, construction paper, scissors, and glue stick.

1. Remind students that each season has its own kind of weather.

2. Have students cut out pictures of outdoor scenes that show different kinds of weather.

3. Have students glue the pictures to the construction paper.

   ▸ If students would like to give their collage a title, such as "The Weather," write it on the paper **before** they begin gluing.
   ▸ Encourage students to arrange the pictures in a random order or by season.

4. Ask the following questions. Answers to questions may vary.

   ▸ What kinds of weather are in your collage?
   ▸ Describe the kind of clothing you would wear for the weather shown in each picture, and why you would wear it.
   ▸ Which picture shows your favorite kind of weather? What do you like to do in this kind of weather?

TIP The amount of time students need to complete this activity will vary. Students need only work for the remaining time of the lesson. If students have more they would like to do, they can complete it at a later time.

Reward: Add a sticker for this unit on the My Accomplishments chart to mark successful completion of the unit.

Objectives
- Respond to text through art, writing, and/or drama.
- Make inferences based on text and/or prior knowledge.
- Support inferences with evidence from text and/or prior knowledge.

Worldly Wisdom

Unit Focus

In this unit, students will explore stories that originate in different countries and impart wisdom. This unit follows the read-aloud instructional approach (see the instructional approaches to reading in the introductory lesson for this program). In this unit, students will

- ▸ Explore how to make and support inferences.
- ▸ Identify story sequence.
- ▸ Self-monitor their understanding of text by retelling the beginning, middle, and end of a story.
- ▸ Learn the characteristics of folktales.
- ▸ Learn to recognize words that indicate a story is from long ago.
- ▸ Practice using context clues to define unknown words.

Unit Plan   〔Offline〕

Lesson 1	Introduce "The Woodpecker, Turtle, and Deer"	**45** minutes a day
Lesson 2	Explore "The Woodpecker, Turtle, and Deer"	
Lesson 3	Introduce "Stone Soup"	
Lesson 4	Explore "Stone Soup"	
Lesson 5	Introduce "Budulinek"	
Lesson 6	Explore "Budulinek"	
Lesson 7	Introduce "Issun Boshi"	
Lesson 8	Explore "Issun Boshi"	
Lesson 9	Your Choice	

Introduce "The Woodpecker, Turtle, and Deer"

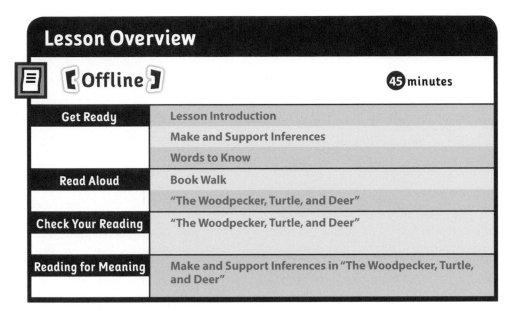

Lesson Overview

Offline — 45 minutes

Get Ready	Lesson Introduction
	Make and Support Inferences
	Words to Know
Read Aloud	Book Walk
	"The Woodpecker, Turtle, and Deer"
Check Your Reading	"The Woodpecker, Turtle, and Deer"
Reading for Meaning	Make and Support Inferences in "The Woodpecker, Turtle, and Deer"

Materials

Supplied

- "The Woodpecker, Turtle, and Deer," *K¹² Classics for Young Readers, Volume A,* pp. 46–53
- Story Card D

Story Synopsis

In this folktale from India, three woodland friends go to great lengths to protect each other from a hunter—because that's what friends do.

Keywords

infer – to use clues and what you already know to make a guess

inference – a guess you make using the clues in a text and what you already know

Advance Preparation

Read "The Woodpecker, Turtle, and Deer" before beginning the Read Aloud to locate Words to Know in the text.

Big Ideas

► Good readers use prior knowledge and text clues to infer or draw conclusions about what is implied but not directly stated in text.

► Verbalizing your thoughts while modeling a reading strategy allows students to see what goes on inside the head of an effective reader; it makes visible the normally hidden process of comprehending text.

► Activating prior knowledge provides a framework for a reader to organize and connect new information to information previously learned; readers that activate prior knowledge before reading are more likely to understand and recall what they read.

 **Offline** ⓸⓹ minutes

Work **together** with students to complete Get Ready, Read Aloud, Check Your Reading, and Reading for Meaning activities.

Get Ready •••

Lesson Introduction

Prepare students for listening to and discussing "The Woodpecker, Turtle, and Deer."

1. Tell students that you are going to read "The Woodpecker, Turtle, and Deer," a story from India about three animal friends who help out each other.

2. Explain that before you read the story, you will get ready by discussing how to make inferences, or figure things out, in a story that the author hints at but doesn't say directly.

Objectives

- Make inferences based on text and/or prior knowledge.
- Support inferences with evidence from text and/or prior knowledge.
- Build vocabulary through listening, reading, and discussion.
- Use new vocabulary in written and spoken sentences.

Make and Support Inferences

Explore making and supporting inferences.

1. Tell students that good readers are able to **infer**, or figure out, things in a story that the author does not say directly. Good readers think about **hints or clues** in the story and pictures and their own **prior knowledge from past experience** to make an inference.

2. Gather Story Card D and have students study the picture.
   Say: I see a man and two children walking together. Personal experience tells me this is probably a family. I also see lots of plants and trees, as well as animals, such as deer and birds. Prior knowledge helps me infer that the family is in the woods or at a park, because that's where I would find these things.

3. Ask the following questions.

   ▶ Do you think it's hot or cold outside? cold   How did you figure that out, or infer that? Students may state that the people are wearing clothing that keeps them warm. They may know from personal experience that this is the kind of clothing people wear when it's a little cold outside.

   ▶ What time of year, or season, is it? spring   How did you make that inference? Students may notice the butterflies and baby animals; they may say that there are lots of plants, and all the trees have leaves on them.

   ▶ How do you think the people in the picture feel? happy   What clues in the pictures helped you infer that? Students may notice that everyone in the picture is smiling, like they're having fun. They may know from personal experience that they smile when they are happy and having fun.

Words to Know

Before reading "The Woodpecker, Turtle, and Deer," go over Words to Know with students.

1. Read aloud each word and have students repeat it.

2. Ask students if they know what each word means.

   ▸ If students know a word's meaning, have them define it and use it in a sentence.

   ▸ If students don't know a word's meaning, read them the definition and discuss the word with them.

gnaw – to chew again and again
gums – the pink flesh around the bottom of your teeth
leather – a tough material made from animal skin
seize – to grab suddenly
trace – a mark or sign that you can see that shows something has happened or that someone has been somewhere

Read Aloud ·

Book Walk

Prepare students for reading by taking them on a Book Walk of "The Woodpecker, Turtle, and Deer." Scan the story together and ask students to make predictions about it. Answers to questions may vary.

1. Turn to the table of contents in *K¹² Classics for Young Readers, Volume A*. Help students find the selection and turn to that page.

2. Point to and read aloud the **title of the story**.

   ▸ What do you think the story is about?

3. Have students look at the **pictures of the story**.

   ▸ Where do you think the story takes place?
   ▸ What do you think might happen in the story?

4. Remind students that thinking and talking about ideas in a story before reading helps us get our brain ready to read and to better understand and remember the story.

5. Tell students that the story you're going to read is about friends that help each other when they are in a difficult situation.

   ▸ Have you ever helped a friend who was in a tough situation? What happened?

   ▸ Were you ever in a tough situation and a friend helped you out? What did they do to help?

6. If students have trouble thinking of a time they helped someone or when a friend helped them, share a story about a time you helped someone in need or somebody helped you.

Objectives

- Activate prior knowledge by previewing text and/or discussing topic.
- Make predictions based on text, illustrations and/or prior knowledge.
- Listen and respond to texts representing a variety of cultures, time periods, and traditions.

"The Woodpecker, Turtle, and Deer"

It's time to read aloud the story.

1. Have students sit next to you so that they can see the pictures and words while you read aloud.

2. Tell students to listen carefully to see if they can figure out some things that the author doesn't say directly.

3. **Read aloud the entire story.** Track with your finger so students can follow along. Emphasize Words to Know as you come to them. If appropriate, use the pictures to help show what each word means.

Check Your Reading

"The Woodpecker, Turtle, and Deer"

Check students' comprehension of "The Woodpecker, Turtle, and Deer."

1. Have students retell "The Woodpecker, Turtle, and Deer" in their own words to develop grammar, vocabulary, comprehension, and fluency skills.

2. Ask students the following questions.

   ▸ Where do the woodpecker, turtle, and deer live? in a forest near a lake
   ▸ What is the hunter's trap made out of? leather
   ▸ What does the woodpecker do when the hunter comes out the front door of his house? flaps his wings in the hunter's face
   ▸ How does the deer get out of the trap? The turtle chews through the leather, and then the deer pulls on the trap until it breaks.
   ▸ What does the deer tell the turtle to do after he tears open the bag and lets the turtle out? to dive into the water

 TIP If students have trouble responding to a question, help them locate the answer in the text or pictures.

Objectives
- Retell or dramatize a story.
- Answer questions requiring literal recall of details.

Reading for Meaning

Make and Support Inferences in "The Woodpecker, Turtle, and Deer"
Explore making inferences with students.

1. Remind students that good readers are able to infer, or figure out, things in a story that the author does not say directly. Good readers use **clues from the story, pictures, and what they know from their own experiences** to make inferences.

2. Ask the following questions to check students' ability to make and support inferences.

   ▸ How do you think the deer feels when he gets trapped? scared
   What clues from your personal experience and the picture helped you figure this out, or infer it? Students may state that the deer has a scared look on his face, and they themselves might be scared if they were trapped and couldn't move.

   ▸ Why does the deer cry out for help when he gets trapped? He hopes his friends, the turtle and woodpecker, will hear him.   What clue in the story and personal experience helped you infer this? The story says they are friends, and friends help each other.

   ▸ Why does the woodpecker flap her wings in the hunter's face when he comes out the door? She's trying to keep the hunter from going back to the deer before the turtle chews through the leather trap; she's trying to slow down the hunter.   What does this tell you about the woodpecker? She's clever or smart; she wants to help her friend.

   ▸ How do you think the hunter feels when the woodpecker flaps her wings in his face? Possible answers: scared; angry; mad; surprised   What clue from the picture at the bottom of page 48 helped you infer this? The hunter has his hands up to protect his face, and his mouth is open like he's yelling.

   ▸ The turtle chews the pieces of leather until his gums bleed. What does this tell you about the turtle? Possible answers: He's a very good friend; he wants to help his friend so much that he's willing to do something difficult and painful.

   ▸ Why is the turtle too weak to move when the hunter returns? He's tired from chewing the leather trap.

   ▸ How do you think the deer feels at the end of the story? happy
   What clues from the story, picture, and your personal experience helped you infer this? Students may notice that the deer is smiling in the picture, which means that he is happy; the deer was trapped and is now free, and he helped the turtle get out of the bag. Students may state that they would be happy if they and their friends were safe.

   ▸ How do you think the hunter feels at the end of the story? Possible answers: unhappy; mad; surprised   What clues from the story and your personal experience helped you infer this? Answers will vary. Students may notice that the man looks surprised and a little mad; they would be surprised to find an empty bag, and they would be unhappy or mad if they lost something that they'd had or were trying to get.

Objectives
- Make inferences based on text and/or prior knowledge.
- Support inferences with evidence from text and/or prior knowledge.

Explore "The Woodpecker, Turtle, and Deer"

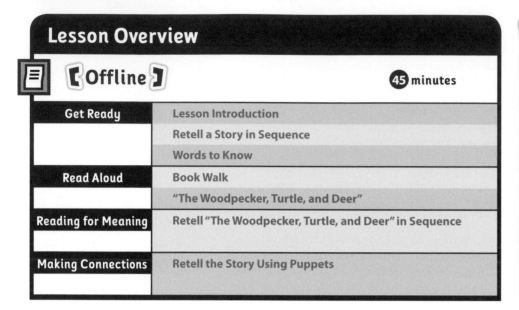

Lesson Overview

Offline — 45 minutes

Get Ready	Lesson Introduction
	Retell a Story in Sequence
	Words to Know
Read Aloud	Book Walk
	"The Woodpecker, Turtle, and Deer"
Reading for Meaning	Retell "The Woodpecker, Turtle, and Deer" in Sequence
Making Connections	Retell the Story Using Puppets

Big Ideas

▸ Comprehension requires the reader to self-monitor understanding.
▸ Comprehension entails an understanding of the organizational patterns of text.

Materials

Supplied

- "The Woodpecker, Turtle, and Deer," *K¹² Classics for Young Readers, Volume A*, pp. 46–53
- *K¹² Language Arts Activity Book*, p. LC 21

Also Needed

- craft sticks
- glue
- scissors, round-end safety

Keywords

retelling – using your own words to tell a story that you have listened to or read

self-monitor – to notice if you do or do not understand what you are reading

sequence – order

 **45 minutes**

Work **together** with students to complete Get Ready, Read Aloud, Reading for Meaning, and Making Connections activities.

Get Ready

Lesson Introduction

Prepare students for listening to and discussing "The Woodpecker, Turtle, and Deer."

1. Tell students that you are going to reread "The Woodpecker, Turtle, and Deer."

2. Explain that before you read the story, you will get ready by discussing

   ▸ Retelling a story as a way to check that you understand what you've read
   ▸ How to retell a story in the order in which things happen

Retell a Story in Sequence

Explore retelling a story in sequence.

1. Tell students that **retelling** means using our own words to tell what happens in a story that we have listened to or read.

   ▸ Retelling a story is a good way to check that we understand what we have read.
   ▸ When we retell a story, we tell the events in sequence, or the order in which they happen.
   ▸ One way to retell the sequence, or order, is to tell the most important things that happen in the beginning, middle, and end of a story.

2. Gather Story Card D and have students review the picture. Read aloud the story.

   Mr. Brodsky and his children, Mira and Vlad, put on warm clothes and got in the family van. After a very cold and snowy winter, they couldn't wait to take a walk in the woods when spring finally came. When they got to the woods, Mira and Vlad jumped out of the van and ran to the family's favorite walking path. Right away, Mira saw a baby deer, and Vlad watched birds building nests in the trees. Mr. Brodsky took pictures of the things the children pointed to while they were walking. In the evening after supper, the family gathered around the computer to look at all the photographs Mr. Brodsky took. Mira put a picture of the baby deer in her scrapbook, while Vlad put a picture of a bluebird on the refrigerator door.

   ▸ What is the first thing that happens in the story? Mr. Brodsky and his children put on warm clothes and get in the van.   Retell that part of the story. Mr. Brodsky and his children get in a van to go to the woods to take a walk.

Objectives

- Identify story sequence.
- Retell the beginning, middle, and end of a story.
- Self-monitor comprehension of text.
- Build vocabulary through listening, reading, and discussion.
- Use new vocabulary in written and spoken sentences.

▸ In what part of the story does Mira see a baby deer? in the middle
Retell that part of the story. The children see animals in the woods, and
Mr. Brodsky takes pictures.

▸ When does Vlad put a picture of a bluebird on the refrigerator door?
at the end   Retell that part of the story. After supper, the family looks at
the pictures Mr. Brodsky took. Mira puts a picture of the baby deer in her
scrapbook, and Vlad puts a picture of a bluebird on the refrigerator.

3. Have students retell the entire story in sequence. The retelling should include
the same information given when they did retellings of the beginning, middle,
and end of the story.

4. Guide students to think about their retelling. Answers to questions may vary.

▸ Did your retelling include the important characters?
▸ Did it include most of the important things that happened?
▸ Did you retell the events in sequence?
▸ Do you think that you understand the story?

Words to Know

Before reading "The Woodpecker, Turtle, and Deer," go over Words to Know
with students.

1. Read aloud each word and have students repeat it.

2. Ask students if they know what each word means.

▸ If students know a word's meaning, have them define it and use it in a
sentence.
▸ If students don't know a word's meaning, read them the definition and
discuss the word with them.

gnaw – to chew again and again
gums – the pink flesh around the bottom of your teeth
leather – a tough material made from animal skin
seize – to grab suddenly
trace – a mark or sign that you can see that shows something has happened or that
someone has been somewhere

Read Aloud

Book Walk

Prepare students by taking them on a Book Walk of "The Woodpecker, Turtle, and Deer." Scan the story together to revisit the characters and events.

1. Turn to the selection in *K¹² Classics for Young Readers, Volume A*. Point to and read aloud the **title of the story**.

2. Have students review the **pictures**.

   ► Who are the characters in the story? deer; woodpecker; turtle; hunter
   ► What are some of the ways that the animals help each other in the story? Possible answers: The turtle helps the deer get out of the hunter's trap; the woodpecker keeps the hunter away from the deer; the deer helps the turtle get out of the bag; the deer tells the turtle to hide in the water.

Objectives

- Activate prior knowledge by previewing text and/or discussing topic.
- Listen and respond to texts representing a variety of cultures, time periods, and traditions.

"The Woodpecker, Turtle, and Deer"

It's time to reread the "The Woodpecker, Turtle, and Deer."

1. Have students sit next to you so that they can see the pictures and words while you read aloud the story.

2. Tell students to listen carefully to hear what happens in the beginning, middle, and end of the story so they can retell it.

3. **Read aloud the entire story.** Track with your finger so students can follow along. Emphasize Words to Know as you come to them. If appropriate, use the pictures to help show what each word means.

Reading for Meaning

Retell "The Woodpecker, Turtle, and Deer" in Sequence

Explore the sequence of a story and retelling to check for understanding.

1. Ask the following sequence questions.

   ► Which happens first: the deer gets trapped, or the woodpecker flaps its wings in the face of the hunter? The deer gets trapped.
   ► Which happens first: the hunter runs after the deer into the forest, or the hunter puts the turtle in a bag? The hunter puts the turtle in a bag.
   ► What happens after the hunter finds the empty bag? He grunts; he goes home.

Objectives

- Identify story sequence.
- Retell the beginning, middle, and end of a story.
- Self-monitor comprehension of text.

2. Remind students of the following:

- ▸ One way readers can check their understanding of a story is by retelling it.
- ▸ Retelling means using your own words to tell what happens in a story that you have listened to or read.
- ▸ A good retelling includes the most important things that happen in the beginning, middle, and end of the story in the order that they happen.
- ▸ A good retelling includes the characters and the things that the characters do.

3. Have students retell the story.

- ▸ Retell the beginning of the story, the part about the deer getting trapped. A deer, woodpecker, and turtle are friends. One day a hunter sets a trap for the deer. The deer gets caught in the trap and calls out to his friends for help.
- ▸ Retell the middle of the story, the part in which the turtle helps the deer get out of the trap. The turtle chews and chews on the leather trap to help the deer get free. The woodpecker flaps his wings in the hunter's face when he tries to leave his house. The deer pulls on the leather trap and gets free just in time, but the turtle is too tired to move.
- ▸ Retell the end of the story, the part in which the hunter puts the turtle in a bag. The hunter puts the turtle in a bag, then chases the deer deep into the forest. The deer slips away and runs out of the forest to help the turtle get out of the bag. The hunter comes back and can't find any of the animals, so he gives up and goes home. All the animal friends are safe.

4. Have students retell the entire story in sequence. The retelling should include the same information given when they did retellings of the beginning, middle, and end of the story.

5. Guide students to think about their retelling. Answers to questions may vary.

- ▸ Did your retelling include the important characters?
- ▸ Did it include most of the important things that happened?
- ▸ Did you retell the events in sequence?
- ▸ Do you think that you understand the story?

TIP If students forgot to mention characters or important events in their retelling, have them retell the story again as you ask questions such as, "Who is in the story? What did they do?" If students don't think they understand the story, reread the story aloud, pausing to let students ask questions as you read.

Making Connections ···

Retell the Story Using Puppets

Check students' understanding of "The Woodpecker, Turtle, and Deer" and their ability to retell a story. Turn to page LC 21 in *K¹² Language Arts Activity Book*.

Objectives
- Retell a story using various media.
- Self-monitor comprehension of text.

1. Have students cut out and glue the pictures to craft sticks to create puppets.

2. Have students use the character puppets to retell the "The Woodpecker, Turtle, and Deer."

   ▶ Be sure students tell important events in the beginning, middle, and end of the story.

3. Ask students the following questions. Answers to questions may vary.

   ▶ Was it easier for you to retell the story with or without the puppets?
   ▶ Which way did you like better? Why?

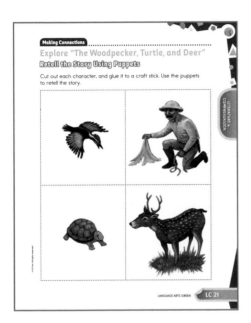

Introduce "Stone Soup"

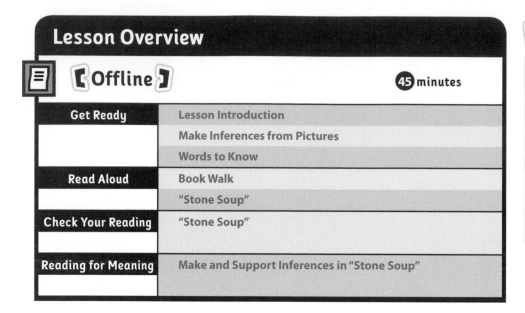

Lesson Overview

Offline   45 minutes

Get Ready	Lesson Introduction
	Make Inferences from Pictures
	Words to Know
Read Aloud	Book Walk
	"Stone Soup"
Check Your Reading	"Stone Soup"
Reading for Meaning	Make and Support Inferences in "Stone Soup"

Advance Preparation

Read "Stone Soup" before beginning the Read Aloud to locate Words to Know in the text.

Big Ideas

▶ Good readers use prior knowledge and text clues to infer or draw conclusions about what is implied but not directly stated in text.

▶ Activating prior knowledge provides a framework for a reader to organize and connect new information to information previously learned; readers that activate prior knowledge before reading are more likely to understand and recall what they read.

Materials

Supplied

- "Stone Soup," *K¹² Classics for Young Readers, Volume A*, pp. 54–67
- *K¹² Language Arts Activity Book*, p. LC 23

Also Needed

- crayons

Story Synopsis

Wary villagers in this French folktale don't want to share their dwindling food supplies with a hungry traveler—not until they hear about his magical soup stone, that is!

Keywords

infer – to use clues and what you already know to make a guess
inference – a guess you make using the clues in a text and what you already know

[Offline] **45** minutes

Work **together** with students to complete Get Ready, Read Aloud, Check Your Reading, and Reading for Meaning activities.

Get Ready

Lesson Introduction

Prepare students for listening to and discussing "Stone Soup."

1. Tell students that you are going to read "Stone Soup," a French folktale about a man who teaches villagers the importance of sharing and working together.

2. Explain that before you read the story, you will get ready by reviewing how to make inferences.

Make Inferences from Pictures

Review how we make inferences. Turn to page LC 23 in *K¹² Language Arts Activity Book.*

1. Remind students we can often figure out, or **infer**, many things about a story even though the author doesn't directly state something.

2. Have students explain what kind of clues they use to make **inferences**.

3. If students have trouble answering, remind them that good readers

   ▸ Use hints or clues in the words and pictures of a story.
   ▸ Use prior knowledge from past experiences to figure out things that the author doesn't directly state, such as why a character does something or how a character feels.

4. Have students study the picture on the Activity Book page.

5. Read aloud the statement in the first text box.

6. Have students decide if the statement is something they can infer from the picture.

   ▸ If the statement is something they can infer from the picture, students should circle the statement.
   ▸ If the statement is **not** something they can infer, students should put an X over the statement.

Objectives

- Make inferences based on text and/or prior knowledge.
- Support inferences with evidence from text and/or prior knowledge.
- Build vocabulary through listening, reading, and discussion.
- Use new vocabulary in written and spoken sentences.

7. Repeat Steps 5 and 6 until all statements have been evaluated.

8. Discuss the clues in the picture and knowledge from their own experiences that helped students make the inferences.

▸ What clues in the picture helped you infer that "Sue likes to build sand castles" and "Sue is enjoying herself"? Students may have noticed that Sue is smiling. Students may have made these inferences because they know that they smile when they are doing something they enjoy.

▸ What clues in the picture helped you infer that "Sue likes the color yellow"? Students may have noticed that Sue's clothes and toys are all yellow. Students may have made this inference because they know that they like to have clothes and toys that are their favorite color.

▸ What clues in the picture helped you infer that "It is a warm day"? Students may have noticed that the sun is out and Sue is wearing a hat. Students may have made this inference because they know that if the sun is out, it is probably a warm day, and people often wear hats to protect themselves on a sunny, warm day.

TIP Keep the Activity Book page in a safe place for later use.

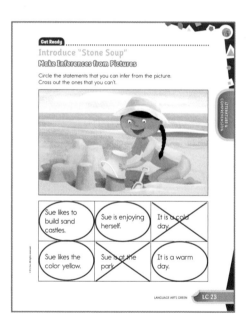

Words to Know

Before reading "Stone Soup," go over Words to Know with students.

1. Read aloud each word or phrase and have students repeat it.

2. Ask students if they know what each word or phrase means.

   ▸ If students know a word's or phrase's meaning, have them define it and use it in a sentence.

   ▸ If students don't know a word's or phrase's meaning, read them the definition and discuss the word or phrase with them.

aroma – a pleasant smell

bouquet – a bunch of flowers

hobble – to walk with difficulty because you are hurt or in pain

ingredient – one of the things that you use to make something to eat, such as an item of food in a recipe

morsel – a very small piece of food

village square – an open space in the center of a town

weary – tired

Read Aloud

Book Walk

Prepare students for reading by taking them on a Book Walk of "Stone Soup." Scan the story together and ask students to make predictions. Answers to questions may vary.

1. Turn to the table of contents in *K¹² Classics for Young Readers, Volume A*. Help students find the selection and turn to that page.

2. Point to and read aloud the **title of the story**.

   ▸ What do you think the story is about?

3. Have students look at the **pictures of the story**.

   ▸ Where do you think the story takes place?

   ▸ What do you think might happen in the story?

4. Remind students that thinking and talking about ideas in a story before reading helps get our brain ready to read and to better understand and remember the story.

   ▸ Have you ever worked with a group of people to do or make something, like wash a car or make a meal? How did it make you feel to work together?

   ▸ Do you like to share with others? How does sharing something of yours make you feel?

Objectives

- Make predictions based on text, illustrations, and/or prior knowledge.
- Activate prior knowledge by previewing text and/or discussing topic.
- Listen and respond to texts representing a variety of cultures, time periods, and traditions.

"Stone Soup"

It's time to read aloud the story.

1. Have students sit next to you so that they can see the pictures and words while you read aloud.

2. Tell students to listen carefully and look at the pictures to see if they can figure out some things that the author doesn't say directly.

3. **Read aloud the entire story.** Track with your finger so students can follow along. Emphasize Words to Know as you come to them. If appropriate, use the pictures to help show what each word means.

Check Your Reading

"Stone Soup"

Check students' comprehension of "Stone Soup."

Objectives

- Retell or dramatize a story.
- Answer questions requiring literal recall of details.

1. Have students retell "Stone Soup" in their own words to develop grammar, vocabulary, comprehension, and fluency skills.

2. Ask students the following questions.

   ▸ Where is the soldier walking to when he stops at the village? home
   ▸ What do the villagers do when they see the soldier walking toward the village? They run into their houses and slam their doors shut.
   ▸ Why do the villagers carefully guard their food? There is very little food left in the land; they don't have much.
   ▸ What does the soldier take out of his pocket for everyone to see while he is standing in the village square? a stone
   ▸ What does the soldier say he's going to make with the stone? a pot of stone soup
   ▸ What's the first thing the soldier asks for to make stone soup? a kettle
     Why doesn't the soldier use the pot that the old woman brings him?
     He says that he needs a bigger one to cook for the whole village.

TIP If students have trouble responding to a question, help them locate the answer in the text or pictures.

Reading for Meaning

Make and Support Inferences in "Stone Soup"

Explore making inferences with students.

1. Remind students that good readers are able to infer, or figure out, things in a story that the author does not say directly. Good readers use **clues from the story, pictures, and what they know from their own experiences** to make inferences.

2. Ask the following questions to check students' ability to make and support inferences.

   ▶ Why do the people of the village run into their houses and slam their doors shut when they see the soldier coming? They don't want to share their food with him.   What clues from the story helped you infer this, or figure this out? Students may state that the story says the people were hungry and that they had started to hide their food from their friends and neighbors.

   ▶ The soldier knocks on every door in the village, looking for food and a place to sleep. What does this tell you about the soldier? He doesn't give up easily; he believes if he keeps asking, someone will help him.   What do you know from personal experience that helped you infer this? Students may explain that when they really want something, they keep asking for it.

   ▶ Why does the soldier say he can make soup for the whole village with just a stone? to get the villagers to share their food   What does this tell you about the soldier? Possible answers: He's clever; he's smart; he thinks the villagers actually have food to share.

   ▶ Why do you think the villagers help the soldier make stone soup? Possible answers: They're curious; they want to see if he can really do it; they're hungry.

   ▶ Why do the villagers laugh and pat the soldier on the back while he's making soup? Possible answers: They're having fun; they like him; they're excited about making stone soup.

   ▶ At the beginning of the story, the villagers say they have no food, but they end up putting carrots, potatoes, beef, barley, and cabbage into the soup kettle. What does this tell you about the villagers? Everyone had some food, but they were saving it for themselves.

   ▶ Why does the mayor give the soldier a new suit of clothes? Possible answer: The mayor wants to do something nice for the soldier because he's making soup for the whole village.   What do you know from personal experience that helped you infer this? Students may explain that when someone shares something with them, they want to do something nice for that person.

   ▶ Why does the soldier give the red-haired girl his stone at the end of the story? He wants the villagers to remember that they can continue to feed everyone if they share their food with each other.

   ▶ How do you think the soldier feels at the end of the story? happy What clue in the picture helped you infer this? The soldier has a big smile on his face.

Objectives
- Make inferences based on text and/or prior knowledge.
- Support inferences with evidence from text and/or prior knowledge.

Explore "Stone Soup"

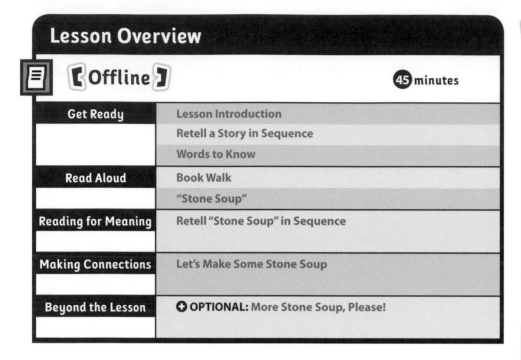

Lesson Overview

Offline   **45** minutes

Get Ready	Lesson Introduction
	Retell a Story in Sequence
	Words to Know
Read Aloud	Book Walk
	"Stone Soup"
Reading for Meaning	Retell "Stone Soup" in Sequence
Making Connections	Let's Make Some Stone Soup
Beyond the Lesson	✚ OPTIONAL: More Stone Soup, Please!

Materials

Supplied

- "Stone Soup," *K¹² Classics for Young Readers, Volume A,* pp. 54–67
- *K¹² Language Arts Activity Book,* pp. LC 23, 25–27

Also Needed

- scissors, round-end safety
- household objects – small cooking pot

Keywords

retelling – using your own words to tell a story that you have listened to or read
self-monitor – to notice if you do or do not understand what you are reading
sequence – order

Advance Preparation

Gather completed page LC 23 (Make Inferences from Pictures) in *K¹² Language Arts Activity Book.*

Big Ideas

▶ Comprehension requires the reader to self-monitor understanding.
▶ Comprehension entails an understanding of the organizational patterns of text.

Offline ⓐ minutes

Work **together** with students to complete Get Ready, Read Aloud, Reading for Meaning, Making Connections, and Beyond the Lesson activities.

Get Ready ....

Lesson Introduction
Prepare students for listening to and discussing "Stone Soup."

1. Tell students that you are going to reread "Stone Soup."

2. Explain that before you read the story, you will get ready by reviewing

   ▸ Retelling a story as a way to check that you understand what you've read
   ▸ How to retell a story in the order in which things happen

---

Retell a Story in Sequence
Review how to retell a story in sequence. Gather completed page LC 23 in *K¹² Language Arts Activity Book*.

1. Remind students that **retelling a story** is a good way to check that we understand what we have read.

2. Have students explain what a **retelling** involves.

3. If students have trouble answering, remind them that a good retelling includes

   ▸ The characters and the setting
   ▸ The most important things that happen in the beginning, middle, and end of a story

4. Have students review the picture on their completed Activity Book page. **Read aloud** this story.

   One day, Sue and her mom decided to go to the beach. Sue got into the car with her new yellow pail and shovel. As soon as they got to the beach, Sue started to build a sand castle. When Sue was finished, Mom came over to take picture of it. A minute later, a big wave knocked over the sand castle. "Lucky I took a picture!" Mom laughed. They went back to the beach blanket and sat down for lunch. Sue spent the rest of the afternoon playing in the water and looking for seashells. Sue was so tired at the end of the day that she fell asleep in the back of the car on the way home.

   ▸ What is the first thing that happens in the story? Sue and her mom decide to go to the beach.   Retell that part of the story. Sue and her mom decide to go to the beach. Sue gets in the car with her new pail and shovel.

> **Objectives**
> - Identify story sequence.
> - Retell the beginning, middle, and end of a story.
> - Self-monitor comprehension of text.
> - Build vocabulary through listening, reading, and discussion.
> - Use new vocabulary in written and spoken sentences.

- ▶ In what part of the story does Sue build a sand castle? in the middle   Retell that part of the story. Sue builds a sand castle when she gets to the beach. Her mom takes a picture of it just before a wave knocks it over.
- ▶ When does Sue look for seashells? at the end   Retell that part of the story. After lunch, Sue plays in the water and looks for seashells. Sue's so tired at the end of the day that she falls asleep in the car on the way home.

5. Have students retell the entire story in sequence. The retelling should include the same information given when they did retellings of the beginning, middle, and end of the story.

6. Guide students to think about their retelling. Answers to questions may vary.

- ▶ Did your retelling include the important characters?
- ▶ Did it include most of the important things that happened?
- ▶ Did you retell the events in sequence?
- ▶ Do you think that you understand the story?

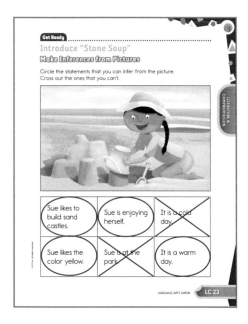

Get Ready

Introduce "Stone Soup"

Make Inferences from Pictures

Circle the statements that you can infer from the picture. Cross out the ones that you can't.

| Sue likes to build sand castles. | Sue is enjoying herself. | It is a cold day. |
| Sue likes the color yellow. | Sue is at the park | It is a warm day. |

LANGUAGE ARTS GREEN   **LC 23**

Words to Know

Before reading "Stone Soup," go over Words to Know with students.

1. Read aloud each word or phrase and have students repeat it.

2. Ask students if they know what each word or phrase means.

   ▶ If students know a word's or phrase's meaning, have them define it and use it in a sentence.
   ▶ If students don't know a word's or phrase's meaning, read them the definition and discuss the word or phrase with them.

aroma – a pleasant smell
bouquet – a bunch of flowers
hobble – to walk with difficulty because you are hurt or in pain
ingredient – one of the things that you use to make something to eat, such as an item of food in a recipe
morsel – a very small piece of food
village square – an open space in the center of a town
weary – tired

Read Aloud

Book Walk

Prepare students by taking them on a Book Walk of "Stone Soup." Scan the story together to revisit the characters and events.

1. Turn to the selection in *K¹² Classics for Young Readers, Volume A*. Point to and read aloud the **title of the story**.

2. Have students review the **pictures**.

3. Point to the picture on page 54.

   ▶ Who is this character? the soldier
   ▶ Why does he knock at every door of the village? He's hungry and wants some food, but each villager tells him to go away.

4. Point to the picture on page 62.

   ▶ Who are these people and what are they doing? villagers; making stone soup
   ▶ When does this event happen in the story? the middle

Objectives
- Activate prior knowledge by previewing text and/or discussing topic.
- Listen and respond to texts representing a variety of cultures, time periods, and traditions.

"Stone Soup"

It's time to reread the story.

1. Have students sit next to you so that they can see the pictures and words while you read aloud the story.

2. Tell students to listen carefully to hear what happens in the beginning, middle, and end of the story so they can retell it.

3. **Read the entire story aloud.** Track with your finger so students can follow along. Emphasize Words to Know as you come to them. If appropriate, use the pictures to help show what each word means.

Reading for Meaning

Retell "Stone Soup" in Sequence

Explore the sequence of a story and retelling to check for understanding.

1. Tell students that we can look for hints in the story and pictures that tell us when a story takes place.

2. Point to and read aloud the first sentence of "Stone Soup" on page 54.

   ▸ What do the words *Once upon a time* tell you? The story happens long ago.

3. Point to the picture on pages 54 and 55.

   ▸ Do people dress like this today? No   Are modern streets usually made out of stone? No   What does this tell you? The story happens long ago.

4. Ask the following questions about the sequence of events.

   ▸ Which happens first: the soldier knocks on doors asking for food, or the soldier takes a stone out of his pocket? The soldier knocks on doors asking for food.
   ▸ Which happens first: the soldier gives a girl his soup stone, or villagers bring ingredients to put in the big kettle? Villagers bring ingredients to put in the big kettle.

5. Remind students of the following:

   ▸ One way readers can check their understanding of a story is by retelling it.
   ▸ Retelling means using your own words to tell what happens in a story that you have listened to or read.
   ▸ A good retelling includes most important things that happen in the beginning, middle, and end of the story in the order that they happen.
   ▸ A good retelling includes the characters and the things that the characters do.

Objectives

- Explain function of recurring phrases in folk and fairy tales.
- Distinguish texts that describe events from long ago from those that describe contemporary events.
- Identify story sequence.
- Retell the beginning, middle, and end of a story.
- Self-monitor comprehension of text.

6. Have students retell the story.

   ▸ Retell the beginning of the story, the part about the soldier coming to a village and asking for food. A hungry soldier comes to a village and knocks on doors, asking the villagers for food. But all the villagers tell him to go away because they have no food to share.

   ▸ Retell the middle of the story, the part in which the soldier and villagers make a pot of stone soup. The soldier pulls a stone out of his pocket and says that he can make stone soup. The villagers are curious and come out of their houses to watch him do it. The soldier asks the villagers if they have things to add to the stone soup, like beef and cabbage, which he adds to the kettle. When the soup is done, everyone eats together until they are full.

   ▸ Retell the end of the story, the part in which the soldier goes on his way. The mayor invites the soldier to sleep at his house. In the morning, the villagers give him a bag filled with food to thank him for showing them how to make stone soup. He thanks them, and then he gives the soup stone to a village girl.

7. Have students retell the entire story in sequence. The retelling should include the same information given when they did retellings of the beginning, middle, and end of the story.

8. Guide students to think about their retelling. Answers to questions may vary.

   ▸ Did your retelling include the important characters?
   ▸ Did it include most of the important things that happened?
   ▸ Did you retell the events in sequence?
   ▸ Do you think that you understand the story?

TIP If students forget to mention characters or important events in their retelling, have them retell the story again as you ask questions such as, "Who is in the story? What did they do?" If students don't think they understand the story, reread the story aloud, pausing to let students ask questions as you read.

Making Connections

Let's Make Some Stone Soup

Check students' comprehension of "Stone Soup" and their understanding of sequence. Turn to pages LC 25–27 in *K¹² Language Arts Activity Book* and gather the small cooking pot.

1. Tell students that they will make an imaginary pot of stone soup to help with retelling the story.

2. Have students name the ingredients on the Activity Book page, one by one.

3. Have students cut out the pictures.

4. Have them retell the story, dropping the ingredients into the pot in the same sequence that they were added in "Stone Soup."

   ▶ If students aren't sure of the order, have them refer back to the story.
   ▶ Be sure students tell important events in the beginning, middle, and end of the story.

TIP If time allows and the necessary ingredients are available, have students help you make a real pot of soup.

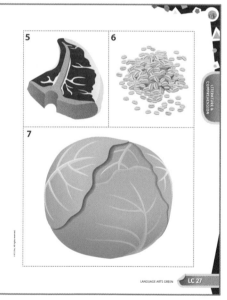

Beyond the Lesson

⊕ OPTIONAL: More Stone Soup, Please!

This activity is OPTIONAL. It is intended for students who have extra time and would enjoy reading another version of "Stone Soup." Feel free to skip this activity.

1. Go to a library and look for a copy of one of the many versions of "Stone Soup."

2. Lead a Book Walk and then read the story aloud.

3. Have students retell the book version of the story, retelling the events in the beginning, middle, and end.

4. Have students describe how the characters and the events of the stories are alike and different.

5. Ask them to tell which version of the story they like best and why.

Objectives

- Retell or dramatize a story.
- Retell the beginning, middle, and end of a story.
- Compare and contrast two texts on the same topic.

Introduce "Budulinek"

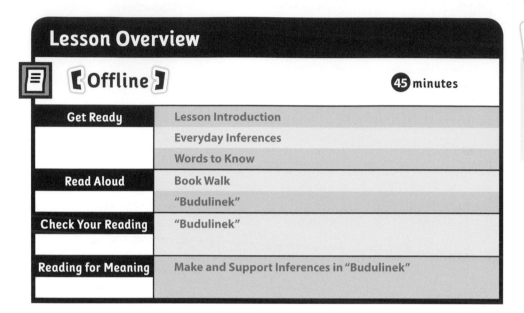

Lesson Overview

Offline		45 minutes
Get Ready	Lesson Introduction	
	Everyday Inferences	
	Words to Know	
Read Aloud	Book Walk	
	"Budulinek"	
Check Your Reading	"Budulinek"	
Reading for Meaning	Make and Support Inferences in "Budulinek"	

Advance Preparation

Read "Budulinek" before beginning the Read Aloud to locate Words to Know
in the text.

Big Ideas

▶ Good readers use prior knowledge and text clues to infer or draw conclusions
about what is implied but not directly stated in text.

▶ Activating prior knowledge provides a framework for a reader to organize
and connect new information to information previously learned; readers that
activate prior knowledge before reading are more likely to understand and
recall what they read.

Materials

Supplied

● "Budulinek," *K12 Classics
for Young Readers,
Volume A*, pp. 68–85

Story Synopsis

In this folktale from
Czechoslovakia, Granny tells
Budulinek many times: "Don't
open the door when your
home alone, no matter who
knocks!" But, Lishka, a clever
fox, tells the naive Budulinek
that she'll take him for a ride
on her tail, if only he would
open the door. Who will
Budulinek listen to?

Keywords

infer – to use clues and what
you already know to make a
guess

inference – a guess you make
using the clues in a text and
what you already know

[Offline] 45 minutes

Work **together** with students to complete Get Ready, Read Aloud, Check Your Reading, and Reading for Meaning activities.

Get Ready

Lesson Introduction
Prepare students for listening to and discussing "Budulinek."

1. Tell students that you are going to read "Budulinek," a story from Czechoslovakia about a boy who is told never to open the door when he's home alone, no matter who knocks.

2. Tell students that before you read the story, you will get ready by reviewing how to make inferences.

 TIP *Budulinek* is pronounced boo-doo-lee-nehk.

Everyday Inferences
Reinforce how we make inferences.

1. Remind students that we can often figure out, or **infer**, many things about a story even though the author doesn't directly state something.

2. Tell students that we also make inferences every day about things that happen in real life.
   Say: It's morning and your sister just walked out of her bedroom, wearing pajamas. She's yawning and her hair is messy.

   ▶ What can you infer? She just woke up.   How did you use personal knowledge to make this inference? Students may state that their hair is messy when they wake up in the morning, and they're wearing pajamas. Students may state that they sometimes yawn when they first wake up.

   Say: You and your friend are watching a movie. Your friend suddenly covers his eyes with his hands.

   ▶ What can you infer about how your friend feels? He's scared. What personal knowledge helped you make this inference? Students may state that they cover their eyes when they don't want to see something that's scary.

Objectives

- Make inferences based on text and/or prior knowledge.
- Support inferences with evidence from text and/or prior knowledge.
- Build vocabulary through listening, reading, and discussion.
- Use new vocabulary in written and spoken sentences.

Words to Know

Before reading "Budulinek," go over Words to Know with students.

1. Read aloud each word or phrase and have students repeat it.

2. Ask students if they know what each word or phrase means.

   ▶ If students know a word's or phrase's meaning, have them define it and use it in a sentence.

   ▶ If students don't know a word's or phrase's meaning, read them the definition and discuss the word or phrase with them.

beg – to ask for strongly

disobey – to do something that you've been told not to do; to break a rule

mind – to listen to

gobble up – to eat quickly

measure – an amount

organ-grinder – a person who walks the streets playing a hand organ to earn money

sly – clever

swiftly – fast; quickly

Read Aloud

Book Walk

Prepare students for reading by taking them on a Book Walk of "Budulinek." Scan the story together and ask students to make predictions about the story. Answers to questions may vary.

1. Turn to the table of contents in *K¹² Classics for Young Readers*. Help students find the selection and turn to that page.

2. Point to and read aloud the **title of the story**.

   ▶ What do you think the story is about?

3. Have students look at the pictures in the story.

   ▶ Where do you think the story takes place?
   ▶ What do you think might happen in the story?

4. Remind students that thinking and talking about ideas in a story before reading helps get our brain ready to read and to better understand and remember the story.

   ▶ What is one of your family rules about staying safe? If students aren't sure, tell them one of the safety rules you had to follow when you were a child, such as not talking to strangers.
   ▶ Why do you think your family has this rule?
   ▶ Did you ever break the rule? What happened?

Objectives

- Make predictions based on text, illustrations, and/or prior knowledge.
- Activate prior knowledge by previewing text and/or discussing topic.
- Listen and respond to texts representing a variety of cultures, time periods, and traditions.

"Budulinek"

It's time to read "Budulinek."

1. Have students sit next to you so that they can see the pictures and words while you read aloud.

2. Tell students to listen for clues about things that the author doesn't directly state.

3. **Read aloud the entire story.** Track with your finger so students can follow along. Emphasize Words to Know as you come to them. If appropriate, use the pictures to help show what each word means.

Check Your Reading

"Budulinek"

Check students' comprehension of "Budulinek."

1. Have students retell "Budulinek" in their own words to develop grammar, vocabulary, comprehension, and fluency skills.

2. Ask students the following questions.

   ▸ Where do Budulinek and Granny live? in a cottage near the forest
   ▸ What does Granny tell Budulinek when she leaves for work? Don't open the door, no matter who knocks.
   ▸ Who is Lishka? a sly old mother fox
   ▸ What does Lishka say she'll do the first time she knocks on the door? She'll give Budulinek a ride on her tail.
   ▸ What does Lishka really do when Budulinek opens the door? She eats all of Budulinek's soup.
   ▸ What does Granny do when she finds out Budulinek opened the door and let Lishka in the house? She tells him not to do it again.
   ▸ What happens the next time that Lishka knocks on the door? Budulinek lets her in again; she eats his food again.

 If students have trouble responding to a question, help them locate the answer in the text or pictures.

> **Objectives**
> • Retell or dramatize a story.
> • Answer questions requiring literal recall of details.

Reading for Meaning

Make and Support Inferences in "Budulinek"
Explore making inferences with students.

> **Objectives**
> - Make inferences based on text and/or prior knowledge.
> - Support inferences with evidence from text and/or prior knowledge.

1. Remind students that good readers are able to **infer**, or figure out, things in a story that the author does not say directly. Good readers use **clues from the story, pictures, and what they know from their own experiences** to make inferences.

2. Ask the following questions to check students' ability to make and support inferences.

   ▸ Why does Granny tell Budulinek not to open the door, no matter who knocks? She's trying to keep Budulinek safe. What do you know from your personal experience that helped you figure this out? Students may share something from their personal experiences about their family's rules for keeping them safe.

   ▸ Why does Lishka tell Budulinek she'll give him a ride on her tail? to get him to open the door What does this tell you about Lishka? Possible answers: She's sly or clever; she can't be trusted; she wants to trick Budulinek.

   ▸ How do you think Budulinek feels when Lishka won't let him out of her hole? Possible answers: scared; upset; sorry he didn't listen to Granny What clues are in the picture on page 77? Budulinek's eyes and mouth are wide open, which makes him look like he's scared; his hand is up, like he's trying to protect himself from the little foxes. What hints from the story and personal experience helped you infer this? Students may state that the three little foxes tease and nip at Budulinek, which would make him upset and scared.

   ▸ Why do you think the organ-grinder tells Granny that he'll keep an eye out for Budulinek? Possible answers: He says "Poor Granny," which sounds like he feels sorry for her; he's kind.

   ▸ Why do you think the organ-grinder puts each fox in a bag? Possible answers: so they can't go back in the hole and warn Lishka; so Lishka will come out of the hole to find out where her little foxes are

   ▸ Do you think Budulinek will follow Granny's rule from now on? Why or why not? Answers will vary. Have students explain the logic behind their answer and give examples from the story, if applicable.

   ▸ Do you think Lishka and her little foxes will leave Budulinek alone like they promised the organ-grinder? Why or why not? Answers will vary. Have students think about how foxes act in other stories that they've heard.

Explore "Budulinek"

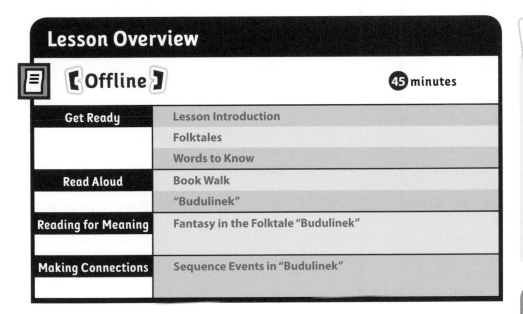

Lesson Overview

[Offline]		**45 minutes**
Get Ready	Lesson Introduction	
	Folktales	
	Words to Know	
Read Aloud	Book Walk	
	"Budulinek"	
Reading for Meaning	Fantasy in the Folktale "Budulinek"	
Making Connections	Sequence Events in "Budulinek"	

Big Ideas

▸ Exposing readers to a wide variety of genres provides them with a wide range of background knowledge and increases their vocabulary.

▸ Comprehension requires the reader to self-monitor understanding.

▸ Comprehension entails an understanding of the organizational patterns of text.

[Materials]

Supplied

- "Budulinek," *K¹² Classics for Young Readers, Volume A*, pp. 68–85
- *K¹² Language Arts Activity Book*, pp. LC 29–31

Also Needed

- scissors, round-end safety
- glue stick

Keywords

folktale – a story passed down through a culture for many years that may have human, animal, or magical characters

genre – a category for classifying literary works

retelling – using your own words to tell a story that you have listened to or read

self-monitor – to notice if you do or do not understand what you are reading

sequence – order

 **Offline** **45** minutes

Work **together** with students to complete Get Ready, Read Aloud, Reading for Meaning, and Making Connections activities.

Get Ready ....

Lesson Introduction

Prepare students for listening to and discussing "Budulinek."

1. Tell students that you are going to reread "Budulinek."

2. Explain that before you read the story, you will get ready by discussing the kind of story called a folktale.

Objectives

- Identify genre.
- Identify characteristics of different genres.
- Distinguish fantasy from realistic text.
- Build vocabulary through listening, reading, and discussion.
- Use new vocabulary in written and spoken sentences.

Folktales

Explore characteristics of folktales.

1. Tell students that there are many kinds of stories. One kind is called a **folktale**. A folktale is a story that has been passed down by a group of people for many years. Folktales come from countries all over the world, such as Russia, France, Brazil, and Australia.

2. Explain that **folktales may have human, animal, or magical characters** and that parts of folktales might be **fantasy**, which means they have make-believe things in them. The parts of a folktale that are fantasy could never happen in the real world. For example, in the real world, animals can't talk.

3. Tell students to listen for parts of a folktale that could not happen in real life. **Say:** One day, the little red hen found a grain of wheat. She asked her animal friends if they would help her plant it. But they all said "I won't," so she did it all by herself. Then the little red hen asked the animals to help her cut the wheat and take it to the mill to make flour. But they all said, "I won't," so she did it all by herself. Then the little red hen baked bread with the flour and asked the animals, "Who will help me eat my bread?" They all shouted, "I will!" But the little red hen said, "Oh, no you won't!" and only shared the bread with her four little chicks.

   ▶ Could a little red hen talk in the real world? No
   ▶ Could a little red hen find a grain of wheat? Yes
   ▶ Could a little red hen plant and cut wheat, then take it to a mill to make flour? No
   ▶ What do we call a part of a story that is make-believe? fantasy
   ▶ What do we call a story that has been told over and over by a group of people and might have parts that are fantasy? a folktale

Words to Know
Before reading "Budulinek," go over Words to Know with students.

1. Read aloud each word or phrase and have students repeat it.

2. Ask students if they know what each word or phrase means.

   ▸ If students know a word's or phrase's meaning, have them define it and use it in a sentence.
   ▸ If students don't know a word's or phrase's meaning, read them the definition and discuss the word with them.

beg – to ask for strongly
disobey – to do something that you've been told not to do; to break a rule
mind – to listen to
gobble up – to eat quickly
measure – an amount
organ-grinder – a person who walks the streets playing a hand organ to earn money
sly – clever
swiftly – fast; quickly

Read Aloud

Book Walk
Prepare students by taking them on a Book Walk "Budulinek." Scan the story together to revisit the characters and events.

1. Turn to the selection in *K¹² Classics for Young Readers, Volume A*. Point to and read aloud the **title of the story**.

   ▸ Explain to students that Czechoslovakia was an old country in Europe. It is split into two countries now called the Czech Republic and Slovakia.

2. Have students review the **pictures**.

3. Point to the picture on page 70.

   ▸ Who are these characters and where are they? Budulinek and Lishka are inside Budulinek's cottage.
   ▸ How did a fox get into the house? She talked Budulinek into opening the door.
   ▸ Could a fox really talk to a boy? No
   ▸ Does a fox wear a scarf on its head in the real world? No
   ▸ What do we call a part of a story that is make-believe? fantasy

Objectives
- Activate prior knowledge by previewing text and/or discussing topic.
- Distinguish fantasy from realistic text.
- Listen and respond to texts representing a variety of cultures, time periods, and traditions.

"Budulinek"

It's time to reread the story.

1. Have students sit next to you so that they can see the pictures and words while you read aloud the story.

2. Tell students to listen for parts of the story that are make-believe, or fantasy.

3. Remind students to listen carefully to hear what happens in the beginning, middle, and end of the story so they can retell it.

4. **Read aloud the entire story.** Track with your finger so students can follow along. Emphasize Words to Know as you come to them. If appropriate, use the pictures to help show what each word means.

Reading for Meaning

Fantasy in the Folktale "Budulinek"

Explore folktales and fantasy with students.

1. Remind students that a **folktale** is a story that has been passed down by a group of people for many years. Parts of a folktale can be fantasy, or make-believe, which means it's something that couldn't happen in the real world.

2. Ask students the following questions.

   ▸ Can a little boy really live in a cottage near a forest? Yes
   ▸ Can a granny have a job? Yes
   ▸ Can a fox be a mother and have little foxes? Yes
   ▸ Lishka tells Budulinek that she will give him a ride on her tail if he would just open the door. Is this fantasy or something that could really happen? fantasy   Why is it fantasy? A fox can't talk, and a little boy can't really go for a ride on a fox's tail.
   ▸ Granny gives the organ-grinder a penny to stop playing music. Later on, each of the little foxes gives the organ-grinder a penny to stop playing music, too. Which part is fantasy? The little foxes giving the organ-grinder a penny to stop playing music.
   ▸ Name something else in the story that is fantasy. Have students explain why the part of the story that they name couldn't happen in the real world.
   ▸ What makes a story a folktale? What are some of the special things about this kind of story? Possible answers: Folktales are stories that have been passed down by a group of people for many years; folktales may have human, animal, or magical characters; folktales can have parts that are fantasy, or make-believe.
   ▸ What makes the story "Budulinek" a folktale? What are some of the special things about this story that make it a folktale? Possible answers: It's an old story from Czechoslovakia; it has animals that talk; a boy goes for a ride on a fox's tail; a boy is trapped in a fox hole and is teased by little foxes.

Objectives

- Distinguish fantasy from realistic text.
- Identify genre.
- Identify characteristics of different genres.

Making Connections

Sequence Events in "Budulinek"

Check students' comprehension of "Budulinek" and their understanding of sequence. Turn to pages LC 29–31 in *K¹² Language Arts Activity Book.*

1. Remind students that the order in which things happen in a story is called the **sequence**. A good retelling mentions the most important events in sequence.

2. Explain that students will use pictures to show the order, or sequence, of the things that happen in "Budulinek."

3. Have students cut out the pictures on page LC 29 and glue them to page LC 31 in the order that they happen in the story.

   ▸ Explain that one picture is from the beginning of the story, three are from the middle, and two are from the end.
   ▸ If students aren't sure of the order, have them refer back to the story.

4. Have students retell the beginning of "Budulinek." There's a boy named Budulinek. His granny goes to work every day, leaves him his dinner, and tells him not to open the door for anyone.

5. Have them retell the middle of "Budulinek." Lishka, a sly mother fox, comes to Budulinek's house and tricks him into opening the door. She does this several times. The last time, she takes Budulinek back to her hole, where her children nip at and tease Budulinek.

6. Have them retell the end of "Budulinek." The organ-grinder tricks the little foxes and then Lishka into coming out of hole. He rescues Budulinek and brings him home to his granny.

Objectives

- Sequence pictures illustrating story events.
- Identify story sequence.
- Retell a story using various media.
- Retell the beginning, middle, and end of a story.
- Self-monitor comprehension of text.

7. Guide students to think about their retelling. Answers to questions may vary.

- ▶ Did your retelling include the important characters?
- ▶ Did it include most of the important things that happened?
- ▶ Did you retell the events in sequence?
- ▶ Do you think that you understand the story?

TIP If students forget to mention characters or important events in their retelling, have them retell the story again as you ask questions such as, "Who is in the story? What does this character do?" If students don't think they understand the story, reread the story aloud, pausing to let students ask questions as you read.

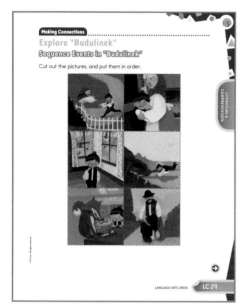

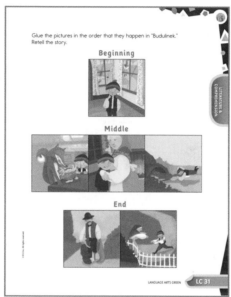

Introduce "Issun Boshi"

Lesson Overview

Materials

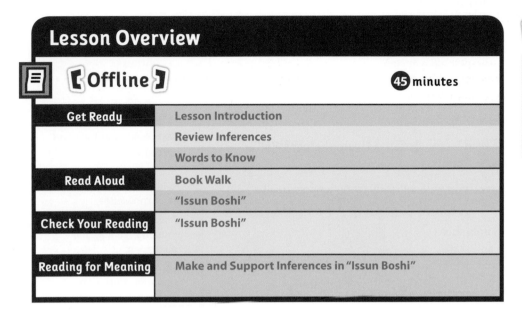

Offline		45 minutes
Get Ready	Lesson Introduction	
	Review Inferences	
	Words to Know	
Read Aloud	Book Walk	
	"Issun Boshi"	
Check Your Reading	"Issun Boshi"	
Reading for Meaning	Make and Support Inferences in "Issun Boshi"	

Advance Preparation

Read "Issun Boshi" before beginning the Read Aloud to locate Words to Know in the text.

Big Ideas

- ▶ Good readers use prior knowledge and text clues to infer or draw conclusions about what is implied but not directly stated in text.
- ▶ Activating prior knowledge provides a framework for a reader to organize and connect new information to information previously learned; readers that activate prior knowledge before reading are more likely to understand and recall what they read.

Supplied

- "Issun Boshi," *K¹² Classics for Young Readers, Volume A*, pp. 86–99

Story Synopsis

In this folktale from Japan, an elderly couple wishes for nothing more than a child. One day, their wish comes true, but their son grows no taller than his father's thumb. His small size does not stop Issun Boshi from traveling to the big city. Issun Boshi has many great adventures, including fighting a monster who has a magic hammer—a magic hammer that can grant wishes. What might Issun Boshi wish for?

Keywords

infer – to use clues and what you already know to make a guess

inference – a guess you make using the clues in a text and what you already know

 **Offline** **45** minutes

Work **together** with students to complete Get Ready, Read Aloud, Check Your Reading, and Reading for Meaning activities.

 Get Ready ....

Lesson Introduction

Prepare students for listening to and discussing "Issun Boshi."

1. Tell students that you are going to read "Issun Boshi," a Japanese story about a boy who is no bigger than his father's thumb.

2. Explain that before you read the story you will get ready by reviewing how to make inferences.

TIP *Issun Boshi* is pronounced ee-sun boh-shee.

Review Inferences

Review how we make inferences.

1. Ask students to tell what helps us make inferences.

2. If students have trouble answering, offer these reminders:

   ▸ We can infer many things about a story by listening for clues in the words and looking for clues in the pictures.
   ▸ We use prior knowledge learned from personal experiences.

3. Have students practice making inferences about actions and emotions.
   Say: Your brother is reading a book and keeps laughing out loud.

   ▸ What can you infer about the book? It's funny.   What prior knowledge helped you make this inference? Answers will vary. Students may indicate that people laugh when they think something is funny.
   ▸ What can you infer about how your brother feels while reading the book? He's happy; he feels good.   What do you know from personal experience that helps you make this inference? Answers will vary. Students may say that people laugh when they feel good or feel happy.

Objectives
- Make inferences based on text and/or prior knowledge.
- Support inferences with evidence from text and/or prior knowledge.
- Build vocabulary through listening, reading, and discussion.
- Use new vocabulary in written and spoken sentences.

Words to Know
Before reading "Issun Boshi," go over Words to Know with students.

1. Read aloud each word and have students repeat it.

2. Ask students if they know what each word means.

   ▶ If students know a word's meaning, have them define it and use it in a sentence.
   ▶ If students don't know a word's meaning, read them the definition and discuss the word with them.

chopstick – a thin stick used for eating food
honor – respect
kimono – a long, loose robe that's worn in Japan
lord – an important man with great power
sayonara – *good-bye* in Japanese
scabbard – a case that holds a sword

Read Aloud

Book Walk
Prepare students for reading by taking them on a Book Walk of "Issun Boshi." Scan the story together and ask students to make predictions about the story. Answers to questions may vary.

1. Turn to the table of contents in *K¹² Classics for Young Readers, Volume A*. Help students find the selection and turn to that page.

2. Point to and read aloud the **title of the story**.

   ▶ What do you think the story is about?

3. Have students look at the pictures in the story.

   ▶ Where do you think the story takes place?
   ▶ What do you think might happen in the story?

4. Remind students that thinking and talking about ideas in a story before reading helps to get our brain ready to read and helps us better understand and remember the story.

   ▶ What do you think the world would look like if you were only as tall as a thumb?
   ▶ What would you use as a bed if you were that small?

Objectives
- Make predictions based on text, illustrations, and/or prior knowledge.
- Activate prior knowledge by previewing text and/or discussing topic.
- Listen and respond to texts representing a variety of cultures, time periods, and traditions.

"Issun Boshi"

It's time to read aloud the story.

1. Have students sit next to you so that they can see the pictures and words while you read aloud.

2. Tell students to listen for clues about things that the author doesn't directly state.

3. **Read aloud the entire story.** Track with your finger so students can follow along. Emphasize Words to Know as you come to them. If appropriate, use the pictures to help show what each word means.

Check Your Reading

"Issun Boshi"

Check students' comprehension of "Issun Boshi."

1. Have students retell "Issun Boshi" in their own words to develop grammar, vocabulary, comprehension, and fluency skills.

2. Ask students the following questions.

   ▸ Why does Issun Boshi leave his parents' home? Possible answers: to go to the great city; to see the world; to bring honor to his family

   ▸ What does Issun Boshi use for a boat? a rice bowl

   ▸ What is one of the jobs Issun Boshi does for the lord? Possible answers: polishes shoes; chases mice and insects; stands on the lord's papers so they won't blow away

   ▸ What do the princess's servants do when the monster, or oni, jumps out from the shadows at the cherry blossom festival? They run away.

   ▸ What does Issun Boshi do when the oni tries to eat him? He stabs the oni in the face over and over with his sword.

   ▸ What does this make the oni do? Possible answers: cry; claw at his eyes; beg Issun Boshi to stop stabbing him; run back into the forest

 TIP If students have trouble responding to a question, help them locate the answer in the text or pictures.

 Objectives
- Retell or dramatize a story.
- Answer questions requiring literal recall of details.

Reading for Meaning

Make and Support Inferences in "Issun Boshi"
Explore making inferences with students.

> **Objectives**
> - Make inferences based on text and/or prior knowledge.
> - Support inferences with evidence from text and/or prior knowledge.

1. Remind students that good readers are able to **infer**, or figure out, things in a story that the author does not say directly. Good readers use **clues from the story, pictures, and what they know from their own experiences** to make inferences.

2. Ask the following questions to check students' ability to make and support inferences.

   ▶ Why does Issun Boshi think the main street of Kyoto is "a forest of legs" and "a sea of feet"? That's what it looks like to him because he's so small.   What do you know from your personal experience that helped you infer this? Answers will vary. Students may refer to how things looked to them when they were small.

   ▶ Why do the princess's servants run away when they see the oni? Possible answers: because they are afraid of him; because they think he will hurt them   What would you do if you saw a scary monster? Answers will vary, but students should explain why they think they'd react this way.

   ▶ What does the princess wish for? to marry Issun Boshi   What does this tell you about the princess? that she loves him   How did you use prior knowledge to make this inference? Answers will vary. Students may say that people marry someone they love.

   ▶ Why does it look like the world is shrinking after Issun Boshi touches the magic hammer? because he is growing taller   What clue is in the picture on page 97? He's taller than the princess in the picture, and he used to be so small he could stand on her shoulder.

   ▶ Why do Issun Boshi's parents cry when he comes back home? They're happy because they haven't seen him for a long time.

   ▶ What words would you use to describe Issun Boshi? Possible answers: brave; adventurous; good worker; good son; friendly   Give examples from the story that explain why you think these words describe him. Possible answers: He fights the monster, even though he's so small; he goes to the big city by himself; he does many jobs for the lord; he brings his parents to live with him in Kyoto; everyone likes him.

Explore "Issun Boshi"

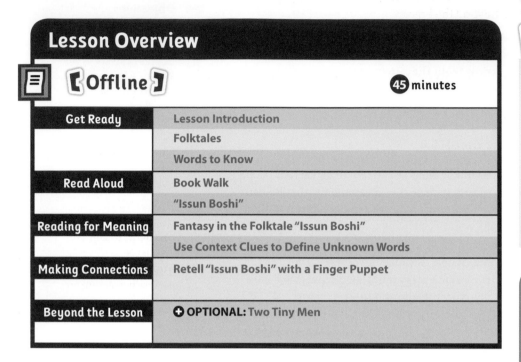

Lesson Overview

[Offline] **45** minutes

Get Ready	Lesson Introduction
	Folktales
	Words to Know
Read Aloud	Book Walk
	"Issun Boshi"
Reading for Meaning	Fantasy in the Folktale "Issun Boshi"
	Use Context Clues to Define Unknown Words
Making Connections	Retell "Issun Boshi" with a Finger Puppet
Beyond the Lesson	⊕ OPTIONAL: Two Tiny Men

Big Ideas

► Exposing readers to a wide variety of genres provides them with a wide range of background knowledge and increases their vocabulary.
► Early learners acquire vocabulary through active exposure (by talking and listening, being read to, and receiving explicit instruction).
► Comprehension requires the reader to self-monitor understanding.
► Comprehension entails an understanding of the organizational patterns of text.

[Materials]

Supplied
● "Issun Boshi," *K¹² Classics for Young Readers, Volume A*, pp. 86–99
● *K¹² Language Arts Activity Book*, p. LC 33

Also Needed
● scissors, round-end safety

Keywords
folktale – a story passed down through a culture for many years that may have human, animal, or magical characters
genre – a category for classifying literary works
retelling – using your own words to tell a story that you have listened to or read
self-monitor – to notice if you do or do not understand what you are reading

[Offline] 45 minutes

Work **together** with students to complete Get Ready, Read Aloud, Reading for Meaning, Making Connections, and Beyond the Lesson activities.

Get Ready

Lesson Introduction

Prepare students for listening to and discussing "Issun Boshi."

1. Tell students that you are going to reread "Issun Boshi."

2. Explain that before you read the story, you will get ready by reviewing the kind of story called a folktale.

Folktales

Review characteristics of folktales.

1. Ask students to explain what makes a story a **folktale**.

2. If necessary, offer students these reminders:

   ▸ Folktales come from countries all over the world.
   ▸ A folktale is a story that has been passed down by a group of people for many years.
   ▸ Folktales may have human, animal, or magical characters.
   ▸ Parts of folktales might be fantasy, which means they have make-believe things in them that could never happen in the real world.

3. Tell students to listen for parts of a folktale that could not happen in real life. **Say:** Listen to this old story from India. Once upon a time, a sleeping rabbit woke up under a palm tree and heard a coconut hit the ground. He thought the loud noise meant the world was breaking into pieces, and he started to run. The rabbit told other animals, and they ran with him. The lion saw them all running and roared to make them stop. The lion and the rabbit went back to the place where the rabbit had been sleeping. The lion figured out that the rabbit had heard the falling coconut and the world was not breaking apart.

   ▸ Could a rabbit fall asleep under a palm tree? Yes
   ▸ Could a coconut fall from a palm tree? Yes
   ▸ Could a rabbit tell other animals that the world was breaking into pieces, or is that make-believe? make-believe   Why is it make-believe? Rabbits can't talk.
   ▸ What do we call a part of a story that is make-believe? fantasy
   ▸ The old story from India begins with *Once upon a time* and has talking animals. What do these things tell you about the story? It's a folktale.

Objectives

- Identify genre.
- Identify characteristics of different genres.
- Distinguish fantasy from realistic text.
- Build vocabulary through listening, reading, and discussion.
- Use new vocabulary in written and spoken sentences.

Words to Know

Before reading "Issun Boshi," go over Words to Know with students.

1. Read aloud each word and have students repeat it.

2. Ask students if they know what each word means.

   ▸ If students know a word's meaning, have them define it and use it in a sentence.
   ▸ If students don't know a word's meaning, read them the definition and discuss the word with them.

chopstick – a thin stick used for eating food
honor – respect
kimono – a long, loose robe that's worn in Japan
lord – an important man with great power
sayonara – *good-bye* in Japanese
scabbard – a case that holds a sword

Read Aloud

Book Walk

Prepare students by taking them on a Book Walk of "Issun Boshi." Scan the story together to revisit the characters and events.

1. Turn to the selection in *K¹² Classics for Young Readers, Volume A*. Point to and read aloud the **title of the story**.

2. Have students review the **pictures**.

3. Point to the picture on page 91.

   ▸ Who are these characters? Issun Boshi and the lord
   ▸ Why does Issun Boshi go to the city? to serve a lord and make a name for himself
   ▸ Could a man be a lord? Yes
   ▸ Could a boy really be only 1 inch tall? No

Objectives

- Activate prior knowledge by previewing text and/or discussing topic.
- Distinguish fantasy from realistic text.
- Listen and respond to texts representing a variety of cultures, time periods, and traditions.

"Issun Boshi"

It's time to reread the story.

1. Have students sit next to you so that they can see the pictures and words while you read aloud the story.

2. Tell students to listen for parts of the story that are make-believe, or fantasy.

3. Remind students to listen carefully to hear what happens in the beginning, middle, and end of the story so they can retell it.

4. **Read aloud the entire story.** Track with your finger so students can follow along. Emphasize Words to Know as you come to them. If appropriate, use the pictures to help show what each word means.

Reading for Meaning

Fantasy in the Folktale "Issun Boshi"
Explore folktales and fantasy elements with students.

1. Remind students that a folktale is a story that has been passed down by a group of people for many years. Parts of a folktale can be fantasy, or make-believe, which means it's something that couldn't happen in the real world.

2. Ask students the following questions.

   ▸ Why does the story begin with *Once upon a time*? to let readers know that the story happened long ago, and that parts of the story are make-believe, or fantasy

   ▸ The name *Issun Boshi* means "One-Inch Boy." Can a boy be only 1 inch tall, or is this make-believe? make-believe   How do you know? There are no 1-inch boys in the real world.   What do we call the parts of a story that are make-believe? fantasy

   ▸ When the princess is walking home from the cherry blossom festival with Issun Boshi, her servants, and some friends, a monster jumps out of the shadows. Which part is fantasy? the monster

   ▸ What do we call a story that has been told over and over by a group of people, begins with *Once upon a time*, and has parts that are fantasy? a folktale

   ▸ What makes the story "Issun Boshi" a folktale? Possible answers: It's an old story from Japan; it starts with the words "Once upon a time"; it has a character that's only 1 inch tall; there's a monster who has a magic hammer that can make wishes come true.

Use Context Clues to Define Unknown Words
Check students' ability to use text and picture clues to determine a word's meaning.

1. Remind students that good readers can sometimes figure out the meaning of unknown words by listening to nearby words and looking at the pictures.

2. Point to the picture on page 89 and read aloud the following sentence from the story.

   "His father and mother gave him a shiny black rice bowl to use as a boat and a chopstick for an oar."

   Say: I'm not sure what *oar* means. The text says that Issun Boshi's parents give him a chopstick to use as an oar, and I see that he's using the chopstick to move the bowl that he's using as a boat. The picture helps me figure out that an *oar* is a kind of paddle.

Objectives
- Distinguish fantasy from realistic text.
- Explain function of recurring phrases in folk and fairy tales.
- Identify genre.
- Identify characteristics of different genres.
- Use context and sentence structure to determine meaning of words, phrases, and/or sentences.
- Use illustrations to aid understanding of text.

3. Turn to page 92 and have students look at the picture at the top of the page. Read aloud the following sentences from the story.

"The bug was almost as big as Issun Boshi. Its stinger was as long as his arm. But, without waiting a moment, Issun Boshi drew his sword and felled the insect with one swift stroke."

▸ What does the word *felled* mean? knocked down   How do the text and picture help you figure this out? The story says Issun Boshi uses his sword, and the insect in the picture looks like it's about to fall over.

4. Turn to page 94 and have the students look at the picture on the page. Read aloud the following sentence from the story.

"As they were walking home, a fierce monster, called an *oni*, jumped out from the shadows, roaring and snarling."

▸ What does the word *fierce* mean? wild; dangerous   What clues are in the text and the picture? The story says the monster roars and snarls, and the picture shows the face of a wild-looking monster with claws and horns.

Making Connections

Retell "Issun Boshi" with a Finger Puppet
Check students' comprehension of the story and its sequence. Turn to page LC 33 in *K¹² Language Arts Activity Book*.

Objectives
- Retell a story using various media.
- Retell the beginning, middle, and end of a story.
- Self-monitor comprehension of text.

1. Help students cut out the finger puppet on the Activity Book page.

2. Cut out the finger holes on the puppet.

   ▸ Demonstrate for students how to put your index and middle fingers through the holes on the puppet so that your fingers act as Issun Boshi's arms.
   ▸ Glue the puppet to a craft stick if tearing is a concern.

3. Have students retell the beginning, middle, and end of "Issun Boshi" with the finger puppet.

   ▸ Retell the beginning of the story, the part in which Issun Boshi is born. An old couple finally have a baby, but he never grows taller than his father's thumb, so they name him "Issun Boshi."
   ▸ Retell the middle of the story, the part in which Issun Boshi meets the lord and begins to work for him. Issun Boshi goes to live in the capital city. When he gets there, he meets a lord and gets a job working for him. One day, when he and the princess are coming back from the cherry blossom festival, a monster called an *oni* jumps out at them and says he's going to eat Issun Boshi. But Issun Boshi stabs him over and over in the face until the monster lets go and runs back into the forest, dropping his magic hammer.
   ▸ Retell the end of the story, the part in which Issun Boshi grows tall. Possible answer: Issun Boshi makes a wish using the magic hammer, and he grows to be a regular-sized man. He becomes famous for fighting the monster. He goes back home to get his parents, and then he marries the princess.

4. Guide students to think about their retelling. Answers to questions may vary.

- ► Did your retelling include the important characters?
- ► Did it include most of the important things that happened?
- ► Did you retell the events in sequence?
- ► Do you think that you understand the story?

 TIP Refer back to the story if students need help recalling events. If students forget to mention characters or important events in their retellings, have them retell the story again as you ask questions such as, "Who is in the story? What does this character do?" If students don't think they understand the story, reread the story aloud, pausing to let students ask questions as you read.

Reward: Add a sticker for this unit on the My Accomplishments chart to mark successful completion of the unit.

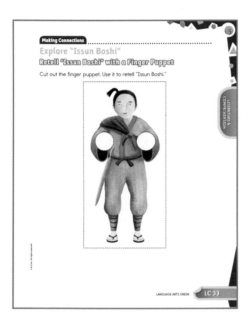

Beyond the Lesson

⊕ OPTIONAL: Two Tiny Men

This activity is OPTIONAL. It is intended for students who have extra time and would enjoy comparing Issun Boshi with Tom Thumb. Feel free to skip this activity.

1. Go to a library for a copy of *Tom Thumb* by Richard Jesse Watson, or any other version of the story.

2. Lead a Book Walk and then read aloud the story.

3. Have students tell how *Tom Thumb* and "Issun Boshi" are alike and different.

4. Ask them to tell which story they like best and why.

 Objectives
- Compare and contrast two texts on the same topic.

Mid-Semester Checkpoint

Unit Focus

In this unit, students will listen to a piece of fiction, a poem, and a nonfiction article. They will demonstrate mastery of content in each genre by listening to a variety of texts, making and checking predictions, identifying story elements and structures of each text, using new vocabulary, comparing and contrasting elements of each text, and retelling.

Unit Plan		[Offline]	[Online]
Lesson 1	Mid-Semester Checkpoint	**45** minutes	varies

Mid-Semester Checkpoint

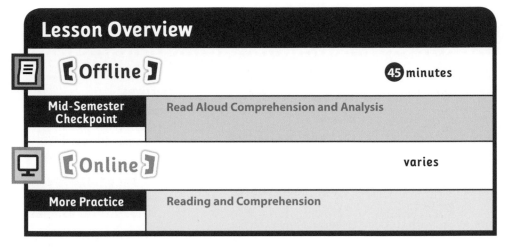

Lesson Overview

Offline		**45** minutes
Mid-Semester Checkpoint	Read Aloud Comprehension and Analysis	
Online		varies
More Practice	Reading and Comprehension	

Materials

Supplied
- *K¹² Language Arts Assessments*, pp. LC 1–27

Also Needed
- crayons
- paper, drawing

Advance Preparation

Read each selection in the Mid-Semester Checkpoint before administering the assessment to locate Words to Know in the text.

 **45** minutes

Work **together** with students to complete the Mid-Semester Checkpoint.

Mid-Semester Checkpoint

Read Aloud Comprehension and Analysis

Explain that students are going to show what they have learned so far this semester.

> ▶ Give students pages LC 5–LC 27 of the Mid-Semester Checkpoint.
> ▶ Read the directions on the students' pages together. Use the Learning Coach instructions on pages LC 1–LC 4 to administer the Checkpoint.
> ▶ Use the Checkpoint pages to record student behaviors and responses.
> ▶ When you have finished, use the Answer Key to score the Checkpoint and then enter the results online.
> ▶ Review each exercise with students. Work with students to correct any exercise that they missed.

Part 1. Fiction: "The Legend of the Hummingbird" Activate Prior Knowledge

Ask students the following questions to activate prior knowledge. Note their responses on the Checkpoint pages.

1. Have you heard of a legend before? Can you name an example of a legend or a characteristic of a legend?

Before reading "The Legend of the Hummingbird," go over Words to Know with students. Read aloud each word and have students repeat it. Ask students if they know what each word means.

> ▶ If students know a word's meaning, have them define it and use it in a sentence.
> ▶ If students don't know a word's meaning, read them the definition and discuss the word with them.

demanded – asked firmly for something
escape – to break free from or get away
plea – a very emotional request

Part 2. Fiction: "The Legend of the Hummingbird" Book Walk and Read Aloud

Gather the Checkpoint pages with "The Legend of the Hummingbird." Have students sit next to you so that they can see the story while you do a Book Walk. Read aloud the title and author of the text. Ask students the following questions and note their responses on the Checkpoint pages.

2. Where is the title of the story? Point to it.

3. What do you think the story will be about?

Explain to students that you will read the story and they will listen carefully.

Read aloud the entire story. Tell students to listen for *demanded*, *escape*, and *plea*.

Objectives
- Complete a Mid-Semester Checkpoint on the elements of poetry, nonfiction, and fiction.

Part 3. Fiction: "The Legend of the Hummingbird" Evaluate Predictions

Read students' predictions to them. Tell students that predictions are not right or wrong; they are just the best guess you can make with the information you have. Ask students the following questions and note their responses on the Checkpoint pages.

4. What helped you make your prediction?

5. What else could help a reader make a prediction?

6. Was your prediction accurate?

Part 4. Fiction: "The Legend of the Hummingbird" Retelling

Have students retell "The Legend of the Hummingbird" in their own words. On the Checkpoint pages, note any key elements that they do not include or that they retell incorrectly.

7. Retell the story in your own words.

Part 5. Fiction: "The Legend of the Hummingbird" Reading Comprehension

Read the questions and possible responses to students and note their responses on the Checkpoint pages. You may let students circle the answers themselves.

Part 6. Fiction: "The Legend of the Hummingbird" Show You Know

Gather paper, pencil, and crayons. Remind students that this story doesn't have any pictures. Tell them that they are going to be the illustrator. Allow five minutes for students to draw a picture (or pictures) to go with the story. Ask students the following questions and note their responses on the Checkpoint pages.

15. What is the job of the illustrator?

16. Draw a picture that goes with the story.

17. Write a sentence that describes the picture. Use the words *demanded*, *escape*, or *plea* in your sentence.

Part 7. Nonfiction: "The Buzz About Hummingbirds" Activate Prior Knowledge

Ask students the following questions to activate prior knowledge. Note their responses on the Checkpoint pages.

18. What is a fact?

19. What is nonfiction?

20. What do you already know about birds?

Before reading "The Buzz About Hummingbirds," go over Words to Know with students. Read each word aloud and have students repeat it. Ask students if they know what each word means.

- ▸ If students know a word's meaning, have them define it and use it in a sentence.
- ▸ If students don't know a word's meaning, read them the definition and discuss the word with them.

beat – to flap with force
dart – to move suddenly and quickly
nectar – a sweet liquid collected from flowers

Part 8. Nonfiction: "The Buzz About Hummingbirds" Book Walk and Read Aloud

Gather the Checkpoint pages with "The Buzz About Hummingbirds." Have students sit next to you so that they can see the story while you do a Book Walk. Read aloud the title and author of the text. Ask students the following questions and note their responses on the Checkpoint pages.

21. What is the title of the article? Point to it.

22. Who is the author of the article? Point to it.

23. What does an author do?

24. What do you think the article will be about?

Part 9. Nonfiction: "The Buzz About Hummingbirds" Evaluate Predictions

Read students' predictions to them. Tell students that predictions are not right or wrong; they are just the best guess you can make with the information you have. Ask students the following questions and note their responses on the Checkpoint pages.

25. What helped you make your prediction?

26. Was your prediction accurate?

Part 10. Nonfiction: "The Buzz About Hummingbirds" Retelling

Have students retell "The Buzz About Hummingbirds" in their own words. On the Checkpoint pages, note any key elements that they do not include or that they retell incorrectly.

27. Retell the story in your own words.

Part 11. Nonfiction: "The Buzz About Hummingbirds" Reading Comprehension

Read the questions and possible responses to students and note their responses on the Checkpoint pages. You may let students circle the answers themselves.

Part 12. Nonfiction: "The Buzz About Hummingbirds" Identify Facts

Read aloud each sentence. Students should tell you whether each statement is a fact or not. Write students' responses on the Checkpoint pages.

33. Hummingbirds are the best birds ever.

34. Hummingbirds are the smallest birds ever.

35. Hummingbirds hum because they are happy.

36. Hummingbirds hum because they beat their wings so fast.

37. Hummingbirds have long, thin bills so they can drink nectar.

38. Hummingbirds have very pretty feathers.

Part 13. Poetry: "The Little Hummingbird" Activate Prior Knowledge

Ask students the following questions to activate prior knowledge. Note their responses on the Checkpoint pages.

39. I've read a story and an article to you. What was their topic?

40. What do you think this poem will be about?

Part 14. Poetry: "The Little Hummingbird" Book Walk and Read Aloud

Gather the Checkpoint pages with "The Little Hummingbird." Have students sit next to you so that they can see the poem while you do a Book Walk. Read aloud the title and author of the text. Ask students the following questions and note their responses on the Checkpoint pages.

41. Where is the title of the poem? Point to it.

42. Who is the author of the poem? Point to the name.

Explain to students that you will read the poem and they will listen carefully. **Read aloud the entire poem**.

Part 15. Poetry: "The Little Hummingbird" Evaluate Predictions

Read students' predictions to them. Tell students that predictions are not right or wrong; they are just the best guess you can make with the information you have. Ask students the following questions and note their responses on the Checkpoint pages.

43. What helped you make your prediction?

44. Was your prediction accurate?

Part 16. Poetry: "The Little Hummingbird" Reading Comprehension

Read the questions and possible responses to students and note their responses on the Checkpoint pages. You may let students circle the answers themselves.

TIP A full list of objectives for the Mid-Semester Checkpoint can be found in the online lesson.

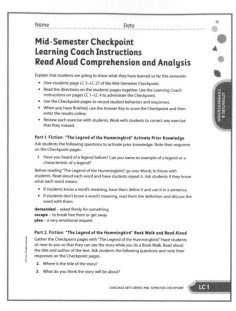

Name Date

Mid-Semester Checkpoint
Learning Coach Instructions
Read Aloud Comprehension and Analysis

Explain that students are going to show what they have learned so far this semester.

- Give students page LC 5–LC 27 of the Mid-Semester Checkpoint.
- Read the directions on the students' pages together. Use the Learning Coach instructions on pages LC 1–LC 4 to administer the Checkpoint.
- Use the Checkpoint pages to record student behaviors and responses.
- When you have finished, use the Answer Key to score the Checkpoint and then enter the results online.
- Review each exercise with students. Work with students to correct any exercise that they missed.

Part 1. Fiction: "The Legend of the Hummingbird" Activate Prior Knowledge

Ask students the following questions to activate prior knowledge. Note their response on the Checkpoint pages.

1. Have you heard of a legend before? Can you name an example of a legend or a characteristic of a legend?

Before reading "The Legend of the Hummingbird," go over Words to Know with students. Read aloud each word and have students repeat it. Ask students if they know what each word means.

- If students know a word's meaning, have them define it and use it in a sentence.
- If students don't know a word's meaning, read them the definition and discuss the word with them.

demanded – asked firmly for something
escape – to break free from or get away
plea – a very emotional request

Part 2. Fiction: "The Legend of the Hummingbird" Book Walk and Read Aloud

Gather the Checkpoint pages with "The Legend of the Hummingbird." Have students sit next to you so that they can see the story while you do a Book Walk. Read aloud the title and author of the text. Ask students the following questions and note their responses on the Checkpoint pages.

2. Where is the title of the story?
3. What do you think the story will be about?

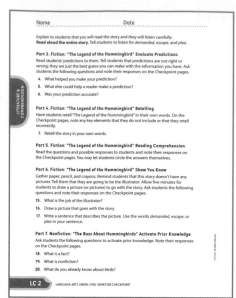

Name Date

Explain to students that you will read the story and they will listen carefully. **Read aloud the entire story.** Tell students to listen for *demanded*, *escape*, and *plea*.

Part 3. Fiction: "The Legend of the Hummingbird" Evaluate Predictions

Read students' predictions to them. Tell students that predictions are not right or wrong; they are just the best guess you can make with the information you have. Ask students the following questions and note their responses on the Checkpoint pages.

4. What helped you make your prediction?
5. What else could help a reader make a prediction?
6. Was your prediction accurate?

Part 4. Fiction: "The Legend of the Hummingbird" Retelling

Have students retell "The Legend of the Hummingbird" in their own words. On the Checkpoint pages, note any key elements that they do not include or that they retell incorrectly.

7. Retell the story in your own words.

Part 5. Fiction: "The Legend of the Hummingbird" Reading Comprehension

Read the questions and possible responses to students and note their responses on the Checkpoint pages. You may let students circle the answers themselves.

Part 6. Fiction: "The Legend of the Hummingbird" Show You Know

Gather paper, pencil, and crayons. Remind students that this story doesn't have any pictures. Tell them that they are going to be the illustrator. Allow five minutes for students to draw a picture (or pictures) to go with the story. Ask students the following questions and note their responses on the Checkpoint pages.

15. What is the job of the illustrator?
16. Draw a picture that goes with the story.
17. Write a sentence that describes the picture. Use the words *demanded*, *escape*, or *plea* in your sentence.

Part 7. Nonfiction: "The Buzz About Hummingbirds" Activate Prior Knowledge

Ask students the following questions to activate prior knowledge. Note their responses on the Checkpoint pages.

18. What is a fact?
19. What is nonfiction?
20. What do you already know about birds?

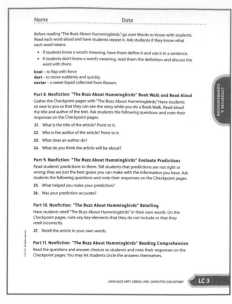

Name Date

Before reading "The Buzz About Hummingbirds," go over Words to Know with students. Read each word aloud and have students repeat it. Ask students if they know what each word means.

- If students know a word's meaning, have them define it and use it in a sentence.
- If students don't know a word's meaning, read them the definition and discuss the word with them.

beat – to flap with force
dart – to move suddenly and quickly
nectar – a sweet liquid collected from flowers

Part 8. Nonfiction: "The Buzz About Hummingbirds" Book Walk and Read Aloud

Gather the Checkpoint pages with "The Buzz About Hummingbirds." Have students sit next to you so that they can see the story while you do a Book Walk. Read aloud the title and author of the text. Ask students the following questions and note their responses on the Checkpoint pages.

21. What is the title of the article? Point to it.
22. Who is the author of the article? Point to it.
23. What does an author do?
24. What do you think the article will be about?

Part 9. Nonfiction: "The Buzz About Hummingbirds" Evaluate Predictions

Read students' predictions to them. Tell students that predictions are not right or wrong; they are just the best guess you can make with the information you have. Ask students the following questions and note their responses on the Checkpoint pages.

25. What helped you make your prediction?
26. Was your prediction accurate?

Part 10. Nonfiction: "The Buzz About Hummingbirds" Retelling

Have students retell "The Buzz About Hummingbirds" in their own words. On the Checkpoint pages, note any key elements that they do not include or that they retell incorrectly.

27. Retell the article in your own words.

Part 11. Nonfiction: "The Buzz About Hummingbirds" Reading Comprehension

Read the questions and answer choices to students and note their responses on the Checkpoint pages. You may let students circle the answers themselves.

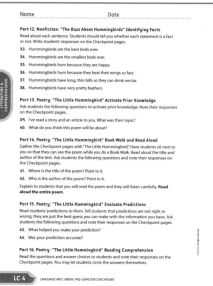

Name Date

Part 12. Nonfiction: "The Buzz About Hummingbirds" Identifying Facts

Read aloud each sentence. Students should tell you whether each statement is a fact or not. Write students' responses on the Checkpoint pages.

33. Hummingbirds are the best birds ever.
34. Hummingbirds are the smallest birds ever.
35. Hummingbirds hum because they are happy.
36. Hummingbirds hum because they beat their wings so fast.
37. Hummingbirds have long, thin bills so they can drink nectar.
38. Hummingbirds have very pretty feathers.

Part 13. Poetry: "The Little Hummingbird" Activate Prior Knowledge

Ask students the following questions to activate prior knowledge. Note their responses on the Checkpoint pages.

39. I've read a story and an article to you. What was their topic?
40. What do you think this poem will be about?

Part 14. Poetry: "The Little Hummingbird" Book Walk and Read Aloud

Gather the Checkpoint pages with "The Little Hummingbird." Have students sit next to you so that they can see the poem while you do a Book Walk. Read aloud the title and author of the text. Ask students the following questions and note their responses on the Checkpoint pages.

41. Where is the title of the poem? Point to it.
42. Who is the author of the poem? Point to it.

Explain to students that you will read the poem and they will listen carefully. **Read aloud the entire poem.**

Part 15. Poetry: "The Little Hummingbird" Evaluate Predictions

Read students' predictions to them. Tell students that predictions are not right or wrong; they are just the best guess you can make with the information you have. Ask students the following questions and note their responses on the Checkpoint pages.

43. What helped you make your prediction?
44. Was your prediction accurate?

Part 16. Poetry: "The Little Hummingbird" Reading Comprehension

Read the questions and answer choices to students and note their responses on the Checkpoint pages. You may let students circle the answers themselves.

Name Date

Mid-Semester Checkpoint Answer Key
Read Aloud Comprehension and Analysis

Part 1. Fiction: "The Legend of the Hummingbird" Activate Prior Knowledge
Get ready to read. Listen to the question, and say your answer.

1. **Possible answers: *The Legend of the Bluebonnet* or "The Legend of the Dipper"; it is a story that is very old and has been told for many years; it may be about a real person, but it can't be proven; it has a character who is a hero.**

Part 2. Fiction: "The Legend of the Hummingbird" Book Walk and Read Aloud
Do a Book Walk. Listen to the question, and say your answer. Then, listen to the story.

2. **"The Legend of the Hummingbird"**
3. **Answers will vary.**

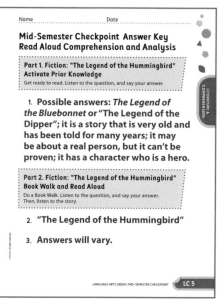

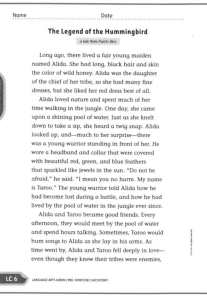

Name Date

The Legend of the Hummingbird

a tale from Puerto Rico

Long ago, there lived a fair young maiden named Alida. She had long, black hair and skin the color of wild honey. Alida was the daughter of the chief of her tribe, so she had many fine dresses, but she liked her red dress best of all.

Alida loved nature and spent much of her time walking in the jungle. One day, she came upon a shining pool of water. Just as she knelt down to take a sip, she heard a twig snap. Alida looked up, and—much to her surprise—there was a young warrior standing in front of her. He wore a headband and collar that were covered with beautiful red, green, and blue feathers that sparkled like jewels in the sun. "Do not be afraid," he said. "I mean you no harm. My name is Taroo." The young warrior told Alida how he had become lost during a battle, and how he had lived by the pool of water in the jungle ever since.

Alida and Taroo became good friends. Every afternoon, they would meet by the pool of water and spend hours talking. Sometimes, Taroo would hum songs to Alida as she lay in his arms. As time went by, Alida and Taroo fell deeply in love—even though they knew their tribes were enemies,

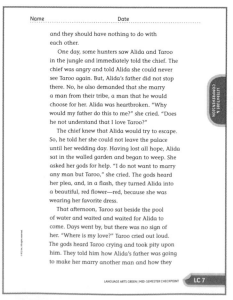

Name Date

and they should have nothing to do with each other.

One day, some hunters saw Alida and Taroo in the jungle and immediately told the chief. The chief was angry and told Alida she could never see Taroo again. But, Alida's father did not stop there. No, he also demanded that she marry a man from their tribe, a man that he would choose for her. Alida was heartbroken. "Why would my father do this to me?" she cried. "Does he not understand that I love Taroo?"

The chief knew that Alida would try to escape. So, he told her she could not leave the palace until her wedding day. Having lost all hope, Alida sat in the walled garden and began to weep. She asked her gods for help. "I do not want to marry any man but Taroo," she cried. The gods heard her plea, and, in a flash, they turned Alida into a beautiful, red flower—red, because she was wearing her favorite dress.

That afternoon, Taroo sat beside the pool of water and waited and waited for Alida to come. Days went by, but there was no sign of her. "Where is my love?" Taroo cried out loud. The gods heard Taroo crying and took pity upon him. They told him how Alida's father was going to make her marry another man and how they

Name Date

had turned her into a red flower. Taroo begged the gods to help him find her. In a flash, Taroo was turned into a hummingbird. The sparkling feathers that once covered his headband and collar now covered his little bird head and chest. When he flapped his tiny wings, it made a humming sound so Alida would know it was him.

To this day, you can hear the hummingbird hum a song as he darts from flower to flower—especially the red ones—still looking for his dear Alida.

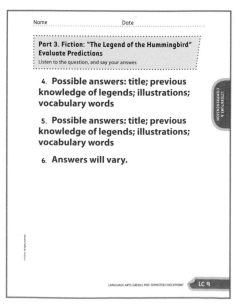

Name Date

Part 3. Fiction: "The Legend of the Hummingbird" Evaluate Predictions
Listen to the question, and say your answer.

4. **Possible answers: title; previous knowledge of legends; illustrations; vocabulary words**
5. **Possible answers: title; previous knowledge of legends; illustrations; vocabulary words**
6. **Answers will vary.**

Name _____ Date _____

7. Answers should accurately retell each of these elements:

Title: "The Legend of the Hummingbird"

Characters: Alida; Taroo; the chief; the gods

Setting: long ago; the jungle

Problem: Alida and Taroo met and fell in love, but the chief would not allow Alida to marry Taroo and demanded she marry a man from her tribe.

Solution: Alida made a plea to the gods, who turned her into a red flower. Then, the gods felt sorry for Taroo, so they turned him into a hummingbird. As a hummingbird, Taroo could be with Alida, the red flower, whenever he wanted.

Name _____ Date _____

8. What is the author's purpose in writing "The Legend of the Hummingbird"?
   A. to teach us about what birds like to eat
   B. to explain why there are hummingbirds
   C. to teach us a lesson about hummingbirds

9. Who are the main characters in "The Legend of the Hummingbird"?
   A. Alida and Taroo
   B. Alida's father and the gods
   C. Taroo and the hunters

10. What did Alida's father demand she do?
   A. marry a man from her tribe
   B. return to the jungle to meet Taroo
   C. stay in her room

Name _____ Date _____

11. What did Alida do after her father told her she couldn't leave the palace?
   A. She married a man from her tribe.
   B. She ran away with Taroo.
   C. She made a plea to the gods.

12. How did Alida feel?
   A. tired   **B.** very sad   C. hungry

13. How do you know Alida felt this way?
   A. The story says, "Alida was heartbroken." It says she cried. It says she began to weep.
   B. The story says Alida and Taroo spent hours talking and fell deeply in love.
   C. The story says Alida had many fine dresses, but she liked her red dress best of all.

14. How is "The Legend of the Hummingbird" similar to other legends?
   A. The story is new and has a hero.
   B. The story is very old and might be about real people, but we can't prove it.
   C. The story is very old and is about real people.

Name _____ Date _____

15. to draw the pictures that go with the story

16. Answers will vary. Students' picture should go with the story and include story elements, such as the characters or the setting.

17. Answers will vary. Students should use the words *demanded*, *escape*, or *plea* in their descriptive sentence.

Name _____ Date _____

18. something you can prove to be true

19. writings about true things

20. Answers may include: Birds fly; they have beaks; they can be big or small; they lay eggs; they have feathers.

Name _____ Date _____

21. "The Buzz About Hummingbirds"

22. Kandee Works

23. writes a story

24. Answers will vary.

Name _____ Date _____

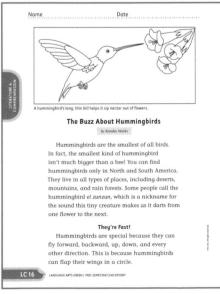

A hummingbird's long, thin bill helps it sip nectar out of flowers.

The Buzz About Hummingbirds
by Kandee Works

Hummingbirds are the smallest of all birds. In fact, the smallest kind of hummingbird isn't much bigger than a bee! You can find hummingbirds only in North and South America. They live in all types of places, including deserts, mountains, and rain forests. Some people call the hummingbird *el zunzun*, which is a nickname for the sound this tiny creature makes as it darts from one flower to the next.

They're Fast!

Hummingbirds are special because they can fly forward, backward, up, down, and every other direction. This is because hummingbirds can flap their wings in a circle.

Name _____ Date _____

Hummingbirds can flap their wings so fast that it makes them look like they're hovering, or standing in the air. They need to do this so that they can reach into flowers to get food.

Because they do everything so quickly, hummingbirds have hearts that beat really fast. A hummingbird's heart beats more than 1,000 times a minute when it's flying. Even when you're playing hard, your heart doesn't beat much more than 200 times a minute. That's quite a difference!

Food

Hummingbirds might be small, but they have giant appetites. That's because they need lots of food to keep going.

Hummingbirds eat only a few things: flower nectar, tree sap, and small insects. These birds love sugar, so they like sipping flower nectar the best—and they spend almost all day doing it.

To drink nectar from flowers, the hummingbird has a long, thin bill. The hummingbird sticks out its skinny tongue and quickly licks the inside of a flower—up to 13 licks a second. Try to move your tongue in and out of your mouth 13 times in one second, and you'll soon see how fast that is.

Name _____ Date _____

Why They Hum

People use their throats when they want to hum. But not hummingbirds! Hummingbirds hum because they beat their wings so fast. A medium-sized hummingbird flaps its wings more than 20 times a second. It moves its wings so fast that it makes the air around its wings vibrate, or shake, which makes a humming sound. But, as soon as a hummingbird sits on a tree branch, the humming sound stops.

Do Hummingbirds Sleep?

Some people think hummingbirds are on the go all the time. But, that's not true. Every day when the sun goes down, hummingbirds perch on tree branches so that they can fall asleep. They breathe much slower at night, and their heart slows down to save energy. In the morning, they warm up their little bodies in the sun, and then they're off again to spend the day sipping nectar, humming all the while.

Literature & Comprehension   **LC 231**

Name _____ Date _____

Part 9. Nonfiction: "The Buzz About Hummingbirds" Evaluate Predictions
Listen to the question, and say your answer.

25. **Answers may include: title; pictures; headers**

26. **Answers will vary.**

Name _____ Date _____

Part 10. Nonfiction: "The Buzz About Hummingbirds" Retelling
Retell the article in your own words.

27. **Answers should accurately retell each of these elements:**

Title: "The Buzz About Hummingbirds"

Topic: hummingbirds

Important details: Hummingbirds are the smallest of all birds; they live only in North and South America; they're fast and can fly up, down, forward, and backward; hummingbirds have hearts that beat very fast; they eat nectar, tree sap, and small insects; their wings beat very fast, and that's what makes the humming noise; they sleep at night.

Name _____ Date _____

Part 11. Nonfiction: "The Buzz About Hummingbirds" Reading Comprehension
Listen to the question, and choose the answer.

28. What is the author's purpose in writing "The Buzz About Hummingbirds"?
(A) to teach us facts about hummingbirds
B. to entertain us with a made-up story
C. to help us understand where hummingbirds come from

29. Why is there a picture in the article?
A. It makes the reader laugh.
(B) It helps the reader visualize the hummingbird.
C. It helps the reader locate information in the article.

30. Where can you find information about this picture?
A. in the text of the article
B. in the table of contents
(C) in the caption

Name _____ Date _____

31. What is nectar?
A. seeds from flowers
(B) sweet liquid from flowers
C. perfume from flowers

32. What does dart mean?
(A) to move suddenly and quickly
B. to run slowly and steadily
C. to fly straight

Part 12. Nonfiction: "The Buzz About Hummingbirds" Identify Facts
Listen to the sentence, and say whether it is a fact or not.

33. **not a fact**

34. **fact**

35. **not a fact**

36. **fact**

Name _____ Date _____

37. **fact**

38. **not a fact**

Part 13. Poetry: "The Little Hummingbird" Activate Prior Knowledge
Get ready to read. Listen to the question, and say your answer.

39. **hummingbirds**

40. **Answers may include: hummingbirds**

Part 14. Poetry: "The Little Hummingbird" Book Walk and Read Aloud
Do a Book Walk. Listen to the question, and say your answer.

41. **"The Little Hummingbird"**

42. **Art Friday**

Name _____ Date _____

The Little Hummingbird
By Art Friday

All day long
He hums his song
The little hummingbird.
Feathers red
Shine on his head
The little hummingbird.
In the sky
She'll watch him fly
The little hummingbird.
"I miss you!"
Red Rose says to
The little hummingbird.
"Oh, my love
From up above"
The little hummingbird.

Name _____ Date _____

Part 15. Poetry: "The Little Hummingbird" Evaluate Predictions
Listen to the question, and say your answer.

43. **Answers may include: title**

44. **Answers will vary.**

Part 16. Poetry: "The Little Hummingbird" Reading Comprehension
Listen to the question, and choose the answer.

45. What is the author's purpose in writing "The Little Hummingbird"?
A. to inform us
(B) to entertain us
C. to test us

46. What does the little hummingbird do?
(A) He hums a song and flies.
B. He sleeps and has a dream.
C. He flies in circles and chases bugs.

Name _____ Date _____

47. What does the hummingbird look like?
A. He is blue and big.
B. He is red and orange.
(C) He is red and small.

48. Who is watching the little hummingbird?
(A) Red Rose
B. Blue Bonnet
C. Green Grass

49. How does Red Rose feel about the little hummingbird?
(A) She misses and loves him.
B. She is angry and annoyed at him.
C. She fears and dislikes him.

50. How do you know this is how Red Rose feels?
A. The poem says, "She'll watch him fly."
(B) The poem says, "I miss you!" She calls him "my love."
C. The poem says "All day long / He hums his song."

Name _____ Date _____

51. Which words rhyme?
(A) long and song
B. song and bird
C. Red Rose

52. Which words repeat throughout the poem?
A. "All day long / He hums his song"
B. "Red Rose"
(C) "The little hummingbird"

53. Which words start with the same sounds?
A. all day long
B. little hummingbird
(C) Red Rose

54. Where does this poem take place?
A. indoors, in someone's bedroom
B. in a school or classroom
(C) outside, maybe in a garden

 **varies**

If necessary, work with students to complete the More Practice activity.

More Practice

Reading and Comprehension

If students scored less than 80 percent on the Mid-Semester Checkpoint, they may benefit from completing another Reader's Choice unit. You can find this list online. Additionally, continue to work with students on skills such as making and evaluating predictions and identifying elements of a given story (title, author, illustrator, characters, setting, problem, solution).

Objectives
- Evaluate Checkpoint results and choose activities to review.

Reward: Add a sticker for this unit on the My Accomplishments chart to mark successful completion of the unit.

You Reap What You Sow

Unit Focus

In this unit, students will explore stories from different countries with a common theme—good deeds are rewarded in the end. This unit follows the read-aloud instructional approach (see the Instructional Approaches to Reading in the introductory lesson for this program). In this unit, students will

- ► Listen to a folktale, a fairy tale, and a legend.
- ► Learn about the strategy of questioning and how it helps readers.
- ► Explore characters and their actions.
- ► Explore problem and solution.
- ► Practice making inferences.
- ► Practice comparing and contrasting story elements.
- ► Explore using text and picture clues to define unknown words.

Unit Plan

[Offline]

Lesson 1	Introduce "The Poor Man's Reward"	**45** minutes a day
Lesson 2	Explore "The Poor Man's Reward"	
Lesson 3	Introduce "The Water of Life"	
Lesson 4	Explore "The Water of Life"	
Lesson 5	Introduce "The Wonderful Brocade"	
Lesson 6	Explore "The Wonderful Brocade"	
Lesson 7	Your Choice	

Introduce "The Poor Man's Reward"

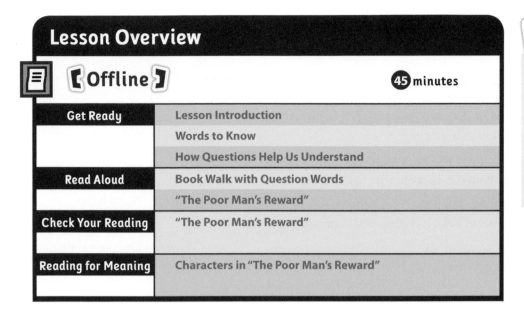

Lesson Overview

[Offline]　　　　　　　　　**45** minutes

Get Ready	Lesson Introduction
	Words to Know
	How Questions Help Us Understand
Read Aloud	Book Walk with Question Words
	"The Poor Man's Reward"
Check Your Reading	"The Poor Man's Reward"
Reading for Meaning	Characters in "The Poor Man's Reward"

Materials

Supplied

- "The Poor Man's Reward," *K¹² Classics for Young Readers, Volume A,* pp. 100–123
- *K¹² Language Arts Activity Book,* pp. LC 35–36

Story Synopsis

A kind but poor man decides to take the few things he owns and walk to another part of the country to try his luck there. On the way, he helps several animals who do not soon forget his generosity.

Keywords

self-monitor – to notice if you do or do not understand what you are reading

self-question – to ask questions of yourself as you read to check your understanding

Advance Preparation

Read "The Poor Man's Reward" before beginning the Read Aloud to locate Words to Know in the text. Review Reading for Meaning to familiarize yourself with the questions and answers.

Big Ideas

- ▶ Comprehension entails asking and answering questions about the text.
- ▶ Comprehension requires the reader to self-monitor understanding.

[Offline] ⏱ **45** minutes

Work **together** with students to complete Get Ready, Read Aloud, Check Your Reading, and Reading for Meaning activities.

Get Ready

Lesson Introduction

Prepare students for listening to and discussing "The Poor Man's Reward," a folktale from West Africa.

1. Tell students that you are going to read "The Poor Man's Reward," a story about a poor man who might be dressed in rags but who has a big heart.

2. Explain that before you read the story, you will get ready by discussing why it's important to ask and answer questions before, during, and after reading.

> ### Objectives
> - Build vocabulary through listening, reading, and discussion.
> - Use new vocabulary in written and spoken sentences.
> - Ask and answer who, what, where, when, why, and how questions.

Words to Know

Before reading "The Poor Man's Reward," go over Words to Know with students.

1. Read aloud each word and have students repeat it.

2. Ask students if they know what each word means.

   ▸ If students know a word's meaning, have them define it and use it in a sentence.

   ▸ If students don't know a word's meaning, read them the definition and discuss the word with them.

gourd – the dried-out shell of a kind of vegetable that's used as a jug or bowl
millet – the seeds of a grass plant that is used for food
noble – having strong character or qualities, such as being honest and fair
platter – a very large plate
scrawny – very thin; skinny
shabby – old and falling apart
task – a chore; something you have to do

How Questions Help Us Understand

Explore self-questioning with students.

1. Tell students that readers **ask questions** before, during, and after they read. Asking questions is important because it gives us a focus when we read so we're more likely to remember what we read. It's also a way to check that we understand what we've read.

2. Explain that questions can begin with **who, what, where, when, why, or how**. Some people call these question words the 5 Ws and H.

3. **Say:** For example, before reading a story called "The Sad, Sad Man," a reader might ask: Who is the sad man? What made the man sad? Where does the sad man live? How will the sad man learn to be happy?

4. Have students imagine that they are going to read a story called "The House Made of Glass." Have them practice using the 5 Ws and H question words to think of questions based on the title of the story.

   ▸ What question could you ask that begins with the word *who*? Possible answers: Who built the house made of glass? Who lives in the house made of glass?

   ▸ What question could you ask that begins with the question word *what*? Possible answer: What is inside the house made of glass?

   ▸ The other question words are *where*, *when*, *why*, and *how*. What are some questions you could ask that begin with those words? Possible answers: Where is the house made of glass? When was the house made of glass built? Why is there a house made of glass? How was a house made out of glass?

TIP Asking questions is an important strategy for improving comprehension. Do not describe a question as "bad" or "wrong" because this may discourage students from asking questions.

Read Aloud

Book Walk with Question Words

Prepare students for reading by taking them on a Book Walk of "The Poor Man's Reward." Scan the story together, and ask students to make predictions about the story. Turn to pages LC 35 and 36 in *K¹² Language Arts Activity Book*.

1. Turn to the **table of contents** in *K¹² Classics for Young Readers, Volume A*. Help students find the selection, and turn to that page.

2. Point to and read aloud the **title of the story**.

   ▸ What do you think the story might be about? Answers will vary.

3. Have students look at the **pictures of the story**.

   ▸ What do you think might happen in the story? Answers will vary.

   ▸ What are some different kinds of rewards? Possible answers: money; extra computer or video game time; stickers

   ▸ Have you ever received a reward? What did you do to earn it? Answers will vary.

4. Remind students of the 5 Ws and H: who, what, where, when, why, and how.

5. Tell students to use the 5 Ws and H question words to think of questions based on the title and pictures of the story.

Objectives

- Make predictions based on text, illustrations, and/or prior knowledge.
- Activate prior knowledge by previewing text and/or discussing topic.
- Ask and answer who, what, where, when, why, and how questions.
- Generate literal level questions.
- Monitor understanding by self-questioning.
- Listen and respond to texts representing a variety of cultures, time periods, and traditions.

6. Read aloud a question starter on the Activity Book page, and write down what students dictate.

7. Repeat Step 6 until all question starters are filled in.

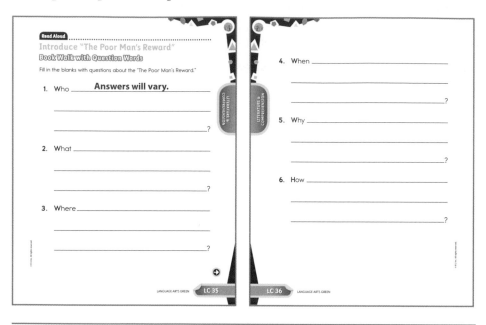

"The Poor Man's Reward"

It's time to read aloud the story.

1. Have students sit next to you so that they can see the pictures and words while you read aloud.

2. Tell students to listen for the answers to the 5 Ws and H questions they asked.

3. **Read aloud the entire story.** Track with your finger so students can follow along. Emphasize Words to Know as you come to them. If appropriate, use the pictures to help show what each word means.

Check Your Reading

"The Poor Man's Reward"

Check students' comprehension of "The Poor Man's Reward." Gather the completed Book Walk with Question Words on pages LC 35 and 36 in *K¹² Language Arts Activity Book.*

1. Have students retell "The Poor Man's Reward" in their own words to develop grammar, vocabulary, comprehension, and fluency skills.

2. Read aloud the questions students dictated and have students answer them.

3. Explain to students that the answers to some of their questions might not have been in the story. However, thinking about the questions and listening for the answers helped students listen carefully to the story and remember it better.

Objectives

- Retell or dramatize a story.
- Answer questions requiring literal recall of details.
- Ask and answer who, what, where, when, why, and how questions.
- Monitor understanding by self-questioning.
- Identify character(s).
- Identify details that explain characters' actions and feelings.

4. Ask students the following questions.

> ▸ Why does the man decide to move to another part of the country?
> He wants to find a better life.
> ▸ What four animals does the man meet? a bird, a hyena, a bee, and
> a crocodile
> ▸ Why do the animals help the man? because the man had helped them

TIP If students have trouble responding to a question, help them locate the answer in the text or pictures.

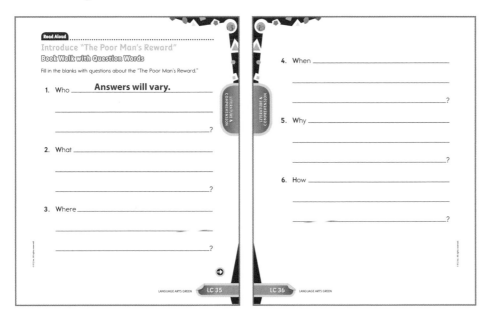

Reading for Meaning

Characters in "The Poor Man's Reward"
Explore the story structure element of characters by using the 5 Ws and H question words.

1. Remind students that characters are the people and animals in a story. The main character is the one who does most of the things in a story.

2. Tell students that we can use the 5 Ws and H question words after we read a story to make sure we understand the story's characters.

3. Ask students the following questions to check their understanding of the main character and the 5Ws and H.

> ▸ Who is the main character? the poor man
> ▸ What does the poor man do to help the animals he meets? He shares his food and water with them.
> ▸ When do the animals help the poor man? when he is trying to complete the tasks the king gives him
> ▸ Where is the poor man going? to a different part of the country
> ▸ Why is the poor man going there? to see if he will have better luck
> ▸ How is the poor man able to complete the tasks that the king asks him to do? with help from the animals

Objectives
- Identify the main character(s).
- Describe character(s).
- Identify details that explain characters' actions and feelings.

4. Ask students the following questions to check their understanding of characters and their actions.

- ▶ What words would you use to describe the poor man? Possible answers: poor; kind; generous; brave   Why do you describe him that way? Give examples from the story. Possible answers: He owns only the clothes on his back; he shares his food and water with the animals; he walks across a bridge made of crocodiles.
- ▶ What words would you use to describe the hyena? Possible answers: hungry; polite; helpful   What does the hyena do to cause you to describe him that way? Give examples from the story. Possible answers: He asks the man for food; he thanks the man for giving him food; he helps the man complete one of the king's tasks.
- ▶ How would you describe the king? Possible answers: rich; mean; protective of his daughter   Why do you describe him that way? Give examples from the story. Possible answers: He lives in a magnificent palace; he makes the man complete difficult tasks when he sees that the man is poor; he makes sure his daughter marries a noble man.

5. Ask students the following questions to check their understanding of self-questioning.

- ▶ What are the 5Ws and H question words? who, what, where, when, why, how
- ▶ Why is it important to ask questions before, during, and after you read? to better understand the characters and the story
- ▶ What is one question that you wrote before reading the story? Answers will vary.   Did you hear the answer to your question while you were listening to the story? Answers will vary.

Explore "The Poor Man's Reward"

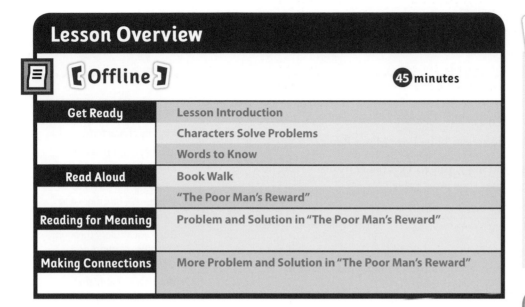

Lesson Overview

[Offline] **45** minutes

Get Ready	Lesson Introduction
	Characters Solve Problems
	Words to Know
Read Aloud	Book Walk
	"The Poor Man's Reward"
Reading for Meaning	Problem and Solution in "The Poor Man's Reward"
Making Connections	More Problem and Solution in "The Poor Man's Reward"

Advance Preparation

Review "The Woodpecker, Turtle, and Deer" to prepare for the Get Ready. Review Reading for Meaning and Making Connections to familiarize yourself with the questions and answers.

Big Ideas

An awareness of story structure elements (setting, characters, plot) provides readers a foundation for constructing meaning when reading new stories and writing their own stories.

Materials

Supplied

- "The Poor Man's Reward," *K¹² Classics for Young Readers, Volume A*, pp. 100–123
- "The Woodpecker, Turtle, and Deer," *K¹² Classics for Young Readers, Volume A*, pp. 46–53
- *K¹² Language Arts Activity Book*, p. LC 37

Keywords

character – a person or animal in a story

problem – an issue a character must solve in a story

solution – how a character solves a problem in a story

 **45** minutes

Work **together** with students to complete Get Ready, Read Aloud, Reading for Meaning, and Making Connections activities.

Get Ready

Lesson Introduction
Prepare students for listening to and discussing "The Poor Man's Reward."

1. Tell students that you are going to reread "The Poor Man's Reward."

2. Explain that before you reread the story, you will get ready by discussing how characters often have problems that they must solve.

 Objectives
- Identify character(s).
- Identify examples of problem and solution.
- Describe story structure elements—problem and solution.
- Build vocabulary through listening, reading, and discussion.
- Use new vocabulary in written and spoken sentences.

Characters Solve Problems
Explore the story structure elements of characters and problem and solution.

1. Tell students that sometimes we have problems that we need to solve.
   Say: For example, if your problem is that you're thirsty, you might solve your problem by getting a glass of water. If your problem is that you're hungry, you might solve your problem by getting something to eat.

   ► What if your problem is that you are bored? How might you solve your problem? Answers will vary.

2. Remind students that the people and animals in a story are called **characters**.

3. Explain that a **character usually needs to solve a problem**. There can be more than one character that needs to solve a problem in a story.

4. Have students recall the story of "The Woodpecker, Turtle, and Deer" to help them understand a character's problem and how it is solved.

5. If necessary, show students the pictures from the story in *K¹² Classics for Young Readers, Volume A*.

6. Remind students that in the story of "The Woodpecker, Turtle, and Deer," the hunter sets a trap for the deer.

   ► Who are the characters in "The Woodpecker, Turtle, and Deer"? woodpecker, turtle, deer
   ► What is the deer's problem? He gets caught in a hunter's trap.
   ► How does the deer solve his problem? He cries for help, and the turtle comes and chews away the leather trap so the deer can free himself.
   ► What is the turtle's problem after he helps free the deer? The hunter puts him in a bag and ties it to a tree.
   ► How does the deer help the turtle solve his problem? The deer leads the hunter into the forest and then returns to free the turtle.

7. Tell students to think about the problems.

Say: As we read, think about the problems the characters have and how the problems are solved.

TIP If students haven't read "The Woodpecker, Turtle, and Deer," have them think of a story that they are familiar with and explain who the main character is and state the problem and solution.

Words to Know

Before reading "The Poor Man's Reward," go over Words to Know with students.

1. Read aloud each word and have students repeat it.

2. Ask students if they know what each word means.

  ▸ If students know a word's meaning, have them define it and use it in a sentence.
  ▸ If students don't know a word's meaning, read them the definition and discuss the word with them.

gourd – the dried-out shell of a kind of vegetable that's used as a jug or bowl
millet – the seeds of a grass plant that is used for food
noble – having strong character or qualities, such as being honest and fair
platter – a very large plate
scrawny – very thin; skinny
shabby – old and falling apart
task – a chore; something you have to do

Read Aloud

Book Walk

Prepare students by taking them on a Book Walk of "The Poor Man's Reward." Scan the story together to revisit the characters and events.

1. Turn to the selection in *K¹² Classics for Young Readers, Volume A*. Point to and read aloud the **title of the story**.

2. Have students review the **pictures**.

  ▸ Where does the story take place? Africa
  ▸ Who is the most important character in the story? the poor man
  ▸ What are some things the poor man does to help the animals he meets on the road? He gives the weaverbird some millet; he gives the hyena some meat; he gives the bee some honey; he gives the crocodile some water.
  ▸ How do the animals repay the man's kindness? They help him complete the king's tasks.

Objectives
- Activate prior knowledge by previewing text and/or discussing topic.
- Listen and respond to texts representing a variety of cultures, time periods, and traditions.

"The Poor Man's Reward"

It's time to reread the story.

1. Have students sit next to you so that they can see the pictures and words while you read aloud.

2. Remind students to listen for the characters' problems and their solutions.

3. **Read aloud the entire story.** Track with your finger so students can follow along. Emphasize Words to Know as you come to them. If appropriate, use the pictures to help show what each word means.

Reading for Meaning

Problem and Solution in "The Poor Man's Reward"

Explore how characters solve problems.

▶ What problem does the man have at the beginning of the story? He's poor and all alone.   How does he try to solve his problem? He walks to another part of the country.

▶ What problem does the weaverbird have? He's starving.   How does he solve his problem? He asks the man for some of his millet.

▶ What problem does the bee have? He can't find any flowers.   How does he solve his problem? He asks the man for some of his honey.

▶ The poor man must figure out which girl is the princess. How does he solve this problem? The bee shows him.

▶ What is the man's problem after he meets the king? The king gives him difficult tasks to complete before he can marry the princess.

▶ At the beginning of the story the poor man is all alone. How does he solve this problem in the end? He does all the tasks and becomes part of the king's family.

Objectives
- Describe story structure elements—problem and solution.

Making Connections

More Problem and Solution in "The Poor Man's Reward"

Have students identify and describe problems and solutions in "The Poor Man's Reward." Turn to page LC 37 in *K¹² Language Arts Activity Book*.

1. Point to each animal and have students tell you the name of the animal.

2. Point to each scene and have students describe the task in the scene.

3. Have students draw a line from an animal to the task that animal helps the poor man complete.

Objectives
- Identify character(s).
- Describe story structure elements—problem and solution.
- Compare and contrast story structure elements within a text.

4. Have students retell how the following animals help the man solve his problem.

   ▸ bird The bird brings hundreds of birds to the courtyard to help the poor man sort a pile of seeds.

   ▸ hyena The hyena brings his family to help eat all the meat.

   ▸ bee The bee buzzes around the princess to show the poor man where she is in the crowd.

   ▸ crocodile The crocodile and his friends help the poor man cross the river to get the feather.

5. Repeat Steps 3 and 4 until students match all characters and tasks and discuss all problems and solutions.

6. Ask the following questions to encourage discussion and comparisons of the animal characters.

   ▸ How are the four animal characters alike? Possible answers: They are all grateful and help the poor man complete the king's tasks; all of them are polite.

   ▸ How are the four animal characters different? Possible answers: Each animal does something different to help the poor man; they are all different types of animals.

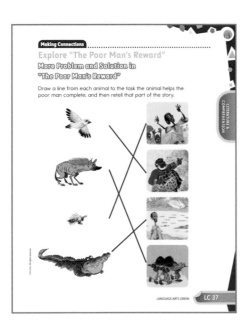

Introduce "The Water of Life"

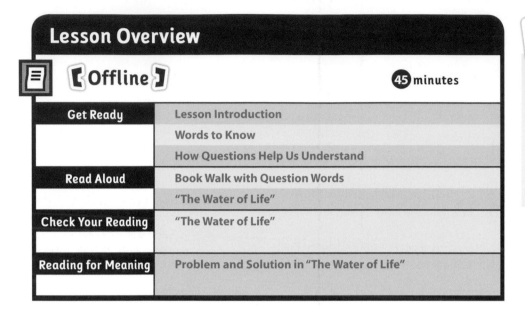

Advance Preparation

Read "The Water of Life" before beginning the Read Aloud to locate Words to Know in the text. Review Reading for Meaning to familiarize yourself with the questions and answers.

Big Ideas

► Comprehension entails asking and answering questions about the text.
► Comprehension requires the reader to self-monitor understanding.

Materials

Supplied

● "The Water of Life," *K¹² Classics for Young Readers, Volume A,* pp. 124–147
● *K¹² Language Arts Activity Book,* pp. LC 39–40

Story Synopsis

Three princes set out—one at a time—to find the water of life that will save their dying father. Success, betrayal, and vindication ensue.

Keywords

inference – a guess you make using the clues in a text and what you already know

problem – an issue a character must solve in a story

self-monitor – to notice if you do or do not understand what you are reading

self-question – to ask questions of yourself as you read to check your understanding

solution – how a character solves a problem in a story

 **45** minutes

Work **together** with students to complete Get Ready, Read Aloud, Check Your Reading, and Reading for Meaning activities.

Get Ready

Lesson Introduction

Prepare students for listening to and discussing "The Water of Life."

1. Tell students that you are going to read "The Water of Life," a story about three brothers who want to save their dying father.

2. Explain that before you read the story, you will get ready by discussing why it's important to ask and answer questions before, during, and after reading.

Words to Know

Before reading "The Water of Life," go over Words to Know with students.

1. Read aloud each word and have students repeat it.

2. Ask students if they know what each word means.

   ▸ If students know a word's meaning, have them define it and use it in a sentence.

   ▸ If students don't know a word's meaning, read them the definition and discuss the word with them.

banish – to force someone to go away
condemn – to order that someone be punished
grieve – to feel deep sadness
haughty – proud; to look down on others
inherit – to get something from someone who has died
remedy – a cure

How Questions Help Us Understand

Review how questions help readers understand a story.

1. Have students explain why it is important to ask questions before, during, and after they read a story.

2. If students have trouble responding, remind them of the following:

   ▸ Asking questions gives us a focus when we read so we're more likely to remember the story.

   ▸ Asking questions is a way to check that we understand what we read.

Objectives

- Build vocabulary through listening, reading, and discussion.
- Use new vocabulary in written and spoken sentences.
- Ask and answer who, what, where, when, why, and how questions.
- Generate literal level questions.
- Monitor understanding by self-questioning.

---

3. **Say:** For example, before reading a story called "The Dog That Found a Treasure," a good reader might ask: Who hid the treasure? What did the dog do with the treasure? Where did the dog find the treasure? How did the dog find the treasure? What is the treasure?

4. Have students imagine that they are going to read a story called "A Box Filled with Feathers." Have students practice using the 5 Ws and H question words to think of questions based on the title of the story.

   ▶ What question could you ask that begins with *who*? Possible answers: Who does the box belong to? Who filled the box with feathers?

   ▶ The other question words are *what, where, when, why,* and *how.* What are some questions you could ask that begin with those words? Possible answers: What kind of feathers are in the box? Where is the box? When was the box filled with feathers? Why is the box filled with feathers? How did the feathers get into the box?

TIP Asking questions is an important strategy for improving comprehension. Do not describe a question as "bad" or "wrong" because this may discourage students from asking questions.

Read Aloud ●●

Book Walk with Question Words

Prepare students for reading by taking them on a Book Walk of "The Water of Life." Scan the story together and ask students to make predictions about the story. Turn to pages LC 39 and 40 in *K¹² Language Arts Activity Book*. Answers to questions may vary.

1. Turn to the **table of contents** in *K¹² Classics for Young Readers, Volume A*. Help students find the selection and turn to that page.

2. Point to and read aloud the **title of the story**.

   ▶ What do you think this story might be about?

3. Have students look at the **pictures of the story**.

   ▶ What do you think might happen in the story?

   ▶ Has anyone in your family ever been sick? Did you do anything to help?

Objectives

- Make predictions based on text, illustrations, and/or prior knowledge.
- Activate prior knowledge by previewing text and/or discussing topic.
- Ask and answer who, what, where, when, why, and how questions.
- Generate literal level questions.
- Monitor understanding by self-questioning.
- Listen and respond to texts representing a variety of cultures, time periods, and traditions.

4. Remind students of the 5 Ws and H: **who, what, where, when, why, and how.**

5. Tell students to use the 5 Ws and H question words to think of questions based on the title and pictures of the story.

6. Read aloud a question starter on the Activity Book page and write down what students dictate.

7. Repeat Step 6 until all question starters have been filled in.

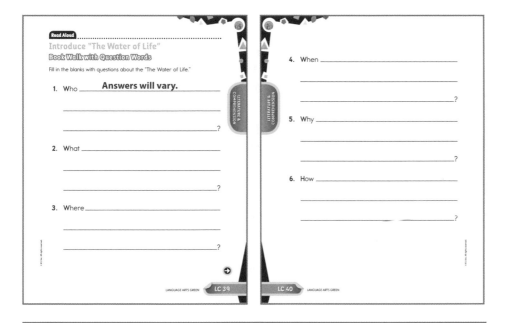

"The Water of Life"
It's time to read aloud the story.

1. Have students sit next to you so that they can see the pictures and words while you read aloud.

2. Tell students to listen for the answers to the 5 Ws and H questions they asked.

3. **Read aloud the entire story.** Track with your finger so students can follow along. Emphasize Words to Know as you come to them. If appropriate, use the pictures to help show what each word means.

Check Your Reading

"The Water of Life"

Check students' comprehension of "The Water of Life." Gather the completed Book Walk with Question Words on pages LC 39 and 40 in *K¹² Language Arts Activity Book*.

1. Have students retell "The Water of Life" in their own words to develop grammar, vocabulary, comprehension, and fluency skills.

2. If you haven't done so already, read aloud each question starter on the Activity Book page and write down what students dictate.

3. Read aloud the questions students dictated and have students answer them.

4. Ask students the following questions.

   ▸ How many sons does the king have? three
   ▸ Who do the princes meet on their way to find the water of life? a dwarf
     How do the two older brothers treat the dwarf? They are mean to him.
     How does the younger brother treat the dwarf? He is nice to the dwarf.
   ▸ What is the road leading to the princess's castle made of? gold
   ▸ Who marries the princess? the youngest prince

TIP If students have trouble responding to a question, help them locate the answer in the text or pictures.

Objectives
- Retell or dramatize a story.
- Answer questions requiring literal recall of details.
- Ask and answer who, what, where, when, why, and how questions.
- Monitor understanding by self-questioning.

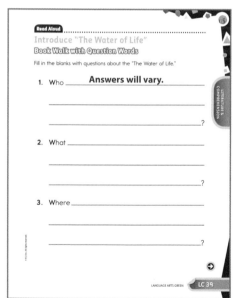
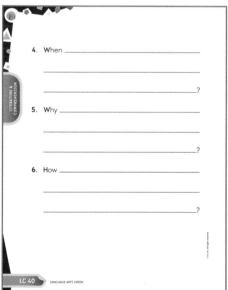

Reading for Meaning

Problem and Solution in "The Water of Life"

Explore how characters solve problems in "The Water of Life."

1. Remind students that characters in a story often have problems that they need to solve.

2. Ask the following questions.

   ▶ What problem do the three princes have at the beginning of the story? They need to find the water of life to save their father.
   ▶ The king does not want to let his sons leave to search for the water of life. How do the princes solve this problem? They beg their father until he agrees to let them go.
   ▶ What problem do the two oldest brothers have after they meet the dwarf? They get trapped.   How do the brothers solve this problem? The youngest brother begs the dwarf to free them.
   ▶ The youngest brother does not know where to find the water of life. How does he solve this problem? He is kind to the dwarf, so the dwarf tells him how to find the water of life.
   ▶ The older brothers think their father will give the kingdom to the youngest son because he found the water of life. What do they do to keep this from happening? The two older brothers pour the water of life from their brother's cup into their own cup.
   ▶ What problem does the youngest brother have after his older brothers tell their father that the youngest brother tried to kill him? He is forced to leave the kingdom, and he needs to find a way to get back.   How does the youngest brother solve this problem? He tells the princess his wish, and she goes to the king and tells him the truth.

Objectives

- Describe story structure elements—problem and solution.

Explore "The Water of Life"

Lesson Overview

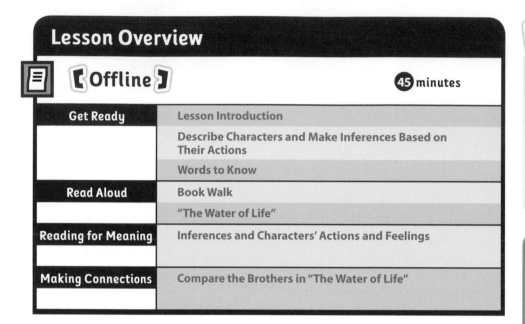

Offline	45 minutes

Get Ready	Lesson Introduction
	Describe Characters and Make Inferences Based on Their Actions
	Words to Know
Read Aloud	Book Walk
	"The Water of Life"
Reading for Meaning	Inferences and Characters' Actions and Feelings
Making Connections	Compare the Brothers in "The Water of Life"

Materials

Supplied
- "The Water of Life," *K¹² Classics for Young Readers, Volume A,* pp. 124–147
- *K¹² Language Arts Activity Book,* p. LC 41

Keywords

character – a person or animal in a story

compare – to explain how two or more things are alike

contrast – to explain how two or more things are different

inference – a guess you make using the clues in a text and what you already know

Advance Preparation

Review Reading for Meaning and Making Connections to familiarize yourself with the questions and answers.

Big Ideas

▶ An awareness of story structure elements (setting, characters, plot) provides readers a foundation for constructing meaning when reading new stories and writing their own stories.

▶ To understand and interpret a story, readers need to understand and describe characters and what they do.

▶ Good readers use prior knowledge and text clues to infer or draw conclusions about what is implied but not directly stated in text.

 **45 minutes**

Work **together** with students to complete Get Ready, Read Aloud, Reading for Meaning, and Making Connections activities.

Get Ready

Lesson Introduction

Prepare students for listening to and discussing "The Water of Life."

1. Tell students that you are going to reread "The Water of Life."

2. Explain that before you reread the story, you will get ready by discussing

   ▸ How characters react in different ways to the same problem
   ▸ How we can make inferences about characters based on what they say and do

---

Describe Characters and Make Inferences Based on Their Actions

Discuss how characters act and respond to the events in a story.

1. Explain that sometimes the same thing can happen to two people, but they will react in different ways.

2. Tell students that one way to better understand characters' actions is to think about our own actions in similar situations.

   ▸ What does the oldest brother do when he meets the dwarf in "The Water of Life"? He is mean to the dwarf; he leaves the dwarf in a cloud of dust. Why do you think he does that? Possible answers: He is rude; he is selfish; he doesn't think of others.
   ▸ What would you do if you were searching for the water of life and you met the dwarf? Answers will vary.   Why would you do that? Answers will vary.

3. Have students practice comparing shared experiences and characters' reactions.

Objectives

- Describe character(s).
- Activate prior knowledge by previewing text and/or discussing topic.
- Make inferences based on text and/or prior knowledge.
- Identify details that explain characters' actions and feelings.
- Compare and contrast story structure elements within a text.
- Build vocabulary through listening, reading, and discussion.
- Use new vocabulary in written and spoken sentences.

4. **Read aloud** the following story.

Blake and Jordan had been playing outside all afternoon. "I'm hungry," Jordan said. "Me, too," Blake replied. "Let's get a snack." Blake and Jordan went to find a snack in the kitchen. They both reached for the last banana on the counter. "Uh oh," Blake said. "This is the last banana. Since we're at my house, I think I should get to eat it." Jordan shook her head. "Wait a minute, Blake. I know how we can both have a banana for a snack," she said. Then Jordan cut the banana in half and gave Blake one piece and kept one piece for herself. Blake and Jordan smiled as they ate their snack.

> ▸ What happens to Blake and Jordan that is the same? They both want to eat a banana for a snack.
> ▸ What does Blake want to do when he sees there is only one banana? keep the banana for himself   What does Blake's reaction tell you about him? Possible answers: He doesn't like to share; he's selfish.
> ▸ What does Jordan want to do when she sees there is only one banana? cut it in half to share with Blake   What does Jordan's reaction tell you about her? Possible answers: She is generous; she likes to share with others.
> ▸ How do you think Blake and Jordan feel at the end of the story? happy Why do you think they feel that way? because they both get to eat the snack they want

---

Words to Know

Before reading "The Water of Life," go over Words to Know with students.

1. Read aloud each word and have students repeat it.

2. Ask students if they know what each word means.

> ▸ If students know a word's meaning, have them define it and use it in a sentence.
> ▸ If students don't know a word's meaning, read them the definition and discuss the word with them.

banish – to force someone to go away
condemn – to order that someone be punished
grieve – to feel deep sadness
haughty – proud; to look down on others
inherit – to get something from someone who has died
remedy – a cure

Read Aloud

Book Walk

Prepare students by taking them on a Book Walk of "The Water of Life." Scan the story together to revisit the characters and events.

1. Turn to the selection in *K¹² Classics for Young Readers, Volume A*. Point to and read aloud the **title of the story.**

2. Look through the story. Have students review the **pictures.**

   ▶ Who are some of the characters in the story? the three brothers; the king; the dwarf; the princess

   ▶ What do the brothers need to do to save their father? find and bring him the water of life

   ▶ What do the two oldest brothers do while the youngest brother is sleeping? They pour the water of life from the youngest brother's cup into their own and fill his cup with seawater.   Why do they do that? They want to give their father the water of life so they can inherit the kingdom.

Objectives

- Activate prior knowledge by previewing text and/or discussing topic.
- Listen and respond to texts representing a variety of cultures, time periods, and traditions.

"The Water of Life"

It's time to reread the story.

1. Have students sit next to you so that they can see the pictures and words while you read the story aloud.

2. Tell students to listen carefully to learn more about the characters and their actions.

3. **Read aloud the entire story.** Track with your finger so students can follow along. Emphasize Words to Know as you come to them. If appropriate, use the pictures to help show what each word means.

Reading for Meaning

Inferences and Characters' Actions and Feelings

Explore inferences and the actions and feelings of characters in "The Water of Life."

1. Tell students that good readers are able to **infer**, or figure out, things in a story that the author does not say directly. Good readers think about **clues in the story and their own prior knowledge from past experience** to make inferences.

Objectives

- Make inferences based on text and/or prior knowledge.
- Support inferences with evidence from text and/or prior knowledge.
- Identify details that explain characters' actions and feelings.

2. Have students practice making an inference.

   ▸ Your friend is talking on the phone and shouts, "Oh, boy!" How do you think your friend might be feeling? Possible answers: happy; excited   How did you infer, or figure that out? Possible answer: People say, "Oh, boy!" when they are happy or excited about something they hear or see.

3. Ask students the following questions.

   ▸ How do you think the dwarf feels about the oldest brother? The dwarf does not like him.   How did you infer that? Give an example from the story. He wishes an evil wish on the oldest brother.
   ▸ Why do you think the dwarf wishes an evil wish on the second brother? because the second brother is mean to him
   ▸ Why do you think the dwarf helps the youngest brother? because the youngest brother is nice to him
   ▸ What words would you use to describe the youngest brother? Possible answers: loving; kind; brave   Give examples from the story to explain why you think those words describe the youngest brother. Possible answers: He goes out to find the water of life to save his father's life; he is nice to the dwarf; he is not afraid of the lions.
   ▸ How do you think the youngest brother feels about his father? He loves him very much.   Why do you think that? Possible answers: He wants to find the water of life to save his father; he cries when his father banishes him from the kingdom.
   ▸ What words would you use to describe the princess? Possible answers: helpful; smart; kind   Give examples from the story to explain why you think those words describe the princess. Possible answers: She tells the youngest prince where to find the water of life; she has a road of gold built leading to her castle to keep out the greedy princes; she tells the king the truth for the youngest prince.
   ▸ How do you think the youngest brother feels when he is sent away from his kingdom? sad   How did you infer that? Give examples from the story. He walks away from the palace with bitter tears.

Making Connections ....

Compare the Brothers in "The Water of Life"

Have students complete a graphic organizer to demonstrate an understanding how characters are alike and different. Turn to page LC 41 in *K¹² Language Arts Activity Book*.

1. Point to and read aloud the first column heading, "Words that describe characters."

2. Write what students dictate in the first row of boxes under the appropriate column heading.

3. Repeat until the chart is completed.

4. Ask the following questions to encourage discussion and comparisons of the characters.

   ▶ How are the older brothers and the youngest brother alike? They all try to find the water of life; they all meet the dwarf; they all go to the princess's castle.

   ▶ How are the older brothers and the youngest brother different? Possible answers: The older brothers are mean, dishonest, and greedy, and the youngest brother is kind and unselfish; the older brothers are mean to the dwarf, and the youngest brother is kind to the dwarf; the older brothers flee from the kingdom in the end, while the youngest brother marries the princess and is reunited with his father.

   ▶ If you had to choose a brother to be friends with, which would you choose and why? Be sure to have students give examples from the stories to support their answer.

Objectives

- Describe character(s).
- Make inferences based on text and/or prior knowledge.
- Compare and contrast story structure elements within a text.
- Demonstrate understanding through graphic organizers.

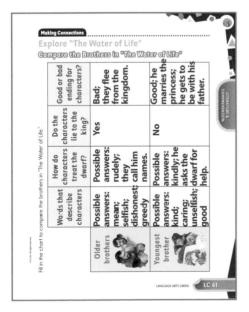

Introduce "The Wonderful Brocade"

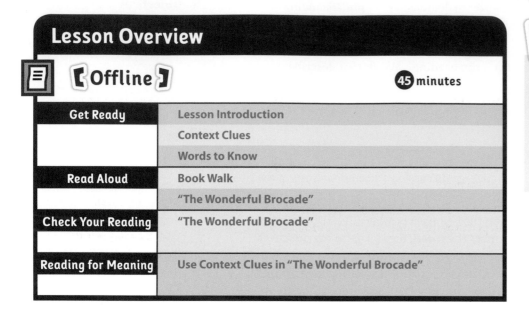

Lesson Overview

[Offline]   45 minutes

Get Ready	Lesson Introduction
	Context Clues
	Words to Know
Read Aloud	Book Walk
	"The Wonderful Brocade"
Check Your Reading	"The Wonderful Brocade"
Reading for Meaning	Use Context Clues in "The Wonderful Brocade"

Advance Preparation

Read "The Wonderful Brocade" before beginning the Read Aloud to locate Words to Know in the text. Review Reading for Meaning to familiarize yourself with the questions and answers.

Big Ideas

▶ Verbalizing your thoughts while modeling a reading strategy allows students to see what goes on inside the head of an effective reader; it makes visible the normally hidden process of comprehending text.

▶ Early learners acquire vocabulary through active exposure (by talking and listening, being read to, and receiving explicit instruction).

[Materials]

Supplied

● "The Wonderful Brocade," *K¹² Classics for Young Readers, Volume A,* pp. 148–173
● Story Card D

Story Synopsis

Three brothers set out—one at a time—to recover the beautiful brocade that will save their mother's life. But each brother must face fire and ice before he can enter the Sun Palace and reclaim the stolen weaving. Will any of them succeed?

Keywords

context – the parts of a sentence or passage surrounding a word

context clue – a word or phrase in a text that helps you figure out the meaning of an unknown word

[Offline] 45 minutes

"The Wonderful Brocade"

Work **together** with students to complete Get Ready, Read Aloud, Check Your
Reading, and Reading for Meaning activities.

Get Ready

Lesson Introduction

Prepare students for listening to and discussing "The Wonderful Brocade."

1. Tell students that you are going to read "The Wonderful Brocade," a story
   about a woman who weaves a beautiful picture that is stolen by the wind.

2. Explain that before you read the story, you will get ready by discussing how
   to use context clues in the text and pictures to figure out the meaning of
   unknown words.

Context Clues

Explore using context clues to figure out the meaning of unknown words.

1. Tell students that good readers can sometimes use clues to figure out the
   meaning of a word. The words, phrases, and sentences around an unfamiliar
   word can give hints to its meaning.

2. Tell students that you will show them how to do this while sharing your
   thoughts aloud. This is so students can know what goes on in the mind of a
   good reader as you figure out what a word means.

3. Show students how to determine the meaning of an unknown word.
   Say: I was reading and came across this sentence: "The mud and stains on
   the soiled carpet were hard to clean up." I'm not sure what *soiled* means. The
   sentence mentions *mud* and *stains*, so these are clues that make me think that
   soiled means dirty.

4. Tell students that you used clues that came before the word *soiled* to help you
   figure out what the word means. But explain that sometimes we get clues **after**
   the unknown word that help us figure out what the word means.
   Say: The brawny man picked up the heavy box. When I read *The brawny man*,
   I'm not sure what *brawny* means. I'm going to read what comes **after** the word
   brawny to see if I can find some clues.

5. Read the phrase *picked up the heavy box*.

6. Explain that *picked up* and *heavy* are clues. The man must be very strong if he
   can pick up a heavy box.

   ▸ Does *very strong* make sense in the sentence? *The very strong man picked up
   the heavy box.* Yes, *very strong* makes sense.

7. Remind students that the clues after the word *brawny* helped you figure out
   that *brawny* means very strong.

Objectives

- Use context and sentence
  structure to determine
  meaning of words, phrases,
  and/or sentences.
- Use illustrations to aid
  understanding of text.
- Build vocabulary through
  listening, reading, and
  discussion.
- Use new vocabulary
  in written and spoken
  sentences.

---

8. Explain to students that looking at the pictures on a page can also help us figure out what an unfamiliar word means.

9. Gather Story Card D. Have students look at the picture of the man and his children.
   Say: The man and his children like to go for walks when the air is brisk.

   ▸ What do you think *brisk* means? Possible answers: cool; cold; chilly

10. Tell students that looking at the man and his children gives clues about how it must feel outside.
    Say: I see that the people are wearing long sleeves, vests, and scarves, but they are not wearing heavy coats, hats, or gloves. These clues make me think that *brisk* means chilly or cool.

Words to Know

Before reading "The Wonderful Brocade," go over Words to Know with students.

1. Read aloud each word and have students repeat it.

2. Ask students if they know what each word means.

   ▸ If students know a word's meaning, have them define it and use it in a sentence.
   ▸ If students don't know a word's meaning, read them the definition and discuss the word with them.

ash – the dust that is left over from a fire
beggar – a person who has no money and has to ask others for things, such as food
boast – to brag
brocade – a woven cloth that has a design with lots of detail on it
shiver – to shake from being cold

Read Aloud

Book Walk

Prepare students for reading by taking them on a Book Walk of "The Wonderful Brocade." Scan the story together and ask students to make predictions about the story. Answers to questions may vary.

1. Turn to the **table of contents** in *K¹² Classics for Young Readers, Volume A*. Help students find the selection and turn to that page.

2. Point to and read aloud the **title of the story**.

   ▸ What do you think the story is about?

3. Have students look at the **pictures of the story**.

   ▸ What do you think might happen in the story?
   ▸ Have you ever helped someone in your family when they were sick? What did you do to help?

Objectives

- Make predictions based on text, illustrations, and/or prior knowledge.
- Activate prior knowledge by previewing text and/or discussing topic.
- Listen and respond to texts representing a variety of cultures, time periods, and traditions.

"The Wonderful Brocade"

It's time to read aloud the story.

1. Have students sit next to you so that they can see the pictures and words while you read aloud.

2. Tell students to listen to the words before and after an unknown word to help figure out what the word means. Remind them to look at the pictures for clues, too.

3. **Read aloud the entire story.** Track with your finger so students can follow along. Emphasize Words to Know as you come to them. If appropriate, use the pictures to help show what each word means.

Check Your Reading

"The Wonderful Brocade"

Check students' comprehension of "The Wonderful Brocade."

1. Have students retell "The Wonderful Brocade" in their own words to develop grammar, vocabulary, comprehension, and fluency skills.

2. Ask students the following questions.

   ▶ Where does the story take place? China
   ▶ How many sons does the old woman have? three
   ▶ Where does the wind carry the old woman's brocade? to the Sun Palace
   ▶ Who do the brothers meet on their way to find their mother's brocade? an old man
   ▶ What does the old man give to the youngest son to help him get to the Sun Palace? his stone horse
   ▶ Who lives in the Sun Palace? 12 fairies
   ▶ Why do the fairies take the brocade? They think that it's so wonderful that they want to make copies of it.

 If students have trouble responding to a question, help them locate the answer in the text or pictures.

> **Objectives**
> • Retell or dramatize a story.
> • Answer questions requiring literal recall of details.

Reading for Meaning

Use Context Clues in "The Wonderful Brocade"

Explore using context clues to define unknown words in "The Wonderful Brocade."

1. Remind students that good readers are able to figure out what unknown words mean by using the words that surround them and the pictures of the story.

2. Read aloud the last paragraph on page 150 while students study the picture at the bottom of the page.
   - ▶ What does the word *merchant* mean? someone who sells things; a shopkeeper
   - ▶ What word or words give you a clue? Guide students to the clue words *buying* and *pennies to buy*.
   - ▶ How does the picture help you figure this out? It shows the mother buying something from the man.

3. Read aloud the second paragraph on page 152.
   - ▶ What does *sorrowful* mean? sad
   - ▶ How do you know what it means? Guide students to the clue words *why do you look so sad?*

4. Read aloud the last sentence on page 156 while students study the picture at the bottom of page 157.
   - ▶ What do you think the word *hut* means? a small house   What clues help you figure it out? the word *doorstep* and the picture of the little house

5. Read aloud the first paragraph on page 169.
   - ▶ What does *swift* mean? fast
   - ▶ What word or words give you a clue? Guide students to the clue word *hurry*.

Objectives
- Use context and sentence structure to determine meaning of words, phrases, and/or sentences.
- Use illustrations to aid understanding of text.

Explore "The Wonderful Brocade"

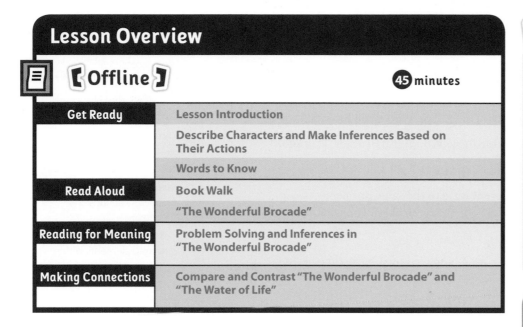

Advance Preparation

Review Reading for Meaning and Making Connections to familiarize yourself with the questions and answers.

Big Ideas

- ▸ An awareness of story structure elements (setting, characters, plot) provides readers a foundation for constructing meaning when reading new stories and writing their own stories.
- ▸ To understand and interpret a story, readers need to understand and describe characters and what they do.
- ▸ Good readers use prior knowledge and text clues to infer or draw conclusions about what is implied but not directly stated in text.

Materials

Supplied

- "The Water of Life," *K¹² Classics for Young Readers, Volume A,* pp. 124–147
- "The Wonderful Brocade," *K¹² Classics for Young Readers, Volume A,* pp. 148–173
- *K¹² Language Arts Activity Book,* pp. LC 43–44

Keywords

character – a person or animal in a story

compare – to explain how two or more things are alike

contrast – to explain how two or more things are different

inference – a guess you make using the clues in a text and what you already know

problem – an issue a character must solve in a story

solution – how a character solves a problem in a story

 **Offline** **45** minutes

Work **together** with students to complete Get Ready, Read Aloud, Reading for
Meaning, and Making Connections activities.

Get Ready ···

Lesson Introduction
Prepare students for listening to and discussing "The Wonderful Brocade."

1. Tell students you are going to reread "The Wonderful Brocade."

2. Explain that before you reread the story, you will get ready by discussing

   ► How characters react in different ways to the same problem
   ► How we can make inferences about characters based on what they say
     and do

Describe Characters and Make Inferences Based on Their Actions
Discuss how characters act and respond to the problems in a story.

1. Tell students that sometimes the same thing can happen to two characters in a
   story, but they will react in different ways.

2. Explain to students that to better understand why characters do
   things differently, it's helpful to think about what we would do in the
   same situation.

   ► What does the oldest brother do when the old man offers him a box of gold
     coins in "The Wonderful Brocade"? He takes the gold and moves to the
     city instead of trying to find his mother's brocade.   Why do you think he
     does that? Possible answers: He's afraid; he's greedy.
   ► What would do if you were searching for the brocade and the old
     man offered you a box of gold coins? Why would you do that?
     Answers will vary.

3. Tell students that different characters may respond to the same problem in
   very different ways.

Objectives
- Describe character(s).
- Make inferences based on text and/or prior knowledge.
- Identify details that explain characters' actions and feelings.
- Compare and contrast story structure elements within a text.
- Describe story structure elements—problem and solution.
- Build vocabulary through listening, reading, and discussion.
- Use new vocabulary in written and spoken sentences.

4. Tell students to listen for how two characters respond to a problem. Then **read aloud** the following story.

Rebecca and Henry were ready to play their favorite board game. Henry opened the box and looked inside. "Some of the pieces are missing," he said. Rebecca looked in the box, too. "You're right. I guess we can't play," she said. "I'm going to draw a picture instead." Henry looked all around for the missing pieces. He finally found them under the couch. "I found the missing pieces," Henry said to Rebecca. She looked at him and smiled. "Thanks. Now we can play our game."

▸ What is the problem when Rebecca and Henry go to play their favorite board game? Pieces are missing.

▸ What does Rebecca do when she sees that some pieces are missing? She decides to draw a picture.

▸ What does Henry do when he sees that some pieces are missing? He looks for them.

5. Explain that a character's actions can tell us a lot about that character. We can make inferences, or guesses, about what characters are like and how they are feeling based on what they do.

6. Tell students that the different ways in which Rebecca and Henry react to the missing game pieces gives us clues about what they are like.

7. Reread the story in Step 4 and have students think about what Rebecca and Henry are like.

▸ Henry searches for the puzzle pieces when he sees that they are missing. What does this tell you about him? Possible answers: He's helpful; he doesn't give up; he really wants to play the game.

▸ Rebecca decides to draw a picture instead. What can you infer, or guess, about Rebecca based on this? Possible answers: She doesn't really care about playing the game; she gives up easily.

▸ How do you think Rebecca feels after Henry finds the missing pieces? happy   What clue did you use to infer this? She smiles.

Words to Know

Before reading "The Wonderful Brocade," go over Words to Know with students.

1. Read aloud each word and have students repeat it.

2. Ask students if they know what each word means.

▸ If students know a word's meaning, have them define it and use it in a sentence.

▸ If students don't know a word's meaning, read them the definition and discuss the word with them.

ash – the dust that is left over from a fire
beggar – a person who has no money and has to ask others for things, such as food
boast – to brag
brocade – a woven cloth that has a design with lots of detail on it
shiver – to shake from being cold

Read Aloud

Book Walk

Prepare students by taking them on a Book Walk of "The Wonderful Brocade." Scan the story together to revisit the characters and events.

1. Turn to the selection in *K¹² Classics for Young Readers, Volume A*. Point to and read aloud the **title of the story**.

2. Look through the story. Have students review the **pictures**.

   ▸ What happens to the old woman when the wind steals her brocade? She thinks she will die; she gets weaker and weaker.

   ▸ What must the brothers do to get their mother's brocade back? go to the Sun Palace; go through the Valley of Fire and the Sea of Ice

   ▸ If you were one of the brothers, what would you have done when the wind took the brocade? Answers will vary.

Objectives

- Activate prior knowledge by previewing text and/or discussing topic.
- Listen and respond to texts representing a variety of cultures, time periods, and traditions.

"The Wonderful Brocade"

It's time to reread the story.

1. Have students sit next to you so that they can see the pictures and words while you read the aloud.

2. Tell students to listen carefully to learn more about the characters and their actions.

3. **Read aloud the entire story.** Track with your finger so students can follow along. Emphasize Words to Know as you come to them. If appropriate, use the pictures to help show what each word means.

Reading for Meaning

Problem Solving and Inferences in "The Wonderful Brocade"

Explore how characters solve problems and make inferences based on characters' actions.

1. Have students retell "The Wonderful Brocade" in their own words to develop grammar, vocabulary, comprehension, and fluency skills.

2. Ask the following questions.

   ▸ What do the older sons do when their mother brings home the painting? They say it was foolish of her; they complain about having to work more. What can you figure out, or infer, about the brothers based on this? They are selfish; they don't like to work.

   ▸ What does the youngest son do when his mother brings home the painting? He says it's beautiful; he asks his mother why she looks sad. What does this tell you about the youngest son? He cares about his mother.

Objectives

- Retell or dramatize a story.
- Compare and contrast story structure elements within a text.
- Make inferences based on text and/or prior knowledge.
- Describe character(s).
- Identify details that explain characters' actions and feelings.
- Describe story structure elements—problem and solution.

► When the mother brings home the painting, the older sons have small piles of twigs at their feet. The youngest son brings home a bag bulging with wood. What can you infer about the sons based on this? The older sons are lazy; the older sons don't work hard; the youngest son is a hard worker.

► The old woman is sad because she wants to live in a beautiful place like the one in her painting. How does she solve her problem? She weaves a copy of the picture so she can feel like she lives there while she works on it.

► What problem do the three brothers have after the wind takes their mother's brocade? They must find it and bring it back so their mother does not die.

► What do the older brothers do when the old man tells them about the Valley of Fire and the Sea of Ice? They take gold coins from the man and run away.   What can you infer about the older brothers based on this? Possible answers: They are cowards; they are greedy; they don't really care about their mother.

► What does the youngest brother do when the old man offers him gold coins like he offered the older brothers? He does not take the gold; he says that gold won't save his mother.   What can you infer about the youngest brother? Possible answers: He is brave; he is not greedy; he loves his mother.

► When the youngest son returns to the old man's hut with his mother's brocade, the old man tells him that he needs to get to his mother quickly. How is this problem solved? The old man gives him boots that get him home in two steps.

Making Connections

Compare and Contrast "The Wonderful Brocade" and "The Water of Life"
Explore the similarities and differences between "The Wonderful Brocade" and "The Water of Life." Turn to pages LC 43 and 44 in *K¹² Language Arts Activity Book.*

1. Look at the chart with students. Point to and read aloud the first row heading, "Setting." Write what students dictate in the first row of boxes under the appropriate story title.

2. Repeat Step 1 until the chart is completed.

Objectives

- Compare and contrast story structure elements across texts.
- Make connections with text: text-to-text, text-to-self, text-to-world.
- Demonstrate understanding through graphic organizers.

3. Ask the following questions to encourage discussion and comparisons of the two stories.

  ▶ How are the two stories alike? Possible answers: Both are about three brothers; the youngest brother is the main character in both; the brothers are trying to save a parent in both; the brothers meet someone who can help them in both stories; the two older brothers run away at the end of both stories.

  ▶ How are the two stories different? Possible answers: One story has fairies and the other has a princess; the brothers are looking for different things in the two stories; one story has a mother who needs help and one story has a father who need helps.

Reward: Add a sticker for this unit on the My Accomplishments chart to mark successful completion of the unit.

Making Connections

Explore "The Wonderful Brocade"
Compare and Contrast "The Wonderful Brocade" and "The Water of Life"

Fill in the chart to compare and contrast two stories.

	"The Wonderful Brocade"	"The Water of Life"
Setting	a kingdom	China
Characters	three brothers; old woman; old man; fairies	three brothers; king; dwarf; princess
Main character	the youngest brother	the youngest brother
What are the brothers trying to do?	find their mother's brocade	find the water of life

	"The Wonderful Brocade"	"The Water of Life"
Who do the brothers need to help?	their mother	their father
Who do the brothers meet that can help them?	an old man	a dwarf
Which brother finds what he is looking for?	the youngest	the youngest
What happens to the brothers at the end of the story?	The two oldest run away; the youngest marries a fairy.	The two oldest run away; the youngest marries a princess.

LANGUAGE ARTS GREEN LC 43

LC 44 LANGUAGE ARTS GREEN

A Whirl of Words

Unit Focus

In this unit, students will explore fun texts that play with sounds, words, and phrases. This unit follows the shared-reading instructional approach. (see the Instructional Approaches to Reading in the introductory lesson for this program). Before you begin this unit, you may want to review the online course introduction. In this unit, students will

▶ Listen to stories, poems, rhymes, and tongue twisters.
▶ Learn about the strategy of summarizing and how it helps readers.
▶ Explore author's purpose.
▶ Explore exclamations and exclamation marks.
▶ Explore the poetic elements of alliteration, repetition, and rhyme.
▶ Practice using a book's table of contents.
▶ Explore imagery and descriptive language.
▶ Explore characters and their actions.
▶ Explore print features.
▶ Learn to identify literal and nonliteral meanings of words and phrases.

Unit Plan   〔Offline〕

Lesson 1	Introduce "Sheep in a Jeep"	45 minutes a day
Lesson 2	Explore "Sheep in a Jeep"	
Lesson 3	Explore Poems About Animals (B)	
Lesson 4	Explore "Did You Ever See . . . ?"	
Lesson 5	Explore "Tongue-Twisters"	
Lesson 6	Introduce "Morris Has a Cold"	
Lesson 7	Explore "Morris Has a Cold"	
Lesson 8	Introduce *Amelia Bedelia*	
Lesson 9	Explore *Amelia Bedelia*	
Lesson 10	Your Choice	

Introduce "Sheep in a Jeep"

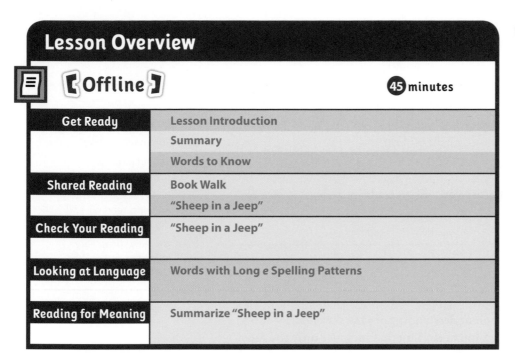

Lesson Overview

[Offline]   45 minutes

Get Ready	Lesson Introduction
	Summary
	Words to Know
Shared Reading	Book Walk
	"Sheep in a Jeep"
Check Your Reading	"Sheep in a Jeep"
Looking at Language	Words with Long *e* Spelling Patterns
Reading for Meaning	Summarize "Sheep in a Jeep"

[Materials]

Supplied
- *Ready . . . Set . . . Read! The Beginning Reader's Treasury,* pp. 12–26
- *K¹² Language Arts Activity Book,* pp. 45–46

Also Needed
- index cards (16)

Story Synopsis
Five sheep in a jeep take the reader on a wild ride.

Keywords
author – a writer
illustrator – the person who draws the pictures that go with a story
summarize – to tell in order the most important ideas or events of a text
summary – a short retelling that includes only the most important ideas or events of a text

Advance Preparation

Read "Sheep in a Jeep" before beginning the Shared Reading to locate Words to Know in the text. For Looking at Language, preview the Reading Aid on pages LC 45 and 46 in *K¹² Language Arts Activity Book* to prepare the materials, and prepare two index cards by writing *sheep* on one and *leap* on another.

Big Ideas

▸ Comprehension requires the reader to self-monitor understanding.
▸ Shared reading allows students to observe and practice the reading behaviors of proficient readers.
▸ During shared-reading activities, students learn more about how print works.
▸ Repeated rereading leads to increased fluency.

 **45** minutes

Work **together** with students to complete Get Ready, Shared Reading, Check Your Reading, Looking at Language, and Reading for Meaning activities.

Get Ready

Lesson Introduction
Prepare students for listening to and discussing "Sheep in a Jeep" by Nancy Shaw.

1. Tell students that you are going to read "Sheep in a Jeep," a story about five sheep that go for a ride.

2. Explain that before you read the story you will get ready by discussing how to do a summary.

Summary
Introduce how to do a summary.

1. Explain that readers can check their understanding of what they read by doing a summary. **A summary is a very short retelling that includes only the most important ideas or events of a text.** Doing a summary is not the same as a full retelling of a story because **a summary does not include very many details**.

2. Tell students that a good way to do a summary is to ask the question, "Who did what?" A reader tries to answer this question after reading parts or all of a story.

3. **Read aloud** the following short story so students can practice summarizing a story.

   It was Jack's turn to load the dishwasher. He scraped the leftover food off the plates, and then he lined them up in the bottom rack. Then he rinsed out the glasses and put them next to the plates. After he put the silverware in the basket, he added detergent, slammed the door shut, and pushed the on button.

   ▸ Who is the story about? Jack
   ▸ What did Jack do? load the dishwasher
   ▸ Summarize the story. Jack loaded the dishwasher.

4. As students read and listen to stories, encourage them to think about and answer the question, "Who did what?"

Objectives
- Summarize a story.
- Self-monitor comprehension of text.
- Build vocabulary through listening, reading, and discussion.
- Use new vocabulary in written and spoken sentences.

Words to Know

Before reading "Sheep in a Jeep," go over Words to Know with students.

1. Read aloud each word and have students repeat it.

2. Ask students if they know what each word means.

    ▸ If students know a word's meaning, have them define it and use it in a
      sentence.
    ▸ If students don't know a word's meaning, read them the definition and
      discuss it with them.

heap – a pile; a stack
shove – to push hard
steep – having a sharp slope
steer – to make something move in a particular direction

TIP To help students better understand the word *steep*, you may want to draw a
picture of a mountain, hill, or other sloped object.

Shared Reading

Book Walk

Prepare students for reading by taking them on a Book Walk of "Sheep in a Jeep."
Scan the story together and ask students to make predictions about it.

1. Turn to the **table of contents** in *Ready . . . Set . . . Read!* Help students find
    "Sheep in a Jeep" and turn to that page.

2. Point to and read aloud the **title of the story**.

    ▸ What do you think this story is about? Answers will vary.

3. Read aloud the **name of the author**.

    ▸ What does an author do? writes a story or book

4. Read aloud the **name of the illustrator**.

    ▸ What does an illustrator do? makes the pictures for a story or book

5. Have students look at the **pictures**. Answers to questions may vary.

    ▸ Where do you think the story takes place?
    ▸ What do you think might happen in the story?
    ▸ Have you ever heard a story about sheep that drive a car? Do you think this
      will be a silly story or a serious story?

Objectives

- Make predictions based on
  text, illustrations, and/or
  prior knowledge.
- Describe role of author and/
  or illustrator.
- Activate prior knowledge
  by previewing text and/or
  discussing topic.
- Read and listen to a variety
  of texts for information and
  pleasure independently or
  as part of a group.

"Sheep in a Jeep"

It's time to read aloud the story.

1. Have students sit next to you so that they can see the pictures and words while you read aloud.

2. Tell students to listen for information that can answer the question, "Who did what?" so that they can do a summary of the story.

3. **Read aloud the entire story.** Track with your finger so students can follow along. Emphasize Words to Know as you come to them. If appropriate, use the pictures to help show what each word means.

Check Your Reading

"Sheep in a Jeep"

Check students' comprehension of "Sheep in a Jeep." Ask students the following questions.

- ▶ Who drives the jeep? a sheep
- ▶ What do the sheep do when the jeep won't go? They push it.
- ▶ What happens when the jeep goes down the hill? It gets stuck in the mud.
- ▶ What do the sheep do when they can't get the jeep out of the mud? They get help.
- ▶ What do the sheep do with the jeep after they crash it? They put up a sign to sell it.

 TIP If students have trouble responding to a question, help them locate the answer in the text or pictures.

Objectives
- Answer questions requiring literal recall of details.

Looking at Language

Words with Long *e* Spelling Patterns

Reread "Sheep in a Jeep" with a focus on spelling patterns for the long *e* sound. Gather the index cards and the Reading Aid on pages LC 45 and 46 in *K¹² Language Arts Activity Book*.

1. Point to the word on each index card and read it aloud, and then have students read each word with you.

- ▶ Do the words *sheep* and *leap* rhyme? Yes
- ▶ What do you notice about how the sound /ēp/ is spelled in these words? In *sheep* it's spelled *eep*, but in *leap* it's spelled *eap*.

Objectives
- Identify and use /ē/ spelling patterns.
- Identify words that rhyme.
- Read aloud grade-level text with appropriate expression, accuracy, and rate.

2. Explain that the spelling patterns *ee* and *ea* are two ways to make the long *e* sound. So the words *sheep* and *leap* both have the same long *e* sound, even though they are spelled differently.

3. Tell students that they will read aloud the story **with** you as you track the words with your finger, paying special attention to the words ending in *–eep* and *–eap*. All of these words will rhyme with *sheep*.

4. Explain that you will stop at certain points in the story to talk about these words and to write them on index cards.

5. As you read aloud, **encourage students to chime in and read with you**.

6. Refer to the Reading Aid.

Reading Aid   Tear out the Reading Aid for this reading selection. Follow the instructions for folding the page, and then use the page as a guide as you reread the selection with students.

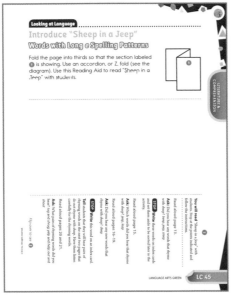

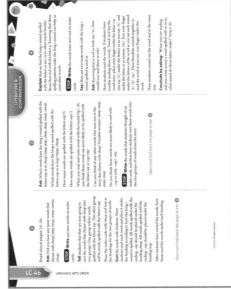

Reading for Meaning

Summarize "Sheep in a Jeep"

Review summarizing with students, and then help them summarize "Sheep in a Jeep."

1. Remind students that a **summary** is a short retelling that includes only the most important ideas or events of a text. A summary answers the question, "Who did what?" Doing a summary is one way readers can check that they understand what they read.

2. Have students practice summarizing.

   ▸ Who is the story about? sheep
   ▸ What do the sheep do? Possible answers: drive a jeep; push the jeep up a hill and into the mud; crash the jeep; put up a sign to sell the jeep
   ▸ How could you summarize the story? Guide students to answer the question, "Who did what?" Example: Sheep drive a jeep, get it stuck in the mud, and crash it.

3. Ask the following questions to check students' comprehension of summarizing.

   ▸ What is a summary? a short retelling that includes only the most important ideas or events of a text
   ▸ What question does a summary answer? Who did what?
   ▸ Were you able to answer the question, "Who did what?" for this story? Answers will vary.   Do you think that you understand the story? Answers will vary.

Objectives
- Summarize a story.
- Self-monitor comprehension of text.

Explore "Sheep in a Jeep"

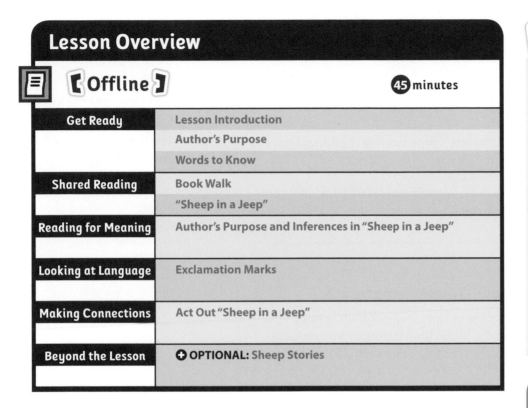

Lesson Overview

Offline — 45 minutes

Get Ready	Lesson Introduction
	Author's Purpose
	Words to Know
Shared Reading	Book Walk
	"Sheep in a Jeep"
Reading for Meaning	Author's Purpose and Inferences in "Sheep in a Jeep"
Looking at Language	Exclamation Marks
Making Connections	Act Out "Sheep in a Jeep"
Beyond the Lesson	⊕ OPTIONAL: Sheep Stories

Materials

Supplied

- *Ready . . . Set . . . Read! The Beginning Reader's Treasury*, pp. 12–26
- *K¹² Language Arts Activity Book*, pp. LC 47–51

Also Needed

- glue
- scissors, adult
- scissors, round-end safety
- tape, clear
- yarn
- household objects – cotton balls, hole punch

Keywords

author's purpose – the reason the author wrote a text: to entertain, to inform, to express an opinion, or to persuade

infer – to use clues and what you already know to make a guess

inference – a guess you make using the clues in a text and what you already know

Advance Preparation

For Looking at Language, cut out the sentence strips on page LC 47, and preview the Reading Aid on pages LC 49 and 50 in *K¹² Language Arts Activity Book* to prepare the materials.

Big Ideas

▸ Shared reading allows students to observe and practice the reading behaviors of proficient readers.

▸ During shared-reading activities, students learn more about how print works.

▸ Good readers use prior knowledge and text clues to infer or draw conclusions about what is implied but not directly stated in text.

▸ Repeated rereading leads to increased fluency.

[Offline] 45 minutes

Work **together** with students to complete Get Ready, Shared Reading, Reading for Meaning, Looking at Language, Making Connections, and Beyond the Lesson activities.

Get Ready

Lesson Introduction

Prepare students for listening to and discussing "Sheep in a Jeep" by Nancy Shaw.

1. Tell students that you are going to reread "Sheep in a Jeep."

2. Explain that before you reread the story, you will get ready by discussing how to identify an author's purpose for writing a story.

Author's Purpose

Introduce students to identifying the author's purpose for writing a text.

1. Explain that an author writes an article or story for a certain reason, or **purpose**. An author's purpose may be to teach something, to entertain, to convince the reader of something, or to tell the reader what the author thinks about something.

2. Read aloud information about a story and model how to determine the author's purpose.
   Say: Listen as I read the title of a story and what it's about. In the story "Squidmore the Squishy Squid," the author tells a funny story about a silly squid named Squidmore. This is a funny story, so I think the author wrote it to entertain us.

3. Have students practice identifying the purpose of a text.
   Say: Listen as I read the title of a text and what it's about. In the text "Apple Pies," the author gives instructions on how to bake an apple pie.
   ► Why do you think the author wrote the text? to teach us
   ► What clues tell you that the author wants to teach us? The text has instructions on how to do something.

Objectives
- Identify the purpose of a text.
- Identify the author's purpose.
- Build vocabulary through listening, reading, and discussion.
- Use new vocabulary in written and spoken sentences.

Words to Know

Before reading "Sheep in a Jeep," go over Words to Know with students.

1. Read aloud each word and have students repeat it.

2. Ask students if they know what each word means.
   ▸ If students know a word's meaning, have them define it and use it in a sentence.
   ▸ If students don't know a word's meaning, read them the definition and discuss the word with them.

heap – a pile; a stack
shove – to push hard
steep – having a sharp slope
steer – to make something move in a particular direction

Shared Reading

Book Walk

Prepare students by taking them on a Book Walk of "Sheep in a Jeep." Scan the story together to revisit the characters and events.

1. Read aloud the **title of the story.**

2. Have students point to the **name of the author and illustrator** while you read the names aloud.

3. Have students review the **pictures**.
   ▸ What happens when the sheep push the jeep? It gets stuck in the mud.
   ▸ What do the sheep do with the jeep after they crash it? They put up a sign to sell it.
   ▸ Look at the picture on pages 20 and 21. Why do you think the illustrator drew such funny pictures? Possible answers: because the story is silly; to make the story funnier

Objectives

- Activate prior knowledge by previewing text and/or discussing topic.
- Read and listen to a variety of texts for information and pleasure independently or as part of a group.

"Sheep in a Jeep"

It's time to reread the story.

1. Have students sit next to you so that they can see the pictures and words while you read the story aloud.

2. Tell students to think about why the author wrote the story while they listen to you read. Remind them to look at the pictures to see how the pictures relate to the story.

3. **Read aloud the entire story.** Track with your finger so students can follow along.

Reading for Meaning

Author's Purpose and Inferences in "Sheep in a Jeep"

Explore author's purpose and make inferences based on the story's illustrations.

1. Remind students that an author has a reason, or purpose, for writing a text.

   ▸ Why did the author write "Sheep in a Jeep"? to entertain us
   ▸ How can you tell the author wrote the story to entertain us? It's funny.

2. Remind students that readers can figure out things the author doesn't state directly by looking for clues in the text and the pictures.

   ▸ Point to the picture on pages 14 and 15. Why do you think the jeep won't go? Possible answers: because the sheep are too heavy; because the jeep is broken
   ▸ Point to the pictures on pages 19 and 20. Why do the sheep need help getting the jeep out of the mud? Possible answers: The mud is very deep; the jeep is heavy.
   ▸ Point to the picture on page 21. How do you think the sheep feel after the pigs help get the jeep out of the mud? happy; excited   What are the sheep doing in the picture to make you think that? They're dancing, hugging, and smiling.
   ▸ Point to the picture on pages 22 and 23. Why do you think the jeep crashes? The driver isn't steering; the driver isn't looking forward.
   ▸ Point to the pictures on pages 24–26. Why are the sheep selling the jeep for cheap? because it's broken

Objectives

- Identify the purpose of a text.
- Identify the author's purpose.
- Make inferences based on text and/or prior knowledge.
- Use illustrations to aid understanding of text.

Looking at Language

Exclamation Marks

Reread "Sheep in a Jeep" with a focus on exclamation marks. Gather the sentence strips that you prepared from page LC 47 and the Reading Aid on pages LC 49 and 50 in *K¹² Language Arts Activity Book*.

1. Point to the two sentences on the sentence strips. Tell students that the sentences have the same words, but when you read them aloud, they will sound different.

2. Track with your finger as you read each sentence. **Read aloud** the sentence that ends with a period in a normal voice and the sentence that ends with an exclamation mark with excitement.

   ▸ Did you notice the difference in the way I read the sentences? Possible answers: The second sentence sounded more exciting; the second sentence had more expression.

3. Tell students that the mark at the end of the second sentence is called an **exclamation mark**. A sentence that ends with an exclamation mark is called an **exclamation**, and it should be read with excitement.

Objectives

- Identify sentences that are exclamations.
- Read aloud grade-level text with appropriate expression, accuracy, and rate.
- Demonstrate one-to-one correspondence (voice-to-print).

4. Have students read aloud the first sentence with you **in a normal voice**.

5. Have students read the second sentence with you **with excitement**. Have them jump up as they read the exclamation to help them associate an exciting physical movement with reading an exclamation in an expressive, exciting way.

6. Tell students that as you reread the story, they should **chime in and read with you**. When they see exclamations—sentences that end in exclamation marks—they should read with excitement. Encourage students to jump up every time they read an exclamation.

7. Refer to the Reading Aid.

Reading Aid Tear out the Reading Aid for this reading selection. Follow the instructions for folding the page, and then use the page as a guide as you reread the selection with students.

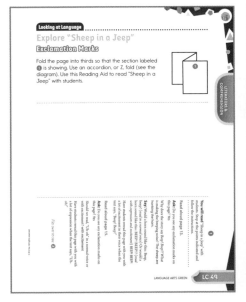
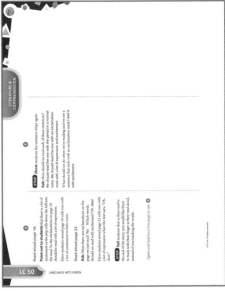

Making Connections

Act Out "Sheep in a Jeep"

Have students act out the story. Turn to page LC 51 in *K¹² Language Arts Activity Book*. Gather the glue, scissors, tape, yarn, cotton balls, and holepunch.

1. Have students glue cotton balls onto the mask and then cut out the mask.

2. Help students cut out the eye holes.

3. Use a hole punch to cut out the holes on the tabs so you can thread yarn through each tab.

4. Reinforce the holes with tape so that the paper doesn't tear. Fold back the tabs.

5. Cut two lengths of yarn for each mask. Loop the yarn through the holes and tie a knot close to the end of each strand of yarn. Have students put on the mask and tie the yarn behind their head.

6. Have students act out "Sheep in a Jeep" as you read aloud the story.

Objectives
- Respond to text through art, writing, and/or drama.
- Retell or dramatize a story.

Beyond the Lesson ....

⊕ OPTIONAL: Sheep Stories

This activity is OPTIONAL. It is intended for students who have extra time and would enjoy reading additional stories by Nancy Shaw. Feel free to skip this activity.

1. Go to a library and look for a copy of any of Nancy Shaw's sheep stories, such as *Sheep Out to Eat* or *Sheep Take a Hike*.

2. Lead a Book Walk and then read aloud the story. As you read aloud, encourage students to chime in and read with you.

3. Have students tell how the stories are alike and different. Be sure students describe how the characters and settings are alike and different.

4. Have students summarize the book.

5. Ask them to tell which book is their favorite and why.

Objectives

- Compare and contrast story structure elements across texts.
- Summarize a story.

Explore Poems About Animals (B)

Lesson Overview

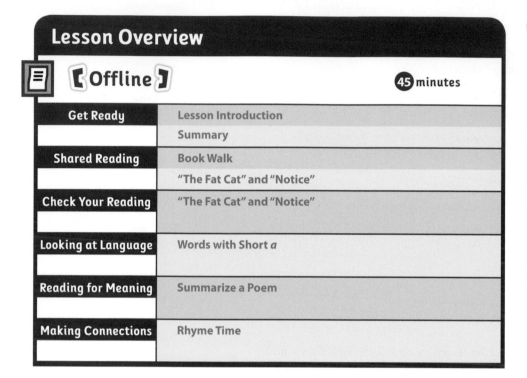

Offline		45 minutes
Get Ready	Lesson Introduction	
	Summary	
Shared Reading	Book Walk	
	"The Fat Cat" and "Notice"	
Check Your Reading	"The Fat Cat" and "Notice"	
Looking at Language	Words with Short *a*	
Reading for Meaning	Summarize a Poem	
Making Connections	Rhyme Time	

Advance Preparation

Cut out and tape together the sentence strip on page LC 53 in *K¹² Language Arts Activity Book* for Looking at Language.

Big Ideas

▶ Shared reading allows students to observe and practice the reading behaviors of proficient readers.
▶ During shared-reading activities, students learn more about how print works.
▶ Comprehension requires the reader to self-monitor understanding.
▶ Repeated rereading leads to increased fluency.

Materials

Supplied

● *Ready ... Set ... Read! The Beginning Reader's Treasury*, pp. 84–85
● *K¹² Language Arts Activity Book*, pp. LC 53, 55

Also Needed

● scissors, adult
● scissors, round-end safety
● tape, clear

Poetry Synopsis

Two poets offer insights about their pets.

Keywords

author's purpose – the reason the author wrote a text: to entertain, to inform, to express an opinion, or to persuade

rhyme – when two or more words have the same ending sounds; for example, *cat* and *hat* rhyme

summarize – to tell in order the most important ideas or events of a text

summary – a short retelling that includes only the most important ideas or events of a text

 **45** minutes

Work **together** with students to complete Get Ready, Shared Reading, Check Your Reading, Looking at Language, Reading for Meaning, and Making Connections activities.

Get Ready

Lesson Introduction

Prepare students for listening to and discussing "The Fat Cat" by Stephanie Calmenson and "Notice" by David McCord.

1. Tell students that you are going to read "The Fat Cat" and "Notice," two poems about pets.

2. Explain that before you read the poems, you will get ready by discussing how to summarize a poem and why it's important to be able to do so.

 Objectives
- Summarize a story.
- Self-monitor comprehension of text.

Summary

Explore how to do a summary.

1. Explain that good readers can check their understanding of what they read by doing a summary. **A summary is a very short retelling that includes only the most important ideas or events of a text.** Doing a summary is not the same as a full retelling a poem or story because **a summary does not include very many details**.

2. Tell students that a good way to do a summary is to ask the question, "Who did what?" A good reader tries to answer this question after reading parts or all of a poem or story.
   Say: For example, if we read a story about a girl who plants a garden and shares the food with the people in her neighborhood, a good summary might be "A girl feeds people in her neighborhood." This summary answers the question, "Who did what?"

3. **Read aloud** the following poem so students can practice summarizing.

   Cody washed his face,
   Then gave his hair a scrub.
   Cody took a bath
   In the great big tub!

   ► Who is the poem about? Cody
   ► What did Cody do? took a bath
   ► Summarize the poem. Cody took a bath.
   ► Does your summary answer the question, "Who did what?" Answers will vary.
   ► Do you think you understand the poem? Answers will vary.

Shared Reading

Book Walk

Prepare students by taking them on a Book Walk of "The Fat Cat" and "Notice." Scan the poems together and ask students to make predictions about the poems. Answers to questions may vary.

1. Turn to the table of contents in *Ready . . . Set . . . Read!*

2. Explain that the **table of contents** is found at the beginning of a book or magazine. It helps the reader find a story, poem, or article. The table of contents lists the name of each story, poem, or article in the order that they appear. Next to the title is the page number where the story, poem, or article can be found.

3. Point to and read aloud "The Fat Cat" and "page 84."

4. Turn to "The Fat Cat."

5. Point to and read aloud the **title of the poem** and the **name of the poet**. Have students repeat the poet's name.

6. Have students look at the **picture**.
   ▸ What do you think the poem is about?
   ▸ Do you like cats? Why or why not?

7. Return to the **table of contents**. Help students locate the title of the second poem, "Notice."

8. Point to and read aloud "Notice" and "page 85."

9. Have students turn to "Notice."

10. Point to and read aloud the **title of the poem** and the **name of the poet**. Have students repeat the poet's name.

11. Have students look at the **picture**.
    ▸ What do you think the poem is about?
    ▸ Do you have a pet? What is it? If you don't have a pet, is there a kind of pet you would like to have?

12. Point to the word *ME*. Explain that the letters in word are written with capital letters so the reader knows to say the word loudly.

Objectives

- Identify the function of and locate information with a table of contents.
- Make predictions based on text, illustrations, and/or prior knowledge.
- Activate prior knowledge by previewing text and/or discussing topic.
- Identify and describe the use of print features: boldface, underlining, highlighting, italic, capital letters.
- Read and discuss poetry.

"The Fat Cat" and "Notice"

It's time to read aloud the poems.

1. Have students sit next to you so that they can see the pictures and words while you read aloud.

2. Tell students to listen for words that rhyme and words that are said over and over.

3. Tell students to listen carefully so they can summarize what the poems are about.

4. Remember to point to and emphasize the word *ME* in "The Fat Cat."

5. **Read aloud both poems.** Track with your finger so students can follow along.

Check Your Reading

"The Fat Cat" and "Notice"

Check students' comprehension of "The "Fat Cat" and "Notice."

1. Ask students the following questions to check their understanding of a table of contents.

   ▸ Where is the table of contents? at the beginning of a book or magazine
   ▸ What does the table of contents list? the titles of stories, poems, or articles and the pages they're on

2. Reread "The Fat Cat."

   ▸ What words rhyme with *fat*? *cat* and *sat*
   ▸ What word is repeated at the beginning of each line of the poem? *fat*
   ▸ Why is the word *ME* written in capital letters? so the reader knows to say it loudly

3. Reread "Notice."

   ▸ What word rhymes with *dog*? *frog*
   ▸ What word rhymes with *cat*? *hat*

 TIP If students have trouble responding to a question, help them locate the answer in the text or pictures.

 Objectives

- Identify the function of and locate information with a table of contents.
- Identify structure of poems and poetic elements: rhyme, rhythm, repetition, and/or alliteration.
- Identify and describe the use of print features: boldface, underlining, highlighting, italic, capital letters.

Looking at Language

Words with Short *a*

Reread "The Fat Cat" and "Notice" with a focus on words with the short *a* sound. Gather the sentence strip that you prepared from page LC 53 in *K¹² Language Arts Activity Book*.

1. Show students the sentence and explain that all the words in the poem "Fat Cat" are in this one sentence.

2. Have students read aloud the sentence with you.

   ▸ What do you notice about most of the words in the sentence? Possible answers: They rhyme; they have the sound /ă/; they say –*at*.

3. Tell students that the words *fat*, *cat*, and *sat* all belong to the –*at* word family.

   ▸ Can you think of any other words in the –*at* word family? Possible answers: *bat; rat; mat; flat; hat*
   ▸ What sound does the letter *a* make in these words? /ă/; the short *a* sound

4. Point to the word *ME*.

   ▸ How should we say this word when we read it aloud? Possible answers: with excitement; loud; louder than normal   Why? because it's written in capital letters

5. Explain that "The Fat Cat" is called a **cumulative poem**. In this kind of poem, words are repeated with something new added to each line.

6. Tell students that they are going to use the words in the sentence strip to build each line of "The Fat Cat" and practice reciting the poem aloud.

7. Have students cut apart the words in the sentence strip "keeping on *ME!*" together, and then ask students to rebuild and read the sentence word by word with you.

   ▸ Lay down *fat*, and have students read the word as you point to it.
   ▸ Lay down *cat* after *fat*. Have students read both words beginning with *fat*.
   ▸ Continue in this manner until students have read aloud each line of the poem and rebuilt the complete sentence.

8. Have students complete the steps again on their own. Have them practice this until they feel they know the poem by heart. Remind them to read the word *ME* in a loud voice.

Objectives

- Identify and use /ă/.
- Identify words that rhyme.
- Read aloud grade-level text with appropriate expression, accuracy, and rate.
- Recite short poems and rhymes.

9. Have students recite the poem from memory.

10. Tell students that they are going to reread the poem "Notice," and they should listen for words with the sound /ă/.

11. Reread "Notice" and have students **chime in with you**.

   ‣ Which words have the short *a* sound? Possible answers: *have; had; cat; hat*

Reading for Meaning •

Summarize a Poem
Explore how to summarize a poem.

1. Remind students that a **summary** is a very short retelling of the most important ideas or events of a text. A summary should answer the question, "Who did what?"

2. Have students summarize "The Fat Cat." Have them practice summarizing.

   ‣ Who is the poem about? a fat cat
   ‣ What does the cat do? sits on someone
   ‣ How would you summarize the poem? Guide students to think about the answers to the questions above.
   ‣ Does your summary answer the question, "Who did what?" Answers will vary.
   ‣ Do you think that you understand the poem? Answers will vary.

Objectives
- Summarize a story.
- Self-monitor comprehension of text.

3. Have students summarize "Notice."

   ▸ Who is the poem about? a boy

   ▸ What does the boy do? talks about his pets

   ▸ How would you summarize the poem? Guide students to think about the answers to the questions above.

   ▸ Does your summary answer the question, "Who did what?" Answers will vary.

   ▸ Do you think that you understand the poem? Answers will vary.

4. Ask the following questions to check students' comprehension of summarizing.

   ▸ What is a summary? a short retelling that includes only the most important ideas or events of a text

   ▸ What question does a summary answer? Who did what?

Making Connections

 Rhyme Time

Have students create a new poem with the same rhyming pattern as "Notice" by David McCord. Turn to page LC 55 in *K¹² Language Arts Activity Book*.

1. **Read aloud** the entire poem "Notice."

2. Tell students to listen as you point to and reread the last word in line 1 and the last word in line 3.

   ▸ What do you notice about these two words? They rhyme.

3. Tell students to listen as you point to and reread the last word in line 2 and the last word in line 4.

   ▸ What do you notice about these two words? They rhyme.

4. Tell students this is called a **rhyming pattern**.

5. Direct students' attention to the Activity Book page.

6. Tell students they will make a poem of their own with the same rhyming pattern as "Notice."

7. Point to the blank lines in the poem. Tell students they will choose words that rhyme to create their own poem, based on "Notice."

8. Read aloud the poem on the Activity Book page, pausing at each blank line so that students can choose a word to complete it.

Objectives
- Identify and replicate the pattern of a poem.
- Demonstrate use of poetic elements of rhyme, rhythm, and/or alliteration.

9. Help students write the missing words in the blanks.

  ▸ Be sure students pick pairs of words that rhyme. If students have trouble thinking of pairs of rhyming words, give students a word and have them think of a word that rhymes with your word. Examples: *bug; fan; map*

  ▸ Remind students of the rhyming pattern: One pair of rhyming words should appear at the ends of lines 1 and 3, and another pair should appear at the ends of lines 2 and 4.

10. Help students write their name on the blank line next to the title. Then have them read aloud the completed poem **with** you as you track the words with your finger.

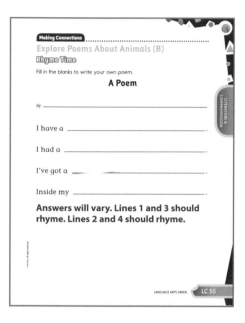

Explore "Did You Ever See . . . ?"

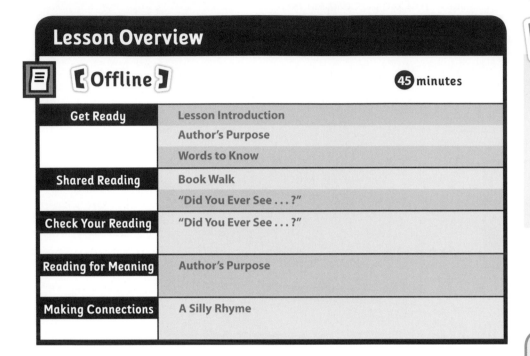

Lesson Overview

Offline — 45 minutes

Get Ready	Lesson Introduction
	Author's Purpose
	Words to Know
Shared Reading	Book Walk
	"Did You Ever See . . . ?"
Check Your Reading	"Did You Ever See . . . ?"
Reading for Meaning	Author's Purpose
Making Connections	A Silly Rhyme

Advance Preparation

Before beginning the Shared Reading, read "Did You Ever See . . . ?" to locate Words to Know in the text.

Big Ideas

Shared reading allows students to observe and practice the reading behaviors of proficient readers.

Materials

Supplied

- *Ready . . . Set . . . Read! The Beginning Reader's Treasury*, pp. 130–134
- *K¹² My Journal*, pp. 2–53

Also Needed

- crayons

Poetry Synopsis

The authors describe fanciful images, such as a goat in a coat and mice on ice.

Keywords

author's purpose – the reason the author wrote a text: to entertain, to inform, to express an opinion, or to persuade

rhyme – when two or more words have the same ending sounds; for example, *cat* and *hat* rhyme

[Offline] 45 minutes

Work **together** with students to complete Get Ready, Shared Reading, Check Your Reading, Reading for Meaning, and Making Connections activities.

Get Ready ....

Lesson Introduction

Prepare students for listening to and discussing "Did You Ever See . . . ?" by Joanna Cole and Stephanie Calmenson.

1. Tell students that you are going to read "Did You Ever See . . . ?" which has rhymes about unusual things.

2. Explain to students that before they hear the rhymes, you will get ready by discussing reasons why an author might write an article or story.

⭐ **Objectives**

- Identify the purpose of a text.
- Identify the author's purpose.
- Build vocabulary through listening, reading, and discussion.
- Use new vocabulary in written and spoken sentences.

Author's Purpose

Explore author's purpose.

1. Explain that an author writes an article or story for a certain reason, or **purpose**. An author's purpose may be to teach something, to entertain, to convince the reader of something, or to tell the reader what the author thinks about something.

2. Read aloud information about a story and model how to determine the author's purpose.
Say: Listen as I read the title of a text and what it's about. In the text "Why You Should Visit Your Local Library," the author talks about the different things people can do at their neighborhood library and gives reasons why people should go. This text is full of reasons why I should go to my neighborhood library, so I think the author wrote it to convince me to do something.

3. Have students practice identifying the purpose of a text.
Say: Listen as I read the title of a story and what it's about. In the story "The Queen Can Only Quack," the author tells a funny story about a queen who forgets how to talk and can only quack like a duck.

   ► Why do you think the author wrote the story? to entertain us
   ► What clues tell you that the author wants to entertain us? The title is silly; a person that quacks is silly.

Words to Know

Before reading "Did You Ever See . . . ?" go over Words to Know with students.

1. Read aloud the word and have students repeat it.

2. Ask students if they know what the word means.

   ▸ If students know the word's meaning, have them define it and use it in a sentence.

   ▸ If students don't know the word's meaning, read them the definition and discuss the word with them.

jig – a lively dance

Shared Reading

Book Walk

Prepare students by taking them on a Book Walk of "Did You Ever See . . . ?" Scan the rhymes together and ask students to make predictions about them. Answers to questions may vary.

1. Turn to the **table of contents** in *Ready . . . Set . . . Read!* Help students find "Did You Ever See . . . ?" and turn to that page.

2. Point to and read aloud the **title of the rhymes**.

   ▸ What do you think these rhymes might be about?

3. Have students look at the **pictures**.

   ▸ Have you ever seen something so silly that it made you laugh out loud?

Objectives
- Make predictions based on text, illustrations, and/or prior knowledge.
- Activate prior knowledge by previewing text and/or discussing topic.
- Read and listen to a variety of texts for information and pleasure independently or as part of a group.

"Did You Ever See . . . ?"

It's time to read aloud the rhymes.

1. Have students sit next to you so that they can see the pictures and words while you read aloud.

2. Tell students to look at the pictures and listen for words that rhyme.

3. Tell students to listen carefully so they can tell why the authors wrote the rhymes.

4. Tell students that these rhymes have many words that they may already know how to read, so they should **chime in and read with you**.

5. **Read aloud all of the rhymes.** Track with your finger so students can follow along and chime in with you.

Check Your Reading

"Did You Ever See . . . ?"

Check students' comprehension of "Did You Ever See . . . ?"

1. Ask students the following question.

   ▶ What happens to the egg after he catches the ball? He falls.

2. Reread the rhymes on page 131.

   ▶ What words rhyme with *goat*? *coat* and *boat*
   ▶ What words rhyme with *ice*? *mice* and *nice*

3. Have students study the picture on page 130 as you reread the text on the page.

   ▶ What is a wig? hair that you can put on and take off

4. Have students study the pictures on page 132 as you reread the text on the page.

   ▶ What is fog? a thick cloud that's close to the ground

5. Have students review all the pictures.

   ▶ Why do you think the illustrator drew such funny pictures? Possible answers: because the rhymes are silly; to make the rhymes funnier

TIP If students have trouble responding to a question, help them locate the answer in the text or pictures.

Objectives

- Answer questions requiring literal recall of details.
- Identify words that rhyme.
- Use illustrations to aid understanding of text.

Reading for Meaning

Author's Purpose

Explore author's purpose.

1. Remind students that an author has a reason, or purpose, for writing a story or article.

2. Ask the following questions.

   ▶ Why did the authors write "Did You Ever See . . . ?" to entertain us
   ▶ How can you tell the authors wrote the rhymes to entertain us? The rhymes are silly.

3. Ask students the following questions to check their comprehension of author's purpose.

   ▶ What do we call the author's reason for writing a story or article? the author's purpose
   ▶ Authors write stories and articles for different reasons. What are some of the reasons? to teach something; to entertain; to convince the reader of something; to tell the reader what the author thinks about something

Objectives

- Identify the purpose of a text.
- Identify the author's purpose.

Making Connections

A Silly Rhyme

Guide students to create their own rhymes. Gather *K¹² My Journal* and have students turn to the next available page for **drawing and writing** in Thoughts and Experiences.

Objectives
- Identify words that rhyme.
- Respond to text through art, writing, and/or drama.

1. Tell students they are going to create their own silly rhymes by completing a sentence that you start.

   ▸ A possible sentence starter might be "A duck . . ."
   ▸ Another possible sentence starter might be "An ape . . ."

2. Have students think of some rhyming words to complete your sentence starter. If students have trouble coming up with their own rhymes to complete your sentence, give them a longer sentence starter and have them think of one rhyming word to complete it.

   ▸ A longer sentence starter might be "A duck driving a truck got . . ."
   ▸ Another longer sentence starter might be "An ape in a cape eating . . ."

3. Have students dictate their rhyme.

4. Write the rhyme students dictate in their journal.

   ▸ If students are ready to write on their own, allow them to do so.

5. Have students read aloud the rhyme **with** you as you track the words with your finger.

6. Have students draw a picture of their rhyme.

TIP The amount of time students need to complete this activity will vary. Students need only work for the remaining time of the lesson. If students have more that they would like to do, they can complete it at a later time.

Explore "Tongue-Twisters"

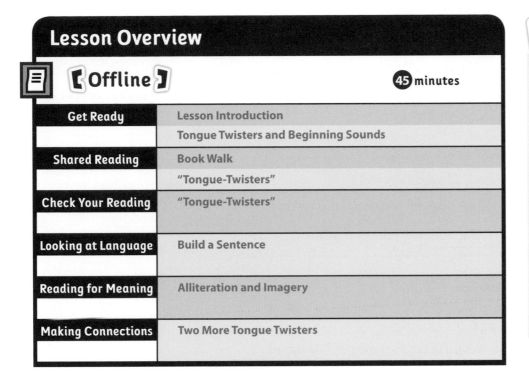

Lesson Overview

[Offline]   **45** minutes

Get Ready	Lesson Introduction
	Tongue Twisters and Beginning Sounds
Shared Reading	Book Walk
	"Tongue-Twisters"
Check Your Reading	"Tongue-Twisters"
Looking at Language	Build a Sentence
Reading for Meaning	Alliteration and Imagery
Making Connections	Two More Tongue Twisters

Advance Preparation

Cut out and tape together the sentence strip on page LC 57 in *K¹² Language Arts Activity Book* for Looking at Language.

Big Ideas

- ▶ Shared reading allows students to observe and practice the reading behaviors of proficient readers.
- ▶ The use of imagery and sensory language creates detailed pictures in the reader's mind, so the reader can understand and appreciate the ideas and feelings the writer conveys.
- ▶ Readers who visualize, or form mental pictures, while they read have better recall of text than those who do not.

[Materials]

Supplied

- *Ready . . . Set . . . Read! The Beginning Reader's Treasury*, pp. 124–127
- *K¹² Language Arts Activity Book*, pp. LC 57, 59
- *K¹² My Journal*, pp. 2–53

Also Needed

- crayons
- index cards
- scissors, adult
- scissors, round-end safety
- tape, clear

Poetry Synopsis

Telling tongue twisters is a tricky treat!

Keywords

alliteration – the use of words with the same or close to the same beginning sounds

table of contents – a list at the start of a book that gives the titles of the book's stories, poems, articles, chapters, or nonfiction pieces and the pages where they can be found

 **Offline** **45** minutes

Work **together** with students to complete Get Ready, Shared Reading, Check Your Reading, Looking at Language, Reading for Meaning, and Making Connections activities.

Get Ready ....

Lesson Introduction

Prepare students for listening to and discussing "Tongue-Twisters" by Joanna Cole and Stephanie Calmenson.

1. Tell students that you are going to read "Tongue-Twisters."

2. Explain that before you read, you will get ready by discussing what makes a sentence a tongue twister.

 Objectives

- Identify structure of poems and poetic elements: rhyme, rhythm, repetition, and/or alliteration.
- Use visualizing to aid understanding of text.

Tongue Twisters and Beginning Sounds

Explore alliteration.

1. Tell students that a **tongue twister** is a sentence in which most of the words begin with the same sound and can be hard to say. For example, "Sid sipped slimy sour soup." All the words in this tongue twister begin with the sound /s/.

2. Explain that saying a tongue twister can be a sort of game. The faster you say a tongue twister, the harder it is to say without stumbling over a word or two.

   ▸ Have students repeat the tongue twister about Sid several times, going faster and faster.

3. Tell students that tongue twisters are not only fun to say, but the words usually paint a picture in your head.

   ▸ What do you see in your head when you hear the tongue twister "Sid sipped slimy sour soup"? Answers will vary.

4. Tell students to listen as you **read aloud** the following tongue twister.

   Hank helped a hairy hog hide his head in hay.

   ▸ What sound do most of the words in the tongue twister begin with? /h/
   ▸ What do you see in your head when you hear the tongue twister? Answers will vary.

TIP Although an objective for this activity is to identify alliteration, there is no need to introduce the term to students at this time.

Shared Reading ....

Book Walk

Prepare students by taking them on a Book Walk of "Tongue-Twisters." Scan the tongue twisters together and ask students to make predictions about the tongue twisters.

1. Turn to the **table of contents** in *Ready . . . Set . . . Read!* Help students find "Tongue-Twisters" and turn to that page.

2. Point to and read aloud the **title**.

   ▸ What do you think these sentences will be like? Possible answers: tongue twisters; they'll be hard to say; they'll have words that start with the same sound.

3. Have students look at the **pictures**. Answers to questions may vary.

   ▸ Have you ever heard the tongue twister "Peter Piper picked a peck of pickled peppers"?
   ▸ Do you know any other tongue twisters?
   ▸ Can you think of five words that start with the sound /f/?

"Tongue-Twisters"

It's time to read aloud the tongue twisters.

1. Have students sit next to you so that they can see the pictures and words while you read aloud.

2. **Read aloud all the tongue twisters.** Track with your finger so students can follow along.

Check Your Reading ....

"Tongue-Twisters"

Check students' comprehension of "Tongue-Twisters."

1. Remind students that some books and magazines have a table of contents.

   ▸ Where is the table of contents? at the beginning of a book or magazine
   ▸ What does the table of contents list? the titles of stories, poems, or articles and the pages they're on
   ▸ Find the table of contents in *Ready . . . Set . . . Read!* On which page does it say "Tongue-Twisters" begins? page 124

2. Reread the tongue twister at the top of page 125.

   ▸ What sound do most of the words in the tongue twister begin with? /b/

3. Ask students the following questions.

   ▸ What did Sue see? sheep in shoes
   ▸ What did Gwen grab? green glue

 If students have trouble responding to a question, help them locate the answer in the text or pictures.

Objectives

- Make predictions based on text, illustrations, and/or prior knowledge.
- Activate prior knowledge by previewing text and/or discussing topic.
- Read and listen to a variety of texts for information and pleasure independently or as part of a group.

Objectives

- Identify the function of and locate information with a table of contents.
- Identify structure of poems and poetic elements: rhyme, rhythm, repetition, and/or alliteration.
- Answer questions requiring literal recall of details.

Looking at Language

Build a Sentence

Reread "Tongue-Twisters" from *Ready . . . Set . . . Read!* with a focus on the word order of a complete sentence. Gather the sentence strip that you prepared from page LC 57 in *K¹² Language Arts Activity Book,* scissors, and index cards.

1. Explain to students that a tongue twister is usually one complete sentence. What makes that sentence a tongue twister is that most of the words in the sentence start with the same sound.

2. Track with your finger as you read aloud the tongue twister on the sentence strip. Then have students read aloud the tongue twister with you.

   ► What sound does each word in the tongue twister start with? /f/

3. Tell students that a complete sentence has a naming part and an action part. Usually the naming part comes first and is followed by the action part. To figure out if our tongue twister is a complete sentence, we can ask ourselves some questions.

   ► Who is the sentence about? Fran
   ► What does Fran do? fries five flat fish
   ► Which word in the action part of the sentence is the action word? fries
   ► Does our sentence have a naming part? Yes
   ► Is the naming part of our sentence followed by an action part? Yes
   ► Is this tongue twister a complete sentence? Yes

4. Explain to students that knowing the parts of a complete sentence can help them to read and write other sentences.

5. Tell them that they are going to break up the tongue twister into individual words. Then they will put it back together by thinking about the order of words in a complete sentence.

6. Explain to students that they will first build a complete sentence with just three of the words, and then they will add describing words to rebuild the complete tongue twister.

7. Have students cut the sentence strip into individual words.

8. Mix up the words and lay them out. Point to and read each word aloud **with students**.

9. Have students rebuild a complete sentence with three words. Ask the following questions to help students with placing the three words in the correct order.

   ► Which word comes first? Who is the sentence about? Fran
   ► Which single word names the action? What does Fran do? fries
   ► Which word tells what Fran fries? fish
   ► What does the sentence say so far? Fran fries fish.

Objectives

- Identify beginning sounds in words.
- Recognize word groups that are sentences.
- Use context and sentence structure to support decoding.
- Use the correct word order in sentences.

10. Tell students that they now have a complete sentence, but they will add the other two words to the sentence and make the tongue twister more interesting and difficult. To do this, they will have to think about where to put describing words in the sentence so that it makes sense.

11. Point to and read the word *five*. Then have students put the word at the end of the complete sentence.

   ▸ Does our sentence make sense if it says *Fran fries fish five*? No
   ▸ Where should we put the word *five* so that our sentence makes sense? in front of *fish*

12. Have students place *five* in front of *fish*.

   ▸ What does the sentence say now? Fran fries five fish.

13. Have students place the word *flat* where they think it belongs in the sentence.

   ▸ If students have placed *flat* in the wrong place, ask them to read the sentence aloud and think about whether or not it sounds right. Have them do this until they are able to put *flat* in the correct place.

14. After students have rebuilt the tongue twister correctly, have them read it aloud while tracking with their finger.

   ▸ Who is the sentence about? Fran
   ▸ What does Fran do? fries five flat fish

15. If time allows, write the words of another tongue twister on index cards and have students rebuild the sentence following the same process.

Reading for Meaning

Alliteration and Mental Imagery

Explore alliteration and mental imagery in "Tongue-Twisters." Gather *K¹² My Journal* and have students turn to the next available page for **drawing and writing** in Thoughts and Experiences.

1. Remind students that most of the words in a tongue twister begin with the same sound, which makes them fun to listen to and hard to say.

2. Reread the tongue twister at the top of page 127.

   ▸ What sound do all of the words in the tongue twister begin with? /g/

3. Reread the tongue twister at the bottom of page 127.

   ▸ What sound do most of the words in the tongue twister begin with? /d/

4. Remind students that the words in tongue twisters usually help readers paint a picture in their heads.

5. Reread the tongue twister at the top of page 125.

   ▸ What word does the author use to describe the bridges? blue
   ▸ What word does the author use to describe the blocks? big
   ▸ Why do you think the author used these words in the tongue twister? Guide students to recognize that the words begin with the sound /b/ and help readers imagine a picture in their heads.

6. Tell students to close their eyes as you **read aloud** the following tongue twister.

   Paul pulled the pink pig from the pail of purple paint.

7. Have students draw a picture in their journal of what they imagine when they hear the tongue twister.

   ▸ Which words help you see this picture in your head? Answers will vary.

Objectives

- Identify beginning sounds in words.
- Respond to poetic devices of rhyme, rhythm, and/or alliteration.
- Identify author's use of imagery and descriptive language.
- Demonstrate visualizing through drawing, discussion, and/or writing.

8. Have students read the tongue twister aloud **with** you as you track the words with your finger.

 The amount of time students need to complete this activity will vary. Students need only work for about 15 minutes. If students have more they would like to do, they can complete it at a later time.

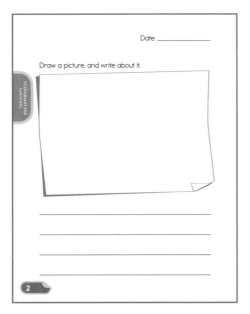

Date _____

Draw a picture, and write about it.

2

Making Connections

Two More Tongue Twisters

Have students create their own tongue twister to demonstrate their understanding of descriptive language. Turn to page LC 59 in *K¹² Language Arts Activity Book*.

1. Tell students they are going to create their own tongue twister by completing the sentence on the Activity Book page.

2. Read aloud the sentence starter and ask students how they would complete it. If necessary, remind students that most of the words in their tongue twister should start with the same sound. If students are having difficulty, help them get started by asking the following questions.

   ▸ What are some action words that start with the letter *b*?
   ▸ Can you think of other words that start with the letter *b*?

3. Write the tongue twister students dictate on the blank lines following the sentence starter.

   ▸ If students are ready to write on their own, allow them to do so.

Objectives
- Create mental imagery using sensory and descriptive language.
- Demonstrate use of poetic elements of rhyme, rhythm, and/or alliteration.

4. Have students read the tongue twister aloud **with** you as you track the words with your finger.

5. Tell students to think of another tongue twister without using a sentence starter.

6. Have students dictate their tongue twister. If students have trouble coming up with their own tongue twister, give them a sentence starter.

   ▸ A possible sentence starter might be "Five fast foxes . . . "
   ▸ Another possible sentence starter might be "Sam saw six seals . . . "

7. Write the tongue twister students dictate on the blank lines.

   ▸ If students are ready to write on their own, allow them to do so.

8. Have students read the tongue twister aloud **with** you as you track the words with your finger.

9. Have students draw a picture of one of the tongue twisters.

TIP The amount of time students need to complete this activity will vary. Students need only work for the remaining time of the lesson. If students have more they would like to do, they can complete it at a later time.

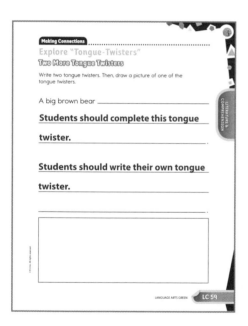

Introduce "Morris Has a Cold"

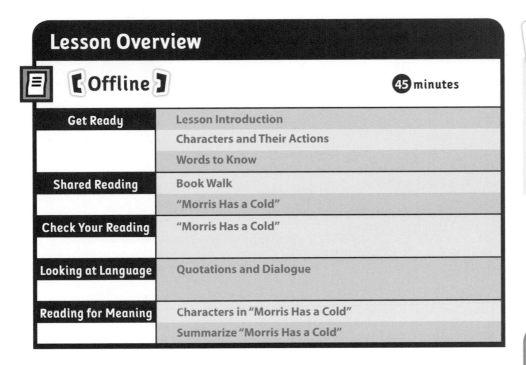

Lesson Overview

[Offline] 45 minutes

Get Ready	Lesson Introduction
	Characters and Their Actions
	Words to Know
Shared Reading	Book Walk
	"Morris Has a Cold"
Check Your Reading	"Morris Has a Cold"
Looking at Language	Quotations and Dialogue
Reading for Meaning	Characters in "Morris Has a Cold"
	Summarize "Morris Has a Cold"

[Materials]

Supplied
- *Ready . . . Set . . . Read! The Beginning Reader's Treasury*, pp. 66–82
- *K¹² Language Arts Activity Book*, pp. LC 61–62

Story Synopsis
Morris the Moose is not only sick with a cold but has trouble communicating with his helpful friend, Boris the Bear.

Keywords
character – a person or animal in a story

self-monitor – to notice if you do or do not understand what you are reading

summarize – to tell in order the most important ideas or events of a text

summary – a short retelling that includes only the most important ideas or events of a text

Advance Preparation

Before beginning the Shared Reading, read "Morris Has a Cold" to locate Words to Know in the text. Preview the Reading Aid on pages LC 61 and 62 in *K¹² Language Arts Activity Book* to prepare the materials for Looking at Language.

In the Looking at Language activity, students take a close look at the use of quotation marks in dialogue. Please note that the ending quotation mark is missing from the sentence *Morris said, "I will see...* Let students know that the author should have closed the quotation marks after the ellipsis.

Big Ideas

- ▶ To understand and interpret a story, readers need to understand and describe characters and what they do.
- ▶ Shared reading allows students to observe and practice the reading behaviors of proficient readers.
- ▶ During shared-reading activities, students learn more about how print works.
- ▶ Comprehension requires the reader to self-monitor understanding.

 **Offline** **45** minutes

Work **together** with students to complete Get Ready, Shared Reading, Check Your Reading, Looking at Language, and Reading for Meaning activities.

Get Ready

Lesson Introduction

Prepare students for listening to and discussing "Morris Has a Cold" by Bernard Wiseman.

1. Tell students that you are going to read "Morris Has a Cold," a story about a moose who is sick and his friend who helps him get better.

2. Explain that before you read the story you will get ready by discussing the story structure element of characters and characters' actions.

 Objectives

- Identify details that explain characters' actions and feelings.
- Build vocabulary through listening, reading, and discussion.
- Use new vocabulary in written and spoken sentences.

Characters and Their Actions

Explore the story structure element of characters and characters' actions.

1. Have students explain what a character is. If students have trouble, remind them that the people and animals in a story are called **characters**.

2. Remind students that we can learn a lot about a story's characters from what they say and do.

3. **Read aloud** the following story.

Miguel is Jesse's older brother. Jesse really likes playing with Miguel, but Miguel spends most of his time hanging out with his friends. One day, Miguel and Jesse were outside. "I really wish I knew how to ride a skateboard," Miguel said. "I can teach you," Jesse replied. He gave Miguel a helmet and spent the rest of the afternoon teaching him how to skateboard. By the end of the day, Miguel was riding around their driveway like a pro. "Thanks, little brother. You're a great teacher!" he said to Jesse with a grin. Jesse smiled back. "I'm glad we had fun together! Next time we'll work on tricks," he said.

- ▸ Who are the characters in the story? Miguel and Jesse
- ▸ How do you think Jesse feels at the end of the story? happy   What did the characters say or do that makes you think this? Possible answers: Miguel was hanging out with Jesse instead of his friends; Miguel called Jesse a great teacher; Jesse was smiling; Jesse said he was glad they had fun together.
- ▸ How do you think Miguel feels at the end of the story? happy   What did the characters do or say that makes you think this? Possible answers: Jesse said he could teach Miguel to skateboard; Miguel was riding around like a pro; Miguel was grinning; Miguel said thanks and called his brother a good teacher.

TIP To help students answer the questions, as necessary, reread the text, emphasizing specific actions of the characters or specific things the characters say.

Words to Know

Before reading "Morris Has a Cold," go over Words to Know with students.

1. Read aloud the word and have students repeat it.

2. Ask students if they know what the word means.

   ▸ If students know the word's meaning, have them define it and use it in a sentence.

   ▸ If students don't know the word's meaning, read them the definition and discuss the word with them.

cold – common sickness that often causes coughing, sneezing, and a runny nose

Shared Reading

Book Walk

Prepare students for reading by taking them on a Book Walk of "Morris Has a Cold." Scan the story together and ask students to make predictions about the story. Answers to questions may vary.

1. Turn to the **table of contents** in *Ready...Set...Read!* Help students find "Morris Has a Cold" and turn to that page.

2. Point to and read aloud the **title of the story**.

3. Have students point to the **name of the author** while you read the name aloud.

   ▸ What do you think this story is about?

4. Have students look at the **pictures**.

   ▸ Where do you think the story takes place?
   ▸ What do you think might happen in the story?
   ▸ How do you feel when you have a cold? What helps you feel better?

Objectives

- Make predictions based on text, illustrations, and/or prior knowledge.
- Activate prior knowledge by previewing text and/or discussing topic.
- Read and listen to a variety of texts for information and pleasure independently or as part of a group.

"Morris Has a Cold"

It's time to read aloud the story.

1. Have students sit next to you so that they can see the pictures and words while you read aloud.

2. Tell students to listen for the way characters act and how they feel in the story.

3. Tell students to listen for information that can answer the question, "Who did what?" so that they can do a summary of the story.

4. **Read aloud the entire story.** Track with your finger so students can follow along.

Check Your Reading

"Morris Has a Cold"

Check students' comprehension of "Morris Has a Cold."

- ▶ Who are the characters in "Morris Has a Cold"? Morris and Boris
- ▶ What kind of animal is Morris? a moose
- ▶ What kind of animal is Boris? a bear
- ▶ What is wrong with Morris? He has a cold; he doesn't feel well.
- ▶ How does Boris help Morris? He gives Morris a bowl of soup; he feeds Morris soup.

 TIP If students have trouble responding to a question, help them locate the answer in the text or pictures.

 Objectives
- Identify character(s).
- Answer questions requiring literal recall of details.

Looking at Language

Quotations and Dialogue

Reread "Morris Has a Cold" with a focus on quotation marks and dialogue. Gather the Reading Aid on pages LC 61 and 62 in *K¹² Language Arts Activity Book*.

1. Before you reread, ask students if they notice that Morris and Boris speak aloud to each other in the story. When characters talk to each other, we call this **dialogue**.

2. Explain that there are clues in the story that let us know a character is speaking aloud. These clues help us know when Morris and Boris are having a conversation, or dialogue.

3. Tell students that they will reread the story with you. As you read aloud together, you will stop at certain points to look at the clues that tell us a character is speaking aloud.

Objectives
- Recognize quotations in dialogue.
- Read aloud grade-level text with appropriate expression, accuracy, and rate.
- Demonstrate one-to-one correspondence (voice-to-print).

4. As you read aloud, **encourage students to chime in and read aloud with you**.

5. Refer to the Reading Aid.

Reading Aid Tear out the Reading Aid for this reading selection. Follow the instructions for folding the page, and then use the page as a guide as you reread the selection with students.

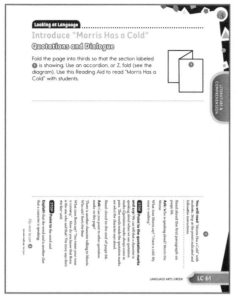
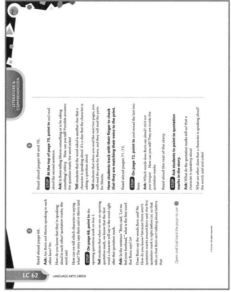

Reading for Meaning

Characters in "Morris Has a Cold"
Explore characters.

1. Remind students that we can learn a lot about characters by their actions— the things they do and why they do them. Thinking about these things helps a reader better understand the characters and the story.

2. Ask the following questions to check students' comprehension of characters and their actions.

   ▶ Why does Boris feel Morris's forehead? to see if Morris's forehead is hot
   ▶ Why does Boris tell Morris to lie down? He wants Morris to get some rest since he is sick.
   ▶ Why does Boris give Morris a bowl of soup? to make Morris feel better
   ▶ Why does Morris want a big breakfast in the morning? because he feels better
   ▶ Is Boris a good friend to Morris? How do you know this? Yes. Possible answers: Boris checks Morris's forehead; Boris wants Morris to rest; Boris makes Morris soup.

Objectives
- Identify details that explain characters' actions and feelings.
- Summarize a story.
- Self-monitor comprehension of text.

Summarize "Morris Has a Cold"

Explore summarizing.

1. Remind students that a **summary** is a very short retelling of the most important ideas or events of a text. A summary should answer the question, "Who did what?"

2. Have students practice summarizing.

   ▸ Who did what in the beginning of the story? Tell what happens in one or two sentences. Example: Morris tells Boris he's sick.
   ▸ Who did what in the middle of the story? Tell what happens in one or two sentences. Example: Boris tries to figure out if Morris is sick. Boris tries to make Morris feel better.
   ▸ Who did what at the end of the story? Tell what happens in one or two sentences. Example: Morris feels better. Boris tells Morris not to get sick again
   ▸ Summarize the whole story in one or two sentences that answer the question, "Who did what?" Example: Morris is sick and Boris tries to make him feel better. Morris gets better and Boris tells him not to get sick again.

3. Ask the following questions to check students' comprehension of summarizing.

   ▸ What is a summary? a short retelling that includes only the most important ideas or events of a text
   ▸ What question does a summary answer? Who did what?
   ▸ Were you able to answer the question, "Who did what?" for this story? Answers will vary.
   ▸ Do you think that you understand the story? Answers will vary.

(TIP) If students don't think they understand the story, reread the story aloud, pausing to let students ask questions as you read.

Explore "Morris Has a Cold"

Lesson Overview

Offline		45 minutes
Get Ready	Lesson Introduction	
	Words to Know	
Shared Reading	Book Walk	
	"Morris Has a Cold"	
Reading for Meaning	Author's Purpose	
	Illustrations Tell About Characters	
Making Connections	What It Sounds Like, What It Means	

Materials

Supplied

- *Ready...Set...Read!
  The Beginning Reader's
  Treasury,* pp. 66–82
- *K¹² Language Arts Activity
  Book,* pp. LC 63–65

Also Needed

- crayons
- index cards (2)

Keywords

author's purpose – the
reason the author wrote a
text: to entertain, to inform,
to express an opinion, or to
persuade

character – a person or
animal in a story

illustration – a drawing

Advance Preparation

For Looking at Language, preview the Reading Aid on pages LC 63 and 64 in
K¹² Language Arts Activity Book to prepare the materials, and prepare two index cards
by writing *no* on one and *NO!* on another.

Big Ideas

- ▶ Readers must focus on the specific language of a text to aid in interpretation.
- ▶ Shared reading allows students to observe and practice the reading behaviors
  of proficient readers.
- ▶ During shared-reading activities, students learn more about how print works.
- ▶ To understand and interpret a story, readers need to understand and describe
  characters and what they do.

 **45 minutes**

Work **together** with students to complete Get Ready, Shared Reading, Reading for Meaning, and Making Connections activities.

Get Ready

Lesson Introduction

Prepare students for listening to and discussing "Morris Has a Cold" by Bernard Wiseman.

1. Tell students that you are going to reread "Morris Has a Cold."

2. Explain that this lesson will focus on the reasons why authors write stories or articles and how illustrations give information about what characters are doing and feeling.

Objectives
- Build vocabulary through listening, reading, and discussion.
- Use new vocabulary in written and spoken sentences.

Words to Know

Before reading "Morris has a Cold," go over Words to Know with students.

1. Read aloud the word and have students repeat it.

2. Ask students if they know what the word means.

   ▸ If students know the word's meaning, have them define it and use it in a sentence.
   ▸ If students don't know the word's meaning, read them the definition and discuss the word with them.

cold – common sickness that often causes coughing, sneezing, and a runny nose

Shared Reading

Book Walk

Prepare students by taking them on a Book Walk of "Morris Has a Cold." Scan the story together to revisit the characters and events.

1. Turn to the selection. Point to and read aloud the **title of the story**.

2. Have students point to the **name of the author** while you read the name aloud.

3. Have students review the **pictures**.

   ▸ Who are the characters in the story? Morris and Boris
   ▸ What's wrong with Morris? He's sick.
   ▸ Why does Boris give Morris a bowl of soup? to help Morris feel better

"Morris Has a Cold"

It's time to reread the story. Tell students that you will reread "Morris Has a Cold" with a focus on clues in the text that tell readers when to read with a loud, raised voice. Gather the index cards and Reading Aid on pages LC 63 and 64 in *K¹² Language Arts Activity Book*.

1. Before you reread, ask students if they noticed that Boris gets frustrated and angry with Morris in the story.

2. Explain that we can see how Boris is feeling by the expression on his face in the illustrations. Along with the illustrations, there are clues in the text that tell us when Boris is getting angry and raising his voice.

3. Point to the index cards with *no* and *NO!* written on them. Tell students that each card has the same word, but when you read them aloud, they will sound different.

4. **Point to and read aloud** the word *no* in lowercase letters in a normal voice and the one in capital letters followed by an exclamation mark with your voice raised.

   ▸ What did you notice about the different ways I read the word *no*? One was in a normal voice, and the other was in a loud voice.
   ▸ Which way do you think somebody says *no* when they are feeling frustrated or angry? in a loud voice

Objectives
- Activate prior knowledge by previewing text and/or discussing topic.
- Read and listen to a variety of texts for information and pleasure independently or as part of a group.
- Identify and describe the use of print features: boldface, underlining, highlighting, italic, capital letters.
- Identify sentences that are exclamations.
- Read aloud grade-level text with appropriate expression, accuracy, and rate.

5. Show students the word *NO!* written in capital letters.

   ▶ What do you notice about how the word is written? It's written in all capital letters; there's an exclamation mark.

6. Tell students that when a word is written all in capital letters, we should read it in a loud voice.

7. Explain that the mark after the word *NO!* in capital letters is called an **exclamation mark**. An exclamation mark is another clue that tells us we should read in an expressive, raised voice.

8. Have students read aloud the first card **with you in a normal voice**. Then have them read aloud the second card **with you with their voice raised**.

9. Tell students that they will **read aloud the story with you**. As you read aloud together, you will stop at certain points to look at the clues that tell us a character is speaking in a loud, raised voice.

10. As you read aloud, **encourage students to chime in and read aloud with you**.

11. Refer to the Reading Aid.

Reading Aid Tear out the Reading Aid for this reading selection. Follow the instructions for folding the page, and then use the page as a guide as you reread the selection with students.

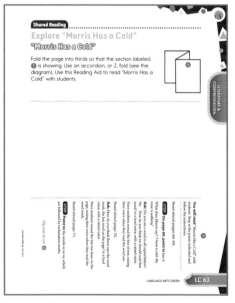
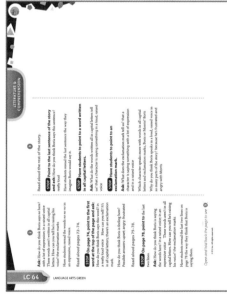

Reading for Meaning

Author's Purpose

Explore the reasons why authors write a text.

1. Remind students that an author has a reason, or purpose, for writing a story or article.

2. Ask the following questions.

   ▸ Why did the author write "Morris Has a Cold"? to entertain us
   ▸ How can you tell the author wrote the story to entertain us? It's silly.

Illustrations Tell About Characters

Explore how illustrations give information about what characters are doing and feeling.

1. Tell students that the pictures in a story can give us extra information about what the characters are doing and how they are feeling.

2. Point to the pictures on pages 70 and 71 and reread the text.

3. Explain that Morris doesn't understand what Boris means when he asks how Morris's throat feels. The pictures help us see that Morris is confused, because one picture shows him touching the outside of his throat and the other picture shows him about to touch the inside of his throat.

4. Point to the picture on page 73 and reread the text.

   ▸ Does Morris understand what Boris wants him to do when he tells Morris to stick out his tongue? No   How do you know that Morris doesn't understand? He's sticking out his tongue in a silly way.
   ▸ Look at Boris in the picture. How do you think he feels? Possible answers: mad; angry; frustrated   What do you see in the picture that makes you think that? He's making a mean face; his fists are clenched.   Why do you think Boris is feeling that way? because Morris doesn't understand him and he keeps doing silly things

5. Point to the pictures on pages 77 and 78 and reread the text.

   ▸ Does Morris understand what Boris means when he tells Morris to use the spoon? No   How do you know that Morris doesn't understand? He's using the spoon the wrong way in both pictures.

6. Point to the picture on page 79.

   ▸ How do you think Boris is feeling? Possible answers: mad; upset; frustrated   Why is he feeling that way? because Morris doesn't know how to use a spoon, so now Boris has to feed him

7. Point to the picture on page 82.

 ▶ How do you think Boris is feeling? mad   What do you see in the pictures
   that makes you think that? His arms are raised and he's leaning over Morris;
   his eyes look angry; his mouth is open like he's yelling at Morris.   Why do
   you think Boris feels that way? It was hard to take care of Morris when he
   was sick because he didn't understand what Boris wanted him to do.

Making Connections ....

What It Sounds Like, What It Means

Guide students to draw pictures of a well-known idiom. Turn to page LC 65 in
K¹² Language Arts Activity Book.

1. Tell students that sometimes we say phrases that sound like they mean one
   thing, but they really mean something else.

2. **Read aloud** the following sentence.

   Everyone ran inside when it started raining cats and dogs.

3. Ask students what the phrase *raining cats and dogs* sounds like it means, and
   what they think it actually means. Guide students to recognize that *raining
   cats and dogs* means it's raining very hard, but it sounds like cats and dogs are
   falling out of the sky.

4. Have students draw two pictures on the Activity Book page. The first picture
   should show what the words in the sample sentence sound like they mean, and
   the second should show what the words actually mean.

TIP The amount of time students need to complete this activity will vary. Students
need only work for the remaining time of the lesson. If students have more they
would like to do, they can complete it at a later time.

> ### Objectives
> - Use context and sentence
>   structure to determine
>   meaning of words, phrases,
>   and/or sentences.
> - Identify and define words'
>   and phrases' literal and
>   nonliteral meanings.

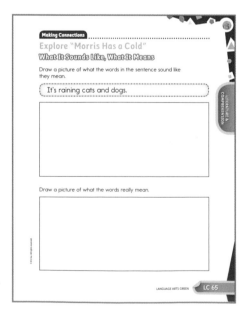

Introduce *Amelia Bedelia*

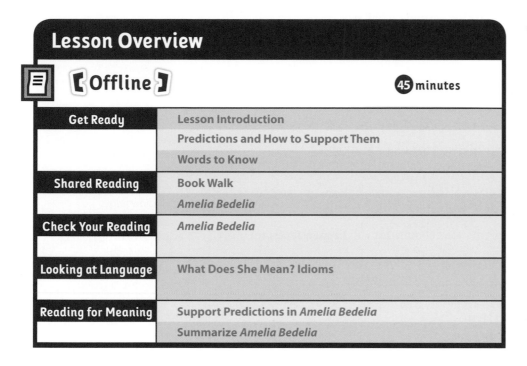

Lesson Overview

[Offline]   45 minutes

Get Ready	Lesson Introduction
	Predictions and How to Support Them
	Words to Know
Shared Reading	Book Walk
	Amelia Bedelia
Check Your Reading	*Amelia Bedelia*
Looking at Language	What Does She Mean? Idioms
Reading for Meaning	Support Predictions in *Amelia Bedelia*
	Summarize *Amelia Bedelia*

Advance Preparation

Before beginning the Shared Reading, read *Amelia Bedelia* to locate Words to Know in the text. Read the Shared Reading directions to be aware of stopping points in the story where students will make predictions. Preview the Reading Aid on pages LC 67 and 68 in *K¹² Language Arts Activity Book* to prepare the materials for Looking at Language.

Big Ideas

▶ Good readers interact with text to make logical predictions before reading; confirm predictions during reading; and revise or make new predictions as they read further.
▶ Shared reading allows students to observe and practice the reading behaviors of proficient readers.
▶ Readers must focus on the specific language of a text to aid in interpretation.

Materials

Supplied

- *Amelia Bedelia* by Peggy Parish
- *K¹² Language Arts Activity Book*, pp. LC 67–68

Story Synopsis

Amelia Bedelia follows directions *exactly*, which leads to hilarious consequences.

Keywords

character – a person or animal in a story

idiom – an expression that cannot be understood from its literal meaning

prediction – a guess about what might happen that is based on information in a story and what you already know

summarize – to tell in order the most important ideas or events of a text

summary – a short retelling that includes only the most important ideas or events of a text

 **45 minutes**

Work **together** with students to complete Get Ready, Shared Reading, Check Your Reading, Looking at Language, and Reading for Meaning activities.

Get Ready

Lesson Introduction
Prepare students for listening to and discussing *Amelia Bedelia* by Peggy Parish.

1. Tell students that you are going to read *Amelia Bedelia*, a story about a housekeeper who misunderstands directions.

2. Explain that before you read the story, you will get ready by discussing how to make a prediction.

3. Tell students that they will make predictions about what will happen at certain points in the story.

Objectives
- Make predictions before and during reading.
- Make predictions based on text, illustrations, and/or prior knowledge.
- Support predictions with evidence from text and/or prior knowledge.
- Build vocabulary through listening, reading, and discussion.
- Use new vocabulary in written and spoken sentences.

Predictions and How to Support Them
Explore how to make and support a prediction.

1. Have students explain what predictions are and how we make them when we read. If students have trouble responding, remind them of the following.

   ▸ **Predictions** are guesses about what will happen in a story.
   ▸ We use clues in the story and what we know from our personal experience to make predictions.

2. Have students explain why we make predictions.

   ▸ If students have trouble responding, remind them that making predictions makes us want to keep reading a story to see if what we predict happens or not.

3. Have students practice making and supporting a prediction. **Read aloud** the following story.

   Claire looked outside to make sure it wasn't raining. Then she put on her shoes and put the leash on her dog.

   ▸ What do you think will happen next? Claire will take her dog for a walk.
   ▸ What clues in the story make you think this? Claire looks outside to make sure it isn't raining, and then she puts the leash on her dog.
   ▸ What clues from your own experience made you predict this? Possible answers: Claire checked to make sure it wasn't raining because most people don't go for walks in the rain; Claire put on her shoes, which is what I do before I go outside; Claire put the leash on her dog and a leash is what people use when they take their dogs on walks.

TIP Predictions are neither right nor wrong. We make the best prediction we can, based on the available information. Do not describe a prediction as "wrong" because this may discourage students from making predictions.

Words to Know

Before reading *Amelia Bedelia*, go over Words to Know with students.

1. Read aloud each word and have students repeat it.

2. Ask students if they know what each word means.

   ► If students know a word's meaning, have them define it and use it in a sentence.
   ► If students don't know a word's meaning, read them the definition and discuss the word with them.

container – something, such as a box, that can hold something else
drapes – a long cloth that covers windows; curtains
fade – to lose color
fire – to let somebody go from a job
icebox – an old-fashioned refrigerator
snip – to cut with scissors

Shared Reading

Book Walk

Prepare students for reading by taking them on a Book Walk of *Amelia Bedelia*. Scan the beginning of the book together, and ask students to make predictions about the story. Answers to questions may vary.

1. Have students look at the picture on the cover. Point to and read aloud the **book title**.

   ► What do you think the book is about?

2. Have students point to the **name of the author and illustrator** while you read the names aloud.

3. Have students look at the **pictures up to page 15**. Then discuss the following questions to prepare for reading.

   ► Where do you think the story takes place?
   ► What do you think might happen in the story?
   ► What do you think it means when someone says they got up on the wrong side of the bed?

Objectives

- Make predictions based on text, illustrations, and/or prior knowledge.
- Activate prior knowledge by previewing text and/or discussing topic.
- Make predictions before and during reading.
- Read and listen to a variety of texts for information and pleasure independently or as part of a group.

Amelia Bedelia

It's time to read aloud the story and ask students to make predictions.

1. Have students sit next to you so that they can see the pictures and words while you read aloud.

2. Tell students to listen for clues in the story about what might happen next.

3. **Begin to read aloud.** Pause at the following points in the story to ask students what they predict will happen next. Jot down their predictions for later reference.

> ► At the end of page 25
> ► At the end of page 29
> ► At the end of page 42
> ► At the end of page 45
> ► At the end of page 58

4. **Continue to read aloud the story.** Track with your finger so students can follow along.

> ► Emphasize Words to Know as you come to them. If appropriate, use the pictures to help show what each word means.
> ► Remember to stop at the points listed in Step 3 and have students make predictions.

Check Your Reading

Amelia Bedelia

Check students' comprehension of *Amelia Bedelia*.

1. Have students retell *Amelia Bedelia* in their own words to develop grammar, vocabulary, comprehension, and fluency skills.

2. Ask students the following questions.

> ► Who are the characters in *Amelia Bedelia*? Amelia Bedelia; Mrs. Rogers; Mr. Rogers
> ► Who is the main character? Amelia Bedelia   How do you know Amelia Bedelia is the main character? She says and does the most in the story.
> ► What surprise does Amelia Bedelia make for Mr. and Mrs. Rogers? a lemon meringue pie
> ► How does Mrs. Rogers feel about the way Amelia Bedelia completes everything on the list? She is mad.
> ► What happens when Mrs. Rogers opens her mouth to fire Amelia Bedelia? Mr. Rogers puts a bite of pie into her mouth.
> ► Why doesn't Mrs. Rogers fire Amelia Bedelia? because she and Mr. Rogers want her to keep making lemon meringue pies for them

 TIP If students have trouble responding to a question, help them locate the answer in the text or pictures.

Objectives
- Retell or dramatize a story.
- Identify character(s).
- Identify the main character(s).
- Answer questions requiring literal recall of details.

Looking at Language

What Does She Mean? Idioms

Reread *Amelia Bedelia* with a focus on literal and nonliteral meanings of phrases. Gather the Reading Aid on pages LC 67 and 68 in *K¹² Language Arts Activity Book*.

1. Explain to students that one of the things that makes *Amelia Bedelia* fun is the unusual way that she understands common phrases.
   Say: If I'm feeling tired, I might say, "I'm going to hit the hay."

   ▸ What do you think I'm going to do? go to bed
   ▸ What would Amelia Bedelia think that I'm going to do? punch or hit a bunch of hay like a horse would eat

2. Tell students that this kind of phrase is called an **idiom**. An idiom is a group of words that does not mean what it actually says. It is a kind of descriptive language that authors use to make a story more interesting.

3. Explain that Amelia Bedelia understands idioms by thinking about what the words actually mean. She doesn't understand that the whole phrase means something different.

4. Tell students that they will reread the story with you. As you **read aloud together**, you will stop at certain points to discuss idioms and what they mean.

5. As you read aloud, **encourage students to chime in and read with you**.

6. Refer to the Reading Aid.

Reading Aid Tear out the Reading Aid for this reading selection. Follow the instructions for folding the page, and then use the page as a guide as you reread the selection with students.

Objectives
- Identify and define words' and phrases' literal and nonliteral meanings.
- Identify author's use of imagery and descriptive language.
- Read aloud grade-level text with appropriate expression, accuracy, and rate.

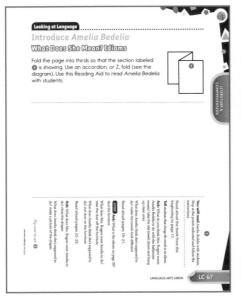
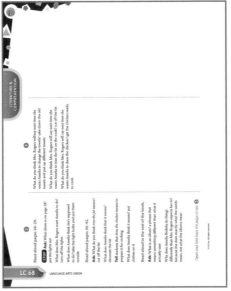

Reading for Meaning

Support Predictions in *Amelia Bedelia*

Revisit the predictions students made while reading the text.

Objectives

- Support predictions with evidence from text and/or prior knowledge.
- Summarize a story.

1. Remind students that good readers make predictions by using clues in the words and pictures when they read a story. Good readers can explain what clues they used to make a prediction.

2. **Have students explain how they made a particular prediction by citing clues from the story and personal experience.** Ask students the following questions. Refer to their predictions you wrote down as necessary. Answers to questions may vary.

   ▶ What did you predict would happen after Amelia Bedelia reads on her list that she needs to draw the drapes? What clues did you use to make this prediction?

   ▶ What did you predict would happen after Amelia Bedelia reads on her list that she needs to put the lights out when she's finished in the living room? What clues did you use to make this prediction?

   ▶ What did you predict would happen after Amelia Bedelia starts to dress the chicken? What clues did you use to make this prediction?

   ▶ What did you predict would happen after Amelia Bedelia meets Mr. and Mrs. Rogers at the door? What clues did you use to make this prediction?

   ▶ What did you predict would happen after Mrs. Rogers sees the way Amelia Bedelia dresses the chicken? What clues did you use to make this prediction?

Summarize *Amelia Bedelia*

Explore summarizing.

1. Have students explain what a summary is and what question a summary answers. If students have trouble, remind them that

   ▶ A summary is a short retelling of the most important ideas or events of a text.

   ▶ A summary answers the question, "Who did what?"

2. Have students practice summarizing.

   ▶ Who is the story about? Amelia Bedelia

   ▶ What does Amelia Bedelia do? Possible answers: She does everything on her list of chores the wrong way; she makes a mess in Mr. and Mrs. Rogers's house.

   ▶ How could you summarize the story? Guide students to answer the question, "Who did what?" Example: Amelia Bedelia does everything on her list of chores the wrong way and ends up making a mess in Mr. and Mrs. Rogers's house.

Explore *Amelia Bedelia*

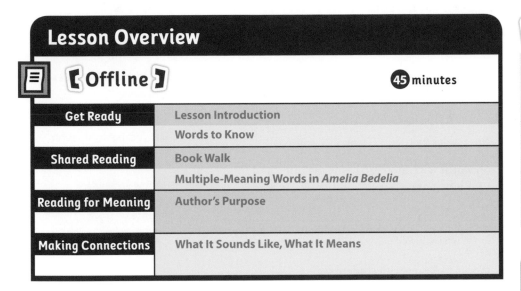

Lesson Overview

[Offline]   **45** minutes

Get Ready	Lesson Introduction
	Words to Know
Shared Reading	Book Walk
	Multiple-Meaning Words in *Amelia Bedelia*
Reading for Meaning	Author's Purpose
Making Connections	What It Sounds Like, What It Means

Advance Preparation

Preview the Reading Aid on pages LC 69 and 70 in *K¹² Language Arts Activity Book* to prepare the materials for the Shared Reading.

Big Ideas

- ▸ Readers must focus on the specific language of a text to aid in interpretation.
- ▸ Shared reading allows students to observe and practice the reading behaviors of proficient readers.
- ▸ To understand and interpret a story, readers need to understand and describe characters and what they do.

[Materials]

Supplied
- *Amelia Bedelia* by Peggy Parish
- *K¹² Language Arts Activity Book*, pp. LC 69–71

Also Needed
- crayons

Keywords

author's purpose – the reason the author wrote a text: to entertain, to inform, to express an opinion, or to persuade

multiple-meaning word – a word that has more than one meaning

 **Offline** **45** minutes

Work **together** with students to complete Get Ready, Shared Reading, Reading for Meaning, and Making Connections activities.

Get Ready

Lesson Introduction

Prepare students for listening to and discussing *Amelia Bedelia*.

1. Tell students you are going to reread *Amelia Bedelia*.

2. Explain that the lesson will focus on words with more than one meaning and on the author's reason, or purpose, for writing the story.

 Objectives

- Build vocabulary through listening, reading, and discussion.
- Use new vocabulary in written and spoken sentences.

Words to Know

Before reading *Amelia Bedelia*, go over Words to Know with students.

1. Read aloud each word and have students repeat it.

2. Ask students if they know what each word means.

   ► If students know a word's meaning, have them define it and use it in a sentence.
   ► If students don't know a word's meaning, read them the definition and discuss the word with them.

container – something, such as a box, that can hold something else
drapes – a long cloth that covers windows; curtains
fade – to lose color
fire – to let somebody go from a job
icebox – an old-fashioned refrigerator
snip – to cut with scissors

Shared Reading

Book Walk

Prepare students by taking them on a Book Walk of *Amelia Bedelia*. Scan the book together to revisit the characters and events.

1. Read aloud the **book title**.

2. Have students point to the **name of the author and illustrator** while you read the names aloud.

3. Look through the book. Have students review the **pictures**.

   ▶ Why does Mrs. Rogers get upset with Amelia Bedelia? because Amelia Bedelia doesn't do the things on her list they way Mrs. Rogers wants her to
   ▶ Why doesn't Mrs. Rogers fire Amelia Bedelia? because Mr. Rogers puts a bite of pie into her mouth; she wants to keep Amelia Bedelia so she will make more lemon meringue pies

Objectives

- Activate prior knowledge by previewing text and/or discussing topic.
- Read and listen to a variety of texts for information and pleasure independently or as part of a group.
- Identify and define multiple-meaning words.
- Read aloud grade-level text with appropriate expression, accuracy, and rate.

Multiple-Meaning Words in *Amelia Bedelia*

It's time to reread the story. Tell students that you will reread *Amelia Bedelia* with a focus on words with more than one meaning. Gather the Reading Aid on pages LC 69 and 70 in *K¹² Language Arts Activity Book*.

1. Before you reread, remind students that one of the things that makes *Amelia Bedelia* fun is the unusual way that Amelia follows directions.

   ▶ Mrs. Rogers asks Amelia to change the towels. What does Mrs. Rogers expect Amelia to do? take down the old towels and put up clean ones
   ▶ What does Amelia do? cuts the towels and makes them different

2. Tell students that the reason Amelia doesn't do what Mrs. Rogers expects is that the word *change* has more than one meaning. It can mean to make something different, and it can mean to replace with something that is the same.

   ▶ Which meaning of *change* is Amelia going by? to make something different
   ▶ Which meaning does Mrs. Rogers have in mind when she asks Amelia to change the towels? to replace something

3. Tell students that they will read the story with you. As you **read aloud together**, you will stop at certain points to discuss words that have more than one meaning.

4. As you read aloud, **encourage students to chime in and read with you**.

5. Refer to the Reading Aid.

Reading Aid Tear out the Reading Aid for this reading selection. Follow the instructions for folding the page, and then use the page as a guide as you reread the selection with students.

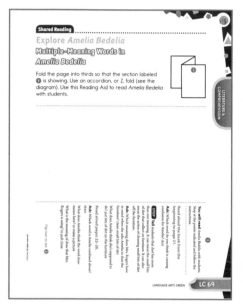
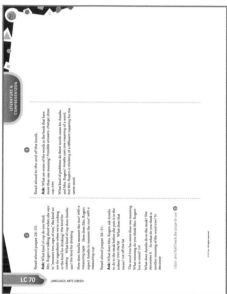

Reading for Meaning

Author's Purpose

Review author's purpose.

1. Remind students that an author has a reason, or purpose, for writing a story or article.

2. Ask the following questions.

   ▸ Why did Peggy Parish write *Amelia Bedelia*? to entertain us
   ▸ How can you tell the author wrote the story to entertain us? It's a silly story.
   ▸ How does Peggy Parish make the story funny? Guide students to recognize that the author plays with words to make the story silly.

3. Ask students the following questions to check their comprehension of author's purpose.

   ▸ What do we call the author's reason for writing a story or article? the author's purpose
   ▸ Authors write stories and articles for different reasons. What are some of the reasons? to teach something; to entertain; to convince the reader of something; to tell the reader what the author thinks about something

> **Objectives**
> • Identify the purpose of a text.
> • Identify the author's purpose.

Making Connections

What It Sounds Like, What It Means

Check students' understanding of the character Amelia Bedelia and her confusion of idioms. Turn to page LC 71 in *K¹² Language Arts Activity Book*.

1. Ask the following questions to check students' understanding of characters and their actions.

   ▸ What words would you use to describe Amelia Bedelia? Possible answers: nice; happy; thoughtful; hard-working   Why do you describe her that way? Give examples from the story. Possible answers: She bakes a pie for Mr. and Mrs. Rogers; she is always smiling; she does all the tasks on Mrs. Rogers's list, even though she does things the wrong way.

   ▸ Mrs. Rogers wants Amelia Bedelia to dust the furniture. What does Amelia Bedelia do? She sprinkles dusting powder on the furniture. Why does Amelia do that? She is thinking of a different meaning for *dust* than Mrs. Rogers is.

   ▸ Mrs. Rogers wants Amelia Bedelia to draw the drapes. What does Amelia Bedelia do? She draws a picture of the drapes.   Why does Amelia do that? She is thinking of a different meaning for *draw* than Mrs. Rogers is.

   ▸ Why does Mrs. Rogers get angry? because Amelia Bedelia doesn't do anything on her list the way Mrs. Rogers expects her to

2. Remind students that an idiom is a phrase that does not mean exactly what it actually says. Amelia doesn't understand idioms, so this causes problems with Mrs. Rogers.

3. **Read aloud** the list of chores on the Activity Book page.

4. Discuss the meaning of each chore on the list and how Amelia might complete each one.

Objectives

- Describe character(s).
- Identify details that explain characters' actions and feelings.
- Identify and define words' and phrases' literal and nonliteral meanings.
- Demonstrate understanding through drawing, discussion, drama, and/or writing.

5. Have students choose one of the chores to draw a picture showing how Amelia would complete the chore.

 TIP The amount of time students need to complete this activity will vary. Students need only work for the remaining time of the lesson. If students have more they would like to do, they can complete it at a later time.

Reward: Add a sticker for this unit on the My Accomplishments chart to mark successful completion of the unit.

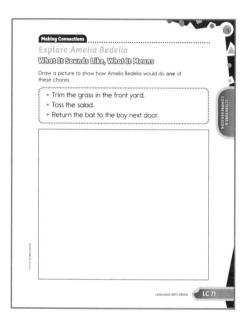

Our Place in Space

Unit Focus

In this unit, students will explore texts that focus on planetary bodies and space exploration. This unit follows the shared-reading instructional approach (see the Instructional Approaches to Reading in the introductory lesson for this program). In this unit, students will

▶ Explore imagery, descriptive language, and similes in poetry.
▶ Learn about the strategy of activating prior knowledge.
▶ Practice setting a purpose before reading.
▶ Explore informational text features.
▶ Learn how to identify the main idea and supporting details of a paragraph.
▶ Explore how time-order words indicate a sequence of events.
▶ Practice the strategy of self-questioning.
▶ Learn strategies to use if they find that they don't understand something they have read.
▶ Explore how to tell the difference between a fact and an opinion.
▶ Learn about when to use capital letters.
▶ Explore /ā/ and /ē/ spelling patterns.

Unit Plan   【Offline】

		45 minutes a day
Lesson 1	Explore Poems About the Weather (D)	
Lesson 2	Introduce "Our Earth in Space"	
Lesson 3	Explore "Our Earth in Space"	
Lesson 4	Introduce "By the Light of the Moon"	
Lesson 5	Explore "By the Light of the Moon"	
Lesson 6	Introduce "The *Eagle* on the Moon"	
Lesson 7	Explore "The *Eagle* on the Moon"	
Lesson 8	Introduce "Women in Space"	
Lesson 9	Explore "Women in Space"	
Lesson 10	Your Choice	

Explore Poems About the Weather (D)

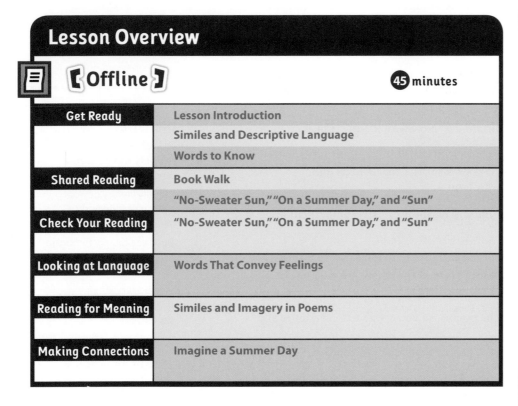

Lesson Overview

[Offline]   **45** minutes

Get Ready	Lesson Introduction
	Similes and Descriptive Language
	Words to Know
Shared Reading	Book Walk
	"No-Sweater Sun," "On a Summer Day," and "Sun"
Check Your Reading	"No-Sweater Sun," "On a Summer Day," and "Sun"
Looking at Language	Words That Convey Feelings
Reading for Meaning	Similes and Imagery in Poems
Making Connections	Imagine a Summer Day

Materials

Supplied

- *Weather: Poems for All Seasons*, pp. 10, 14–17
- *K¹² Language Arts Activity Book*, pp. LC 73–75

Also Needed

- sticky notes
- crayons

Poetry Synopsis

Three poets use vivid imagery and descriptive language to express different aspects of a sunny day.

Keywords

imagery – language that helps readers imagine how something looks, sounds, smells, feels, or tastes

simile – a comparison between two things using the words *like* or *as*; for example, "He was as quiet as a mouse."

tone – the author's feelings toward the subject and characters of a text

visualize – to picture things in your mind as you read

Advance Preparation

Before beginning the Shared Reading, read the poems to locate Words to Know in the text. Use sticky notes to number the lines in "No-Sweater Sun." Preview the Reading Aid on pages LC 73 and 74 in *K¹² Language Arts Activity Book* to prepare the materials for Looking at Language.

Big Ideas

- ► The use of imagery and sensory language creates detailed pictures in the reader's mind, so the reader can understand and appreciate the ideas and feelings the writer conveys.
- ► Readers who visualize, or form mental pictures, when they read have better recall of text than those who do not.
- ► Readers must focus on the specific language of a text to aid in interpretation.
- ► Shared reading allows students to observe and practice the reading behaviors of proficient readers.
- ► Repeated rereading leads to increased fluency.

 **45 minutes**

Work **together** with students to complete Get Ready, Shared Reading, Check Your Reading, Looking at Language, Reading for Meaning, and Making Connections activities.

Get Ready

Lesson Introduction
Prepare students for listening to and discussing "No-Sweater Sun," "On a Summer Day," and "Sun."

1. Tell students you are going to read poems called "No-Sweater Sun," "On a Summer Day," and "Sun."

   ▸ What do you think these poems will be about? Answers may include: the weather; the sun.

2. Tell students that you will read the poems more than once. Explain that when you're learning to read, it's important to reread the poems because each time you read, you

   ▸ Become more familiar with the poems, so you are able to read more and more of the words on your own.
   ▸ Learn something new about the poems that you didn't consider during the first reading.
   ▸ Build your confidence as a reader.

3. Explain to students that before you read the poems, you will get ready by discussing how poets sometimes

   ▸ Compare two things that are not alike to make a vivid picture in your mind.
   ▸ Use descriptive language to help you imagine what the poet wants you to see.

 Objectives
- Identify author's use of imagery and descriptive language.
- Identify literary devices: personification and/or simile.
- Build vocabulary through listening, reading, and discussion.
- Use new vocabulary in written and spoken sentences.

Similes and Descriptive Language
Explore the literary device of similes and the use of descriptive language to create mental imagery.

1. Ask students if they have ever heard anyone described as being *as busy as a bee*. By saying that someone is *as busy as a bee*, we mean that the person is working quickly, going from task to task, much like a bee moving from flower to flower gathering pollen. We know that the person we're describing is not a bee, but making the comparison gives a vivid picture of that person.

2. Tell students that poets make these same types of comparisons in their poems. They often compare two things that are not alike by using the words *like* or *as*. For example, a poet might say that a mother's hug is *like a warm blanket*.

3. Explain that poets also use descriptive words and phrases that help us imagine pictures in our head. This makes the poem more interesting and helps us visualize what the poet wants us to imagine. Instead of saying a flower is white, a poet might say the flower is *whiter than new-fallen snow* to help us see the white flower in our head.

4. Tell students to listen for ways a poet might compare two things.
   Say: The cookie was as hard as a rock.

   ► What is being compared? a cookie and a rock   What does it make you imagine? a really hard cookie that wouldn't be good to eat

5. Tell students to listen for ways a poet uses words to paint a picture in their head.
   Say: The fluffy, pink clouds drifted in the evening sky.

   ► What words does the poet use to describe the clouds? *fluffy; pink* Why does the poet use these words? to help us imagine what the clouds look like

 There is no need to teach students the term *simile* at this time.

Words to Know

Before reading "No-Sweater Sun," "On a Summer Day," and "Sun," go over Words to Know with students.

1. Read aloud each word and have students repeat it.

2. Ask students if they know what each word means.

   ► If students know a word's meaning, have them define it and use it in a sentence.
   ► If students don't know a word's meaning, read them the definition and discuss the word with them.

cartwheel – a sideways handspring
giddy – dizzy with excitement
mane – the long hair on the sides and back of the neck of lions and horses
noon – twelve o'clock; in the middle of the day
scorch – to dry out something with heat

Shared Reading

Book Walk

Prepare students by taking them on a Book Walk of "No-Sweater Sun," "On a Summer Day," and "Sun." Scan the poems together and ask students to make predictions about the poems. Answers to questions may vary.

1. Turn to "No-Sweater Sun" on page 10.

2. Point to and read aloud the **title of the poem** and the **name of the poet**.

3. Have students study the **picture**.

   ▸ What do you think the poem is about?
   ▸ What do you like to do outside on a sunny day?

4. Turn to "On a Summer Day" on pages 14 and 15.

5. Point to and read aloud the **title of the poem** and the **name of the poet**.

6. Have students study the **picture**.

   ▸ What do you think the poem is about?
   ▸ Why do you think the picture is mostly yellow and orange?
   ▸ What do the colors make you think about or feel?

7. Turn to "Sun" on pages 16 and 17.

8. Point to and read aloud the **title of the poem** and the **name of the poet**.

9. Have students study the **picture**.

   ▸ What do you think the poem is about?
   ▸ Why do you think the picture is mostly yellow and orange?
   ▸ How does a hot day make you feel?

Objectives

- Make predictions based on text, illustrations, and/or prior knowledge.
- Activate prior knowledge by previewing text and/or discussing topic.
- Read and discuss poetry.

"No-Sweater Sun," "On a Summer Day," and "Sun"

It's time to read aloud.

1. Have students sit next to you so that they can see the pictures and words while you read aloud.

2. Tell students to listen carefully to the words the poets use to describe things in the poems.

3. **Read aloud all three poems.** Track with your finger so students can follow along. Emphasize Words to Know as you come to them. If appropriate, use the pictures to help show what each word means.

Check Your Reading

"No-Sweater Sun," "On a Summer Day," and "Sun"
Check students' comprehension of the poems.

1. Reread "No-Sweater Sun" aloud, **encouraging students to chime in and read with you**. Then have students tell what the poem is about in their own words.

   ▶ What kind of day is a "No-Sweater Sun" day? a day that is warm enough to go outside without wearing a sweater
   ▶ What is something the poet says you *have* to do during the first no-sweater sun? run; turn a thousand cartwheels; sing

2. Reread "On a Summer Day" aloud, **encouraging students to chime in and read with you**. Then have students tell what the poem is about in their own words.

   ▶ What kind of day is this poem about? a hot summer day
   ▶ What do the bugs in the poem want? rain

3. Reread "Sun" aloud, **encouraging students to chime in and read with you**. Then have students tell what the poem is about in their own words.

   ▶ What color are the squares of sun on the floor? yellow
   ▶ What animal in the poem likes to curl and purr in the sun? the cat

TIP If students have trouble responding to a question, help them locate the answer in the text or pictures.

Objectives
- Read and discuss poetry.
- Answer questions requiring literal recall of details.

Looking at Language

Words That Convey Feelings
Reread the poem "No-Sweater Sun" with a focus on words that reveal the feeling of the poem. Gather the Reading Aid on pages LC 73 and 74 in *K¹² Language Arts Activity Book*.

1. Remind students that poets choose their words carefully to help readers imagine pictures in their head. In addition, poets often use words to express what they were feeling when they wrote a poem.

2. Tell students to listen to the following sentence and think about how it makes them feel.
   Say: The little boy cried when his kitten ran away.

   ▶ How does the sentence make you feel? Students may bring up feelings of sadness.
   ▶ Which words make you feel sad? Answers will vary. Discuss the words *cried* and *ran away*.

Objectives
- Identify words and phrases that reveal the tone of a text.
- Read and discuss poetry.
- Read aloud grade-level text with appropriate expression, accuracy, and rate.

3. Tell students that you are going to change some of the words in the sentence. **Say:** The little boy laughed when his kitten jumped in his lap.

   ▶ How does the sentence make you feel now? Answers will vary. Guide students to discuss how changing some of the words changed the feeling of the sentence from sad to happy.

   ▶ Which words make you feel happy? Answers will vary. Discuss the words *laughed* and *jumped*.

4. Tell students that you will reread "No-Sweater Sun," pausing at certain points to discuss what the poet was feeling and how the words of the poem make them feel.

5. Encourage students to **chime in and read aloud with you** as much as they can.

6. Refer to the Reading Aid.

Reading Aid   Tear out the Reading Aid for this reading selection. Follow the instructions for folding the page, and then use the page as a guide as you reread the selection with students.

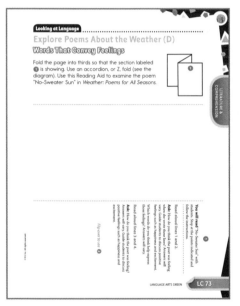

Reading for Meaning

Similes and Imagery in Poems

Explore similes and descriptive language in poems.

1. Remind students that poets make poems interesting by comparing two things that are not alike and using words to paint a picture in our head.

2. Check students' ability to recognize and comprehend similes in "No-Sweater Sun."
   Say: Listen as I read a line from "No-Sweater Sun."
   Read aloud: "Your arms feel new as growing grass . . ."

   ▸ What two things does the poet compare in this line? arms and growing grass   Why does the poet do this? to help us imagine how our arms feel when we don't have to wear a sweater because it's warm

   Say: Listen as I read another line from "No-Sweater Sun."
   Read aloud: "Your legs feel light as rising air . . ."

   ▸ What two things does the poet compare in this line? legs and air Why does the poet do this? to help us think of how light our legs can feel when we're playing outside

3. Check students' ability to recognize descriptive language in "On a Summer Day."

   ▸ In "On a Summer Day," the poet describes the sun as having a lion's face and an "orangy" mane. What do you imagine when you hear this description? Answers will vary.   Why do you think the poet describes the sun this way? Possible answers: to help us imagine what the sun looks like; to paint a picture in the our head

   ▸ The poet says the sun's "tongue scorches leaves." Does the sun really have a tongue? No   What do you think the poet wants you to imagine when you hear that the sun's "tongue scorches leaves"? the sun being so hot that the leaves dry up and look burnt

4. Check students' ability to recognize and comprehend similes and descriptive language in "Sun."

   ▸ In "Sun," the poet says the sun is "a leaping fire." Why do you think the poet describes the sun this way? Possible answers: to help us think of how hot the sun is; to help us think of how the sun and fire are alike

   ▸ The poet says the sun will lie on the floor "like a flat quilt." Why do you think the poet compares the sun to a quilt? Possible answers: to help us imagine seeing squares of sunshine on the floor like quilt squares; to help us imagine how the sun keeps us warm like a quilt

Objectives

- Identify literary devices: personification and/or simile.

- Identify author's use of imagery and descriptive language.

- Read and discuss poetry.

Making Connections

Imagine a Summer Day

Check students' understanding of imagery and their ability to visualize. Turn to page LC 75 in *K¹² Language Arts Activity Book.*

1. Remind students that in "On a Summer Day," the poet uses words to help paint a picture in the reader's head.

2. Tell students to close their eyes and think about what they see in their head as they listen to you reread the poem.

3. On the Activity Book page, have students draw a picture of what they see in their head.

4. Ask students to describe their drawing.

   ▶ Which words in the poem do you think helped you imagine this picture? Answers will vary. Students may indicate descriptive phrases such as *lion-faced, orangy mane,* and *tongue scorches.*

5. Read aloud the sentence starter on the Activity Book page and ask students how they would complete the sentence.

6. As needed, help students write the words to complete the sentence.

7. Have students read aloud the completed sentence **with** you as you track the words with your finger.

Objectives

- Identify author's use of imagery and descriptive language.
- Demonstrate visualizing through drawing, discussion, and/or writing.

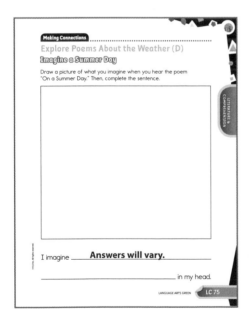

Introduce "Our Earth in Space"

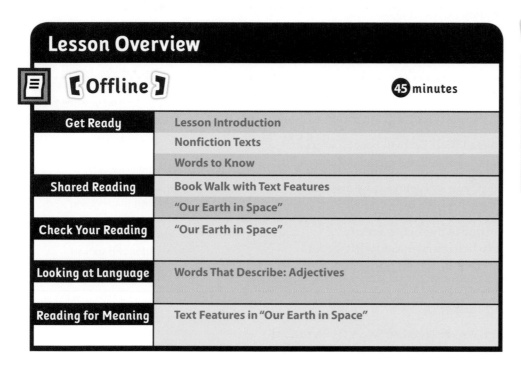

Lesson Overview

[Offline] 45 minutes

Get Ready	Lesson Introduction
	Nonfiction Texts
	Words to Know
Shared Reading	Book Walk with Text Features
	"Our Earth in Space"
Check Your Reading	"Our Earth in Space"
Looking at Language	Words That Describe: Adjectives
Reading for Meaning	Text Features in "Our Earth in Space"

Advance Preparation

Before beginning the Shared Reading, read "Our Earth in Space" to locate Words to Know in the text. Preview the Reading Aid on pages LC 77 and 78 in *K¹² Language Arts Activity Book* to prepare the materials for Looking at Language.

Big Ideas

- ▶ Exposing readers to a wide variety of genres provides them with a wide range of background knowledge and increases their vocabulary.
- ▶ Nonfiction texts differ from fiction texts in that they describe real or true things in life, rather than things made up by the author.
- ▶ Comprehension is facilitated by an understanding of physical presentation (for example, headings, subheads, graphics, and other features).
- ▶ Activating prior knowledge provides a framework for a reader to organize and connect new information to information previously learned; readers that activate prior knowledge before reading are more likely to understand and recall what they read.
- ▶ Shared reading allows students to observe and practice the reading behaviors of proficient readers.
- ▶ During shared-reading activities, students learn more about how print works.

[Materials]

Supplied

- *Ready . . . Set . . . Read! The Beginning Reader's Treasury*, pp. 50–65
- *K¹² Language Arts Activity Book*, pp. LC 77–78

Story Synopsis

Long ago, people thought the earth was flat. Today we know the earth isn't flat, it's round! What else have we learned about our planet since the days of long ago? (Note that this text, written in 1990, states that there are nine planets. In 2006, scientists determined that Pluto is not a planet, reducing the total number of planets to eight.)

Keywords

informational text – text written to explain and give information on a topic

nonfiction – writings about true things

prior knowledge – things you already know from past experience

text feature – part of a text that helps a reader locate information and determine what is most important; some examples are the title, table of contents, headings, pictures, and glossary

topic – the subject of a text

visual text support – a graphic feature that helps a reader better understand text, such as a picture, chart, or map

 **45 minutes**

Work **together** with students to complete Get Ready, Shared Reading, Check Your Reading, Looking at Language, and Reading for Meaning activities.

Get Ready

Lesson Introduction

Prepare students for listening to and discussing "Our Earth in Space" by Joanna Cole.

1. Tell students that you are going to read "Our Earth in Space," a text that explains how our understanding of the earth has changed over the years.

2. Explain that before you read the text, you will get ready by discussing

   ▸ A kind of writing called nonfiction, or informational text
   ▸ Some specific features that we find in nonfiction text
   ▸ How we use prior knowledge to better understand what we read

 Objectives
- Identify the topic.
- Increase concept and content vocabulary.
- Build vocabulary through listening, reading, and discussion.
- Use new vocabulary in written and spoken sentences.

Nonfiction Texts

Explore the genre of nonfiction.

1. Explain that some texts are about real things. This kind of writing is called **nonfiction**. It is also called **informational text**.

2. Tell students that something true and real is called a **fact**. We can prove facts are true. Nonfiction texts are about real things, so they are filled with facts.

3. Explain that every nonfiction text has a **topic**. The topic is what the text is about. Good readers can figure out the topic by thinking about the title of a text and asking, "What is this text mostly about?"

4. Have students practice naming the topic of a text.
   Say: Listen carefully as I read the title of a nonfiction text and what it's about. In the text "Learning About Lizards," the author tells interesting facts about many different kinds of lizards.

   ▸ What do you think is the topic of the text "Learning About Lizards"?
   lizards

TIP Although an objective for this lesson is to identify genre, there is no need to introduce the term to students at this time.

Words to Know

Before reading "Our Earth in Space," go over Words to Know with students.

1. Read aloud each word aloud and have students repeat it.

2. Ask students if they know what each word means.

   ▸ If students know a word's meaning, have them define it and use it in a sentence.

   ▸ If students don't know a word's meaning, read them the definition and discuss the word with them.

notice – observe; come to understand
telescope – an instrument shaped like a long tube that makes faraway things appear closer when you look through it
top – a toy that spins on its point

Shared Reading

Book Walk with Text Features

Prepare students for reading by taking them on a Book Walk of "Our Earth in Space." Scan the text together to point out text features and ask students to make predictions about the text. Answers to questions may vary.

1. Turn to the **table of contents** in *Ready ... Set ... Read!* Help students find "Our Earth in Space" and turn to that page.

2. Tell students that nonfiction texts have features that help readers better understand the information in the text.

3. Point to and read aloud the **title of the text**. Explain that the title usually tells us what the text is about.

   ▸ What do you think this text is about?

4. Have students point to the **name of the author and illustrator** while you read the names aloud.

5. Point to the **picture on pages 56 and 57**. Explain that pictures help show ideas that are in the text.
   Say: This picture helps the reader better understand how people long ago thought the sun moved each day.

6. Point to the words in the picture on pages 62 and 63. Tell students that the words in the picture are **labels**. They tell what the objects are in the picture. Read aloud the labels.

Objectives
- Make predictions based on text, illustrations, and/or prior knowledge.
- Activate prior knowledge by previewing text and/or discussing topic.
- Read for information.

7. Explain that, in addition to using text features to better understand text, good readers use **prior knowledge**, or things we know from past experience, to make sense of text. We do the same thing to help us understand the world around us.

   Say: Imagine that it's dark outside and you see a small animal in front of you. It has four legs and a long tail. What could it be? Answers will vary.   Now imagine the animal starts barking. What kind of animal is it? a dog   Using your prior knowledge about dogs helps you figure out that the unknown animal is a dog.

8. Tell students that when we read, thinking about our prior knowledge helps us connect new information in a text to things that we already know. This helps us better understand and remember what we've read.

9. Tell students that the text you will read is about the earth, so thinking about what they already know about the earth will help them to understand the text.

10. Have students share a few things they know about the earth. If students have trouble thinking of something, encourage them to think about

    ▸ the shape of the planet round
    ▸ what provides light for the planet during the day the sun
    ▸ what they see when they look at the night sky the moon; stars

---

"Our Earth in Space"
It's time to read aloud.

1. Have students sit next to you so that they can see the pictures and words while you read aloud.

2. Tell students to look at the pictures to see how they explain the information in the text.

3. **Read aloud the entire text.** Track with your finger so students can follow along. Emphasize Words to Know as you come to them. If appropriate, use the pictures to help show what each word means.

Check Your Reading

"Our Earth in Space"

Check students' comprehension of "Our Earth in Space."

▶ What type of text is this? nonfiction; informational text
▶ What is the topic of the text? the earth
▶ What question did you ask yourself to figure out the topic? What is this text mostly about?
▶ How do we get pictures of the earth floating in space? Spaceships send them.
▶ Is the sun bigger or smaller than the earth? bigger   Why does the sun look small from earth? because it is so far away
▶ What does the earth do that makes day and night? spins around the sun
▶ Many stars are bigger than the sun. Why do they look smaller than the sun from earth? because they are much farther away
▶ Which of these statements is a fact? The earth is round, or the earth is the best planet. The earth is round.

TIP If students have trouble responding to a question, help them locate the answer in the text or pictures.

> **Objectives**
> • Identify genre.
> • Identify the topic.
> • Identify important details in informational text.
> • Identify facts in informational text.

Looking at Language

Words That Describe: Adjectives

Reread "Our Earth in Space" with a focus on adjectives. Gather the Reading Aid on pages LC 77 and 78 in *K¹² Language Arts Activity Book*.

1. Explain to students that describing words make what we read more interesting. **Say:** As I say the following sentences, think about which one is more interesting and descriptive.

   ▶ The stars look like lights.
   ▶ The distant stars look like tiny, shimmering lights.

2. Discuss with students which sentence they think is more interesting and why.

3. Tell students that a describing word is called an *adjective*. Adjectives make stories more interesting because they add descriptive details to the story. Because adjectives describe things, they help us better imagine pictures in our head as we read.

> **Objectives**
> • Identify adjectives.
> • Use adjectives to describe someone or something.
> • Identify author's use of imagery and descriptive language.
> • Read aloud grade-level text with appropriate expression, accuracy, and rate.

4. Give examples of some of the types of information that adjectives can add:

   ▸ Size: I saw a tiny butterfly; I saw a humongous frog. The words *tiny* and *humongous* are adjectives.

   ▸ Looks: My shirt is green and purple; the girl has long, red hair. The words *green*, *purple*, *long*, and *red* are adjectives.

   ▸ Taste: I ate some salty pretzels; I ate some sweet chocolate cookies. The words *salty*, *sweet*, and *chocolate* are adjectives.

5. Tell students that they will **read aloud the story with you**. As you read aloud together, you will stop at certain points to look at adjectives.

6. Refer to the Reading Aid.

TIP If students are reading fluently, allow them to read aloud to you on their own.

Reading Aid Tear out the Reading Aid for this reading selection. Follow the instructions for folding the page, and then use the page as a guide as you reread the selection with students.

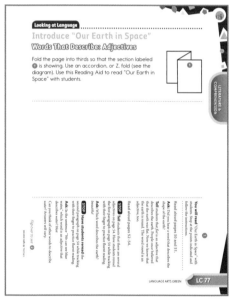
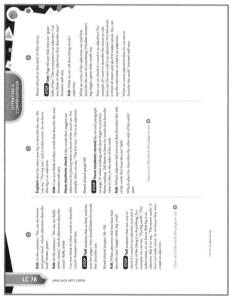

Reading for Meaning

Text Features in "Our Earth in Space"

Check students' understanding of text features in nonfiction texts.

1. Remind students that text features, such as titles, pictures, and labels, can help us better understand the information in a nonfiction text.

2. Point to the title of the text on page 50.

   ▸ What is this called? the title   What does the title tell the reader? what the topic is; what the text is about

3. Point to the picture on pages 56 and 57.

   ▸ How does this picture help us understand information in the text? It shows how people long ago thought the sun moved.

4. Turn to the picture on page 58. Point to and read aloud the labels.

   ▸ What are these two words called? labels   What do the labels tell us? the names of the two objects in the picture
   ▸ Which is bigger, the earth or the sun? the sun

5. Point to the picture on page 59.

   ▸ What does this picture show us? Possible answers: which direction the earth spins; how one side of the earth is dark while the other side is light

6. Point to the picture on pages 62 and 63.

   ▸ How many labels are in this picture? 11
   ▸ What does this picture show us? Possible answers: how far each planet is from the sun; the names of the planets; what the planets look like; the path that each planet travels around the sun
   ▸ Based on this picture, which planet is closest to the sun? Mercury
   ▸ Which planets have rings? Jupiter, Saturn, and Uranus

Objectives

- Identify features of informational text.
- Identify purpose of and information provided by informational text features.
- Interpret information from visual text supports: graphs, tables, charts, cartoons.

Explore "Our Earth in Space"

Lesson Overview

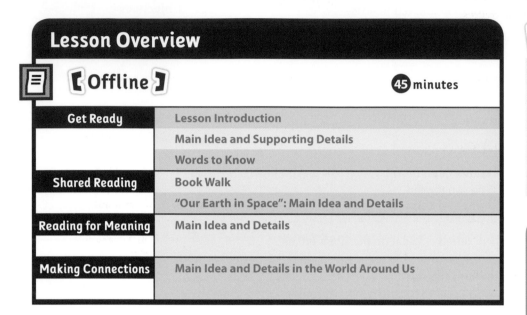

[Offline]   **45** minutes

Get Ready	Lesson Introduction
	Main Idea and Supporting Details
	Words to Know
Shared Reading	Book Walk
	"Our Earth in Space": Main Idea and Details
Reading for Meaning	Main Idea and Details
Making Connections	Main Idea and Details in the World Around Us

Materials

Supplied

- *Ready ... Set ... Read! The Beginning Reader's Treasury*, pp. 50–65
- *K¹² Language Arts Activity Book*, pp. LC 79–81

Keywords

main idea – the most important idea in a paragraph or text

supporting detail – a detail that gives more information about a main idea

topic – the subject of a text

Advance Preparation

Preview the Reading Aid on pages LC 79 and 80 in *K¹² Language Arts Activity Book* to prepare the materials for the Shared Reading.

Big Ideas

- ► Nonfiction texts differ from fiction texts in that they describe real or true things in life, rather than things made up by the author.
- ► Comprehension entails an understanding of the organizational patterns of text.
- ► During shared-reading activities, students learn more about how print works.

 **45 minutes**

Work **together** with students to complete Get Ready, Shared Reading, Reading for Meaning, and Making Connections activities.

Get Ready ···

Lesson Introduction

Prepare students for listening to and discussing "Our Earth in Space."

1. Tell students that you are going to reread "Our Earth in Space."

2. Explain that before you read the text, you will get ready by discussing main idea and supporting details.

Main Idea and Supporting Details

Introduce identifying the main idea and supporting details.

1. Remind students that texts about real things are called **nonfiction**.

2. Explain that in nonfiction texts, most paragraphs have a **main idea**. The main idea is what the paragraph is mostly about. The other sentences in a paragraph give information, or **details**, about the main idea.

3. Read aloud the following paragraph, and then model how to determine the main idea.

   Read aloud: Carson's room is messy. There are books on the floor. His bed is unmade. Piles of clothes are everywhere.

   Say: This paragraph gives information about Carson's messy room. So I think the main idea is, "Carson's room is messy." I can make sure that this is the main idea by checking if most of the other sentences give details about Carson's messy room.

   ▸ Does the sentence, "There are books on the floor," talk about Carson's messy room? Yes

   ▸ Does the sentence, "His bed is unmade," talk about Carson's messy room? Yes

   ▸ Does the sentence, "Piles of clothes are everywhere," talk about Carson's messy room? Yes

   Say: The other sentences give details about Carson's messy room. So, I can confirm that, "Carson's room is messy," is the main idea of the paragraph. We call the details that give information about Carson's messy room *supporting details*.

> **Objectives**
> - Identify the main idea.
> - Identify main idea and supporting details.
> - Increase concept and content vocabulary.
> - Build vocabulary through listening, reading, and discussion.
> - Use new vocabulary in written and spoken sentences.

4. Read aloud the following paragraph, and then have students practice identifying the main idea and supporting details.

Read aloud: Lions spend much of their time relaxing. They spend up to 21 hours a day sleeping or resting. Sometimes they relax on the ground. Sometimes they relax in trees.

- ► What do you think is the main idea of the paragraph? Lions spend a lot of time relaxing.
- ► Do the other sentences in the paragraph give details about how lions relax? Yes
- ► What are some of the details about how lions relax? They spend 21 hours a day sleeping or resting; they rest on the ground; they rest in trees.

Say: Since the other sentences give supporting details about how lions relax, we can confirm that the main idea is, "Lions spend a lot of time relaxing."

5. Tell students that when they read nonfiction texts they should look for main ideas and supporting details.

Words to Know

Before reading "Our Earth in Space," go over Words to Know with students.

1. Read aloud each word and have students repeat it.

2. Ask students if they know what each word means.

- ► If students know a word's meaning, have them define it and use it in a sentence.
- ► If students don't know a word's meaning, read them the definition and discuss the word with them.

notice – observe; come to understand
telescope – an instrument shaped like a long tube that makes faraway things appear closer when you look through it
top – a toy that spins on its point

Shared Reading

Book Walk

Prepare students by taking them on a Book Walk of "Our Earth in Space." Scan the selection together to revisit the text.

1. Turn to the selection.

2. Point to and read aloud the **title of the text**.

3. Have students point to the **name of the author and illustrator** while you read the names aloud.

4. Have students look at the **pictures in the text**.

5. Remind students that thinking about their prior knowledge will help them connect new information they learn to things that they already know. This will help them to better understand and remember what they read.

6. Ask the following questions to help students think about what they already know about the earth.

   ▸ What can we see in pictures of earth taken from space? Possible answers: blue water; brown and green land; clouds; how the earth is round
   ▸ Why is one of the sides of the earth light while the other side is dark? The side that faces the sun is light and the side that is not facing the sun is dark.

7. Turn to the picture on page 58.

   ▸ What does this picture show? the size of the earth compared to the sun
   ▸ Why does the sun look so small when we see it from the earth? because it is so far away

Objectives

- Activate prior knowledge by previewing text and/or discussing topic.
- Read for information.
- Identify the main idea.
- Identify main idea and supporting details.
- Identify the topic.

"Our Earth in Space": Main Idea and Details

It's time to reread the story. Tell students that they will reread "Our Earth in Space" with a focus on main idea and supporting details. Gather the Reading Aid on pages LC 79 and 80 in *K¹² Language Arts Activity Book*.

1. Have students sit next to you so that they can see the pictures and words while you read aloud.

2. Tell students that they will **read aloud the story with you**. As you read aloud together, you will stop at certain points to figure out the main idea and supporting details of some of the paragraphs.

3. Refer to the Reading Aid.

Reading Aid Tear out the Reading Aid for this reading selection. Follow the instructions for folding the page, and then use the page as a guide as you reread the selection with students.

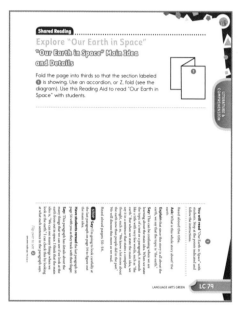

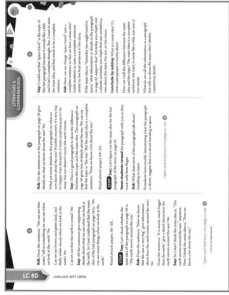

Reading for Meaning

Main Idea and Details

Check students' understanding of main idea and supporting details.

1. Remind students that the **main idea** of a paragraph is what a paragraph is mostly about. Most of the other sentences in a paragraph give information, or supporting details, about the main idea.

2. Turn to and read aloud pages 56 and 57 of "Our Earth in Space."

   ▸ What is the main idea of this paragraph? Long ago, people thought the sun moved and the earth stayed still.

   ▸ Name two details in this paragraph that support the main idea, "Long ago, people thought the sun moved and the earth stayed still." Possible answers: The sun seemed to rise in the east; it looked like the sun moved across the sky; the sun looked like it sank in the west; the earth seemed to stay still.

3. Turn to page 60 and read aloud the paragraph.

   ▸ What is the main idea of this paragraph? Stars are very big, not tiny.

   ▸ Name two supporting details about stars from this paragraph. Possible answers: Stars are giant balls of fire; the sun is a star; many stars are bigger than the sun; the stars that are bigger than the sun look smaller because they are farther away.

4. Turn to page 62 and read aloud the paragraph.

   ▸ What is the main idea of this paragraph? We can see planets in the night sky.

   ▸ Name two details from this paragraph that support the main idea, "We can see planets in the night sky." They look like stars if we look at them without a telescope; the planets are really worlds.

Objectives
- Identify the main idea.
- Identify main idea and supporting details.

Making Connections

Main Idea and Details in the World Around Us

Check students' ability to determine the main idea and supporting details of a picture. Gather page LC 81 in *K¹² Language Arts Activity Book*.

1. Explain to students that we identify main ideas and supporting details even when we're not reading a text. We figure out the main idea and details of events in our lives each day.

2. Have students look at the picture on the Activity Book page and describe what they see.

Objectives
- Identify the main idea.
- Identify main idea and supporting details.
- Demonstrate understanding through graphic organizers.

3. Have students tell you the main idea, or what the picture is mostly about. If students are having difficulty, ask the following questions to help them determine the main idea.

   ► What are the two children doing in the picture? riding bikes
   ► Can you say what the picture is about in one sentence? Two children are riding their bikes.

4. Write the main idea students dictate in the box on the Activity Book page.

   ► If students are ready to write on their own, allow them to do so.

5. Have students look at the picture and tell you two details, or other things, about the picture. If students are having difficulty, ask the following questions to help them determine supporting details.

   ► What color are the bikes? The girl's bike is red; the boy's bike is green.
   ► What are the children wearing? helmets; shorts; short-sleeved shirts
   ► Where are the children riding their bikes? outside; in the park

6. Write the supporting details students dictate in the boxes on the Activity Book page.

   ► If students are ready to write on their own, allow them to do so.

7. Have students read aloud the main idea and supporting details **with** you as you track the words with your finger.

Introduce "By the Light of the Moon"

Materials

Supplied
- "By the Light of the Moon," *K¹² World: Earth and Sky*, pp. 12–23
- *K¹² Language Arts Activity Book*, pp. LC 82–84

Also Needed
- index cards (20)

Lesson Overview

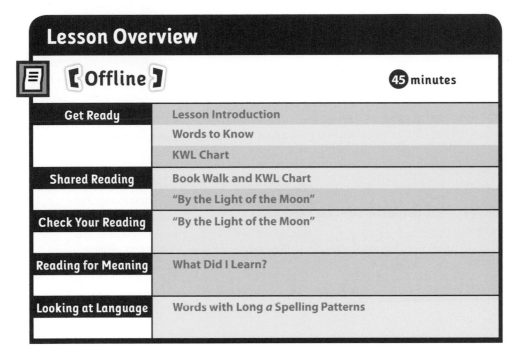

Offline — **45** minutes

Get Ready	Lesson Introduction
	Words to Know
	KWL Chart
Shared Reading	Book Walk and KWL Chart
	"By the Light of the Moon"
Check Your Reading	"By the Light of the Moon"
Reading for Meaning	What Did I Learn?
Looking at Language	Words with Long *a* Spelling Patterns

Article Synopsis

The moon is the earth's closest neighbor in space, but it's a very different place. Students will learn about the moon's surface and phases, and find out some of the questions that remain unanswered.

Keywords

prior knowledge – things you already know from past experience

Advance Preparation

Before beginning the Shared Reading, read "By the Light of the Moon" to locate Words to Know in the text. For Looking at Language, preview the Reading Aid on pages LC 83 and 84 in *K¹² Language Arts Activity Book* to prepare the materials, and prepare two index cards by writing *pay* on one and *make* on the other.

Big Ideas

- ► Activating prior knowledge provides a framework for a reader to organize and connect new information to information previously learned; readers that activate prior knowledge before reading are more likely to understand and recall what they read.
- ► Comprehension entails having and knowing a purpose for reading.
- ► During shared-reading activities, students learn more about how print works.

Offline **45** minutes

Work **together** with students to complete Get Ready, Shared Reading, Check Your Reading, Reading for Meaning, and Looking at Language activities.

Get Ready

Lesson Introduction

Prepare students for listening to and discussing "By the Light of the Moon."

1. Tell students that you are going to read "By the Light of the Moon," a nonfiction magazine article that gives information about the moon.

2. Explain that before you read the article, you will get ready by discussing

   ▸ An activity that can help readers get ready to read by thinking about their prior knowledge related to the text
   ▸ How asking questions about a text before reading gives a reader a purpose, or a reason, for reading a text

> **Objectives**
> - Build vocabulary through listening, reading, and discussion.
> - Use new vocabulary in written and spoken sentences.
> - Increase concept and content vocabulary.

Words to Know

Before reading "By the Light of the Moon," go over Words to Know with students.

1. Read aloud each word and have students repeat it.

2. Ask students if they know what each word means.

   ▸ If students know a word's meaning, have them define it and use it in a sentence.
   ▸ If students don't know a word's meaning, read them the definition and discuss the word with them.

astronaut – a person trained to travel and work in space
meteorite – a large piece of rock or metal that falls to earth or to the moon from space
reflect – to bounce something back from a surface; for example, light and heat can reflect off a surface
spacecraft – a vehicle made to travel in outer space
surface – the outside or top part of something
telescope – an instrument shaped like a long tube that makes faraway things appear closer when you look through it

KWL Chart

Explore prereading activities and reading for a specific purpose. Turn to page LC 82 *K¹² Language Arts Activity Book.*

1. Direct students' attention to the KWL chart (Know/Want to know/Learn chart) on the Activity Book page.
   Say: This is called a KWL chart. It will help us get ready to read. It will also help us organize our thoughts on what we want to know.

2. Point to the K column.
   Say: The K stands for **know**. Good readers ask, "What do I already know about this subject?" before they read an article.

3. Tell students that what we already know is our **prior knowledge**. Thinking about what we already know about a subject helps get our brain ready to learn more about the subject.

   ▸ Review the K example that is provided on the Activity Book page.

4. Point to the W column.
   Say: The W stands for **want to know.** Good readers ask, "What do I want to know, or wonder, about this subject?" before they read an article.

5. Tell students that good readers ask questions and then look for the answers while they read. Looking for the answers to our questions is the **purpose** for reading this article.

6. Explain that asking questions helps readers to understand what they read because they focus on the important information to answer their questions. They're also motivated to read to find answers to their questions.

   ▸ Read the W question on the Activity Book page.

7. Point to the L column.
   Say: The L stands for **learn**. Good readers think about what they've learned after they read an article.

8. Tell students that before they read "By the Light of the Moon," they will work on the K and W columns of the chart. They will complete the L column after they read.

TIP Students will not complete the chart at this time. Keep the Activity Book page in a safe place for later use.

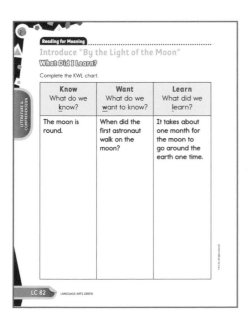

Shared Reading

Book Walk and KWL Chart

Prepare students by taking them on a Book Walk of "By the Light of the Moon." Scan the magazine article together and ask students to make predictions about the text. Gather the KWL chart. Answers to questions may vary.

1. Turn to the **table of contents** in *K¹² World: Earth and Sky*. Help students find the selection and turn to that page.

2. Point to and read aloud the **title of the article**.

   ▸ What do you think the article will be about?

3. Have students look at the **pictures of the article**. Explain that as they look through the article, you will help them begin filling out the KWL chart.

   ▸ If students are ready to write on their own, allow them to do so.

4. Tell students to think about their prior knowledge, or what they already know about the moon. Explain that this will help them get their brain ready to read about the moon.

   ▸ What do you already know about the moon? (Write each fact students dictate in the K column of the KWL chart.)

5. Tell students that they will set a purpose for reading by thinking of questions about the moon.

   ▸ What are three things that you want to know, or wonder, about the moon? (Write what students dictate in the W column of the KWL chart.)
   ▸ If students have difficulty thinking of things they'd like to know, suggest one or more of the following questions: Why does the moon's shape look different from week to week? Why does the moon look like it moves across the sky? When did the first astronaut walk on the moon?

Objectives

- Make predictions based on text, illustrations, and/or prior knowledge.
- Activate prior knowledge by previewing text and/or discussing topic.
- Generate questions and seek information to answer questions.
- Set a purpose for reading.
- Demonstrate understanding through graphic organizers.
- Read for information.

6. Point to and read aloud any headers, captions, or other features that stand out.

   ▸ What do you think the article might tell us about the moon?

TIP Students will not complete the chart at this time. Keep the Activity Book page in a safe place for later use.

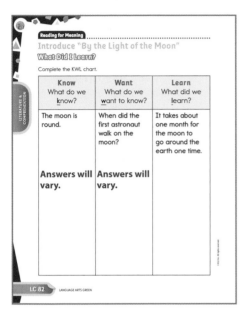

"By the Light of the Moon"

It's time to read aloud.

1. Have students sit next to you so that they can see the pictures and words while you read aloud.

2. Tell students to listen carefully to hear if the article answers any of their questions.

3. **Read aloud the entire article.** Track with your finger so students can follow along. Emphasize Words to Know as you come to them. If appropriate, use the pictures to help show what each word means.

Check Your Reading

"By the Light of the Moon"

Check students' comprehension of "By the Light of the Moon."

▶ How long does it take the moon to go around the earth one time? about a month
▶ What are craters? deep holes on the moon's surface
▶ How do scientists think craters were formed? by meteorites crashing into the moon
▶ Why does the moon look like it changes shape? because it reflects different amounts of sunlight as it goes around the earth
▶ How many phases does the moon go through? four
▶ How do astronauts breathe on the moon? They carry air in their space suits.
▶ Which one of these statements is a fact? The moon reflects light from the sun, or it's fun to look at the moon through a telescope. The moon reflects light from the sun.

(TIP) If students have trouble responding to a question, help them locate the answer in the text or pictures.

Objectives
- Identify important details in informational text.
- Identify facts in informational text.

Reading for Meaning

What Did I Learn?

Have students use the KWL chart to record answers to the questions they previously generated and what they learned from the article. Gather the KWL chart.

1. Read aloud the first question written in the W column. If students are ready, have them write their answers in the KWL chart; otherwise, write their answers for them.

   ▶ Ask students if they heard the answer in the article. If students know the answer, write it in the L column of the chart across from the question.
   ▶ If the answer is in the article but students cannot remember it, return to the article and help students locate the answer. Then write it in the L column across from the question.
   ▶ If the answer to a question is not in the article, leave the area across from the question blank. Explain to students that we don't always find the answers to our questions in the articles we read. But asking the questions helps us become better readers because it motivates us to read or listen carefully to a text.

Objectives
- Demonstrate understanding through graphic organizers.
- Generate questions and seek information to answer questions.
- Identify facts in informational text.

2. Repeat Step 1 for each of the remaining questions in the W column.

3. After the last question is answered, have students tell any additional facts that they learned about the moon, and write them at the end of the L column.

TIP Keep the Activity Book page in a safe place for later use.

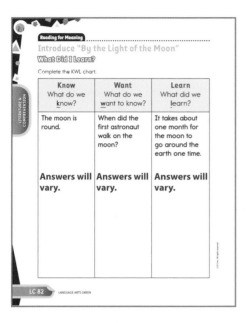

Looking at Language

Words with Long *a* Spelling Patterns

Reread "Our Earth in Space" with a focus on spelling patterns for the long *a* sound. Gather the index cards and the Reading Aid on pages LC 83 and 84 in *K¹² Language Arts Activity Book*.

1. Point to the word on each index card and read it aloud. Then have students read each word with you.

   ▶ What vowel sound do the words *pay* and *make* both have? long *a*

2. Tell students that there is more than one way to spell the long *a* sound. In the word *pay*, the spelling pattern *ay* makes the sound /ā/. In the word *make*, the silent *e* on the end causes the letter *a* to make the sound /ā/.

3. Explain that the spelling patterns *ay* and *a* with the silent *e* both make the long *a* sound. So the words *pay* and *make* both have the same long *a* sound even though they are spelled differently.

4. Tell students that they will **read aloud the article with you**. As you read aloud together, they should listen for words with the long *a* sound.

Objectives
- Identify and use the sound /ā/.
- Identify and use /ā/ spelling patterns.
- Read aloud grade-level text with appropriate expression, accuracy, and rate.

5. Tell students that you will stop at certain points to have them hunt for words with the long *a* sound and write those words on index cards. Explain that there will be many words with the same spelling patterns as *pay* and *make*, but there will also be some words with the long *a* sound spelled in other ways.

6. Refer to the Reading Aid.

TIP When students point out long *a* words with the plural *s*, such as *places,* or with a past tense verb ending, such as *shaped*, write the word on the index card without the ending. Explain to students that this will make it easier to see the spelling patterns and sort the words.

Reading Aid Tear out the Reading Aid for this reading selection. Follow the instructions for folding the page, and then use the page as a guide as you reread the selection with students.

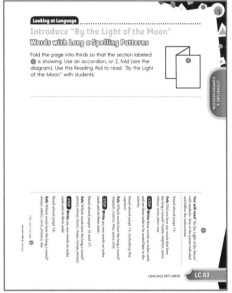

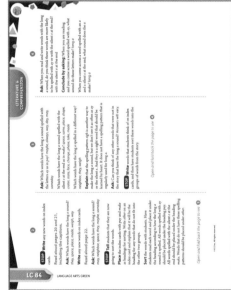

Explore "By the Light of the Moon"

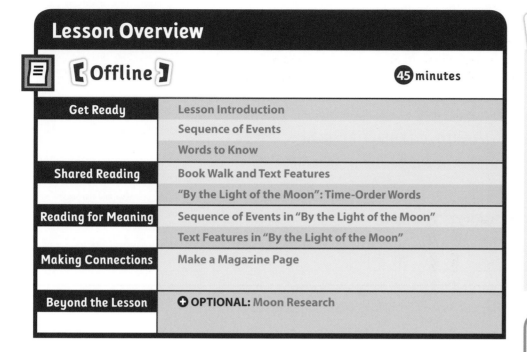

Lesson Overview	
Offline	**45** minutes
Get Ready	Lesson Introduction
	Sequence of Events
	Words to Know
Shared Reading	Book Walk and Text Features
	"By the Light of the Moon": Time-Order Words
Reading for Meaning	Sequence of Events in "By the Light of the Moon"
	Text Features in "By the Light of the Moon"
Making Connections	Make a Magazine Page
Beyond the Lesson	⊕ OPTIONAL: Moon Research

Materials

Supplied
- "By the Light of the Moon," *K¹² World: Earth and Sky*, pp. 12–23
- *K¹² Language Arts Activity Book*, pp. LC 82 (optional), 85–87

Also Needed
- glue stick
- paper, drawing
- scissors, round-end safety

Keywords

sequence – order

text feature – part of a text that helps a reader locate information and determine what is most important; some examples are the title, table of contents, headings, pictures, and glossary

visual text support – a graphic feature that helps a reader better understand text, such as a picture, chart, or map

Advance Preparation

Preview the Reading Aid on pages LC 85 and 86 in *K¹² Language Arts Activity Book* to prepare the materials for the Shared Reading.

Big Ideas

- ▶ Nonfiction texts differ from fiction texts in that they describe real or true things in life, rather than things made up by the author.
- ▶ Comprehension entails an understanding of the organizational patterns of text.
- ▶ Comprehension is facilitated by an understanding of physical presentation (for example, headings, subheads, graphics, and other features).
- ▶ During shared-reading activities, students learn more about how print works.

 **Offline** ⓐ minutes

Work **together** with students to complete Get Ready, Shared Reading, Reading for Meaning, Making Connections, and Beyond the Lesson activities.

Get Ready

Lesson Introduction
Prepare students for listening to and discussing "By the Light of the Moon."

1. Tell students that you are going to reread "By the Light of the Moon."

2. Explain that before you read the article, you will get ready by discussing sequence of events in a text.

Objectives
- Identify sequence of events in informational text.
- Increase concept and content vocabulary.
- Build vocabulary through listening, reading, and discussion.
- Use new vocabulary in written and spoken sentences.

Sequence of Events
Explore the order of events in a text.

1. Tell students that the order in which things happen in a story or article is called the **sequence**. Words like *first*, *next*, *last*, *before*, *after*, *then*, and *finally* help tell the sequence.

2. Have students practice identifying the sequence of events in a short paragraph. **Say:** Listen for words that tell the sequence, or the order in which things happen: *First*, Maria dug a small hole. *Then*, she put some flower seeds in the hole. *Next*, she covered the seeds with soil. *Last*, Maria watered the seeds.

   ▸ What happened first? Maria dug a small hole.
   ▸ What happened last? Maria watered the seeds.

Words to Know
Before reading "By the Light of the Moon," go over Words to Know with students.

1. Read aloud each word and have students repeat it.

2. Ask students if they know what each word means.

   ▸ If students know a word's meaning, have them define it and use it in a sentence.
   ▸ If students don't know a word's meaning, read them the definition and discuss the word with them.

astronaut – a person trained to travel and work in space
meteorite – a large piece of rock or metal that falls to earth or to the moon from space
reflect – to bounce something back from a surface; for example, light and heat can reflect off a surface
spacecraft – a vehicle made to travel in outer space
surface – the outside or top part of something
telescope – an instrument shaped like a long tube that makes faraway things appear closer when you look through it

Shared Reading

Book Walk and Text Features

Prepare students by taking them on a Book Walk of "By the Light of the Moon." Scan the magazine article together to revisit the text and point out text features.

1. Remind students that magazine articles have features that help readers better understand the information in the article.

2. Turn to page 13 and point to and read aloud the **title of the article**. Explain that the title usually tells us what the article is about.

3. Point to the **picture** of craters on page 15. Explain that pictures help show ideas that are in the article.
   Say: This picture shows craters on the moon. It helps the reader better understand how big some of the craters are.

4. Point to the text below the picture of the craters on page 15. Tell students that the text below the picture is called a **caption**. It gives information about the picture. Read aloud the caption.

5. Point to the word *reflects* on page 16. Explain that some words in the article are darker, or bold, so that we will notice them. This word is bold because it's an important word in the article. We can find out what this word means in the glossary at the back of the magazine on pages 51 and 52.
   Say: Let's read the definition for the word *reflects*: to bounce something back from a surface; for example, light and heat can reflect off a surface. Can you make up a sentence using the word *reflects*? Answers will vary. If students are not using the word correctly, give an example sentence that uses the word correctly and discuss the sentence to clear up any misunderstandings.

6. Turn to page 18 and point to the **heading**. Explain that articles can be broken up into sections, and a heading tells what a section is about. An article's headings can help us figure out where to find certain information.
   Say: This heading tells readers that this section of the article explains phases of the moon. If I want to find information about the moon's different shapes, this is the section I would look in.

7. Remind students that thinking about their prior knowledge will help them connect new information in the article to things that they already know.

8. Ask the following questions to help students think about what they already know about the moon.

   ▸ Why does the moon seem to glow with light? because it reflects light from the sun
   ▸ Why do astronauts carry air to breathe in their space suits when they go to the moon? because the moon does not have air to breathe

Objectives
- Activate prior knowledge by previewing text and/or discussing topic.
- Read for information.
- Identify sequence of events in informational text.
- Use time-order words.
- Interpret information from visual text supports: graphs, tables, charts, cartoons.

"By the Light of the Moon": Time-Order Words

It's time to reread the article. Tell students that they will reread "By the Light of the Moon" with a focus on text and text features that indicate time and sequence. Gather the Reading Aid on pages LC 85 and 86 in *K¹² Language Arts Activity Book*.

1. Have students sit next to you so that they can see the pictures and words while you read aloud.

2. Tell students that **they will read aloud the article with you**. As you read aloud together, you will stop at certain points to discuss time-order words and sequence.

3. Refer to the Reading Aid.

Reading Aid Tear out the Reading Aid for this reading selection. Follow the instructions for folding the page, and then use the page as a guide as you reread the selection with students.

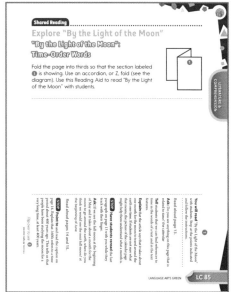
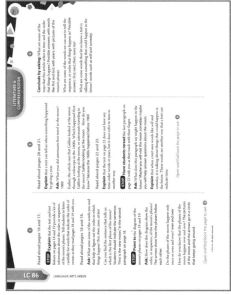

Reading for Meaning

Sequence of Events in "By the Light of the Moon"
Check students' understanding of sequence.

1. Remind students that the words *first*, *next*, *after*, and *then* are sequence words. They help tell the order of things that happen.

2. Read aloud page 18, and then prompt students with these questions.

   ▸ How many phases does the moon go through? four
   ▸ What is the first phase of the moon? new moon
   ▸ What phase comes after the new moon? crescent moon
   ▸ What is the next phase of the moon? half-moon
   ▸ What is the last phase of the moon? full moon

3. Have students look at the picture on pages 18 and 19.

   ▸ What do the arrows in the picture show? They show the order of the moon's phases.
   ▸ Does the moon get bigger or smaller after the full moon? smaller

---

Text Features in "By the Light of the Moon"
Check students' understanding of text features.

1. Point to the picture on page 14 of the magazine and read aloud the caption below it.

   ▸ What information does this picture and caption give us? They tell us about the first person to use a telescope to look at the moon.

2. Point to the word *meteorites* on page 15.

   ▸ Why is this word darker than the other words? It's an important word in the article.   Where can we find out what this word means? in the back of the magazine

3. Point to and read aloud the heading on page 18.

   ▸ What is this called? a heading
   ▸ What does this heading tell us? that this part of the article is about the moon's phases

4. Point to the picture on pages 18 and 19 of the magazine.

   ▸ Do we see more of the moon reflected when it's a new moon or a half-moon? half-moon

5. Where should I look if I want to find information about astronauts walking on the moon? the section on page 21

Objectives
- Identify sequence of events in informational text.
- Interpret information from visual text supports: graphs, tables, charts, cartoons.
- Identify features of informational text.
- Identify purpose of and information provided by informational text features.
- Locate information using features of text and electronic media.

Making Connections

Make a Magazine Page

Check students' understanding of the placement of text features in a nonfiction article. Turn to page LC 87 in K^{12} *Language Arts Activity Book* and gather the drawing paper, scissors, and glue stick.

1. Remind students that good readers use text features, such as headings, pictures, and captions, to better understand the information in a magazine article.

2. Tell students they will create their own magazine page by cutting out and arranging text features.

3. Have students point to and name the text features on the Activity Book page and then cut them out.

4. Have students place the text features where they think the features should go on the drawing paper and explain why they placed them where they did. If students have trouble arranging the features appropriately, ask the following questions.

   ▸ Where does a caption belong? near a picture
   ▸ What belongs under a heading? text; paragraphs

5. Have students glue down the text features. Magazine page layouts will vary, but students should glue the title at the top of the page; the block of text should be below the heading; and the caption should be below the picture.

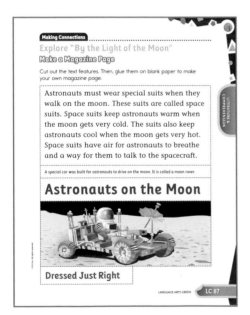

Beyond the Lesson

⊕ OPTIONAL: Moon Research

This activity is OPTIONAL. It is intended for students who have extra time and would benefit from further research on the moon. Feel free to skip this activity. Gather the completed KWL chart on page LC 82 in *K¹² Language Arts Activity Book.*

1. Help students look for answers to their unanswered questions about the moon on their KWL chart. Use one or more of the following sources:

   ▶ the Further Reading section of *K¹² World: Earth and Sky*
   ▶ encyclopedias
   ▶ science magazines, such as *National Geographic Kids*
   ▶ nonfiction library books about the moon
   ▶ the Internet, using the search words "moon facts"

2. When looking at sources of information, have students point out any text features that may help them locate information, such as titles, headings, pictures, and captions.

3. If students find an answer, write it in the L column next to the question in the W column of the chart.

4. If students find additional information about the moon that they find interesting, write these facts at the end of the L column in the chart.

   ▶ What is something that you have learned about the moon that you did not know before? Answers will vary.   Where did you find that information? Answers will vary.

Objectives

- Demonstrate understanding through graphic organizers.
- Identify important details in informational text.
- Generate questions and seek information to answer questions.
- Locate information using features of text and electronic media.

Introduce "The *Eagle* on the Moon"

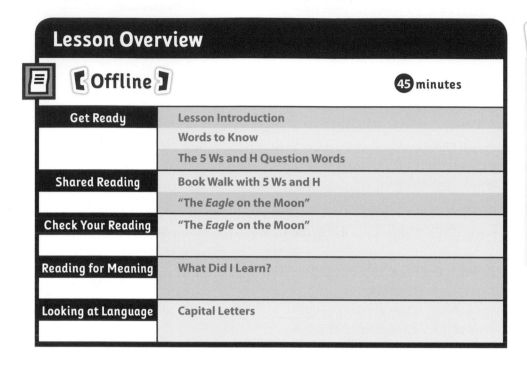

Lesson Overview

Offline   45 minutes

Get Ready	Lesson Introduction
	Words to Know
	The 5 Ws and H Question Words
Shared Reading	Book Walk with 5 Ws and H
	"The *Eagle* on the Moon"
Check Your Reading	"The *Eagle* on the Moon"
Reading for Meaning	What Did I Learn?
Looking at Language	Capital Letters

Materials

Supplied
- "The *Eagle* on the Moon," *K¹² World: Earth and Sky*, pp. 24–37
- *K¹² Language Arts Activity Book*, pp. LC 89–94

Also Needed
- scissors, adult
- tape, clear

Article Synopsis

Neil Armstrong, Buzz Aldrin, and Mike Collins were the first astronauts to fly to the moon. Learn about their journey—from training for their trip to walking on the moon.

Keywords

self-monitor – to notice if you do or do not understand what you are reading

self-question – to ask questions of yourself as you read to check your understanding

Advance Preparation

Before beginning the Shared Reading, read "The *Eagle* on the Moon" to locate Words to Know in the text. For Looking at Language, cut out and tape together the sentence strips on page LC 91, and preview the Reading Aid on pages LC 93 and 94 in *K¹² Language Arts Activity Book* to prepare the materials.

Big Ideas

- ▸ Comprehension entails having and knowing a purpose for reading.
- ▸ Self-questioning improves comprehension and ensures that reading is an interactive process.
- ▸ Comprehension requires the reader to self-monitor understanding.
- ▸ During shared-reading activities, students learn more about how print works.

 **45** minutes

Work **together** with students to complete Get Ready, Shared Reading, Check Your Reading, Reading for Meaning, and Looking at Language activities.

Get Ready

Lesson Introduction
Prepare students for listening to and discussing "The *Eagle* on the Moon."

1. Tell students that you are going to read "The *Eagle* on the Moon," a nonfiction magazine article that gives information about the first astronauts to travel to the moon.

2. Explain that before you read the article, you will get ready by discussing

   ▸ Why it's important to ask and answer questions before, during, and after reading
   ▸ How to set a purpose, or a reason, for reading and why it is important to do so

> **Objectives**
> - Increase concept and content vocabulary.
> - Build vocabulary through listening, reading, and discussion.
> - Use new vocabulary in written and spoken sentences.
> - Ask and answer who, what, where, when, why, and how questions.

Words to Know
Before reading "The *Eagle* on the Moon," go over Words to Know with students.

1. Read aloud each word and have students repeat it.

2. Ask students if they know what each word means.

   ▸ If students know a word's meaning, have them define it and use it in a sentence.
   ▸ If students don't know a word's meaning, read them the definition and discuss the word with them.

astronaut – a person trained to travel and work in space
experiment – a carefully planned test used to discover something unknown
fuel – something that is burned to supply heat or power; gasoline, coal, and oil are types of fuel
hatch – an opening in a vehicle, which people and things can go through; hatches are usually found on ships
mission – a special job or task
orbit – the curved path in space that an object follows as it goes around a planet, moon, or star; for example, the earth travels in orbit around the sun
surface – the outside or top part of something

The 5 Ws and H Question Words

Explore self-questioning.

1. Tell students that **good readers ask questions** before, during, and after they read. Asking questions is important because it helps us focus on the important information as we look for the answers to our questions while we read. If we ask questions and look for the answers, we're more likely to remember what we read. It's also a way to check that we understand what we've read.

2. Explain that questions can begin with **who**, **what**, **where**, **when**, **why**, or **how**. Some people call these question words the 5 Ws and H.
   Say: For example, before reading a story called "The Surprise," a reader might ask: Who is the surprise for? What is the surprise? Where did the surprise happen? When did the surprise happen? Why did someone get a surprise? How will the person feel about the surprise?

3. Have students imagine that they are going to read a story called "Alone in the Cold." Have students practice using the 5 Ws and H question words to think of questions based on the title of the story.

   ▸ What question could you ask that begins with the word *who*? Possible answer: Who is alone in the cold?

   ▸ What question could you ask that begins with the question word *what*? Possible answer: What will the person do to stay warm?

   ▸ The other question words are *where*, *when*, *why*, and *how*. What are some questions you could ask that begin with those words? Possible answers: Where is the person alone in the cold? When will the person get out of the cold? Why is the person alone? How does the person feel about being alone?

(TIP) Asking questions is an important strategy for improving comprehension. Do not describe a question as "bad" or "wrong" because this may discourage students from asking questions.

Shared Reading

Book Walk with 5 Ws and H

Prepare students by taking them on a Book Walk of "The *Eagle* on the Moon." Scan the magazine article together and ask students to make predictions about the text. Turn to pages LC 89 and 90 in *K¹² Language Arts Activity Book*. Answers to questions may vary.

1. Turn to the table of contents in *K¹² World: Earth and Sky*. Help students find "The *Eagle* on the Moon" and turn to that page.

2. Point to and read aloud the **title of the article**.

3. Have students look at the **pictures** in the article.

   ▸ What do you think the article is about?
   ▸ What do you think a trip to the moon would be like?

4. Point to and read aloud any headers, captions, or other features that stand out.

   ▸ What do you think the article might tell us about the first astronauts to travel to the moon?

5. Remind students of the 5 Ws and H: who, what, where, when, why, and how.

6. Tell students to use the 5 Ws and H question words to think of questions based on the title and pictures of the article.

7. On the Activity Book page, read aloud a question starter and write down what students dictate. Repeat this step until all questions are complete.

   ▸ If students are ready to write on their own, allow them to do so.

8. Explain to students that they will listen for answers to their 5 Ws and H questions as you read aloud "The *Eagle* on the Moon."

9. Tell students that good readers usually have a **purpose**, or reason, for reading a text. Having a reason for reading helps readers focus on the important information in a text and remember what they read.

Objectives

- Make predictions based on text, illustrations, and/or prior knowledge.
- Activate prior knowledge by previewing text and/or discussing topic.
- Ask and answer who, what, where, when, why, and how questions.
- Generate literal level questions.
- Monitor understanding by self-questioning.
- Set a purpose for reading.
- Read for information.

10. Explain to students that listening for the answers to their questions is their purpose, or reason, for listening to "The *Eagle* on the Moon."

TIP Keep the Activity Book pages in a safe place so you can add to it later.

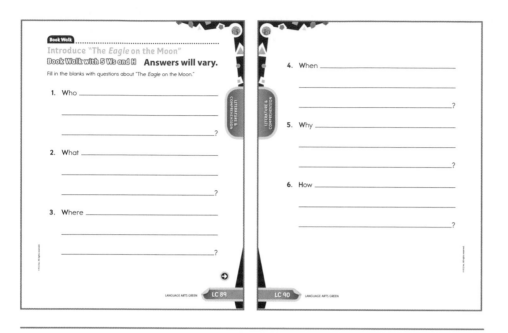

"The *Eagle* on the Moon"

It's time to read aloud.

1. Have students sit next to you so that they can see the pictures and words while you read aloud.

2. Tell students to listen for the answers to the 5 Ws and H questions they asked.

3. **Read aloud the entire article.** Track with your finger so students can follow along. Emphasize Words to Know as you come to them. If appropriate, use the pictures to help show what each word means.

Check Your Reading

"The *Eagle* on the Moon"

Check students' comprehension of "The *Eagle* on the Moon."

Objectives
- Identify the topic.
- Identify important details in informational text.
- Identify facts in informational text.

- ► What is the topic of the article? the first astronauts to travel to the moon
- ► Who were the first astronauts to go to the moon? Neil Armstrong, Buzz Aldrin, and Mike Collins
- ► What was the name of the ship that landed on the surface of the moon? the *Eagle*
- ► How did people on earth see the astronauts on the moon? on television
- ► Which astronaut was the first to walk on the moon? Neil Armstrong
- ► Which astronaut was second to walk on the moon? Buzz Aldrin
- ► What did Neil Armstrong and Buzz Aldrin put up on the moon? an American flag

TIP If students have trouble responding to a question, help them locate the answer in the text or pictures.

Reading for Meaning

Objectives
- Ask and answer who, what, where, when, why, and how questions.
- Monitor understanding by self-questioning.

What Did I Learn?

Check students' ability to answer their prereading questions. Gather completed pages LC 89 and 90 in *K¹² Language Arts Activity Book.*

1. Remind students that good readers **ask questions** before, during, and after they read. Asking questions is important because it gives us a focus when we read so we're more likely to remember what we read. It's also a way to check that we understand what we've read.

2. Read aloud the questions students dictated to you on the Activity Book page and have students answer them verbally.

3. Explain to students that the answers to some of their questions might not have been in the article. However, thinking about the questions and listening for the answers still helps them become better readers because they listen carefully to the article and remember it better.

TIP Keep the list of questions handy so students can use it to do more research later.

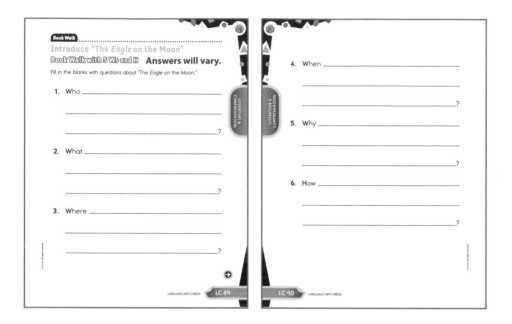

Looking at Language

Capital Letters

Reread "The *Eagle* on the Moon" with a focus on the uses of capital letters. Gather the sentence strip that you prepared from page LC 91 and the Reading Aid on pages LC 93 and 94 in *K¹² Language Arts Activity Book*.

1. Explain to students that different words in a sentence begin with capital letters for different reasons.

   ► Can you tell me some of the rules for when we use capital letters? at the beginning of a sentence; at the beginning of a name

2. If students are not able to provide any rules for when to use capital letters, tell them not to worry because you will teach them the rules as you reread the article together.

3. Gather the sentence strip and track with your finger as you read aloud the sentence. Then have students read aloud the sentence with you.

4. Tell students that the word *They* begins with a capital letter because it is the beginning of the sentence. The words *Mike*, *Neil*, and *Buzz* begin with capital letters because they are the specific names of people.

Objectives
- Recall uses of capital letters.
- Recognize when to use a capital letter.
- Recognize that a sentence begins with a capital letter.
- Read aloud grade-level text with appropriate expression, accuracy, and rate.

5. Tell students that they will **read aloud the article with you**. As you read aloud together, you will stop at certain points to discuss why certain words begin with capital letters.

6. As you read aloud, encourage students to pay attention to words that begin with capital letters.

7. Refer to the Reading Aid.

Reading Aid Tear out the Reading Aid for this reading selection. Follow the instructions for folding the page, and then use the page as a guide as you reread the selection with students.

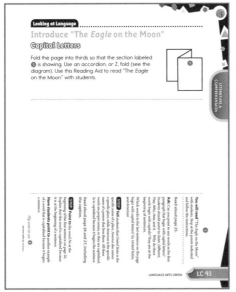
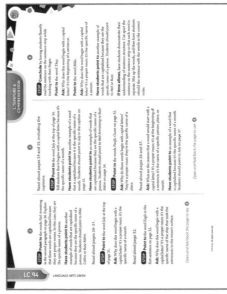

Explore "The *Eagle* on the Moon"

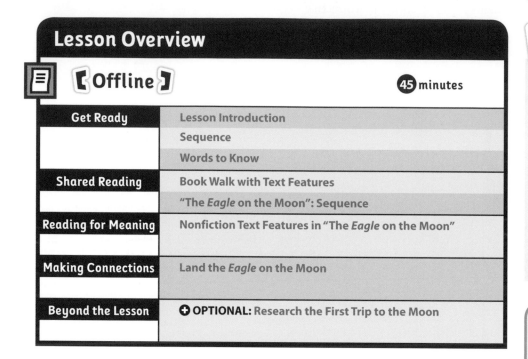

Lesson Overview

[Offline]   45 minutes

Get Ready	Lesson Introduction
	Sequence
	Words to Know
Shared Reading	Book Walk with Text Features
	"The *Eagle* on the Moon": Sequence
Reading for Meaning	Nonfiction Text Features in "The *Eagle* on the Moon"
Making Connections	Land the *Eagle* on the Moon
Beyond the Lesson	⊕ OPTIONAL: Research the First Trip to the Moon

[Materials]

Supplied

- "The *Eagle* on the Moon," *K¹² World: Earth and Sky*, pp. 24–37
- *K¹² Language Arts Activity Book*, pp. LC 89–90 (optional), 95–99

Also Needed

- glue stick
- scissors, round-end safety

Keywords

sequence – order

text feature – part of a text that helps a reader locate information and determine what is most important; some examples are the title, table of contents, headings, pictures, and glossary

visual text support – a graphic feature that helps a reader better understand text, such as a picture, chart, or map

Advance Preparation

Preview the Reading Aid on pages LC 95 and 96 in *K¹² Language Arts Activity Book* to prepare the materials for the Shared Reading.

Big Ideas

- ▶ Comprehension entails an understanding of the organizational patterns of text.
- ▶ Comprehension is facilitated by an understanding of physical presentation (for example, headings, subheads, graphics, and other features).
- ▶ Shared reading allows students to observe and practice the reading behaviors of proficient readers.
- ▶ During shared-reading activities, students learn more about how print works.

⟦ Offline ⟧ **45** minutes

Work **together** with students to complete Get Ready, Shared Reading, Reading for Meaning, Making Connections, and Beyond the Lesson activities.

Get Ready

Lesson Introduction

Prepare students for listening to and discussing "The *Eagle* on the Moon."

1. Tell students that you are going to reread "The *Eagle* on the Moon."

2. Explain that before you read the article, you will get ready by discussing sequence of events in nonfiction text.

Sequence

Explore the order of events in a text.

1. Remind students that the order in which things happen in a story or article is called the **sequence**. Words like *first*, *after*, and *finally* help tell the sequence.

2. Explain that many nonfiction texts also include the years that certain events happened. Paying attention to the years mentioned in a text helps us identify the sequence, or order, in which things happen.

3. Have students practice identifying the sequence of events in a short paragraph. **Say:** Listen for years or words that tell the order in which things happen: Henry was born in 2006. His little sister was born in 2008. In 2010, the last member of Henry's family arrived—his puppy named Spot!

   ▸ What happened first? Henry was born.
   ▸ What happened last? Spot joined the family.

Words to Know

Before reading "The *Eagle* on the Moon," go over Words to Know with students.

1. Read aloud each word and have students repeat it.

2. Ask students if they know what each word means.
   ▸ If students know a word's meaning, have them define it and use it in a sentence.
   ▸ If students don't know a word's meaning, read them the definition and discuss the word with them.

> **Objectives**
> - Identify sequence of events in informational text.
> - Increase concept and content vocabulary.
> - Build vocabulary through listening, reading, and discussion.
> - Use new vocabulary in written and spoken sentences.

astronaut – a person trained to travel and work in space

experiment – a carefully planned test used to discover something unknown

fuel – something that is burned to supply heat or power; gasoline, coal, and oil are types of fuel

hatch – an opening in a vehicle, which people and things can go through; hatches are usually found on ships

mission – a special job or task

orbit – the curved path in space that an object follows as it goes around a planet, moon, or star; for example, the earth travels in orbit around the sun

surface – the outside or top part of something

Shared Reading

Book Walk with Text Features

Prepare students by taking them on a Book Walk of "The *Eagle* on the Moon." Scan the magazine article together to revisit the text and point out text features.

1. Remind students that magazine articles have features that help readers better understand the information in the article.

2. Turn to page 24 and point to and read aloud the **title of the article**. Explain that the title usually tells us what the article is about.

3. Point to the word **pilots** on page 26. Explain that some words in the article are darker, or bold, so that we will notice them. This word is bold because it's an important word in the article. We can find out what this word means in the glossary at the back of the magazine on pages 51 and 52.

4. Point to the pictures on page 29. Explain that pictures help show ideas that are in the article.
   Say: These pictures help the reader better understand how the astronauts prepared to go to the moon.

5. Point to the text below the pictures on page 29. Tell students that the text below the pictures is a **caption**. It gives information about the pictures. Read aloud the caption.

6. Turn to page 31 and point to the heading. Explain that articles can be broken up into sections, and a **heading** tells what a section is about. An article's headings can help us figure out where to find certain information.
   Say: This heading tells readers that this section of the article is about the beginning of the astronauts' trip to the moon. If I want to find out the date the astronauts left earth to go to the moon, this is the section I would look in.

Objectives
- Activate prior knowledge by previewing text and/or discussing topic.
- Read for information.
- Identify sequence of events in informational text.
- Read aloud grade-level text with appropriate expression, accuracy, and rate.

7. Point to the time line on pages 36 and 37. Tell students that the time line lists in order some important events of the space race. Read aloud the dates and events on the time line.

8. Remind students that thinking about their prior knowledge will help them connect new information in the article to things that they already know. This will help them better understand and remember the information in the article.

9. Ask the following questions to help students think about what they already know about the first trip to the moon.
   ▸ Who were the first three astronauts to go to the moon? Neil Armstrong, Buzz Aldrin, and Mike Collins
   ▸ Which two astronauts walked on the moon? Neil Armstrong and Buzz Aldrin
   ▸ What was the name of the small ship that Neil Armstrong landed on the moon? the *Eagle*

"The *Eagle* on the Moon": Sequence

It's time to reread the article. Tell students that they will reread "The *Eagle* on the Moon" with a focus on text and text features that indicate time and sequence. Gather the Reading Aid on pages LC 95 and 96 in *K¹² Language Arts Activity Book*.

1. Remind students that we can tell the order of events in an article when we see words such as *first*, *next*, *then*, and even *soon*. We call these **signal words** because they signal when things happen.

2. Explain that we can also tell the sequence of events when an article mentions years. When an article has most of the important events organized in the order in which they happened, we say that the article is organized **in sequence**.

3. Have students sit next to you so that they can see the pictures and words while you read aloud.

4. Tell students that **they will read aloud the article with you**. As you read aloud together, you will stop at certain points to discuss clues in the text that indicate the sequence in which things happened.

5. Refer to the Reading Aid.

Reading Aid Tear out the Reading Aid for this reading selection. Follow the instructions for folding the page, and then use the page as a guide as you reread the selection with students.

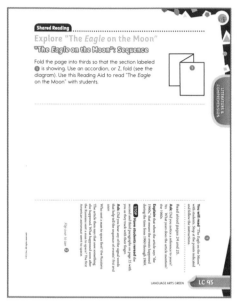
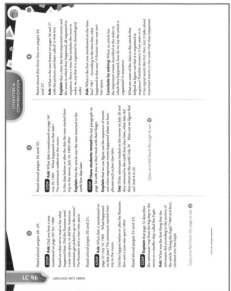

Reading for Meaning

Nonfiction Text Features in "The *Eagle* on the Moon"

Check students' understanding of text features in "The *Eagle* on the Moon."

1. Remind students that good readers use text features, such as headings, pictures, and captions, to better understand the information in a magazine article.

2. Point to the word **astronaut** on page 25.

   ► Why is this word darker than the other words? It's an important word in the article.   Where can we find out what this word means? in the back of the magazine

3. Point to the pictures on pages 26 and 27 of the magazine and read aloud the captions below them.

   ► What information do these pictures and captions give us? They tell us more about each of the astronauts.

Objectives

- Identify features of informational text.
- Identify purpose of and information provided by informational text features.
- Identify sequence of events in informational text.
- Create and/or interpret a time line.

---

4. Point to the pictures on pages 28 and 29 of the magazine and read aloud the caption below them.

   ▸ What information do these pictures and caption give us? They tell us how the astronauts prepared for their mission.

5. Remind students that articles can be broken up into sections, and a heading tells what a section is about. An article's headings can help us figure out where to find certain information

   ▸ Where should I look if I want to read about the day the astronauts left for the moon? the section on page 31

6. Point to the time line on pages 36 and 37.

   ▸ What is the purpose of this time line? to list in order important events of the space race
   ▸ Based on the time line, when did the first man go to space? 1961
   ▸ Based on the time line, when were Neil Armstrong, Buzz Aldrin, and Mike Collins chosen to go to the moon? 1968
   ▸ Based on the time line, on what date did Neil Armstrong and Buzz Aldrin walk on the moon? July 20, 1969
   ▸ Based on the time line, which happened first—Neil, Buzz, and Mike were picked to go to the moon, or Neil, Buzz, and Mike became astronauts? Neil, Buzz, and Mike became astronauts.

Making Connections

Land the *Eagle* on the Moon
Check students' understanding of the sequence of the events involved in flying the *Eagle* from the main ship to the moon's surface. Turn to pages LC 97–99 in *K¹² Language Arts Activity Book,* and gather the scissors and glue stick.

1. Remind students that an article's headings can help us figure out where to find certain information.

   ▸ In which section of the article would you find information about the astronauts flying the *Eagle* to the surface of the moon? the section on page 32

2. Remind students that the order in which things happen in a story or article is called the **sequence**. One way that readers can check whether they understand what they read is by telling the sequence of events.

Objectives
- Identify relevant sources of information.
- Sequence pictures illustrating story events.
- Identify sequence of events in informational text.
- Follow two- or three-step written directions.
- Retell a story using various media.

3. Explain that students will use pictures to show the sequence of events involved in flying the *Eagle* from the main ship to the moon's surface. They will also practice reading and following simple directions.

4. Have students complete the Activity Book page, helping them with the instructions as needed.

5. Have students retell the sequence of events using the pictures as a guide.

TIP Refer back to page 32 of "The *Eagle* on the Moon" if students have trouble recalling the order of events in flying the *Eagle* from the main ship to the moon's surface.

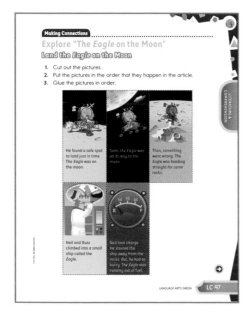

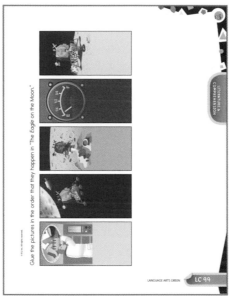

Beyond the Lesson

⊕ OPTIONAL: Research the First Trip to the Moon

This activity is OPTIONAL. It is intended for students who have extra time and would benefit from further research on the first trip to the moon. Feel free to skip this activity. Gather completed pages LC 89 and 90 in *K¹² Language Arts Activity Book.*

1. Help students look for answers to their unanswered questions about the first trip to the moon. Use one or more of the following sources:

   ▸ the Further Reading section of *K¹² World: Earth and Sky*
   ▸ encyclopedias
   ▸ science magazines, such as *National Geographic Kids*
   ▸ nonfiction library books about the first trip to the moon
   ▸ the Internet, using the search words "first trip to the moon"

2. Remind students to use the headings in the science magazines or websites to help them locate information to answer their questions.

3. Discuss any answers students are able to find.

4. Discuss any other interesting information that students find in their search. Answers to questions may vary.

   ▸ What is something new that you learned about the astronauts' first trip to the moon? Where did you find that information?

Objectives

- Locate information using features of text and electronic media.
- Identify important details in informational text.
- Generate questions and seek information to answer questions.
- Identify relevant sources of information.

Introduce "Women in Space"

Lesson Overview

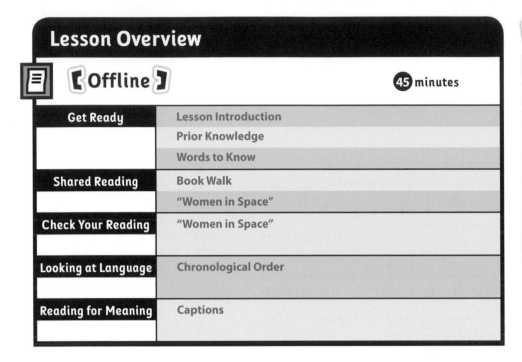

[Offline]   **45** minutes

Get Ready	Lesson Introduction
	Prior Knowledge
	Words to Know
Shared Reading	Book Walk
	"Women in Space"
Check Your Reading	"Women in Space"
Looking at Language	Chronological Order
Reading for Meaning	Captions

[Materials]

Supplied
- "Women in Space," *K¹² World: Earth and Sky,* pp. 38–49
- *K¹² Language Arts Activity Book,* pp. LC 101–102
- *K¹² My Journal,* pp. 2–53

Also Needed
- index cards (5)

Article Synopsis

NASA first allowed women to become astronauts in 1978. Since then, women have become an important part of the space program.

Keywords

caption – writing under a picture that describes the picture

prior knowledge – things you already know from past experience

Advance Preparation

Before beginning the Shared Reading, read "Women in Space" to locate Words to Know in the text. Preview the Reading Aid on pages LC 101 and 102 in *K¹² Language Arts Activity Book* to prepare the materials for Looking at Language.

Big Ideas

▸ Activating prior knowledge provides a framework for a reader to organize and connect new information to information previously learned; readers that activate prior knowledge before reading are more likely to understand and recall what they read.

▸ Comprehension entails having and knowing a purpose for reading.

▸ Self-questioning improves comprehension and ensures that reading is an interactive process.

▸ Comprehension is facilitated by an understanding of physical presentation (for example, headings, subheads, graphics, and other features).

▸ Shared reading allows students to observe and practice the reading behaviors of proficient readers.

▸ During shared-reading activities, students learn more about how print works.

 **45** minutes

Work **together** with students to complete Get Ready, Shared Reading, Check Your Reading, Looking at Language, and Reading for Meaning activities.

Get Ready

Lesson Introduction
Prepare students for listening to and discussing "Women in Space."

1. Tell students that you are going to read "Women in Space," a nonfiction magazine article that gives information about several female astronauts.

2. Explain that before you read the article, you will get ready by discussing how and why we activate prior knowledge when we read.

 Objectives

- Activate prior knowledge by previewing text and/or discussing topic.
- Increase concept and content vocabulary.
- Build vocabulary through listening, reading, and discussion.
- Use new vocabulary in written and spoken sentences.

Prior Knowledge
Explore the strategy of activating prior knowledge.

1. Tell students that good readers think about what they already know when reading a new text. We use **prior knowledge**, or things we know from past experience, to help us better understand a text. We do the same thing to help us understand the world around us.
   Say: Imagine you're in your room and you hear a loud pop in the next room. You go into the next room and see two balloons floating, each with a piece of string tied to it. You also see a piece of string on the floor.

   ▶ What do you think caused the loud noise? a balloon popping

   Say: Using your prior knowledge about balloons probably helped you figure out that the unknown noise was a balloon popping.

2. Explain that the text you will read is about women astronauts. So students' prior knowledge about astronauts and space travel will help them understand the new text.

3. Have students tell you some things they already know about astronauts and space travel. If students have trouble thinking of something, encourage them to think about

   ▶ How astronauts travel in space in spaceships
   ▶ What astronauts wear when they travel in space space suits
   ▶ The first astronauts to travel to the moon Neil Armstrong, Buzz Aldrin, and Mike Collins

4. Explain that when we read, thinking about our prior knowledge helps us get our brain ready to read. It helps us connect new information in a text to things that we already know that are stored in our brain. This helps us better understand and remember what we've read.

Words to Know

Before reading "Women in Space," go over Words to Know with students.

1. Read aloud each word and have students repeat it.

2. Ask students if they know what each word means.

   ▸ If students know a word's meaning, have them define it and use it in a sentence.
   ▸ If students don't know a word's meaning, read them the definition and discuss the word with them.

astronaut – a person trained to travel and work in space

experiment – a carefully planned test used to discover something unknown

international – having to do with more than one country

laboratory – a place where people do scientific experiments

NASA – a U.S. government organization involved with space travel; stands for National Aeronautics and Space Administration

orbit – the curved path in space that an object follows as it goes around a planet, moon, or star; for example, the earth travels in orbit around the sun

shuttle – a vehicle that travels the same route back and forth

space walk – when an astronaut leaves a spacecraft and works outside of it while in outer space

Shared Reading

Book Walk

Prepare students by taking them on a Book Walk of "Women in Space." Scan the magazine article together and ask students to make predictions about the text. Gather *K¹² My Journal* and have students turn to the next available page for **writing** in Thoughts and Experiences. Answers to questions may vary.

1. Turn to the table of contents in *K¹² World: Earth and Sky.* Help students find the selection and turn to that page

2. Point to and read aloud the **title of the article**.

3. Have students look at the **pictures of the article**.

   ▸ Do you know of any astronauts that are women?

4. Point to and read aloud any headers, captions, or other features that stand out.

   ▸ What do you think the article might tell us about female astronauts?

Objectives

- Make predictions based on text, illustrations, and/or prior knowledge.
- Activate prior knowledge by previewing text and/or discussing topic.
- Set a purpose for reading.
- Generate questions and seek information to answer questions.
- Read for information.

5. Have students tell you two questions that they'd like to have answered by the article. Write the questions students dictate in their journal.

   ▸ If students are ready to write on their own, allow them to do so.

6. Tell students that good readers usually have a **purpose**, or reason, for reading a text. Having a reason for reading helps readers to focus on what's important and remember what they read.

7. Explain to students that listening for the answers to their questions is their purpose, or reason, for listening to "Women in Space."

TIP Keep students' journal page in a safe place so you can refer to it later.

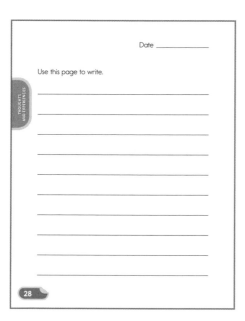

"Women in Space"

It's time to read aloud.

1. Have students sit next to you so that they can see the pictures and words while you read aloud.

2. Tell students to listen for information that answers their questions.

3. **Read aloud the entire article.** Track with your finger so students can follow along. Emphasize Words to Know as you come to them. If appropriate, use the pictures to help show what each word means.

Check Your Reading

"Women in Space"

Check students' comprehension of "Women in Space." Gather the page in Thoughts and Experiences in *K¹² My Journal* with students' questions about the article.

1. Help students read aloud their questions. Have them answer the questions if the answers were in the article.

2. Explain to students that the answers to their questions might not have been in the article. However, thinking about the questions and listening for the answers helped them listen carefully to the article and remember it better.

3. Ask the following questions.

   ▸ What is the topic of this article? female astronauts
   ▸ Why weren't women allowed to be astronauts until 1978? because people at NASA thought being an astronaut was too dangerous and hard for women
   ▸ Who was the first American woman in space? Sally Ride
   ▸ On Sally Ride's second trip to space, Kathryn Sullivan was part of the space crew. What was Kathryn Sullivan's special job on this trip? a space walk
   ▸ When she was a girl, why did some people think Mae Jemison could never be an astronaut? because she was an African American and a girl

TIP If students have trouble responding to a question, help them locate the answer in the text or pictures.

Objectives
- Identify the topic.
- Identify facts in informational text.

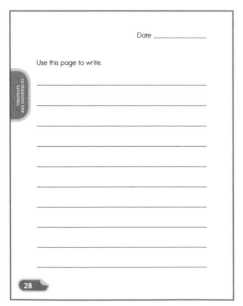

Looking at Language ....

Chronological Order

Reread "Women in Space" with a focus on chronological order. Gather the index cards and the Reading Aid on pages LC 101 and 102 in *K¹² Language Arts Activity Book*.

1. Explain to students that there are different ways that an author can organize information in an article.

   ▸ Some articles are organized by cause and effect, which means that the article explains how some events can cause other things to happen.
   ▸ Some articles are organized by problem and solution, which means that the article describes problems and how those problems have been or are being solved.

2. Tell students that "Women in Space" explains events that have happened over a period of many years. The article has references to years, such as 1978 and 1983, and describes the events that happened in those years. Most of this article is organized in **chronological order**. That means that the article tells us when important events happened and the order in which they happened.

3. Tell students that they will **read aloud the article with you**. As you read aloud together, you will stop at certain points to discuss the major events described in the article and the years those events happened.

4. Explain that as you come across years listed in the article, you will write each year on an index card along with information about the events that happened in that year. You will use the index cards to build a time line after reading the article.

5. As you read, encourage students to pay attention to when the article mentions years.

Objectives
- Identify chronological order.
- Identify sequence of events in informational text.
- Read aloud grade-level text with appropriate expression, accuracy, and rate.
- Create and/or interpret a time line.
- Demonstrate one-to-one correspondence (voice-to-print).

6. Refer to the Reading Aid.

Reading Aid Tear out the Reading Aid for this reading selection. Follow the instructions for folding the page, and then use the page as a guide as you reread the selection with students.

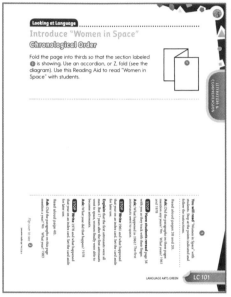
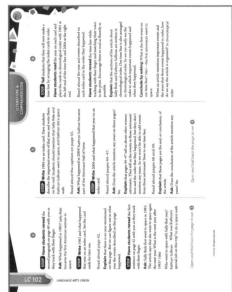

Reading for Meaning

Captions

Explore captions in "Women in Space."

1. Point to the caption under the photo on page 39.

   ▶ What do we call this text feature? a caption   What kind of information do we find in captions? information that explains the photo that the caption is near

2. Remind students that captions explain photos in magazine articles, and sometimes captions provide additional information that may not be in the text.

> **Objectives**
> - Identify features of informational text.
> - Identify purpose of and information provided by informational text features.

3. Point to and read aloud the caption on page 43.

   ▸ What information does this caption provide that isn't in the article text?
     that Kathryn Sullivan became part of the Astronaut Hall of Fame in 2004

4. Point to and read aloud the caption on page 44.

   ▸ What information does this caption provide that isn't in the article text?
     that Mae Jemison studied the human body in space

5. Point to and read aloud the caption on page 46.

   ▸ What information does this caption provide that isn't in the article text?
     that Ellen Ochoa was the first Hispanic American woman in space

6. Point to and read aloud the caption on page 47.
   ▸ What information does this caption provide that isn't in the article text?
     that Ellen Ochoa visited the International Space Station, which is 200 miles
     above the earth

Explore "Women in Space"

Lesson Overview

[Offline]		45 minutes
Get Ready	Lesson Introduction	
	Facts and Opinions	
	Words to Know	
Shared Reading	Book Walk	
	"Women in Space": Repair Comprehension	
Reading for Meaning	Facts and Opinions in "Women in Space"	
Making Connections	How Do They Compare?	

Advance Preparation

Preview the Reading Aid on pages LC 105 and 106 in *K¹² Language Arts Activity Book* to prepare the materials for the Shared Reading.

Big Ideas

▸ Readers must focus on the specific language of a text to aid in interpretation.

▸ Shared reading allows students to observe and practice the reading behaviors of proficient readers.

▸ Comprehension strategies can be taught through explicit instruction.

▸ Self-questioning improves comprehension and ensures that reading is an interactive process.

▸ Verbalizing your thoughts while modeling a reading strategy allows students to see what goes on inside the head of an effective reader; it makes visible the normally hidden process of comprehending text.

▸ Comprehension is facilitated when readers connect new information to information previously learned.

Materials

Supplied

● "Women in Space," *K¹² World: Earth and Sky*, pp. 38–49

● *K¹² Language Arts Activity Book*, pp. LC 103–108

Also Needed

● household objects – beach ball, basketball (optional)

Keywords

compare – to explain how two or more things are alike

contrast – to explain how two or more things are different

fact – something that can be proven true

opinion – something that a person thinks or believes, but which cannot be proven to be true

 **45** minutes

Work **together** with students to complete Get Ready, Shared Reading, Reading for Meaning, and Making Connections activities.

Get Ready

Lesson Introduction

Prepare students for listening to and discussing "Women in Space."

1. Tell students that you are going to reread "Women in Space."

2. Explain that before you read the article, you will get ready by discussing the difference between facts and opinions.

Facts and Opinions

Explore how to identify opinions. Turn to page LC 103 in *K¹² Language Arts Activity Book.*

1. Show students the picture of the beach ball and the basketball on the Activity Book page. (You may show students a real beach ball and basketball if they are available.) Then make the following statements to introduce the difference between a fact and an opinion:

   ▶ This beach ball is round.
   ▶ It's more fun to play with a beach ball than a basketball.

2. Tell students that it is a fact that the beach ball is round. We can look at it and know that it's true.

3. Explain that the statement, "It's more fun to play with a beach ball than a basketball," is an opinion. **An opinion is something that a person feels or believes.** You cannot prove it to be true. While one person may feel that beach balls are more fun to play with than basketballs, someone else may think that basketballs are more fun to play with.

4. Tell students that nonfiction articles are filled with facts. But sometimes authors of nonfiction articles include opinions or feelings about the subject. It's important to know the difference between a fact and an opinion so that we can identify what is true from what somebody feels or believes.

5. Ask students if the following statements are facts or opinions.

   ▶ Fish live in water. fact
   ▶ I think goldfish are the prettiest kind of fish. opinion

Objectives
- Identify opinions.
- Distinguish fact from opinion.
- Increase concept and content vocabulary.
- Build vocabulary through listening, reading, and discussion.
- Use new vocabulary in written and spoken sentences.

6. Point out that we can prove that fish live in water, so this is a fact. However, some people may not believe that goldfish are the prettiest kind of fish, so this is an opinion.

7. Explain that certain words are clues that a statement is an opinion. These words include *think*, *believe*, and *feel*. Also, some phrases, such as *some people say*, are hints that a statement is an opinion.

8. Read the following paragraph to have students practice identifying facts and opinions.
   Say: Listen carefully to hear the facts and opinions in the following paragraph.

   Maya has a cat. Her cat is orange and white. Maya thinks cats are great pets, and she thinks her cat is the best cat in the world.

9. Ask students the following questions to check their understanding of facts and opinions.

   ▸ Maya has a cat. Is this a fact or an opinion? a fact   Why is it a fact? because you can prove it's true

   ▸ Maya thinks cats are great pets. Is this a fact or an opinion? an opinion   Why is it an opinion? Possible answers: You can't prove it's true; someone might think a different animal is a better pet; it has the word *think*.

   ▸ Maya can prove her cat is orange and white. What do we call something that we can prove is true? a fact

   ▸ Maya thinks her cat is the best cat in the world. Is this statement a fact or an opinion? an opinion   Why? Possible answers: You can't prove it; you could say that another cat is the best in the world; it has the word *thinks*.

Words to Know

Before reading "Women in Space," go over Words to Know with students.

1. Read aloud each word and have students repeat it.

2. Ask students if they know what each word means.

   ▸ If students know a word's meaning, have them define it and use it in a sentence.
   ▸ If students don't know a word's meaning, read them the definition and discuss the word with them.

astronaut – a person trained to travel and work in space

experiment – a carefully planned test used to discover something unknown

international – having to do with more than one country

laboratory – a place where people do scientific experiments

NASA – a U.S. government organization involved with space travel; stands for National Aeronautics and Space Administration

orbit – the curved path in space that an object follows as it goes around a planet, moon, or star; for example, the earth travels in orbit around the sun

shuttle – a vehicle that travels the same route back and forth

space walk – when an astronaut leaves a spacecraft and works outside of it while in outer space

Shared Reading

Book Walk

Prepare students by taking them on a Book Walk of "Women in Space." Scan the magazine article together to revisit the text.

1. Turn to the selection.

2. Point to and read aloud the **title of the article**.

3. Have students look at the **pictures of the article**.

4. Remind students that thinking about their prior knowledge will help them connect new information in the article to things that they already know.

5. Ask the following questions to help students think about what they already know about female astronauts.

   ▸ Why didn't people at NASA allow women to be astronauts until 1978? They thought being an astronaut was too dangerous and too hard for women.
   ▸ Who was the first American woman in space? Sally Ride
   ▸ Who was the first American woman to do a space walk? Kathryn Sullivan
   ▸ Who is Mae Jemison? the first African American woman in space

6. Point to the four pictures of female astronauts on page 39.

   ▸ Why do you think these pictures are in this section of the article? to show the astronauts that the article is going to talk about

Objectives
- Activate prior knowledge by previewing text and/or discussing topic.
- Read for information.
- Repair comprehension using strategies: reread, use prior knowledge, self-question.
- Read aloud grade-level text with appropriate expression, accuracy, and rate.

"Women in Space": Repair Comprehension

It's time to reread the article. Tell students that they will reread "Women in Space" with a focus on what to do if they don't understand something they are reading. Gather the Reading Aid on pages LC 105 and 106 in *K¹² Language Arts Activity Book*.

1. Tell students that sometimes when we're reading, we realize that we're confused, and we don't understand something in the story or article we're reading.

2. Explain that there are strategies we can use to help us figure out what we don't understand.

   ▸ Sometimes all we need to do is go back and reread a part of the article more slowly and carefully.

   ▸ Other times it's helpful to ask yourself a question about something you're trying to figure out, and then go back and reread.

3. Tell students that when good readers do these things, you can't see what they're doing because it's happening in their head.

4. Explain that you will show students how to use these strategies, while sharing your thoughts aloud. That way they can learn what goes on in the head of a good reader.

5. Have students sit next to you so that they can see the pictures and words while you read aloud.

6. Tell students that **they will read aloud the article with you**. As you read aloud together, you will stop at certain points to show students how to use strategies to help you figure out something that is causing you confusion while reading.

7. Refer to the Reading Aid.

Reading Aid   Tear out the Reading Aid for this reading selection. Follow the instructions for folding the page, and then use the page as a guide as you reread the selection with students.

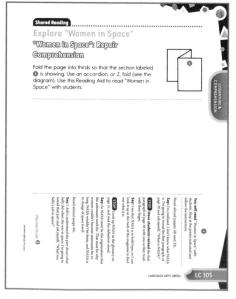
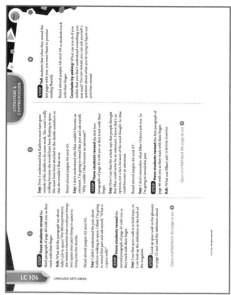

Reading for Meaning

Facts and Opinions in "Women in Space"

Explore facts and opinions in "Women in Space."

1. Remind students that a fact is something you can prove is true. If a statement tells what somebody feels or believes, it is an opinion.

2. Ask the following questions to check students' ability to distinguish fact from opinion.

   ▶ The article says that Sally Ride was the first American woman in space. Is this a fact or an opinion? a fact   How do you know? You can prove it; it's true

   ▶ The article says that people at NASA thought it was too hard for women to be astronauts. Is this a fact or an opinion? an opinion   How do you know? It says that people thought it; other people may have thought that it wasn't too hard for women to become astronauts.

   ▶ The article says that Kathryn Sullivan was the first American woman to do a space walk. Is this a fact or an opinion? a fact

   ▶ The article says that Mae Jemison became a doctor. Is this a fact or an opinion? a fact

   ▶ The article says that people thought Mae Jemison would never be an astronaut. Is this a fact or an opinion? an opinion

   ▶ The article says that Ellen Ochoa was a scientist. Is this a fact or an opinion? a fact

   ▶ The article says that more than 50 women have gone to space. Is this a fact or an opinion? a fact

TIP If students are confused as to whether a statement is a fact or opinion, pause and explain the answer.

Objectives

- Identify opinions.
- Identify facts in informational text.
- Distinguish fact from opinion.

Making Connections

How Do They Compare?

Explore the similarities and differences between an astronaut from "The *Eagle* on the Moon" and an astronaut from "Women in Space." Turn to pages LC 107 and 108 in *K¹² Language Arts Activity Book*

1. Look at the chart with students. Point to and read aloud the first row heading, "Year became an astronaut." Write what students dictate in the first row of boxes under the appropriate astronaut's name. Repeat until the chart is complete.

   ▶ If students are ready to write on their own, allow them to do so.

2. Have students tell you one fact and one opinion about each astronaut. Write what students dictate under the chart.

   ▶ If students have trouble stating an opinion about each astronaut, provide them with a sentence starter such as, "I think Neil Armstrong was . . ." or "I believe that Sally Ride was . . ."

Objectives

- Compare and contrast elements across informational texts.
- Demonstrate understanding through graphic organizers.
- Identify facts.
- Identify opinions.
- Make connections with text: text-to-text, text-to-self, text-to-world.

3. Ask the following questions to encourage discussion and comparisons of the two astronauts.

▸ How are Neil Armstrong and Sally Ride alike? Possible answers: Both are astronauts; both waited several years between becoming an astronaut and going to space; both went to space more than once; both were the first to do something.

▸ How are the two astronauts different? Possible answers: Neil Armstrong is a man and Sally Ride is a woman; Neil Armstrong became an astronaut first; Neil Armstrong went to space sooner after becoming an astronaut than Sally Ride; Neil Armstrong was the first astronaut to walk on the moon; Sally Ride was the first American woman in space.

Reward: Add a sticker for this unit on the My Accomplishments chart to mark successful completion of the unit.

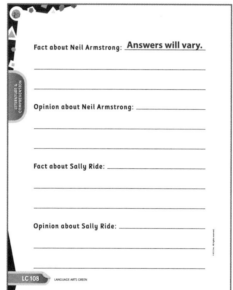

If You're Happy and You Know It

Unit Focus

In this unit, students will explore fables and folktales with a common theme—be happy with what you have. This unit follows the shared-reading instructional approach (see the Instructional Approaches to Reading in the introductory lesson for this program). In this unit, students will

- ► Listen to fables and folktales.
- ► Explore the characteristics of fables.
- ► Explore author's purpose.
- ► Explore story structure elements.
- ► Explore characters' actions and feelings.
- ► Practice using text and picture clues to define unknown words.
- ► Explore exclamations and questions.
- ► Learn the skill of distinguishing important details from less important details.

Unit Plan   【Offline】

Lesson 1	Introduce "The Pine Tree and Its Needles"	45 minutes a day
Lesson 2	Explore "The Pine Tree and Its Needles"	
Lesson 3	Introduce "The Little Rabbit Who Wanted Red Wings"	
Lesson 4	Explore "The Little Rabbit Who Wanted Red Wings"	
Lesson 5	Introduce "The Country Mouse and the City Mouse"	
Lesson 6	Explore "The Country Mouse and the City Mouse"	
Lesson 7	Introduce "The Cap that Mother Made"	
Lesson 8	Explore "The Cap that Mother Made"	
Lesson 9	Your Choice	

Introduce "The Pine Tree and Its Needles"

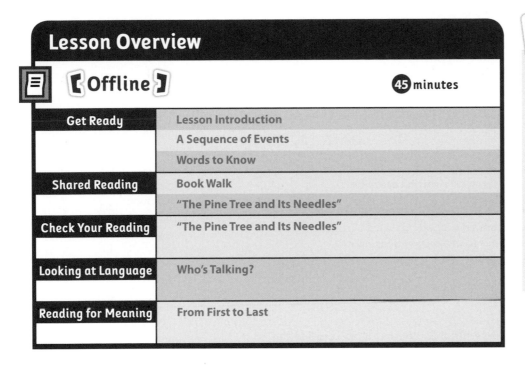

Lesson Overview

Offline — 45 minutes

Get Ready	Lesson Introduction
	A Sequence of Events
	Words to Know
Shared Reading	Book Walk
	"The Pine Tree and Its Needles"
Check Your Reading	"The Pine Tree and Its Needles"
Looking at Language	Who's Talking?
Reading for Meaning	From First to Last

Advance Preparation

Before beginning the Shared Reading, read "The Pine Tree and Its Needles" to locate Words to Know in the text. Use sticky notes to number the paragraphs in the story. Preview the Reading Aid on pages LC 109 and 110 in *K¹² Language Arts Activity Book* to prepare the materials for Looking at Language.

Big Ideas

▶ Comprehension requires an understanding of story structure.
▶ Repeated rereading leads to increased fluency.
▶ During shared-reading activities, students learn more about how print works.

Materials

Supplied

● "The Pine Tree and Its Needles," *K¹² Classics for Young Readers, Volume A,* pp. 174–179
● *K¹² Language Arts Activity Book,* pp. LC 109–113

Also Needed

● sticky notes
● scissors, round-end safety
● glue stick

Story Synopsis

A little pine tree has big dreams. But the little tree learns the hard way that it's best to be yourself.

Keywords

sequence – order

 **45 minutes**

Work **together** with students to complete Get Ready, Shared Reading, Check Your Reading, Looking at Language, and Reading for Meaning activities.

Get Ready

Lesson Introduction

Prepare students for listening to and discussing "The Pine Tree and Its Needles."

1. Tell students that you are going to read "The Pine Tree and Its Needles," a story about a little pine tree that wants to change its needles.

2. Explain that before you read the story, you will get ready by

   ▸ Discussing how the events of a story happen in a certain order
   ▸ Practicing reading aloud sentences that are repeated throughout the story

Objectives

- Identify story sequence.
- Use time-order words.
- Build vocabulary through listening, reading, and discussion.
- Use new vocabulary in written and spoken sentences.

A Sequence of Events

Explore a story's sequence of events.

1. Tell students that the order in which things happen in a story is called the **sequence**. Thinking about the sequence, or order, of events helps good readers check their understanding of what they're reading.

2. Explain that a story might have words like *first*, *next*, and *then* to help tell the sequence. While not all stories have these words, readers can still figure out the order in which things happen by looking for clues. For example, words such as *morning*, *afternoon*, and *night* are clues that show the passing of time and tell us when things happen.

3. Explain a sequence of events.
   Say: Listen carefully to the order in which things happen in this short story.

   Carla went into the kitchen to make a sandwich. First, she spread peanut butter on a slice of bread. Next, she put jam on another slice. Then, she put the two slices of bread together. Finally, Carla took a big bite out of her sandwich.

4. Tell students the sequence, or order, in which things happened:

   ▸ Carla went into the kitchen to make a sandwich.
   ▸ First, Carla put peanut butter on a slice of bread.
   ▸ Next, Carla put jam on another slice of bread.
   ▸ Then, Carla put the two slices of bread together.
   ▸ Finally, Carla took a big bite out of her sandwich.

5. Tell students that it's now their turn. Reread the short story in Step 3, and then ask students to tell you the order of events. Encourage them to use words such as *first*, *next*, and *then*.

TIP Words such as *first*, *next*, and *then* are called **signal words** because they signal that a new event is about to happen.

Words to Know
Before reading "The Pine Tree and Its Needles," go over Words to Know
with students.

1. Read aloud each word and have students repeat it.

2. Ask students if they know what each word means.

   ▸ If students know a word's meaning, have them define it and use it in
     a sentence.
   ▸ If students don't know a word's meaning, read them the definition and
     discuss the word with them.

fairy – a magical creature, usually a very small person with wings
needles – long, very thin, pointy leaves on certain trees, such as pines
woods – a place where many trees grow; the forest

Shared Reading

Book Walk
Prepare students for reading by taking them on a Book Walk of "The Pine Tree and
Its Needles." Scan the story together and ask students to make predictions about the
story. Answers to questions may vary.

1. Turn to the **table of contents** in *K¹² Classics for Young Readers, Volume A*. Help
   students find the selection and turn to that page.

2. Point to and read aloud the **title of the story**.

   ▸ What do you think the story is about?

3. Have students look at the story's **pictures**.

   ▸ Where do you think the story takes place?
   ▸ What do you think might happen in the story?
   ▸ Have you ever wished to look different? If so, what did you want to
     change? Why?

4. **Point to and have students practice reading aloud** the first occurrence of the
   following sentences with you.

   ▸ Night came.
   ▸ "Little pine tree," she said, "you may have your wish."
   ▸ "How beautiful I am!" it said.

5. Tell students that they will hear these sentences repeated many times in
   the story.

Objectives
- Make predictions based on
  text, illustrations, and/or
  prior knowledge.
- Activate prior knowledge
  by previewing text and/or
  discussing topic.
- Read and respond to texts
  representing a variety of
  cultures, time periods, and
  traditions.

"The Pine Tree and Its Needles"
It's time to read aloud.

1. Have students sit next to you so that they can see the pictures and words while
   you read aloud.

2. Tell students to pay attention to the order in which the story events happen.

3. Encourage students to **chime in and read aloud** the sentences they practiced reading during the Book Walk, whenever those sentences appear in the story.

4. **Begin to read aloud the story.** Pause after each time the pine tree wishes for a new type of leaf, and discuss the following questions. Answers to questions may vary.

   ▸ What does the little pine tree wish for? Why?

5. Continue to read to the end of the story. Track with your finger so students can follow along. Emphasize Words to Know as you come to them. If appropriate, use the pictures to help show what each word means.

Check Your Reading

"The Pine Tree and Its Needles"

Check students' comprehension of "The Pine Tree and Its Needles."

1. Have students retell "The Pine Tree and Its Needles" in their own words to develop grammar, vocabulary, comprehension, and fluency skills.

2. Ask students the following questions.

   ▸ Where does the little pine tree live? in the woods
   ▸ What kind of leaves does the little pine tree have at the beginning of the story? needles
   ▸ Who hears the little pine tree wish for gold leaves? the Fairy of the Trees
   ▸ What does the Fairy of the Trees say to the little pine tree each time it wishes for different leaves? "Little pine tree, you may have your wish."
   ▸ What does the little pine tree say each time it gets new leaves? "How beautiful I am!"
   ▸ What kind of leaves does the little pine tree have at the end of the story? needles

 If students have trouble responding to a question, help them locate the answer in the text or pictures.

Objectives
- Retell or dramatize a story.
- Answer questions requiring literal recall of details.

Looking at Language

Who's Talking?

Reread "The Pine Tree and Its Needles" with a focus on quotation marks. Gather the Reading Aid on pages LC 109 and 110 in *K¹² Language Arts Activity Book*.

1. Ask students if they noticed that the Fairy and the little pine tree speak in parts of the story. Tell them that there are clues in the story that let us know that a character is speaking.

2. Tell students that they will **read aloud the story with you**. As you read aloud together, you will pause at certain points to look at the clues that tell us that a character is speaking.

3. As you read aloud, **encourage students to chime in and read with you**.

4. Refer to the Reading Aid.

Reading Aid Tear out the Reading Aid for this reading selection. Follow the instructions for folding the page, and then use the page as a guide as you reread the selection with students.

Objectives

- Read and respond to texts representing a variety of cultures, time periods, and traditions.
- Read aloud grade-level text with appropriate expression, accuracy, and rate.
- Recognize quotations in dialogue.

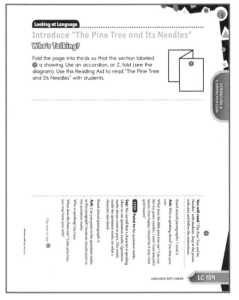
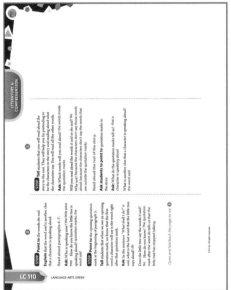

Reading for Meaning

From First to Last

Check students' ability to recall a sequence of events and read simple instructions. Turn to pages LC 111–113 in *K¹² Language Arts Activity Book,* and gather the scissors and glue stick.

1. Have students read and follow the directions for cutting out and putting in order pictures from "The Pine Tree and Its Needles."

   ▸ Help students read the directions, if necessary.

2. Have students refer to the pictures to retell in order the types of leaves that the little pine tree wishes for. Encourage student to use time-order words such as *first*, *next*, *then*, and *finally*.

TIP Refer back to "The Pine Tree and Its Needles" if students have trouble recalling the order of events in the story.

Objectives

- Identify story sequence.
- Sequence pictures illustrating story events.
- Use time-order words.
- Follow written directions.
- Follow two- or three-step written directions.

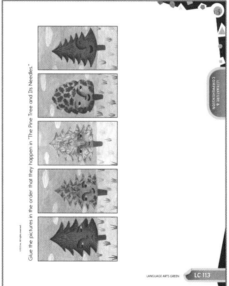

Explore "The Pine Tree and Its Needles"

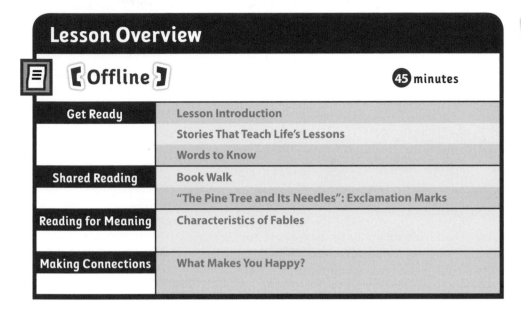

Lesson Overview

[Offline] 45 minutes

Get Ready	Lesson Introduction
	Stories That Teach Life's Lessons
	Words to Know
Shared Reading	Book Walk
	"The Pine Tree and Its Needles": Exclamation Marks
Reading for Meaning	Characteristics of Fables
Making Connections	What Makes You Happy?

Advance Preparation

For the Shared Reading, cut out the sentence strips on page LC 115, and preview the Reading Aid on pages LC 117 and 118 in *K¹² Language Arts Activity Book* to prepare the materials.

Big Ideas

- ► Exposing readers to a wide variety of genres provides them with a wide range of background knowledge and increases their vocabulary.
- ► Interpreting text requires close attention to content and literary elements.
- ► Repeated rereading leads to increased fluency.
- ► During shared-reading activities, students learn more about how print works.

Materials

Supplied
- "The Pine Tree and Its Needles," *K¹² Classics for Young Readers, Volume A*, pp. 174–179
- *K¹² Language Arts Activity Book*, pp. LC 115–118

Also Needed
- scissors, adult
- paper, construction – white
- glue stick
- scissors, round-end safety
- household objects – magazines, photographs, small items that can be glued to a poster

Keywords

author's purpose – the reason the author wrote a text: to entertain, to inform, to express an opinion, or to persuade

exclamation – a kind of sentence that shows strong feeling

fable – a story that teaches a lesson and may contain animal characters

genre – a category for classifying literary works

moral – the lesson of a story, particularly a fable

 **Offline** **45** minutes

Work **together** with students to complete Get Ready, Shared Reading, Reading for Meaning, and Making Connections activities.

Get Ready

Lesson Introduction

Prepare students for reading and discussing "The Pine Tree and Its Needles."

1. Tell students that you are going to reread "The Pine Tree and Its Needles."

2. Explain that before you reread the story, you will get ready by discussing:

   ▸ The reasons an author writes a story
   ▸ A type of story called a *fable*, which teaches a lesson

3. Tell students that because they are now familiar with the story, they should be able to chime in and read aloud much of the story with you. Rereading familiar stories like this will help them recognize words more quickly and read more fluently.

Objectives
- Identify the author's purpose.
- Identify genre.
- Identify the moral or lesson of a text.
- Increase concept and content vocabulary.
- Build vocabulary through listening, reading, and discussion.
- Use new vocabulary in written and spoken sentences.

Stories That Teach Life's Lessons

Introduce students to the reasons why an author writes a text and characteristics of fables.

1. Tell students that an author writes a text for a certain reason, or **purpose**. Good readers can figure out the purpose of a text by asking questions.

   ▸ Does the author give facts or explain something? If so, the author wrote the text to teach us something.
   ▸ Does the author tell a made-up story with characters? If so, the author wrote the story to entertain us.
   ▸ Does the author want us believe something? If so, the author wrote the text to convince us of something or to tell us his or her opinion.

2. Tell students that sometimes an author writes a text for more than one reason. For example, an author might write a story to entertain but also to teach something.

3. Explain to students that a kind of story that both entertains and teaches a lesson about life is called a **fable**. A fable often has animal characters that act like people. Sometimes a character might be something unexpected, such as a gingerbread cookie or a tree.

4. Tell students that the lesson a fable teaches is called a **moral**. Some well-known morals are "Look before you leap" and "You can't judge a book by its cover."

5. Have students practice figuring out why an author wrote a story, and what the moral of a fable is.

Say: Listen to this story.

One day, Ant went to the river to get a sip of water. But Ant slipped and fell in. Ant was about to drown when Robin, who had seen poor Ant slip, plucked a leaf from a tree and dropped it next to Ant in the river. Ant climbed onto the leaf and sailed safely back to shore. "Thank you for saving my life, dear Robin!" shouted Ant.

The next day, a hunter built a trap under a tree to catch Robin. Just as the unaware Robin was about to step inside, Ant stung the hunter so hard on his foot that the hunter kicked over the trap. The startled Robin quickly flew up into the tree and shouted, "Thank you for saving my life, dear Ant!"

▸ Why do you think the author wrote the story? to entertain
▸ Does the story also teach a lesson? Yes
▸ What do we call a story that has animals as characters and teaches a lesson? a fable
▸ What do we call the lesson that the fable teaches? a moral
▸ What lesson does this story teach us? One good turn deserves another. Guide students to understand that the lesson is that when someone helps you, it's the right thing to do to help that person, too.

Words to Know

Before reading "The Pine Tree and Its Needles," go over Words to Know with students.

1. Read aloud each word and have students repeat it.

2. Ask students if they know what each word means.

   ▸ If students know a word's meaning, have them define it and use it in a sentence.
   ▸ If students don't know a word's meaning, read them the definition and discuss the word with them.

fairy – a magical creature, usually a very small person with wings
needles – long, very thin, pointy leaves on certain trees, such as pines
woods – a place where many trees grow; the forest

Shared Reading

Book Walk

Prepare students by taking them on a Book Walk of "The Pine Tree and Its Needles." Scan the story together to revisit the characters and events.

1. Turn to the selection in *K¹² Classics for Young Readers, Volume A*. Read aloud the **title of the story**.

2. Have students review the **pictures**.

   ▸ Who are the characters in the story? the little pine tree; the Fairy of the Woods
   ▸ What does the little pine tree wish for? to have different leaves
   ▸ Why do you think the little pine tree wanted different leaves? Answers will vary.

Objectives

- Activate prior knowledge by previewing text and/or discussing topic.
- Read and respond to texts representing a variety of cultures, time periods, and traditions.
- Read aloud grade-level text with appropriate expression, accuracy, and rate.
- Identify sentences that are exclamations.

"The Pine Tree and Its Needles": Exclamation Marks

It's time to reread the story. Tell students that they will reread "The Pine Tree and Its Needles" with a focus on exclamation marks. Gather the sentence strips that you prepared from page LC 115 and the Reading Aid on pages LC 117 and 118 in *K¹² Language Arts Activity Book*.

1. Point to the two sentences on the sentence strips. Tell students that the sentences have the same words, but when you read them aloud, they will sound different.

2. Track with your finger as you read each sentence. Read aloud the sentence ending with a period in a normal voice and the sentence ending with an exclamation mark with excitement.

   ▸ Did you notice a difference in the way I read the sentences? Possible answers: The second sentence sounded more exciting; the second sentence had more expression.
   ▸ What do you see at the end of each sentence? Guide students to notice the period and exclamation mark.

3. Remind students that the mark at the end of the second sentence is an **exclamation mark** and a sentence that ends with an exclamation mark is an **exclamation**.

   ▸ How should we read a sentence with an exclamation mark? with excitement; with lots of expression

4. Have students read aloud the sentence ending with a period **with you in a normal voice**.

5. Have students read aloud the sentence ending with an exclamation mark **with you in an excited voice**. Ask students to jump up as they read this sentence to help them associate an exciting physical movement with the excitement of a sentence that ends with an exclamation mark.

6. Tell students that they will **read aloud the story with you**. As you read aloud together, you will stop at certain points to discuss how to read sentences that end with exclamation marks.

7. Refer to the Reading Aid.

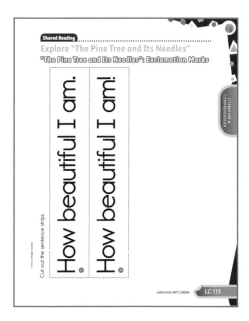

Reading Aid Tear out the Reading Aid for this reading selection. Follow the instructions for folding the page, and then use the page as a guide as you reread the selection with students.

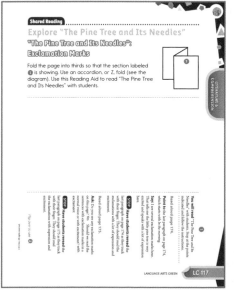

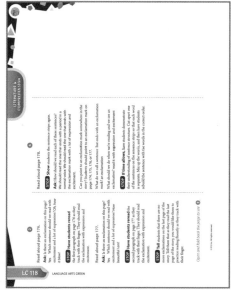

Reading for Meaning

Characteristics of Fables

Check students' understanding of the characteristics of fables.

1. Have students retell the story in their own words to develop grammar, vocabulary, comprehension, and fluency skills.

2. Ask students the following questions.

   ► Why do you think the author wrote "The Pine Tree and Its Needles"? to entertain; to teach a lesson
   ► Does the story also teach a lesson? Yes
   ► What kinds of characters are in the story? a tree; a fairy
   ► What do we call a story that has these kinds of things as characters and also teaches a lesson? a fable
   ► What do we call the lesson that a fable teaches? a moral
   ► What is the moral of the fable "The Pine Tree and Its Needles"? Possible answers: It's best to be yourself; you should be happy the way you are.
   ► What does the moral mean? Answers may vary. Guide students to understand that the moral means that we should love and accept ourselves for what we are.

Objectives

- Retell or dramatize a story.
- Identify the author's purpose.
- Identify genre.
- Identify the moral or lesson of a text.
- Increase concept and content vocabulary.

Making Connections

What Makes You Happy?

Check students' ability to make a personal connection to "The Pine Tree and Its Needles." Gather the construction paper, glue stick, scissors, and household objects.

1. Ask the following questions.

   ► How does the little pine tree feel at the end of the story? happy
   ► What makes the pine tree happy in the end? It has needles again.
   ► If the story were to continue, do you think the little pine tree would want to try another type of leaf? Why or why not? Answers will vary.

2. Tell students to think about things that make them happy.

Objectives

- Make connections with text: text-to-text, text-to-self, text-to-world.
- Demonstrate understanding through drawing, discussion, drama, and/or writing.

3. Have students create a poster showing things that make them happy. Students should use a piece of white construction paper for the poster. They may doing any of the following:

    ▸ Draw pictures.
    ▸ Glue down photographs.
    ▸ Glue down pictures cut out of magazines.
    ▸ Glue down items that represent other things (for example, a feather to represent a pet bird).

4. Help them write "Things That Make Me Happy" at the top or bottom of their poster.

5. Ask the following question.

    ▸ Why does each of these items make you happy? Answers will vary.

6. Remind students that at the beginning of the story, the little pine tree was not happy with its needles. But it was happy to have needles in the end. Answers to questions may vary.

    ▸ Was there ever a time that you were not happy with an item that's on your poster? Why not?
    ▸ Why does it make you happy now, when it didn't make you happy before?

Introduce "The Little Rabbit Who Wanted Red Wings"

Lesson Overview

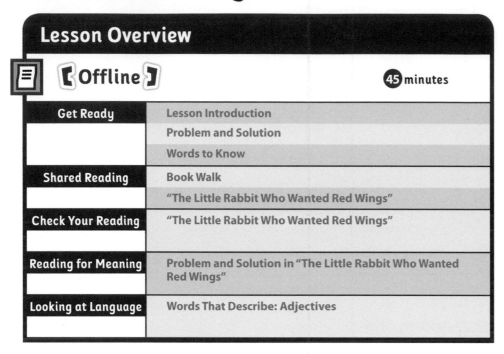

	Offline	**45** minutes
Get Ready	Lesson Introduction	
	Problem and Solution	
	Words to Know	
Shared Reading	Book Walk	
	"The Little Rabbit Who Wanted Red Wings"	
Check Your Reading	"The Little Rabbit Who Wanted Red Wings"	
Reading for Meaning	Problem and Solution in "The Little Rabbit Who Wanted Red Wings"	
Looking at Language	Words That Describe: Adjectives	

Materials

Supplied

- "The Little Rabbit Who Wanted Red Wings," *K¹² Classics for Young Readers, Volume A,* pp. 180–183
- *K¹² Language Arts Activity Book,* pp. LC 119–120

Story Synopsis

A little rabbit makes a wish to change his looks. But the little rabbit learns the hard way that it's best to be yourself.

Keywords

adjective – a word that describes a noun or a pronoun

problem – an issue a character must solve in a story

solution – how a character solves a problem in a story

Advance Preparation

Before beginning the Shared Reading, read "The Little Rabbit Who Wanted Red Wings" to locate Words to Know in the text. Preview the Reading Aid on pages LC 119 and 120 in *K¹² Language Arts Activity Book* to prepare the materials for Looking at Language.

Big Ideas

- ▶ Comprehension requires an understanding of story structure.
- ▶ During shared-reading activities, students learn more about how print works.
- ▶ Readers must focus on the specific language of a text to aid in interpretation.

 **45** minutes

Work **together** with students to complete Get Ready, Shared Reading, Check Your Reading, Reading for Meaning, and Looking at Language activities.

Get Ready

Lesson Introduction

Prepare students for listening to and discussing "The Little Rabbit Who Wanted Red Wings," an American folktale retold by Betty Erickson.

1. Tell students that you are going to read "The Little Rabbit Who Wanted Red Wings," a story about a rabbit who makes a wish to look different.

2. Explain that before you read the story, you will get ready by discussing how characters often have problems that they must solve.

Problem and Solution

Explore the story elements of problem and solution.

1. Tell students that sometimes we have problems that we need to solve.
   Say: For example, if your problem is that you're tired, you might take a nap. If your problem is that your hands are dirty, you might solve your problem by washing them.

   ► What if you couldn't go outside to play because it's raining? How might you solve your problem? Answers will vary.

2. Explain that a character in a story usually needs to solve a problem. There can be more than one character in a story who needs to solve a problem.

3. Have students recall the story of "The Poor Man's Reward" to help them understand a character's problem and how it is solved. If necessary, show students the pictures from the story in the *K¹² Classics for Young Readers, Volume A*, pages 100–123.

4. Remind students that in "The Poor Man's Reward," the poor man sets off to another part of his country in search of a better life. He meets a princess and wants to marry her, but the king is not sure the poor man will make a good husband for his daughter.

   ► What is the poor man's problem after he meets the king? The king gives him difficult tasks to complete before he can marry the princess.
   ► How does the poor man solve his problem? The animals he met on his journey help him with the tasks.

5. Tell students that as they read stories, they should listen for characters' problems and what the characters do to solve their problems.

 If students haven't read "The Poor Man's Reward," refer to a familiar story such as "Cinderella" that has a problem and solution that are easy to identify.

Objectives

- Identify examples of problem and solution.
- Describe story structure elements—problem and solution.
- Build vocabulary through listening, reading, and discussion.
- Use new vocabulary in written and spoken sentences.

Words to Know
Before reading "The Little Rabbit Who Wanted Red Wings," go over Words to Know with students.

1. Read aloud each word and have students repeat it.

2. Ask students if they know what each word means.

   ▸ If students know a word's meaning, have them define it and use it in a sentence.
   ▸ If students don't know a word's meaning, read them the definition and discuss the word with them.

groundhog – an animal with a thick body and shaggy brown fur; a woodchuck
pond – a small body of water, usually smaller than a lake

Shared Reading

Book Walk
Prepare students for reading by taking them on a Book Walk of "The Little Rabbit Who Wanted Red Wings." Scan the story together and ask students to make predictions about the story. Answers to questions may vary.

Objectives
- Make predictions based on text, illustrations, and/or prior knowledge.
- Activate prior knowledge by previewing text and/or discussing topic.
- Read and respond to texts representing a variety of cultures, time periods, and traditions.

1. Turn to the **table of contents** in *K¹² Classics for Young Readers, Volume A*. Help students find "The Little Rabbit Who Wanted Red Wings" and turn to that page.

2. Point to and read aloud the **title of the story**.

   ▸ What do you think this story might be about?

3. Have students point to the **name of the author** while you read the name aloud.

4. Have students look at the **pictures**.

   ▸ What do you think might happen in the story?
   ▸ Have you ever wished you looked different in some way? What do you think would happen if you got your wish?

"The Little Rabbit Who Wanted Red Wings"
It's time to read aloud.

1. Have students sit next to you so that they can see the pictures and words while you read aloud.

2. Tell students to listen for the characters' problems and how they solve their problems.

3. **Read aloud the entire story.** Track with your finger so students can follow along. Emphasize Words to Know as you come to them. If appropriate, use the pictures to help show what each word means.

Check Your Reading

"The Little Rabbit Who Wanted Red Wings"
Check students' comprehension of "The Little Rabbit Who Wanted Red Wings."

1. Have students retell "The Little Rabbit Who Wanted Red Wings" in their own words to develop grammar, vocabulary, comprehension, and fluency skills.

2. Ask students the following questions.

   ▸ Where does this story take place? at a pond
   ▸ Who are some of the characters? Little Rabbit; Groundhog; Mother Rabbit
   ▸ Who is the main character? Little Rabbit
   ▸ What does Little Rabbit wish for at the Wishing Pond? red wings
   ▸ What happens after Little Rabbit's wish comes true and he goes to show his mother his red wings? His mother doesn't recognize him.
   ▸ What does Little Rabbit wish for at the end of the story? to go back to the way he was   Why does he wish for that? He wasn't happy with wings.

TIP If students have trouble responding to a question, help them locate the answer in the text or pictures.

Objectives
- Retell or dramatize a story.
- Answer questions requiring literal recall of details.
- Identify setting.
- Identify character(s).
- Identify the main character(s).

Reading for Meaning

Problem and Solution in "The Little Rabbit Who Wanted Red Wings"
Explore how characters solve problems in "The Little Rabbit Who Wanted Red Wings."

▸ What problem does Little Rabbit have at the beginning of the story? He doesn't like the way he looks.   How does he solve his problem? He wishes for red wings at the Wishing Pond.
▸ What problem does Little Rabbit have when he goes home to show Mother Rabbit his red wings? His mother doesn't recognize him.
▸ Little Rabbit doesn't have a place to sleep when Mother Rabbit and Porcupine don't recognize him. How does he solve his problem? He sleeps at Groundhog's house.
▸ What problem does Little Rabbit have when he tries to use his wings? They don't work.
▸ Little Rabbit is not happy with his wings. How does he solve his problem? He returns to the Wishing Pond and wishes to be himself again.

Objectives
- Describe story structure elements—problem and solution.

Looking at Language

Words That Describe: Adjectives

Reread "The Little Rabbit Who Wanted Red Wings" with a focus on adjectives. Gather the Reading Aid on pages LC 119 and 120 in *K¹² Language Arts Activity Book*.

1. Remind students that describing words, or **adjectives**, make stories more interesting.
   Say: As I say the following sentences, think about which one is more interesting and descriptive.

   - The rabbit has fur.
   - The little rabbit has fluffy fur that feels silky and soft.

2. Discuss with students which sentence they think is more interesting and why. Point out that the words *little, fluffy, silky,* and *soft* are all describing words, or adjectives, that probably helped students imagine how the rabbit looks and feels.

3. Have students explain how adjectives make stories more interesting. If students don't recall, remind them that

   - Adjectives make stories more descriptive.
   - Because adjectives describe things, they help us better imagine pictures in our head as we're reading.

4. Give examples of some of the types of information that adjectives can add.

   - Size: I saw a little rabbit; I saw a gigantic elephant. The words *little* and *gigantic* are adjectives.
   - How things feel: My shirt was rough and scratchy; the mattress was hard and uncomfortable. The words *rough, scratchy, hard,* and *uncomfortable* are adjectives.

Objectives

- Identify adjectives.
- Use adjectives to describe someone or something.
- Identify author's use of imagery and descriptive language.
- Read aloud grade-level text with appropriate expression, accuracy, and rate.

5. Tell students that they will **read aloud the story with you**. As you read aloud together, you will stop at certain points to discuss adjectives.

6. Refer to the Reading Aid.

Reading Aid Tear out the Reading Aid for this reading selection. Follow the instructions for folding the page, and then use the page as a guide as you reread the selection with students.

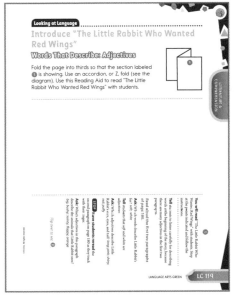

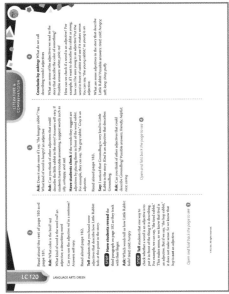

Explore "The Little Rabbit Who Wanted Red Wings"

Lesson Overview

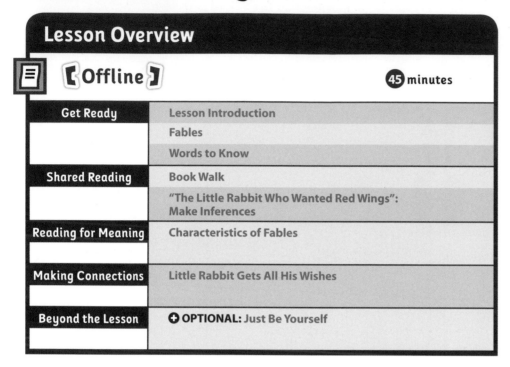

[Offline] **45** minutes

Get Ready	Lesson Introduction
	Fables
	Words to Know
Shared Reading	Book Walk
	"The Little Rabbit Who Wanted Red Wings": Make Inferences
Reading for Meaning	Characteristics of Fables
Making Connections	Little Rabbit Gets All His Wishes
Beyond the Lesson	⊕ OPTIONAL: Just Be Yourself

Materials

Supplied

- "The Little Rabbit Who Wanted Red Wings," *K¹² Classics for Young Readers, Volume A,* pp. 180–183
- *K¹² Language Arts Activity Book,* pp. LC 121–123

Also Needed

- crayons
- glue stick
- household objects – cotton balls, toothpicks, sponge

Keywords

author's purpose – the reason the author wrote a text: to entertain, to inform, to express an opinion, or to persuade

fable – a story that teaches a lesson and may contain animal characters

genre – a category for classifying literary works

infer – to use clues and what you already know to make a guess

inference – a guess you make using the clues in a text and what you already know

moral – the lesson of a story, particularly a fable

Advance Preparation

Preview the Reading Aid on pages LC 121 and 122 in *K¹² Language Arts Activity Book* to prepare the materials for the Shared Reading.

Big Ideas

- ▶ Exposing readers to a wide variety of genres provides them with a wide range of background knowledge and increases their vocabulary.
- ▶ Good readers use prior knowledge and text clues to infer or draw conclusions about what is implied but not directly stated in text.
- ▶ Verbalizing your thoughts while modeling a reading strategy allows students to see what goes on inside the head of an effective reader; it makes visible the normally hidden process of comprehending text.
- ▶ Shared reading allows students to observe and practice the reading behaviors of proficient readers.

[Offline] 45 minutes

Work **together** with students to complete Get Ready, Shared Reading, Reading for Meaning, Making Connections, and Beyond the Lesson activities.

Get Ready ....

Lesson Introduction

Prepare students for listening to and discussing "The Little Rabbit Who Wanted Red Wings."

1. Tell students that you are going to reread "The Little Rabbit Who Wanted Red Wings."

2. Explain that before you reread the story, you will get ready by discussing the kind of story called a fable.

⭐ Objectives
- Identify genre.
- Identify the moral or lesson of a text.
- Build vocabulary through listening, reading, and discussion.
- Use new vocabulary in written and spoken sentences.

Fables

Explore characteristics of fables.

1. Explain that a story can be written to teach a lesson. This kind of story is a **fable**. A fable often has animal characters that act like people.

2. Tell students that the lesson a fable teaches is called a **moral**. Some well-known morals are "Better safe than sorry"; "If at first you don't succeed, try, try again"; and "Honesty is the best policy."

3. Have students practice figuring out the moral of a fable.
   Say: Listen to this fable.

   A lion caught a mouse and was about to eat him. The mouse begged the lion to let him live and promised to pay back the lion's kindness. The lion laughed at the idea that the little mouse could ever help the powerful lion, but he freed the mouse anyway. One day, the mouse found the lion caught in a hunter's trap made of rope. The mouse, remembering his promise, chewed through the rope and set the lion free.

   ▸ Does this story teach a lesson? Yes   What do you think is the lesson, or moral, of this fable? Answers will vary. Guide students to recognize that the moral could be "No act of kindness is ever wasted" or "No matter how small you are, you can always help others."
   ▸ What do we call a story that has animals that act like people and teaches a lesson? a fable

TIP Although an objective for this lesson is to identify genre, there is no need to introduce that term to students.

Words to Know

Before rereading "The Little Rabbit Who Wanted Red Wings," go over Words to Know with students.

1. Read aloud each word and have students repeat it.

2. Ask students if they know what each word means.

   ▸ If students know a word's meaning, have them define it and use it in a sentence.
   ▸ If students don't know a word's meaning, read them the definition and discuss the word with them.

groundhog – an animal with a thick body and shaggy brown fur; woodchuck
pond – a small body of water, usually smaller than a lake

Shared Reading

Book Walk

Prepare students by taking them on a Book Walk of "The Little Rabbit Who Wanted Red Wings." Scan the story together to revisit the characters and events.

1. Turn to the selection in *K¹² Classics for Young Readers, Volume A*. Read aloud the **title of the story**.

2. Have students point to the **name of the author** as you read it aloud.

3. Have students review the **pictures**.

   ▸ Why does Little Rabbit go to the Wishing Pond? He wants to change how he looks.
   ▸ What happens when Little Rabbit goes home to show Mother Rabbit his red wings? She doesn't recognize him.
   ▸ What happens when Little Rabbit tries to use his wings? They don't work.
   ▸ What does Little Rabbit wish for at the end of the story? to go back to the way he was   Why does he wish for that? He isn't happy with wings.

Objectives

- Activate prior knowledge by previewing text and/or discussing topic.
- Read and respond to texts representing a variety of cultures, time periods, and traditions.
- Make inferences based on text and/or prior knowledge.
- Support inferences with evidence from text and/or prior knowledge.
- Demonstrate understanding by thinking aloud.
- Identify details that explain characters' actions and feelings.

"The Little Rabbit Who Wanted Red Wings": Make Inferences

It's time to reread the story. Tell students that you will reread "The Little Rabbit Who Wanted Red Wings" with a focus on clues that help readers make inferences. Gather the Reading Aid on pages LC 121 and 122 in *K¹² Language Arts Activity Book*.

1. Remind students that readers can make **inferences**, or guesses, about things that the author doesn't state directly in a text.
   ▸ What kinds of information, or clues, do we use to make inferences? clues in the text and pictures; information from a reader's personal experiences

2. If students don't recall the type of information that a reader uses to make inferences, tell them that inferences are guesses. However, they are not wild guesses. They are logical guesses based on the following information:
   ▸ The words and pictures of a story
   ▸ The reader's prior knowledge learned from past experiences

3. Tell students that they will reread the story with you. As you **read aloud together**, you will stop at certain points to discuss clues that can help them make inferences.

4. Explain that when readers make an inference, we cannot see how they do it because it's all happening in their head.

5. Tell students that as they reread the story with you, you will explain to them how you make inferences while sharing your thoughts aloud. That way, they can learn what goes on in the head of a good reader. This is called **thinking aloud**.

6. Have students sit next to you so that they can see the pictures and words while they read aloud with you.

7. Refer to the Reading Aid.

Reading Aid Tear out the Reading Aid for this reading selection. Follow the instructions for folding the page, and then use the page as a guide as you reread the selection with students.

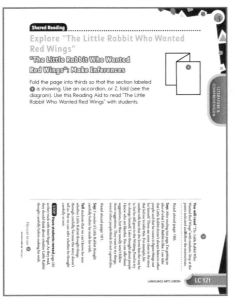
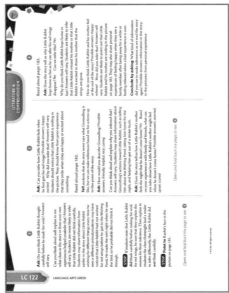

Reading for Meaning

Characteristics of Fables

Check students' understanding of fables, including the reasons an author would write a fable.

1. Have students retell "The Little Rabbit Who Wanted Red Wings" in their own words to develop grammar, vocabulary, comprehension, and fluency skills.

2. Ask the following questions.
   ▸ What kind of story is "The Little Rabbit Who Wanted Red Wings"? a fable How can you tell? It teaches a lesson; animals act like people in the story.
   ▸ What is the moral of this fable? It's best to be yourself.
   ▸ What does the moral mean? Answers may vary. Guide students to understand that the moral means that we should love and accept ourselves for who we are.
   ▸ Have you ever wanted to change something about yourself? Answers will vary.
   ▸ After reading this story, do you still want to change something about yourself, or stay the way you are? Why? Answers will vary.

3. Remind students that an author writes a text for a certain reason, or purpose. Sometimes an author writes a text for more than one reason.
   ▸ What are some of the reasons why an author writes a story? to teach something, to entertain, to convince the reader of something, or to tell the reader what the author thinks about something
   ▸ "The Little Rabbit Who Wanted Red Wings" is a fable, so one of the author's purposes is to teach a lesson. What is the other reason that the author wrote this fable? to entertain

Objectives
- Retell or dramatize a story.
- Identify genre.
- Identify the moral or lesson of a text.
- Make connections with text: text-to-text, text-to-self, text-to-world.
- Identify the author's purpose.

Making Connections

Little Rabbit Gets All His Wishes

Check students' understanding of "The Little Rabbit Who Wanted Red Wings" and their ability to make inferences. Turn to page LC 123 in *K¹² Language Arts Activity Book*, and gather the crayons, glue stick, and household objects.

1. Remind students that at the beginning of the story, Little Rabbit wishes to look like other animals.
   ▸ What are some of the things that Little Rabbit likes about other animals? Possible answers: Squirrel's big, bushy tail; Porcupine's pointy quills; Duck's floppy orange feet

2. If students don't recall what Little Rabbit likes about other animals, refer to the second paragraph on page 180 of the story.

3. Tell students that they are going to fulfill Little Rabbit's wishes.

Objectives
- Demonstrate understanding through drawing, discussion, drama, and/or writing.
- Make inferences based on text and/or prior knowledge.
- Support inferences with evidence from text and/or prior knowledge.

4. Have students brainstorm materials they could use to make Little Rabbit look like the animals he admires. For example, they could use cotton balls for the squirrel's tail, toothpicks for the porcupine's quills, and construction paper or sponges for the duck's feet.

5. Have students draw or glue down household objects to show what they think Little Rabbit would look like if he got all his wishes.

6. Ask the following question to encourage discussion. Answers to questions may vary.

   ▸ Do you think Little Rabbit would be happy like this? Why or why not?
   ▸ What activities do you think would be easier for Little Rabbit if he got his wishes? Why?
   ▸ What activities do you think would be more difficult if Little Rabbit got his wishes? Why?

Beyond the Lesson

⊕ OPTIONAL: Just Be Yourself

This activity is OPTIONAL. It is intended for students who have extra time and would enjoy reading a story similar to "The Little Rabbit Who Wanted Red Wings." Feel free to skip this activity.

1. Go to a library and look for a copy of Eric Carle's *The Mixed-Up Chameleon*.

2. Lead a Book Walk, and then read aloud the story. As you read aloud, encourage students to chime in and read with you.

3. Have students tell how *The Mixed-Up Chameleon* is both like and not like "The Little Rabbit Who Wanted Red Wings." Be sure students describe how the stories' characters are alike and different, and the moral of each story.

4. Ask them to tell which story is their favorite and why.

Objectives

- Compare and contrast story structure elements across texts.

- Compare and contrast two texts on the same topic.

Introduce "The Country Mouse and the City Mouse"

Lesson Overview

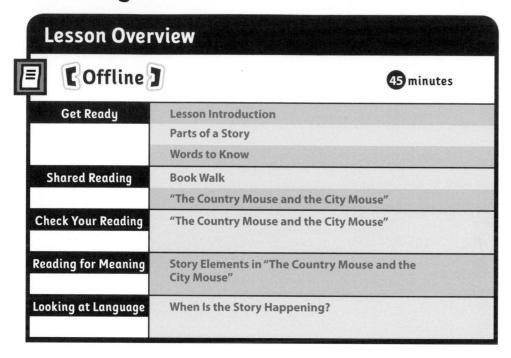

Offline   **45** minutes

Get Ready	Lesson Introduction
	Parts of a Story
	Words to Know
Shared Reading	Book Walk
	"The Country Mouse and the City Mouse"
Check Your Reading	"The Country Mouse and the City Mouse"
Reading for Meaning	Story Elements in "The Country Mouse and the City Mouse"
Looking at Language	When Is the Story Happening?

Advance Preparation

Before beginning the Shared Reading, read "The Country Mouse and the City Mouse" to locate Words to Know in the text. Preview the Reading Aid on pages LC 125 and 126 in *K¹² Language Arts Activity Book* to prepare the materials for Looking at Language.

Big Ideas

- ▶ An awareness of story structure elements (setting, characters, plot) provides readers a foundation for constructing meaning when reading new stories and writing their own stories.
- ▶ Comprehension requires an understanding of story structure.
- ▶ During shared-reading activities, students learn more about how print works.

Materials

Supplied

- "The Country Mouse and the City Mouse," *K¹² Classics for Young Readers, Volume A,* pp. 184–187
- *K¹² Language Arts Activity Book,* pp. LC 125–126

Story Synopsis

The Country Mouse visits the City Mouse and learns very quickly that city life isn't for everyone. (Note that there is a brief reference to the fact that a mouse trap can kill a mouse.)

Keywords

character – a person or animal in a story

plot – what happens in a story

problem – an issue a character must solve in a story

setting – when and where a story takes place

solution – how a character solves a problem in a story

verb – a word that shows action or a state of being

[Offline] **45** minutes

Work **together** with students to complete Get Ready, Shared Reading, Check Your Reading, Reading for Meaning, and Looking at Language activities.

Get Ready ....

Lesson Introduction

Prepare students for listening to and discussing "The Country Mouse and the City Mouse."

1. Tell students that you are going to read "The Country Mouse and the City Mouse," a story about two mice who live very different lives.

2. Explain that before you read the story, you will get ready by discussing the parts of a story.

Parts of a Story

Explore story structure elements.

1. Tell students that every story has certain parts, or elements.

   ▸ The **characters** are the people or animals in a story.
   ▸ The **setting** is where and when a story takes place.
   ▸ The **problem** is the issue a character must solve in a story.
   ▸ The **solution** is what the character does to solve the problem.
   ▸ The **plot** is all the important events that happen in a story.

2. Help students practice naming the characters, setting, problem, and solution of a familiar story.
   Say: Think of "The Princess and the Pea." This is the plot for "The Princess and the Pea."

   A prince is having trouble finding a real princess to marry. One night, a princess shows up at his castle to get out of the rain. The prince's mother wants to find out if the young woman is a real princess, so she puts a pea in the bed the princess will sleep in, and then covers the pea with 20 mattresses and 20 featherbeds. The next morning, the princess says she slept poorly because there was something hard in her bed. The prince's mother knows that only a true princess could feel a pea through all of the mattresses, so the prince and princess get married.

   ▸ Who are the characters? the prince; the princess; the prince's mother
   ▸ What is the setting? the prince's castle
   ▸ What is the prince's problem in the story? He can't find a real princess to marry.
   ▸ How is the prince's problem solved? His mother tests the princess by stacking 20 mattresses and 20 featherbeds on a pea for the princess to sleep on.

Objectives

- Describe story structure elements—problem and solution.
- Identify story structure elements—plot, setting, character(s).
- Build vocabulary through listening, reading, and discussion.
- Use new vocabulary in written and spoken sentences.

Words to Know

Before reading "The Country Mouse and the City Mouse," go over Words to Know with students.

1. Read aloud each word and have students repeat it.

2. Ask students if they know what each word means.

   ► If students know a word's meaning, have them define it and use it in a sentence.
   ► If students don't know a word's meaning, read them the definition and discuss the word with them.

cellar – a room built underground, often used for storage; a basement
trap – a device for catching things, usually animals

Shared Reading

Book Walk

Prepare students for reading by taking them on a Book Walk of "The Country Mouse and the City Mouse." Scan the story together and ask students to make predictions. Answers to questions may vary.

1. Turn to the **table of contents** in *K¹² Classics for Young Readers, Volume A*. Help students find "The Country Mouse and the City Mouse" and turn to that page.

2. Point to and read aloud the **title of the story**.

   ► What do you think this story is about?

3. Have students look at the **pictures**.

   ► Where do you think the story takes place?
   ► What do you think might happen in the story?
   ► Have you ever been to a place where things were very different from what you're used to? How did you feel while you were there?

> **Objectives**
> - Make predictions based on text, illustrations, and/or prior knowledge.
> - Activate prior knowledge by previewing text and/or discussing topic.
> - Read and respond to texts representing a variety of cultures, time periods, and traditions.

"The Country Mouse and the City Mouse"

It's time to read aloud.

1. Have students sit next to you so that they can see the pictures and words while you read aloud.

2. Tell students to listen for the story elements.

3. **Read aloud the entire story.** Track with your finger so students can follow along. Emphasize Words to Know as you come to them. If appropriate, use the pictures to help show what each word means.

Check Your Reading

"The Country Mouse and the City Mouse"
Check students' comprehension of "The Country Mouse and the City Mouse."

1. Have students retell "The Country Mouse and the City Mouse" in their own words to develop grammar, vocabulary, comprehension, and fluency skills.

2. Ask students the following questions.

   ▶ What does the Country Mouse make for dinner? corn and beans
   ▶ What does the cook make at the City Mouse's house? a pie
   ▶ Why do the mice run away just as they are beginning to eat the pie? They hear the cat.
   ▶ Why don't the mice eat the cheese in the cellar? because it's in a trap
   ▶ Why doesn't the Country Mouse like the City Mouse's house? because there's a cat in the kitchen and a trap in the cellar

TIP If students have trouble responding to a question, help them locate the answer in the text or pictures.

Objectives
- Retell or dramatize a story.
- Answer questions requiring literal recall of details.

Reading for Meaning

Story Elements in "The Country Mouse and the City Mouse"
Check students' ability to identify and describe story structure elements.

1. Remind students that a story has certain parts, or elements. These parts include the characters, setting, problem, solution, and plot.

2. Ask the following questions.

   ▶ Who are the characters? Country Mouse; City Mouse
   ▶ Where does this story take place? at the City Mouse's house; at the Country Mouse's house
   ▶ When the mice get to the City Mouse's house, they're hungry. How do they solve their problem? They go to the kitchen to see what the cook has made.
   ▶ What problem do the mice have when they start eating the pie? The cat finds them. How do they solve their problem? They run.
   ▶ What is the plot of the story? The Country Mouse and City Mouse are cousins. The City Mouse invites the Country Mouse to visit her house. During the visit, the two mice are chased by a cat and must avoid a mouse trap. The Country Mouse decides she likes her house in the country better than her cousin's house in the city.

Objectives
- Describe story structure elements—problem and solution.
- Identify story structure elements—plot, setting, character(s).
- Retell a story naming plot, setting, character(s), problem, and solution.

Looking at Language

When Is the Story Happening?

Reread "The Country Mouse and the City Mouse" with a focus on action words that indicate when the story is happening. Gather the Reading Aid on pages LC 125 and 126 in *K¹² Language Arts Activity Book*.

1. Tell students that we can tell when the events in a story happen by certain words that the author uses.

2. **Say:** Listen to the following sentences and think about which one tells us something that is happening now and which one tells us something that already happened. The City Mouse is eating pie. The City Mouse ate pie.

   ▶ Which sentence tells us something that is happening now? The City Mouse is eating pie.

   ▶ Which sentence tells us something that happened in the past? The City Mouse ate pie.

3. Explain that the action words, or **verbs**, are the words that help us figure out when a story happens. We can tell that something in a story is happening now because of action words such as *eat* or *is eating*. We can tell that something has already happened because of verbs such as *ate*.

4. Tell students that they will **read the story aloud with you**. You will stop at certain points to discuss the action words, or verbs, that let us know when the story is happening.

5. Refer to the Reading Aid.

Reading Aid Tear out the Reading Aid for this reading selection. Follow the instructions for folding the page, and then use the page as a guide as you reread the selection with students.

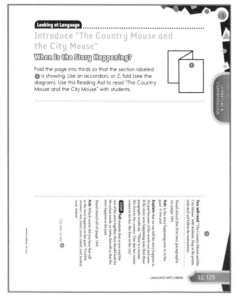
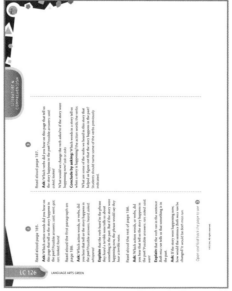

Objectives

- Identify verbs in sentences.
- Recognize the past tense of verbs.
- Recognize and use the past tense of irregular verbs.
- Read aloud grade-level text with appropriate expression, accuracy, and rate.

Explore "The Country Mouse and the City Mouse"

Lesson Overview

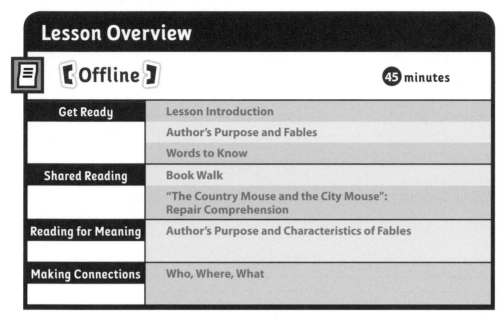

[Offline] **45** minutes

Get Ready	Lesson Introduction
	Author's Purpose and Fables
	Words to Know
Shared Reading	Book Walk
	"The Country Mouse and the City Mouse": Repair Comprehension
Reading for Meaning	Author's Purpose and Characteristics of Fables
Making Connections	Who, Where, What

Materials

Supplied

- "The Country Mouse and the City Mouse," *K¹² Classics for Young Readers, Volume A*, pp. 184–187
- *K¹² Language Arts Activity Book*, pp. LC 127–129

Keywords

author's purpose – the reason the author wrote a text: to entertain, to inform, to express an opinion, or to persuade

fable – a story that teaches a lesson and may contain animal characters

genre – a category for classifying literary works

moral – the lesson of a story, particularly a fable

prior knowledge – things you already know from past experience

Advance Preparation

Preview the Reading Aid on pages LC 127 and 128 in *K¹² Language Arts Activity Book* to prepare the materials for the Shared Reading.

Big Ideas

- ▶ Exposing readers to a wide variety of genres provides them with a wide range of background knowledge and increases their vocabulary.
- ▶ An awareness of story structure elements (setting, characters, plot) provides readers a foundation for constructing meaning when reading new stories and writing their own stories.
- ▶ Comprehension requires an understanding of story structure.
- ▶ Verbalizing your thoughts while modeling a reading strategy allows students to see what goes on inside the head of an effective reader; it makes visible the normally hidden process of comprehending text.
- ▶ Shared reading allows students to observe and practice the reading behaviors of proficient readers.

 **45 minutes**

Work **together** with students to complete Get Ready, Shared Reading, Reading for Meaning, and Making Connections activities.

Get Ready ....

Lesson Introduction

Prepare students for listening to and discussing "The Country Mouse and the City Mouse."

1. Tell students that you are going to reread "The Country Mouse and the City Mouse."

2. Explain that before you reread the story, you will get ready by reviewing

   ▸ The reasons that an author writes a text
   ▸ The characteristics of fables

Objectives
- Identify the author's purpose.
- Identify the moral or lesson of a text.
- Identify genre.
- Build vocabulary through listening, reading, and discussion.
- Use new vocabulary in written and spoken sentences.

Author's Purpose and Fables

Review author's purpose and the characteristics of fables.

1. Have students tell you the reasons why an author writes an article or story.

2. If students don't recall the purposes an author has for writing a text, remind them that

   ▸ An author's purpose may be to teach something, to entertain, to convince the reader of something, or to tell the reader what the author thinks about something.

3. Tell students that sometimes an author writes a text for more than one reason. One type of story where this happens is called a **fable**. A fable both entertains and teaches a lesson about life. A fable often has animal characters that act like people.

   ▸ What do we call the lesson that a fable teaches? a moral

4. If students don't remember what we call the lesson a fable teaches, remind them that it is called a **moral**. Some well-known morals are "Never leave till tomorrow what you can do today" and "It's best to be yourself."

5. Have students practice figuring out why an author wrote a story and what the moral of a fable is.
   Say: Listen to this story.

   A dog was carrying a bone in his mouth as he walked home. As the dog crossed a stream, he looked down into the water. When he saw his reflection, he thought it was another dog with a bigger bone. The dog let go of his bone to try to steal the larger bone. By the time the dog realized that the larger bone was only a reflection, it was too late; his own bone was floating away in the stream.

   ‣ Why do you think the author wrote the story? to entertain and to teach a lesson
   ‣ What do we call a story that has animal characters and teaches a lesson? a fable
   ‣ What do we call the lesson that the fable teaches? a moral
   ‣ What is the moral of this story? Possible answers: Don't be greedy; be happy with what you have; a bird in the hand is worth two in the bush.

Words to Know

Before reading "The Country Mouse and the City Mouse," go over Words to Know with students.

1. Read aloud each word and have students repeat it.

2. Ask students if they know what each word means.

   ‣ If students know a word's meaning, have them define it and use it in a sentence.
   ‣ If students don't know a word's meaning, read them the definition and discuss the word with them.

cellar – a room built underground, often used for storage; a basement
trap – a device for catching things, usually animals

Shared Reading

Book Walk

Prepare students by taking them on a Book Walk of "The Country Mouse and the City Mouse." Scan the story together to revisit the characters and events.

1. Turn to the selection in *K¹² Classics for Young Readers, Volume A*. Read aloud the **title of the story**.

2. Have students review the **pictures**.

   ▶ What does the Country Mouse make for dinner? corn and beans
   ▶ What kinds of food is the City Mouse used to eating? cake and cheese
   ▶ Why don't the mice finish eating the pie at the City Mouse's house? because a cat comes into the kitchen
   ▶ Why can't the mice eat the cheese in the cellar? It's in a trap.
   ▶ If you were a mouse, do you think you would enjoy living in the City Mouse's house? Why or why not? Answers will vary.

Objectives

- Activate prior knowledge by previewing text and/or discussing topic.
- Repair comprehension using strategies: reread, use prior knowledge, self-question.
- Read aloud grade-level text with appropriate expression, accuracy, and rate.
- Demonstrate one-to-one correspondence (voice-to-print).
- Read and respond to texts representing a variety of cultures, time periods, and traditions.

"The Country Mouse and the City Mouse": Repair Comprehension

It's time to reread the story. Tell students that they will reread "The Country Mouse and the City Mouse" with a focus on what to do if they don't understand something they are reading. Gather the Reading Aid on pages LC 127 and 128 in *K¹² Language Arts Activity Book*.

1. Remind students that sometimes when we're reading, we realize that we're confused because we don't understand something in the story.

2. Explain that there are strategies we can use to help us figure out what we don't understand.

   ▶ Sometimes all we need to do is go back and reread a part of the story more slowly and carefully.
   ▶ Other times it's helpful to think about our prior knowledge. If we can connect something we already know to something in the story, it can help us figure out a part of the story that is confusing.

3. Tell students that when good readers do these things, you can't see what they're doing because it's happening in their head.

4. Explain that you will show students how to use these strategies, while sharing your thoughts aloud. That way they can learn what goes on in the head of a good reader.

5. Have students sit next to you so that they can see the pictures and words while you read aloud.

6. Tell students that **they will read aloud the story with you**. As you read aloud together, you will stop at certain points to show students how to use strategies to help you figure out something that is causing you confusion.

7. Refer to the Reading Aid.

Reading Aid Tear out the Reading Aid for this reading selection. Follow the instructions for folding the page, and then use the page as a guide as you reread the selection with students.

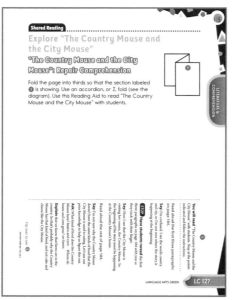
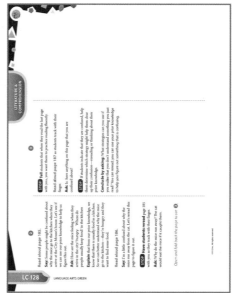

Reading for Meaning

Author's Purpose and Characteristics of Fables
Explore the author's purpose and characteristics of fables.

1. Ask the following questions to check students' understanding of the author's purpose.

   ▶ What do we call the author's reason for writing a story or article? the author's purpose
   ▶ Authors write stories and articles for different reasons. What are some of the reasons? to teach something; to entertain; to convince the reader of something; to tell the reader what the author thinks about something
   ▶ Why do you think the author wrote "The Country Mouse and the City Mouse"? to entertain and to teach a lesson

Objectives
- Identify the author's purpose.
- Identify the moral or lesson of a text.
- Identify genre.

2. Ask the following questions to check students' understanding of the characteristics of fables.

> ▶ What is the lesson of the story "The Country Mouse and the City Mouse"? Possible answers: Be happy with what you have; what's good for one is not always good for another.
> ▶ What kind of story is this? a fable
> ▶ How do you know this story is a fable? It has animal characters and teaches a lesson.
> ▶ What do we call the lesson a fable teaches? a moral

Making Connections

Who, Where, What

Check students' understanding of story structure elements and important details in the story "The Country Mouse and the City Mouse." Turn to page LC 129 in *K¹² Language Arts Activity Book*.

1. Ask the following questions to review the story structure elements of "The Country Mouse and the City Mouse."

> ▶ Who are the characters in the story? Country Mouse and City Mouse
> ▶ Where does the story begin? What is the setting? Country Mouse's house
> ▶ What does the City Mouse think of the Country Mouse's dinner? She thinks it's funny. Why does the City Mouse think the Country Mouse's dinner is funny? because it's not what she's used to eating for dinner
> ▶ What is the setting of the story after the mice leave the country? City Mouse's house
> ▶ What happens when the mice start to eat the pie? They hear the cat.
> ▶ What do the mice do when they hear the cat? They run. Why do the mice run from the cat? because the cat might eat them
> ▶ Why does the cook put cheese in the mouse trap? to catch mice
> ▶ Why doesn't the Country Mouse like the City Mouse's house? because it has a cat and a trap

Objectives
- Identify details that explain characters' actions and feelings.
- Identify important details and/or events of a story.
- Follow two- or three-step written directions.
- Retell a story naming plot, setting, character(s).
- Demonstrate understanding through graphic organizers.

2. Tell students that they will now use information they gave about the story to complete a story map.

3. Have students read aloud the instructions at the top of the Activity Book page.

4. Point to and read aloud the story title in the center of the map.

5. Point to the Characters box and read aloud the label. Have students say the names of the characters and write what students dictate.

   ▸ If students are ready to write on their own, allow them to do so.

6. Repeat Step 5 for each box in the story map.

7. Have students retell the story using the story map as a guide.

TIP If students enjoy drawing, an alternative is to read aloud the box labels and have students draw what goes inside each box.

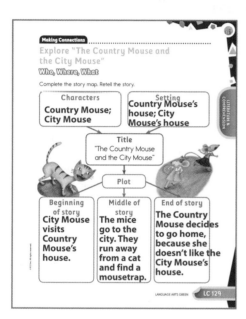

Introduce "The Cap that Mother Made"

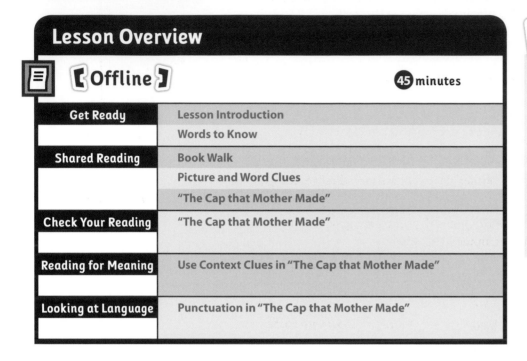

Lesson Overview

Offline   **45 minutes**

Get Ready	Lesson Introduction
	Words to Know
Shared Reading	Book Walk
	Picture and Word Clues
	"The Cap that Mother Made"
Check Your Reading	"The Cap that Mother Made"
Reading for Meaning	Use Context Clues in "The Cap that Mother Made"
Looking at Language	Punctuation in "The Cap that Mother Made"

Advance Preparation

Before beginning the Shared Reading, read "The Cap that Mother Made" to locate Words to Know in the text. Preview the Reading Aid on pages LC 131 and 132 in *K¹² Language Arts Activity Book* to prepare the materials for Looking at Language.

Big Ideas

▶ An awareness of story structure elements (setting, characters, plot) provides readers a foundation for constructing meaning when reading new stories and writing their own stories.

▶ Early learners acquire vocabulary through active exposure (by talking and listening, being read to, and receiving explicit instruction).

▶ During shared-reading activities, students learn more about how print works.

Materials

Supplied

- "The Cap that Mother Made," *K¹² Classics for Young Readers, Volume A,* pp. 188–201
- *K¹² Language Arts Activity Book,* pp. LC131–132

Also Needed

- whiteboard (optional)

Story Synopsis

Anders loves the cap his mother made him more than anything in the world. Everyone he meets loves it, too, and they offer him wonderful things to trade for it. Will any of their offers convince Anders to give up his treasured cap? (Note that this selection includes references to a boy carrying a pocket knife and soldiers holding guns.)

Keywords

context – the parts of a sentence or passage surrounding a word

context clue – a word or phrase in a text that helps you figure out the meaning of an unknown word

 **45 minutes**

Work **together** with students to complete Get Ready, Shared Reading, Check Your Reading, Reading for Meaning, and Looking at Language activities.

Get Ready

Lesson Introduction

Prepare students for listening to and discussing "The Cap that Mother Made," adapted from Carolyn Sherwin Bailey.

1. Tell students that you are going to read "The Cap that Mother Made," a story about a boy who values a cap his mother made for him more than anything in the world.

2. Explain that before you read the story, you will practice using word and picture clues to figure out the meaning of unknown words.

Objectives

- Build vocabulary through listening, reading, and discussion.
- Use new vocabulary in written and spoken sentences.

Words to Know

Before reading "The Cap that Mother Made," go over Words to Know with students.

1. Read aloud each word and have students repeat it.

2. Ask students if they know what each word means.

   ▶ If students know a word's meaning, have them define it and use it in a sentence.
   ▶ If students don't know a word's meaning, read them the definition and discuss the word with them.

ball – a large party with formal dancing
eel – a long fish that looks like a snake
uniform – a special suit worn by all members of a particular group, such as the police or army

Shared Reading

Book Walk

Prepare students for reading by taking them on a Book Walk of "The Cap that Mother Made." Scan the story together and ask students to make predictions about the story. Answers to questions may vary.

1. Turn to the **table of contents** in *K¹² Classics for Young Readers, Volume A*. Help students find "The Cap that Mother Made" and turn to that page.

2. Point to and read aloud the **title of the story**.

   ▸ What do you think this story might be about?

3. Have students look at the **pictures**.

   ▸ Where do you think the story takes place?
   ▸ What do you think might happen in the story?
   ▸ Have you ever had something that you loved very much? Why was it special to you?

Picture and Word Clues

Explore using picture and word clues to define unknown words.

1. Explain to students that sometimes the words and pictures in a story can help a reader figure out what an unknown word means.

2. Tell students that you will show them how to figure out the meaning of a word by explaining to them what you are thinking as you do it. This will help them know what goes on in a good reader's mind as the reader figures out the meaning of a word.

3. Read aloud page 188 in *K¹² Classics for Young Readers, Volume A*.
   Say: I'm not sure what *tassel* means in the sentence "A blue tassel sat on top." All the sentences in this paragraph are about a hat, and I see in the picture that there is a bunch of blue threads tied together at one end on top of the hat. I think that a *tassel* is a decoration made of threads that are tied together at one end.

   ▸ Does "a decoration made of threads tied together at one end" make sense in the sentence, *A blue decoration made of threads tied together at one end sat on top*"? Yes

Objectives

- Make predictions based on text, illustrations, and/or prior knowledge.
- Activate prior knowledge by previewing text and/or discussing topic.
- Use context and sentence structure to determine meaning of words, phrases, and/or sentences.
- Use illustrations to aid understanding of text.
- Read and respond to texts representing a variety of cultures, time periods, and traditions.

"The Cap that Mother Made"

It's time to read aloud.

1. Have students sit next to you so that they can see the pictures and words while you read aloud.

2. Tell students to listen to the words before and after an unknown word to help figure out what the word means. Remind them to look at the pictures for clues, too.

3. **Read aloud the entire story.** Track with your finger so students can follow along. Emphasize Words to Know as you come to them. If appropriate, use the pictures to help show what each word means.

Check Your Reading

"The Cap that Mother Made"

Check students' comprehension of "The Cap that Mother Made."

1. Have students retell "The Cap that Mother Made" in their own words to develop grammar, vocabulary, comprehension, and fluency skills.

2. Ask students the following questions.

   ▸ Who are some of the characters? Possible answers: Anders; Anders's mother; Lars; the princess; the king

   ▸ Who is the main character? Anders

   ▸ Where does the story take place? Possible answers: at Anders's house; on a road; at the king's palace

   ▸ Why doesn't Anders trade his cap for a ride on the farmer's wagon or for Lars's pocketknife? He doesn't think a ride on a wagon or the pocketknife are as nice as the cap his mother made.

   ▸ Why does the princess fill Anders's pockets with cakes, put her gold chain around his neck, and kiss him? She wants Anders to give her his cap.

   ▸ Why does Anders's big brother think Anders should have traded his cap for the king's crown? His brother thinks Anders could sell the gold crown for enough money to buy a house full of caps.

TIP If students have trouble responding to a question, help them locate the answer in the text or pictures.

Objectives

- Retell or dramatize a story.
- Identify character(s).
- Identify the main character(s).
- Identify setting.
- Identify details that explain characters' actions and feelings.
- Answer questions requiring literal recall of details.

Reading for Meaning ●●●

Use Context Clues in "The Cap that Mother Made"

Explore using context clues to define unknown words in "The Cap that Mother Made."

1. Remind students that readers can sometimes figure out what unfamiliar words mean by using the words that surround them as well as the pictures in the story.

2. Read aloud the last paragraph on page 189 while students study the picture at the bottom of the page.

   ▸ What do you think *bow* means? to bend forward at the waist toward somebody   What word or words give you a clue? Guide students to the clue words *head nearly touched the ground.*   How does the picture help you figure this out? It shows the farmer bending over in front of Anders and Anders smiling.

3. Read aloud the second paragraph on page 192 while students study the picture at the bottom of the page.

   ▸ What do you think *curtsied* means? bent slightly while holding out a dress   How does the picture help you figure this out? It shows the woman looking slightly bent and holding out her dress.

4. Read aloud the paragraph on page 199 while students study the picture on the page.

   ▸ What do you think *cottage* means? a small house   How did you figure this out? The story says that Anders rushed into his cottage, and the picture shows a little house.

Objectives
- Use context and sentence structure to determine meaning of words, phrases, and/or sentences.
- Use illustrations to aid understanding of text.

Looking at Language ●●●

Punctuation in "The Cap that Mother Made"

Reread "The Cap that Mother Made" with a focus on punctuation marks. Gather the Reading Aid on pages LC 131 and 132 in *K¹² Language Arts Activity Book.*

1. Explain that while the words in a story are important, there are other marks on the page that also help us understand what we're reading.

2. Write a period, a question mark, and a set of quotation marks on a whiteboard or sheet of paper.

3. Tell students the name of each punctuation mark. Explain that you will look at each of these while rereading the story.

Objectives
- Recognize that a statement ends with a period.
- Recognize questions.
- Recognize that a question ends with a question mark.
- Recognize quotations in dialogue.
- Read aloud grade-level text with appropriate expression, accuracy, and rate.

4. Read aloud the following paragraph, which has no periods, in an exaggerated and rushed voice to illustrate how difficult it is to understand a paragraph without any pauses.
   Say: I'm going to read aloud a paragraph. I want you to think about what is wrong with how I read the paragraph.

   Read aloud: Once there was a boy with a new cap his mother made the cap it was red and green it had a blue tassel everybody liked his new cap

   ▸ What did you notice as I read the paragraph? Answers will vary. Students may notice that you read with no pauses; some students may notice that you didn't stop and pause at places where there should be periods; students may say that all the words ran together and it was hard to understand.

   ▸ What do you think would make the paragraph easier to read and understand? Answers will vary. Guide students to recognize that it would be easier to understand if you took brief pauses so they could hear separate ideas.

5. Tell students that you read the paragraph without any periods. Periods are one type of punctuation mark. They are important because they let us know when one sentence ends and another begins. They separate the ideas in a story.

6. Read aloud the same paragraph in a more natural way, pausing at the periods.
   Say: I'm going to read the same paragraph. Listen closely so you can hear the difference.

   Read aloud: Once there was a boy with a new cap. His mother made the cap. It was red and green. It had a blue tassel. Everybody liked his new cap.

   ▸ What did you notice when I read the paragraph this time? Students should recognize that you paused at certain points in the paragraph.

7. Explain that you know where to pause because of the periods. The periods separate the sentences and the ideas in a paragraph so it's easier to understand.

8. Tell students that in addition to periods, there are other types of punctuation marks that help readers understand a story.

  ▶ What kind of mark is used to let us know that somebody is asking a question? a question mark
  ▶ How do we know that somebody is speaking in a story? quotation marks

9. Tell students that they will **read aloud the story with you**. You will stop at certain points to discuss the different punctuation marks and how they help us understand a story and influence our expression when we read aloud.

10. Refer to the Reading Aid.

Reading Aid Tear out the Reading Aid for this reading selection. Follow the instructions for folding the page, and then use the page as a guide as you reread the selection with students.

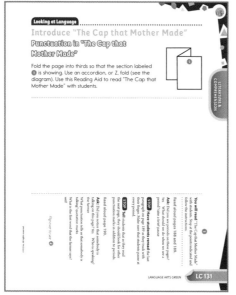

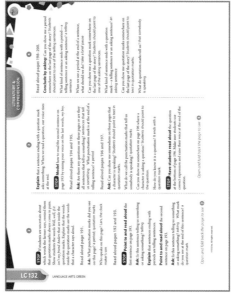

Explore "The Cap that Mother Made"

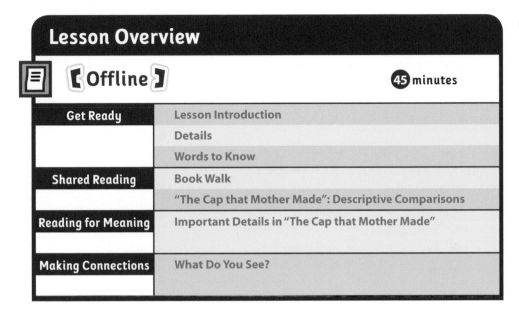

Lesson Overview

Offline	**45** minutes

Get Ready	Lesson Introduction
	Details
	Words to Know
Shared Reading	Book Walk
	"The Cap that Mother Made": Descriptive Comparisons
Reading for Meaning	Important Details in "The Cap that Mother Made"
Making Connections	What Do You See?

Big Ideas

▸ Readers must focus on the specific language of a text to aid in interpretation.
▸ The use of imagery and sensory language creates detailed pictures in the reader's mind, so the reader can understand and appreciate the ideas and feelings the writer conveys.
▸ Readers who visualize, or form mental pictures, while they read have better recall of text than those who do not.
▸ During shared-reading activities, students learn more about how print works.

Materials

Supplied

- "The Cap that Mother Made," *K¹² Classics for Young Readers, Volume A,* pp. 188–201
- *K¹² Language Arts Activity Book,* p. LC 133

Also Needed

- crayons

Keywords

detail – a piece of information in a text
simile – a comparison between two things using the words *like* or *as*; for example: "He was as quiet as a mouse."
visualize – to picture things in your mind as you read

 **Offline** **45** minutes

Work **together** with students to complete Get Ready, Shared Reading, Reading for Meaning, and Making Connections activities.

Get Ready

Lesson Introduction

Prepare students for listening to and discussing "The Cap that Mother Made."

1. Tell students that you are going to reread "The Cap that Mother Made."

2. Explain that before you reread the story, you will get ready by discussing how to determine which details in a story are important.

Details

Help students recognize important details in a text.

1. Tell students that stories are filled with details. However, details are not all equally important. Details that help readers better understand the story's characters and events are important. Other details might be interesting, but they aren't essential to remember.

2. **Read aloud:** Jermaine hurt his ankle yesterday. He was playing outside with his dog and he tripped on a rock. His dog licked his face to try to make him feel better. Now Jermaine can't play in his soccer game.
   Say: It's important to know that Jermaine hurt his ankle by tripping on a rock. It's interesting to know that his dog licked his face to try to make him feel better, but it doesn't help us learn more about Jermaine or his hurt ankle.

3. Tell students that learning to recognize the most important details helps good readers sort through information and make decisions about what they should remember about a story.

4. Have students practice picking out an important detail.
   Say: Listen to this story.

   Celeste was sad because she lost her favorite book. She liked to read the book every night before bed. The book had a brown cover with red letters. Now Celeste would have to find a new book to read before bed.

   ▸ Which detail is more important: Celeste liked to read the book every night before bed, or the book had a brown cover with red letters? Celeste liked to read the book every night before bed.

5. Explain that the detail *Celeste liked to read the book every night before bed* is more important because it helps us to understand why she is so sad that she lost the book.

6. Tell students that as they read a story, they should think about which details are really important because the details help them understand the story.

Objectives
- Identify important details and/or events of a story.
- Distinguish the most important details from less important details in text.
- Build vocabulary through listening, reading, and discussion.
- Use new vocabulary in written and spoken sentences.

Words to Know
Before reading "The Cap that Mother Made," go over Words to Know with students.

1. Read aloud each word and have students repeat it.

2. Ask students if they know what each word means.
   ▸ If students know a word's meaning, have them define it and use it in a sentence.
   ▸ If students don't know a word's meaning, read them the definition and discuss the word with them.

ball – a large party with formal dancing
eel – a long fish that looks like a snake
uniform – a special suit worn by all members of a particular group, such as the police or army

Shared Reading

Book Walk
Prepare students by taking them on a Book Walk of "The Cap that Mother Made." Scan the story together to revisit the characters and events.

1. Turn to the selection in *K¹² Classics for Young Readers, Volume A*. Read aloud the **title of the story**.

2. Have students review the **pictures**.
   ▸ Why is Anders's cap so special? His mother made it.
   ▸ Why won't Anders trade anything for his cap, even the king's crown? He doesn't think that anything is as good as the cap that his mother made.
   ▸ What does Anders's big brother think about Anders not trading his cap for the king's crown? He thinks Anders is silly; he thinks Anders should have traded his cap.

> **Objectives**
> - Activate prior knowledge by previewing text and/or discussing topic.
> - Read and respond to texts representing a variety of cultures, time periods, and traditions.
> - Identify literary devices: personification and/or simile.
> - Use visualizing to aid understanding of text.

"The Cap that Mother Made": Descriptive Comparisons
It's time to reread the story. Tell students that they will reread "The Cap that Mother Made" with a focus on descriptive ways that the author compares things.

1. Ask students if they have ever heard anyone described as being "as quiet as a mouse." Saying that someone is "as quiet as a mouse" is a descriptive way of saying that somebody is very quiet. We know that the person we're describing is not a mouse, but making the comparison gives us a vivid picture of that person.

2. Tell students that authors make these same types of comparisons in their stories. They often compare two things that are not alike by using the words *like* or *as*. For example, an author might say that a character "eats like a bird" to describe someone who eats very little.

3. Explain that authors use these kinds of descriptive comparisons to help readers visualize what's happening in a story. This makes a story more interesting. Instead of saying a character laughs loudly, an author might say that the character "laughs like a hyena" to help readers imagine what that character's laugh sounds like.

   ► What do you think it would sound like if somebody "laughs like a hyena?" Answers will vary.

4. Tell students that they will **read the story aloud with you**. You will stop at certain points to discuss descriptive comparisons.

5. Read aloud pages 188–197, and then pause before continuing.

6. Tell students that they should listen for descriptive comparisons that use the words *like* or *as* when they hear the next page.

7. Read aloud page 198.

   ► How did the author describe Anders as he runs away from the palace? darted like an arrow; twisted like an eel; jumped like a rabbit
   ► How do you imagine Anders is moving as he "darts like an arrow"? Answers will vary.
   ► How do you imagine Anders moves as he "twists like an eel" between the arms of the people attending the royal ball? Answers will vary. If students don't remember what an eel is, remind them that it is a long, thin fish that resembles a snake.
   ► What do you visualize when the story says Anders "jumped like a rabbit" past the soldiers?" Answer will vary.

8. Read aloud to the end of the story.

9. Point out that there is one more descriptive comparison on the last page that uses the word *as*.

   ► How does the author describe Anders's face in the middle of page 200? as red as a tomato   Why do you think Anders's face turned red? He was embarrassed.

10. Conclude by asking the following question.

    ► Why do you think the author described Anders with these unusual comparisons, instead of saying something like "Anders ran really fast" or "Anders's face turned red?" Answers will vary. Students should mention that the comparisons make the story more interesting and help readers imagine pictures in their head.

Reading for Meaning

Important Details in "The Cap that Mother Made"

Check students' understanding of the most important details in "The Cap that Mother Made."

1. Have students retell "The Cap that Mother Made" in their own words to develop grammar, vocabulary, comprehension, and fluency skills.

2. Remind students that some details in a story are more important than others. Details that help readers better understand the story's characters and events are important. Other details might be interesting, but they aren't essential to remember.

3. Tell students to listen to the following sentences and think about which detail is more important.
   Say: Lars wanted to trade his cap and pocketknife for Anders's cap. Lars was the clock maker's son.

   ▸ Which detail is more important? Lars wanted to trade his cap and pocketknife for Anders's cap.
   ▸ Why do you think that detail is more important? because it makes it clear that Anders's cap is so nice, everybody wants to trade him for it

4. Tell students to listen to the following sentences and think about which detail is more important.
   Say: The princess was dressed in a white silk gown. The princess took Anders into the palace.

   ▸ Which detail is more important? The princess took Anders into the palace.
   ▸ Why do you think that detail is more important? because Anders couldn't have gotten into the royal ball if the princess hadn't taken him into the palace

5. Tell students to listen to the following sentences and think about which detail is more important.
   Say: The king wore a great purple robe. The king reached out his hand to grab Anders's cap.

   ▸ Which detail is more important? The king reached out his hand to grab Anders's cap.
   ▸ Why do you think that detail is more important? because it makes it clear that Anders's cap is so wonderful that even the king wants it

Objectives

- Retell or dramatize a story.
- Identify important details and/or events of a story.
- Distinguish the most important details from less important details in text.

Making Connections

What Do You See?

Check students' understanding of descriptive comparisons. Turn to page LC 133 in *K¹² Language Arts Activity Book*.

1. Remind students that authors often compare two things that are not alike by using the words *like* or *as*.

2. Read aloud the list of similes on the Activity Book page.

3. Discuss the meaning of each simile on the list.

4. Have students choose two of the similes to draw pictures of. The pictures should show what students see in their head when they hear the comparisons.

5. Ask students to describe their drawings.

 Reward: Add a sticker for this unit on the My Accomplishments chart to mark successful completion of the unit.

Objectives

- Use visualizing to aid understanding of text.
- Demonstrate visualizing through drawing, discussion, and/or writing.

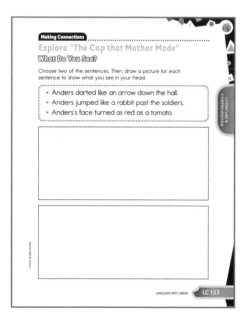

Making Connections

Explore "The Cap that Mother Made"

What Do You See?

Choose two of the sentences. Then, draw a picture for each sentence to show what you see in your head.

- Anders darted like an arrow down the hall.
- Anders jumped like a rabbit past the soldiers.
- Anders's face turned as red as a tomato.

LANGUAGE ARTS GREEN   LC 133

Semester Review and Checkpoint

Unit Focus

In this unit, students will review elements of poetry, nonfiction, and fiction. Students will listen to and share the reading of a piece of fiction, a nonfiction article, and a poem. They will demonstrate mastery of content in each genre by making and checking predictions, identifying story elements and structures of each text, using new vocabulary, comparing and contrasting elements of each text, and summarizing.

Unit Plan		[Offline]	[Online]
Lesson 1	Semester Review	**45** minutes	
Lesson 2	Semester Checkpoint	**45** minutes	varies

Semester Review

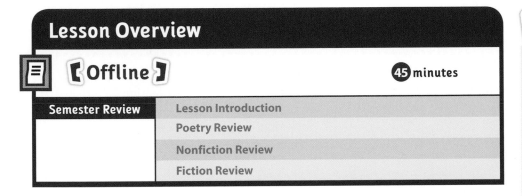

Lesson Overview

Offline 45 minutes

Semester Review	Lesson Introduction
	Poetry Review
	Nonfiction Review
	Fiction Review

Materials

Supplied

- "The Poor Man's Reward," *K¹² Classics for Young Readers, Volume A*, pp. 100–123
- "The *Eagle* on the Moon," *K¹² World: Earth and Sky*, pp. 24–37
- *Weather: Poems for All Seasons*, pp. 16–17
- *K¹² Language Arts Activity Book*, p. LC 135

Also Needed

- scissors, round-end safety

Offline ⏱ 45 minutes

Work **together** with students to complete the Semester Review.

Semester Review ··

Lesson Introduction

Prepare students for reviewing what they have learned about poems, stories, and nonfiction articles.

1. Tell students that they will reread the poem "Sun" and review poetic elements such as imagery and personification.

2. Tell them that they will reread the article "The *Eagle* on the Moon" and review features of nonfiction text, such as charts, graphs, and time lines.

3. Tell them that they will reread the story "The Poor Man's Reward" and discuss story structure elements such as characters, plot, and setting.

Objectives

- Complete a Semester Review on the elements of poetry, nonfiction, and fiction.

Poetry Review

Reread "Sun" by Valerie Worth in *Weather: Poems for All Seasons* to students and then review imagery, descriptive language, and personification.

1. Have students sit next to you so that they can see the pictures and words while you read aloud.

2. **Read aloud the entire poem.** Track with your finger so students can follow along. Encourage students to use pictures and other words on the page to figure out what unfamiliar words mean.

3. Remind students that authors have a purpose when they write.

   ▸ Why did the author write this piece? to entertain us

4. Tell students that the author uses a lot of descriptive language in the poem.

   ▸ What are some phrases that help you picture the poem in your head? Answers will vary but should include *the sun is a leaping fire, it lies down in warm yellow square,* or *like a flat quilt.*

5. Tell students that the author tells readers that the sun lies down on the floor, just like a person can lie down on the floor.

   ▸ What does the author mean? Possible answers: The sun comes in through the window and you can see it on the floor; it's like it is lying there.

   ▸ Does this poem have rhyming? No

Nonfiction Review

Reread "The *Eagle* on the Moon" in K^{12} *World: Earth and Sky* to students and then review features of nonfiction text.

1. Have students sit next to you so that they can see the pictures and words while you read aloud.

2. **Read aloud the entire article.** Track with your finger so students can follow along. Encourage students to use pictures and other words on the page to figure out what unfamiliar words mean.

   ▸ Why did the author write this piece? to teach us about the history of astronauts going to space

3. On page 24, point to the caption, "Could Americans send a man to the moon?"

   ▸ Why is this text in bold? Answers will vary, but guide students to understand that it's an important question, it's something the author wanted readers to notice, and it helps set the purpose for the article.

4. On pages 26 and 27, point to the captions under each picture of the astronauts.

   ▸ Why is this information here? to tell us who is in each picture

5. On page 31, point to the cartoon audience at the bottom of the page and read the text bubble.

   ▸ Why did the illustrator add this cartoon here? It shows us that people were excited and cheered when the spaceship launched.

6. On pages 36 and 37, ask students to point to the time line.

   ▸ What does the time line show us? important information about the history of the first astronauts traveling into space

7. On page 37, point to the cartoon at the bottom right of the page. Read the caption and the labels in the illustration.

   ▸ Can we drive from the earth to the moon? No
   ▸ Why did the illustrator add this cartoon here? to show us how far the earth is from the moon

---

Fiction Review

Reread "The Poor Man's Reward" in K^{12} *Classics for Young Readers, Volume A*, to students and then review story structure elements.

1. Have students sit next to you so that they can see the pictures and words while you read aloud.

2. **Read aloud the entire story.** Track with your finger so students can follow along. Encourage students to use pictures and other words on the page to figure out what unfamiliar words mean.

> ▸ Why did the author write this? Answers may include: to entertain us, to teach us a lesson about helping others.
> ▸ Who are the characters? the poor man; the weaverbird; the hyena; the bee; the crocodile; the king; the princess
> ▸ What is the setting? the wide plains of Africa; the king's palace
> ▸ What is the poor man's problem? He was poor and hungry.
> ▸ How did the poor man solve his problem? He set off to see if he had better luck in another part of the country.

3. Have students summarize "The Poor Man's Reward." Possible answer: A poor man owns nothing and he's hungry. He decides to try his luck in another part of the country. On his journey, even though he doesn't have much food or drink, he shares with different animals that are hungry or thirsty. They all tell him they won't forget his kindness. When the poor man reaches the palace and tries to win the hand of the princess, the animals come back and help him. The poor man is no longer poor!

4. Turn to page LC 135 in *K¹² Language Arts Activity Book*. Have students cut out the pictures on the Activity Book page and sequence them in the correct order. When students have finished the task, have them use the pictures to retell the story of "The Poor Man's Reward."

TIP A full list of objectives covered in the Semester Review can be found in the online lesson.

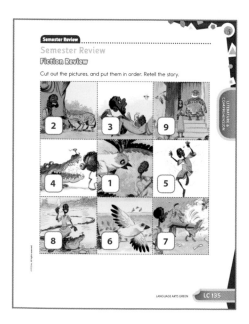

Semester Checkpoint

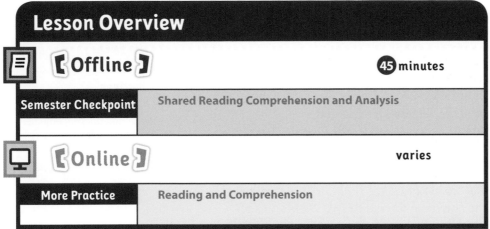

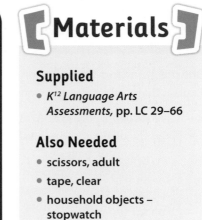

Materials

Supplied
- *K¹² Language Arts Assessments*, pp. LC 29–66

Also Needed
- scissors, adult
- tape, clear
- household objects – stopwatch

Advance Preparation

Read each selection in the Semester Checkpoint before administering the assessment to locate Words to Know in the text. Cut out the sentence strips on pages LC 41–43 and tape them together to make sentences. Cut out the picture cards on page LC 49.

 **45 minutes**

Work **together** with students to complete the Semester Checkpoint.

Semester Checkpoint

Objectives

- Complete a Semester Checkpoint on the elements of poetry, nonfiction, and fiction.

Shared Reading Comprehension and Analysis

Explain that students are going to show what they have learned this semester.

- ▶ Give students pages LC 37–LC 66 of the Semester Checkpoint.
- ▶ Read the directions on the students' pages together. Use the Learning Coach instructions on pages LC 29–LC 35 to administer the Checkpoint.
- ▶ Use the Checkpoint pages to record student behaviors and responses.
- ▶ When you have finished, use the Answer Key to score the Checkpoint and then enter the results online.
- ▶ Review each exercise with students. Work with students to correct any exercise that they missed.

Part 1. Fiction: "The Frog and the Lizard" Activate Prior Knowledge

Ask students the following questions to activate prior knowledge. Note their responses on the Checkpoint pages.

1. What would it be like to live in a rain forest—very wet or very dry?

2. What would it be like to live in a desert—very wet or very dry?

Before reading "The Frog and the Lizard," go over Words to Know with students. Read aloud each word and have students repeat it. Ask students if they know what each word means.

- ▶ If students know a word's meaning, have them define it and use it in a sentence.
- ▶ If students don't know a word's meaning, read them the definition and discuss the word with them.

desert – dry land with few plants and very little rain
gulp – a mouthful of something to swallow

Part 2. Fiction: "The Frog and the Lizard" Book Walk

Gather the Checkpoint pages with "The Frog and the Lizard." Have students sit next to you so that they can see the story while you do a Book Walk. Read aloud the title and author of the text. Ask students the following questions and note their responses on the Checkpoint pages.

3. What do you think the story will be about?

4. What does an author do?

5. What does an illustrator do?

6. Was this story written to teach us about frogs, or was it written to entertain us?

7. Is this story going to be fiction or nonfiction?

Part 3. Fiction: "The Frog and the Lizard" Shared Reading

Cut out the sentence strips on pages LC 41–43 and tape them together to make sentences. Show them to students. Point to each word as you read aloud the sentences. **Say:** "'Rain, rain, every day,' the frog said." A frog is doing the talking here.

Reread the sentence strip again, pointing to each word as you read aloud the entire sentence strip. Then point to the words indicated and ask students to read them.

- ▸ Circle any words that students read incorrectly.
- ▸ If students have trouble with a word, say, "This is the sight word [*word*]. Say [*word*]."

8. the

9. said

10. is

11. I

12. would

13. love

14. to

15. in

16. a

Refer to the story. **In paragraph 5**, point to the sentence, "The desert is a very dry place." Read aloud the sentence, pointing to each word. Explain to students that they will follow along as you read. When you come to this particular sentence, students should chime in and read aloud the sentence.

Begin to read aloud the story. Emphasize the words *desert* and *gulps* when you come to them.

In paragraph 5, point to the sentence "The desert is a very dry place" to remind students to chime in. Circle any words that students read incorrectly.

17. Read aloud the sentence, "The desert is a very dry place."

Pause after reading paragraph 11. Ask students the following questions and note their responses on the Checkpoint pages.
Say: The lizard sees something very colorful in the sky. The sun is shining. The water from the waterfall is splashing up in the sky.

18. What does the lizard see?

Read the next paragraph.
Say: The lizard sees a rainbow.

19. What clues in the text let readers know that the lizard is looking at a rainbow?

Finish reading the story.

Part 4. Fiction: "The Frog and the Lizard" Evaluate Predictions

Read students' predictions to them. Tell students that predictions are not right or wrong; they are just the best guess you can make with the information you have. Ask students the following questions and note their responses on the Checkpoint pages.

20. What helped you make your prediction?

21. What else could help a reader make a prediction?

22. Was your prediction accurate?

Part 5. Fiction: "The Frog and the Lizard" Summarizing

Have students summarize "The Frog and the Lizard." Remind students that a summary answers the question, "Who did what?" Note students' response on the Checkpoint pages.

23. Summarize the story.

Part 6. Fiction: "The Frog and the Lizard" Reading Comprehension

Read the questions on the Checkpoint pages to students. Students should write the answers themselves. If necessary, allow them to dictate their responses to you.

Part 7. Fiction: "The Frog and the Lizard" Show You Know

Cut out the picture cards on page LC 49 and give them to students. Have students use the cards to retell the story and explain the lesson the frog learned. Note their responses on the Checkpoint pages.

31. Put the cards in order so they tell the story.

32. Use the pictures to retell the story.

33. What lesson do you think the frog learns in this story?

Part 8. Nonfiction: "A Trip to the Amazon Rain Forest" Preview the Article

Show students "A Trip to the Amazon Rain Forest." Point to and read aloud the title of the article. Preview the article with students. Have students find the time line.

34. Point to the time line.

Point to the heading **Big, Warm, and Wet**. Explain that the bold print is used to call attention to the text. This is a heading, and it gives us clues about the next paragraph. Have students read the heading and make a prediction. Note their responses on the Checkpoint pages.

35. Read the heading.

36. What do you think this selection will be about?

Have students locate other headings in the text. As students point to a heading, read it aloud. Note students' responses on the Checkpoint pages.

37. Point to the headings.

38. Why are the headings in bold print?

39. What is the topic of this article?

Part 9. Nonfiction: "A Trip to the Amazon Rain Forest" KWL Chart

Gather the KWL chart (Know/Want to know/Learn chart) on page LC 57. Read the directions to students. Students should write under KNOW and WANT on the KWL chart, or if necessary, dictate their answers to you.

40. Read aloud the heading of each column.

41. Write what you know about the rain forest under KNOW.

42. Write what you want to know under WANT.

If necessary, allow students to dictate their answers to you. Tell students that they will complete the LEARN column of the KWL chart after reading the article.

Before reading "A Trip to the Amazon Rain Forest," go over Words to Know with students. Read aloud each word or phrase and have students repeat it. Ask students if they know what each word or phrase means.

- ▸ If students know a word's or phrase's meaning, have them define it and use it in a sentence.
- ▸ If students don't know a word's or phrase's meaning, read them the definition and discuss the word or phrase with them.

rain forest – a tropical woodland where a lot of rain falls
steamboat – a boat that runs on steam
travel – to go from place to place; to take a trip

Part 10. Nonfiction: "A Trip to the Amazon Rain Forest" Shared Reading

It's time to read the article. Have students sit next to you so that they can see the words while you read aloud the text. Emphasize the words *rain forest*, *steamboat*, and *travel* when you come to them.

Pause after reading the section Plants, Animals, and People to ask the following questions. Note students' response on the Checkpoint pages.

43. What is the main idea of this section?

44. What are some details that support the main idea?

Refer to the KWL chart. Have students think about what they learned from the article. Students should write at least three facts on the KWL chart or, if necessary, dictate their answers to you.

45. Write three facts you learned about the Amazon rain forest under LEARN.

Part 11. Nonfiction: "A Trip to the Amazon Rain Forest" Reading Comprehension

Read the questions and answer choices to students and note their responses on the Checkpoint pages. You may allow students to circle the answers.

Part 12. Nonfiction: "A Trip to the Amazon Rain Forest" Text Supports

Show students the article. Ask students the following questions. Write students' responses on the Checkpoint pages. Explain that like many nonfiction articles, this article includes pictures to help support the text. The article contains a map, a chart, and a time line.

51. Where should someone look to find out where the Amazon rain forest is located: the map, the chart, or the time line?

Point to the time line.

52. What does the time line show us?

53. Look at the time line. When did the first highway open in the Amazon rain forest?

Turn to the chart.

54. What does the chart show us?

55. Look at the chart. Where does more rain fall: the Amazon rain forest or Washington, D.C.?

Part 13. Poetry: "Forest Full of Life" Activate Prior Knowledge

Explain to students that they will read a poem with you. Ask students the following questions to activate prior knowledge. Note their responses on the Checkpoint pages.

56. What do you know about poems?

57. I've read a story and an article to you. What was their topic?

58. What do you think this poem will be about?

Part 14. Poetry: "Forest Full of Life" Shared Reading and Fluency Check

Follow the instructions in the Semester Checkpoint for assessing students' fluency.

Part 15. Poetry: "Forest Full of Life" Summarizing

Have students summarize the poem. Note students' response on the Checkpoint pages.

65. What is the poem about?

Part 16. Poetry: "Forest Full of Life" Evaluate Predictions

Read students' predictions to them. Ask students the following questions and note their responses on the Checkpoint pages.

66. What helped you make your prediction?

67. Was your prediction accurate?

Part 17. Poetry: "Forest Full of Life" Reading Comprehension

Read the questions on the Checkpoint pages to students. Students should write the answers themselves. If necessary, allow them to dictate their responses to you.

Part 18. Poetry: "Forest Full of Life" Visualization and Imagery

Ask students the following question and note their response on the Checkpoint pages.

74. Which words help you picture the rain forest?

TIP A full list of objectives for the Semester Checkpoint can be found in the online lesson.

Name .... Date ....

Semester Checkpoint Learning Coach Instructions Shared Reading Comprehension and Analysis

Explain that students are going to show what they have learned this semester.

- Give students pages LC 37–LC 66 of the Semester Checkpoint.
- Read the directions on the students' pages together. Use the Learning Coach instructions on pages LC 29–LC 35 to administer the Checkpoint.
- Use the Checkpoint pages to record student behaviors and responses.
- When you have finished, use the Answer Key to score the Checkpoint and then enter the results online.
- Review each exercise with students. Work with students to correct any exercise that they missed.

Part 1. Fiction: "The Frog and the Lizard" Activate Prior Knowledge

Ask students the following questions to activate prior knowledge. Note their responses on the Checkpoint pages.

1. What would it be like to live in a rain forest—very wet or very dry?
2. What would it be like to live in a desert—very wet or very dry?

Before reading "The Frog and the Lizard," go over Words to Know with students. Read aloud each word and have students repeat it. Ask students if they know what each word means.

- If students know a word's meaning, have them define it and use it in a sentence.
- If students don't know a word's meaning, read them the definition and discuss the word with them.

desert – dry land with few plants and very little rain
gulp – a mouthful of something to swallow

Part 2. Fiction: "The Frog and the Lizard" Book Walk

Gather the Checkpoint pages with "The Frog and the Lizard." Have students sit next to you so that they can see the story while you do a Book Walk. Read aloud the title and author of the text. Ask students the following questions and note their responses on the Checkpoint pages.

3. What do you think the story will be about?
4. What does an author do?

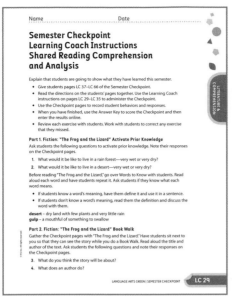

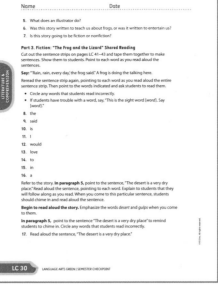

Name .... Date ....

5. What does an illustrator do?
6. Was this story written to teach us about frogs, or was it written to entertain us?
7. Is this story going to be fiction or nonfiction?

Part 3. Fiction: "The Frog and the Lizard" Shared Reading

Cut out the sentence strips on pages LC 41–43 and tape them together to make sentences. Show them to students. Point to each word as you read aloud the sentences.

Say: "'Rain, rain, every day,' the frog said." A frog is doing the talking here.

Reread the sentence strip again, pointing to each word as you read aloud the entire sentence strip. Then point to the words indicated and ask students to read them.

- Circle any words that students read incorrectly.
- If students have trouble with a word, say, "This is the sight word [*word*]. Say [*word*]."

8. the
9. said
10. is
11. I
12. would
13. love
14. to
15. in
16. a

Refer to the story. **In paragraph 5,** point to the sentence, "The desert is a very dry place." Read aloud the sentence, pointing to each word. Explain to students that they will follow along as you read. When you come to this particular sentence, students should chime in and read aloud the sentence.

Begin to read aloud the story. Emphasize the words *desert* and *gulps* when you come to them.

In paragraph 5, point to the sentence "The desert is a very dry place" to remind students to chime in. Circle any words that students read incorrectly.

17. Read aloud the sentence, "The desert is a very dry place."

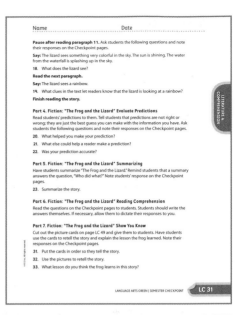

Name .... Date ....

Pause after reading paragraph 11. Ask students the following questions and note their responses on the Checkpoint pages.

Say: The lizard sees something very colorful in the sky. The sun is shining. The water from the waterfall is splashing up in the sky.

18. What does the lizard see?

Read the next paragraph.

Say: The lizard sees a rainbow.

19. What clues in the text let readers know that the lizard is looking at a rainbow?

Finish reading the story.

Part 4. Fiction: "The Frog and the Lizard" Evaluate Predictions

Read students' predictions to them. Tell students that predictions are not right or wrong; they are just the best guess you can make with the information you have. Ask students the following questions and note their responses on the Checkpoint pages.

20. What helped you make your prediction?
21. What else could help a reader make a prediction?
22. Was your prediction accurate?

Part 5. Fiction: "The Frog and the Lizard" Summarizing

Have students summarize "The Frog and the Lizard." Remind students that a summary answers the question, "Who did what?" Note students' response on the Checkpoint pages.

23. Summarize the story.

Part 6. Fiction: "The Frog and the Lizard" Reading Comprehension

Read the questions on the Checkpoint pages to students. Students should write the answers themselves. If necessary, allow them to dictate their responses to you.

Part 7. Fiction: "The Frog and the Lizard" Show You Know

Cut out the picture cards on page LC 49 and give them to students. Have students use the cards to retell the story and explain the lesson the frog learned. Note their responses on the Checkpoint pages.

31. Put the cards in order so they tell the story.
32. Use the pictures to retell the story.
33. What lesson do you think the frog learns in this story?

Name .... Date ....

Part 8. Nonfiction: "A Trip to the Amazon Rain Forest" Preview the Article

Show students "A Trip to the Amazon Rain Forest." Point to and read aloud the title of the article. Preview the article with students. Have students find the time line.

34. Point to the time line.

Point to the heading **Big, Warm, and Wet**. Explain that the bold print is used to call attention to the text. This is a heading, and it gives us clues about the next paragraph. Have students read the heading and make a prediction. Note their responses on the Checkpoint pages.

35. Read the heading.
36. What do you think this selection will be about?

Have students locate other headings in the text. As students point to a heading, read it aloud. Note students' responses on the Checkpoint pages.

37. Point to the headings.
38. Why are the headings in bold print?
39. What is the topic of this article?

Part 9. Nonfiction: "A Trip to the Amazon Rain Forest" KWL Chart

Gather the KWL chart (Know/Want to know/Learn chart) on page LC 57. Read the directions to students. Students should write under KNOW and WANT on the KWL chart, or if necessary, dictate their answers to you.

40. Read aloud the heading of each column.
41. Write what you know about the rain forest under KNOW.
42. Write what you want to know under WANT.

If necessary, allow students to dictate their answers to you. Tell students that they will complete the LEARN column of the KWL chart after reading the article.

Before reading "A Trip to the Amazon Rain Forest," go over Words to Know with students. Read aloud each word or phrase and have students repeat it. Ask students if they know what each word or phrase means.

- If students know a word's or phrase's meaning, have them define it and use it in a sentence.
- If students don't know a word's or phrase's meaning, read them the definition and discuss the word or phrase with them.

rain forest – a tropical woodland where a lot of rain falls
steamboat – a boat that runs on steam
travel – to go from place to place; to take a trip

Name .... Date ....

Part 10. Nonfiction: "A Trip to the Amazon Rain Forest" Shared Reading

It's time to read the article. Have students sit next to you so that they can see the words while you read aloud the text. Emphasize the words *rain forest*, *steamboat*, and *travel* when you come to them.

Pause after reading the section Plants, Animals, and People to ask the following questions. Note students' responses on the Checkpoint pages.

43. What is the main idea of this section?
44. What are some details that support the main idea?

Refer to the KWL chart. Have students think about what they learned from the article. Students should write at least three facts on the KWL chart or, if necessary, dictate their answers to you.

45. Write three facts you learned about the Amazon rain forest under LEARN.

Part 11. Nonfiction: "A Trip to the Amazon Rain Forest" Reading Comprehension

Read the questions and answer choices to students and note their responses on the Checkpoint pages. You may allow students to circle the answers.

Part 12. Nonfiction: "A Trip to the Amazon Rain Forest" Text Supports

Show students the article. Ask students the following questions. Write students' responses on the Checkpoint pages. Explain that like many nonfiction articles, this article includes pictures to help support the text. This article contains a map, a chart, and a time line.

51. Where should someone look to find out where the Amazon rain forest is located: the map, the chart, or the time line?

Point to the time line.

52. What does the time line show us?
53. Look at the time line. When did the first highway open in the Amazon rain forest?

Turn to the chart.

54. What does the chart show us?
55. Look at the chart. Where does more rain fall: the Amazon rain forest or Washington, D.C.?

Part 13. Poetry: "Forest Full of Life" Activate Prior Knowledge

Explain to students that they will read a poem with you. Ask students the following questions to activate prior knowledge. Note their responses on the Checkpoint pages.

56. What do you know about poems?
57. I've read a story and an article to you. What was their topic?
58. What do you think this poem will be about?

Name .... Date ....

Part 14. Poetry: "Forest Full of Life" Shared Reading and Fluency Check

Gather the Checkpoint page with "Forest Full of Life." Cut out the two copies of the poem and give one to students. Use your copy of "Forest Full of Life" to

- Note the kinds of errors that students make as they read.
- Determine students' reading rate.

Read aloud the title of the poem, pointing to each word as you read. Then have students read aloud the title of the poem, pointing to each word as they read.

Tell students that the title is the same as the first sentence in each stanza. Explain that a lot of the words in the poem repeat and that they should listen carefully and follow along as you read aloud the first stanza.

Allow students to read the poem silently before they read aloud to you. When students are ready to read aloud, **start a timer** to keep track of the time in seconds it takes students to read aloud the entire poem. Stop the timer as soon as students read the last word and write the time in seconds in the time box in Question 59.

As you listen, you may choose to mark up your copy of the poem where students have difficulty reading. Make a mark or a note for the following types of errors:

Listen for these types of errors	How many times?	Examples
Reads word incorrectly, does not self-correct.		
Skips a word, does not self-correct.		
Rereads before reading correctly.		
Guesses before reading correctly.		

Name .... Date ....

59. Determine percentage of errors by dividing errors by number of words. Record this number.

[ ]	÷	69	=	[ ]
Errors		Words		Error Rate

60. Determine words per minute by dividing number of words by time in seconds and multiplying by 60. Record this number.

69	÷	[ ]	× 60 =	[ ]
Words		Time (in seconds)		Words per minute

Circle *Yes* or *No* for each question.

61. Did students read with a pace that sounds natural? Yes / No
62. Did students read with appropriate volume? Yes / No
63. Did students pause for periods? Yes / No
64. Did students read with expression? Yes / No

Part 15. Poetry: "Forest Full of Life" Summarizing

Have students summarize the poem. Note students' response on the Checkpoint pages.

65. What is the poem about?

Part 16. Poetry: "Forest Full of Life" Evaluate Predictions

Read students' predictions to them. Ask students the following questions and note their responses on the Checkpoint pages.

66. What helped you make your prediction?
67. Was your prediction accurate?

Part 17. Poetry: "Forest Full of Life" Reading Comprehension

Read the questions on the Checkpoint pages to students. Students should write the answers themselves. If necessary, allow them to dictate their responses to you.

Part 18. Poetry: "Forest Full of Life" Visualization and Imagery

Ask students the following question and note their response on the Checkpoint pages.

74. Which words help you picture the rain forest?

Name .... Date ....

Semester Checkpoint Answer Key Shared Reading Comprehension and Analysis

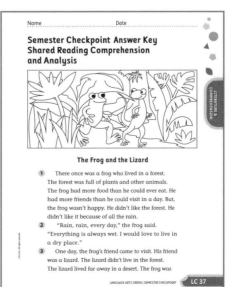

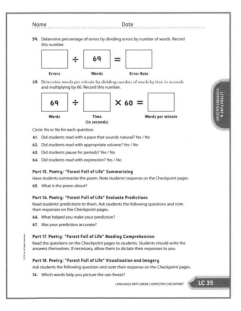

The Frog and the Lizard

1 There once was a frog who lived in a forest. The forest was full of plants and other animals. The frog had more food than he could ever eat. He had more friends than he could visit in a day. But, the frog wasn't happy. He didn't like the forest. He didn't like it because of all the rain.

2 "Rain, rain, every day," the frog said. "Everything is always wet. I would love to live in a dry place."

3 One day, the frog's friend came to visit. His friend was a lizard. The lizard didn't live in the forest. The lizard lived far away in a desert. The frog was

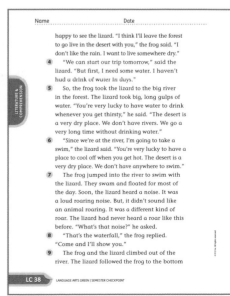

Name .... Date ....

happy to see the lizard. "I think I'll leave the forest to go live in the desert with you," the frog said. "I don't like the rain. I want to live somewhere dry."

4 "We can start our trip tomorrow," said the lizard. "But first, I need some water. I haven't had a drink of water in days."

5 So, the frog took the lizard to the big river in the forest. The lizard took big, long gulps of water. "You're very lucky to have water to drink whenever you get thirsty," he said. "The desert is a very dry place. We don't have rivers. We go a very long time without drinking water."

6 "Since we're at the river, I'm going to take a swim," the lizard said. "You're very lucky to have a place to cool off when you get hot. The desert is a very dry place. We don't have anywhere to swim."

7 The frog jumped into the river to swim with the lizard. They swam and floated for most of the day. Soon, the lizard heard a noise. It was a loud roaring noise. But, it didn't sound like an animal roaring. It was a different kind of roar. The lizard had never heard a roar like this before. "What's that noise?" he asked.

8 "That's the waterfall," the frog replied. "Come and I'll show you."

9 The frog and the lizard climbed out of the river. The lizard followed the frog to the bottom

---

Card LC 39:

Name _____ Date _____

of the waterfall. They looked up at the water falling from high above. They listened to the roaring sound the water made as it crashed into the water at the bottom. They felt the cool drops of water that splashed out from the waterfall.

10 "All of this water is amazing," the lizard said. "The desert is a very dry place. We don't get enough water for a river or a waterfall. You're lucky to have both."

11 Then, the lizard saw something in the sky. It was something he had never seen before. It was colorful and stretched from one side of the waterfall to the other. "What's that?" he asked the frog.

12 "That's a rainbow," the frog replied. "We see those all the time in the forest."

13 The lizard stared at the rainbow a while longer. The frog looked at it, too. He thought about everything the lizard had told him about the desert.

14 "I don't think I'll go with you to the desert tomorrow," the frog said to the lizard. "The desert is a very dry place. You don't have rivers or waterfalls or rainbows. I don't think I would like living in such a dry place. I like the forest. I like all the water."

15 And the frog and the lizard spent the rest of the day enjoying the water in the forest.

LANGUAGE ARTS GREEN | SEMESTER CHECKPOINT LC 39

Card LC 40:

Name _____ Date _____

Part 1. Fiction: "The Frog and the Lizard"
Activate Prior Knowledge
Get ready to read. Listen to the question, and say your answer.

1. The rain forest would be very wet.

2. The desert would be very dry.

Part 2. Fiction: "The Frog and the Lizard"
Book Walk
Do a Book Walk. Listen to the question, and say your answer.

3. Answers will vary.

4. An author writes a story.

5. An illustrator draws the pictures.

6. to entertain us

7. fiction

LC 40 LANGUAGE ARTS GREEN | SEMESTER CHECKPOINT

Card LC 41:

Name _____ Date _____

Part 3. Fiction: "The Frog and the Lizard"
Shared Reading
Cut out the sentence strips. Read along when prompted.

"Rain, rain, every day," the frog said. "Everything is

LANGUAGE ARTS GREEN | SEMESTER CHECKPOINT LC 41

Card LC 43:

Name _____ Date _____

always wet. I would love to live in a dry place."

LANGUAGE ARTS GREEN | SEMESTER CHECKPOINT LC 43

Card LC 45:

Name _____ Date _____

8. the

9. said

10. is

11. I

12. would

13. love

14. to

15. in

16. a

17. The desert is a very dry place.

18. a rainbow

19. Possible answers: It is in the sky; it is colorful; it stretches from one side of the waterfall to the other.

LANGUAGE ARTS GREEN | SEMESTER CHECKPOINT LC 45

Card LC 46:

Name _____ Date _____

Part 4. Fiction: "The Frog and the Lizard"
Evaluate Predictions
Listen to the question, and say your answer.

20. Possible answers: title; the illustration; vocabulary words
21. Possible answers: title; illustrations; vocabulary words
22. Answers will vary.

Part 5. Fiction: "The Frog and the Lizard"
Summarizing
Summarize the story.

23. Answers should include the major events of the story, but not every detail. Possible answer: The frog wants to go to the desert. The lizard comes to visit. The frog and the lizard walk through the rain forest. The lizard tells the frog that in the desert, they go a long time without drinking, they don't have a place to swim, they don't have rivers or waterfalls, and they don't have rainbows. The frog decides he wants to stay in the rain forest.

LC 46 LANGUAGE ARTS GREEN | SEMESTER CHECKPOINT

Card LC 47:

Name _____ Date _____

Part 6. Fiction: "The Frog and the Lizard"
Reading Comprehension
Listen to the question, and write the answer.

24. Who are the characters in the story?
the frog; the lizard

25. Describe the frog. What is he like?
The frog is not happy; he is sad that he lives in a place that is so wet and rainy.

26. Where does the story take place?
in the rain forest

27. What is the frog's problem in this story?
The lizard tells him they have no water to drink, no swimming, no rivers, and no rainbows in the desert. The frog realizes he likes the water.

LANGUAGE ARTS GREEN | SEMESTER CHECKPOINT LC 47

Card LC 48:

Name _____ Date _____

28. Why does the frog change his mind?
The lizard tells him they have no water to drink, no swimming, no rivers, and no rainbows in the desert. The frog realizes he likes the water.

29. Compare the place where the lizard lives to the place where the frog lives. Are they alike or different? Give examples from the story.
They are very different. The lizard lives in a dry desert that has no water. The frog lives in a wet rain forest that has rain, rivers, and waterfalls.

30. What does gulp mean?
a mouthful of something to swallow

LC 48 LANGUAGE ARTS GREEN | SEMESTER CHECKPOINT

Card LC 49:

Name _____ Date _____

Part 7. Fiction: "The Frog and the Lizard"
Show You Know
Cut out the pictures. Then, put them in order and retell the story.

31.

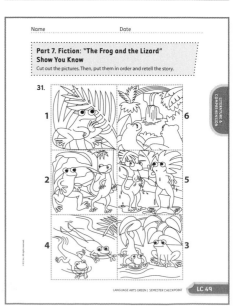

LANGUAGE ARTS GREEN | SEMESTER CHECKPOINT LC 49

Name _____ Date _____

32. Students should use the pictures to retell the story correctly.

33. Answers will vary.

Name _____ Date _____

A Trip to the Amazon Rain Forest
By F. Keen

Imagine that you are in a warm, wet forest. The trees around you are very tall. They grow close together. Their branches touch and block out most of the sunlight. But, there is enough light for you to look around. You see plants you've never seen before. You hear animal sounds you've never heard before. You hear water flowing close by. Where are you? You're in the Amazon rain forest!

Big, Warm, and Wet

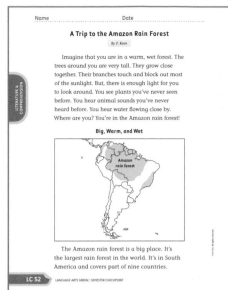

The Amazon rain forest is a big place. It's the largest rain forest in the world. It's in South America and covers part of nine countries.

Name _____ Date _____

Because of where it is in the world, the Amazon rain forest is a warm place. It's warm all day and night. With the word *rain* in its name, you might have guessed that it's a wet place, too. It's not just a little wet. It's really wet! It rains most days of the year there. In one year, it rains about 100 inches. Imagine pouring that much rain into a very tall tube. If you stood next to the tube, the water would be much higher than your head. Even if you raised your arms above your head, the water would still be higher than your fingertips. That's a lot of rain!

Plants, Animals, and People

The rain forest is home to many kinds of plants and animals. Many of the plants that grow there don't grow anywhere else in the world. Many of the animals that live there don't live anywhere else in the world, either. Scientists have spent years learning about the plants and animals. But, they haven't learned about all of them. That's because there are so many. One thing they have learned is that some of the plants are very helpful. Scientists can use the plants to make medicine. These medicines help people all over the world.

Name _____ Date _____

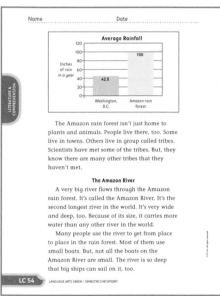

The Amazon rain forest isn't just home to plants and animals. People live there, too. Some live in towns. Others live in group called tribes. Scientists have met some of the tribes. But, they know there are many other tribes that they haven't met.

The Amazon River

A very big river flows through the Amazon rain forest. It's called the Amazon River. It's the second longest river in the world. It's very wide and deep, too. Because of its size, it carries more water than any other river in the world.

Many people use the river to get from place to place in the rain forest. Most of them use small boats. But, not all the boats on the Amazon River are small. The river is so deep that big ships can sail on it, too.

Name _____ Date _____

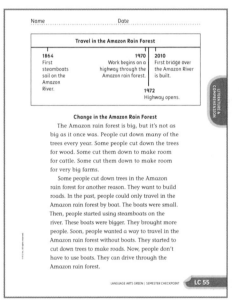

Change in the Amazon Rain Forest

The Amazon rain forest is big, but it's not as big as it once was. People cut down many of the trees every year. Some people cut down the trees for wood. Some cut them down to make room for cattle. Some cut them down to make room for very big farms.

Some people cut down trees in the Amazon rain forest for another reason. They want to build roads. In the past, people could only travel in the Amazon rain forest by boat. The boats were small. Then, people started using steamboats on the river. These boats were bigger. They brought more people. Soon, people wanted a way to travel in the Amazon rain forest without boats. They started to cut down trees to make roads. Now, people don't have to use boats. They can drive through the Amazon rain forest.

Name _____ Date _____

Part 8. Nonfiction: "A Trip to the Amazon Rain Forest" Preview the Article
Listen to the question, and say your answer.

34. Students should point to the time line.

35. Big, Warm, and Wet

36. Answers may include: information about the Amazon rain forest—how big it is, how warm it is, how wet it is

37. Plants, Animals, and People; The Amazon River; Change in the Amazon Rain Forest

38. to call them out; to make them stand out to the reader

39. the Amazon rain forest

Name _____ Date _____

Part 9. Nonfiction: "A Trip to the Amazon Rain Forest" KWL Chart
Write what you know about the Amazon rain forest under **KNOW**.
Write what you want to know under **WANT**.
Write what you learn from the article under **LEARN**.

40. Students should read the column headings and directions.

Know What do I know?	Want What do I want to know?	Learn What did I learn?
41. Answers will vary.	**42.** Answers will vary.	**45.** Answers will vary, but students should write three facts.

Name _____ Date _____

Part 10. Nonfiction: "A Trip to the Amazon Rain Forest" Shared Reading
Listen to the question, and say your answer. Then, listen to the article.

43. The Amazon rain forest is home to many different people, animals, and plants.

44. Answers may include: Many of the people, plants, and animals that live there can't be found anywhere else in the world; scientists have spent a long time studying the plants and animals but haven't learned about all of them yet.

Name _____ Date _____

Part 11. Nonfiction: "A Trip to the Amazon Rain Forest" Reading Comprehension
Listen to the question, and choose the answer.

46. What is the purpose of this article?
A. to teach us about rain
B. to teach us about the rain forest *(circled)*
C. to tell us a story about the rain forest

47. What does the phrase *rain forest* mean?
A. a dry place with few trees
B. a cool, damp place with lots of trees
C. a warm, wet place with lots of trees *(circled)*

48. How much rain falls in the Amazon rain forest each year?
A. 100 inches *(circled)*   B. 10 inches   C. 40 inches

49. What is the name of the body of water found in the Amazon rain forest?
A. the Amazon Lake
B. the Amazon Ocean
C. the Amazon River *(circled)*

Literature & Comprehension

Name _____ Date _____

50. When was the first bridge built in the Amazon rain forest?
A. 1990   B. 2000   Ⓒ 2010

Part 12. Nonfiction: "A Trip to the Amazon Rain Forest" Text Supports
Listen to the question, and say your answer.

51. **map**

52. **The time line shows us travel in the Amazon rain forest.**

53. **1972**

54. **The chart shows us how much rain falls in the Amazon rain forest and in Washington, D.C.**

55. **the Amazon rain forest**

Forest Full of Life

Forest full of life,
All lush and green.
Home to many plants
The world has never seen.

Forest full of life,
All lush and green.
Home to many animals
The world has never seen.

Forest full of life,
All lush and green.
Home to many people
The world has never seen.

Amazing Amazon rain forest,
All lush and green.
So much of your life
The world has never seen.

Forest Full of Life

Forest full of life,
All lush and green.
Home to many plants
The world has never seen.

Forest full of life,
All lush and green.
Home to many animals
The world has never seen.

Forest full of life,
All lush and green.
Home to many people
The world has never seen.

Amazing Amazon rain forest,
All lush and green.
So much of your life
The world has never seen.

Name _____ Date _____

Part 13. Poetry: "Forest Full of Life" Activate Prior Knowledge
Get ready to read. Listen to the question, and say your answer.

56. **Answers may include: They have rhyming words; they're short; they have descriptive language; they have patterns.**

57. **the Amazon rain forest**

58. **Answers may vary, but students should understand that the poem will be about the rain forest as well.**

Part 14. Poetry: "Forest Full of Life" Shared Reading and Fluency Check
Read aloud the poem.

59.–64.

Name _____ Date _____

Part 15. Poetry: "Forest Full of Life" Summarizing
Listen to the question, and say your answer.

65. **The lush and green Amazon rain forest is home to many plants, animals, and people that the world has never seen.**

Part 16. Poetry: "Forest Full of Life" Evaluate Predictions
Listen to the question, and say your answer.

66. **Answers may include: title; previous readings**

67. **Answers will vary.**

Name _____ Date _____

Part 17. Poetry: "Forest Full of Life" Reading Comprehension
Listen to the question, and write your answer.

68. Which words rhyme?
   green and *seen*

69. What phrases repeat throughout the poem?
   Forest full of life,
   All lush and green.
   Home to many
   The world has never seen.

70. What is the pattern of this poem?
   The second and fourth lines
   rhyme.

Name _____ Date _____

71. According to the poem, what is the Amazon rain forest home to?
   many plants, many people, and
   many animals

72. Has the world seen everything that the Amazon rain forest has in it?
   No

73. What does the word *lush* mean?
   thick growth, thick bushes

Part 18. Poetry: "Forest Full of Life" Visualization and Imagery
Listen to the question, and say your answer.

74. **Answers may include:** *full of life;* *lush and green; home to many*
